ESCAPE FROM THE ANTHILL

HUBERT BUTLER was born in Kilkenny in 1900. He was educated at Charterhouse and at St John's College, Oxford, where he was senior classical scholar. After work with the Irish County Libraries, starting the Co. Derry libraries from Coleraine in the mid-1920s, he travelled in Europe and ta
In 1934 he wer
ship from the

Since his f
Kilkenny, w
Archaeologic
1954 he orga
staged annu
Dunboyne, h
he edits.

His books include translations from the Russian of Leonid Leonov's *The Thief* (1931) and Chekhov's *The Cherry Orchard* (written for performance at London's Old Vic in 1934, published the same year), and *Ten Thousand Saints: A Study in Irish and European Origins* (1972). He has broadcast for Radio Éireann and the BBC and written for several Irish and English periodicals, including *The Dublin Magazine*, *The Bell* (of which he was review editor under Peadar O'Donnell), *New Blackfriars* and *The Twentieth Century*.

In June 1986 he won the American-Irish Foundation Award for literature.

THESE ESSAYS share in the great humanist tradition of European letters, in the spirit of Montaigne, of Swift and of Orwell. They form an important contribution to Ireland's social and intellectual history, and they have an integrity and music all their own.

FOR PEGGY

By the same author

HISTORY

Ten Thousand Saints: A Study in Irish and European Origins (Kilkenny: Wellbrook Press, 1972)

TRANSLATION

The Thief by Leonid Leonov (London: Martin Secker, 1931)

The Cherry Orchard by Chekhov (London: H. W. Deane, 1934)

ESCAPE FROM THE ANTHILL

HUBERT BUTLER

With a Foreword by
MAURICE CRAIG

THE LILLIPUT PRESS
MULLINGAR
1986

First published in 1985 by
THE LILLIPUT PRESS LTD
Gigginstown, Mullingar,
Co. Westmeath, Ireland.
Paperback edition, revised with corrections,
published 1986.

British Library Cataloguing in Publication Data

Butler, Hubert
Escape from the anthill
I. Title
082 PR6052. u81/

ISBN 0-946640-16-5

Cover design by Jarlath Hayes
Set in 10 on 12 Palatino by
Koinonia Ltd of Manchester
and printed in England by
Richard Clay Ltd.
of Bungay, Suffolk

CONTENTS

ACKNOWLEDGMENTS

Thanks and acknowledgments are due to the editors and publishers of the following books, periodicals and newspapers in which various parts of this volume first appeared:

'Henry and Frances': *The Dublin Magazine*, April 1950.
'New Geneva in Waterford': *Journal of the Royal Society of Antiquaries of Ireland*, December 1947.
'The Bishop': *The Twentieth Century*, February 1960.
'The Country House After the Union': A Radio Éireann Thomas Davis Lecture 1957, published in R. B. McDowell (ed.), *Social Life in Ireland 1800-45* (Cork 1957) under title 'The Country House – The Life of the Gentry'.
'An Irish Ecumenical Movement': *The Irish Times*, 18 December 1964.
'The Eggman and the Fairies': *The Twentieth Century*, July 1960.
'Anglo-Irish Twilight': *Journal of the Butler Society*, 1978/9, under title 'Anglo-Irish Twilight, the last Ormonde War'.
'Beside the Nore': *Ireland of the Welcomes*, May-June 1970, under title 'Nore and Barrow'.
'Divided Loyalties': *An Cosantoir*, The Irish Army Journal, August 1979.
'The Invader Wore Slippers': *The Bell*, November 1945.
'Portrait of a Minority': *The Bell*, June 1954.
'A House of God': *The Twentieth Century*, May 1955.
'Boycott Village': *The Twentieth Century*, January 1958.

'*The Bell:* An Anglo-Irish View': *Irish University Review*, Spring 1976.
'*Envoy* and Mr Kavanagh': *The Bell*, September 1951.
'Graham Greene and Stephen Spender: The Sense of Evil and the Sense of Guilt': *The Bell*, November and December 1951.
'Two Critics: E. M. Forster and Edmund Wilson': *The Bell*, March 1952.
'Three Friends: Eoin O'Mahony, Owen Sheehy-Skeffington and Elizabeth Bowen': *The Irish Times*, 21 February 1970; memorial addresses 11 June 1971 (Examination Hall, TCD), 18 October 1979 (Farahy Church, Co. Cork).
'A Visit to Hesse and Some Thoughts About Princes': *The Irish Times*, 20 September 1968, and *Journal of the Butler Society*, 1978/9.
'Without the Bible in Spain': *The Twentieth Century*, December 1958.
'Return to Hellas': *The Twentieth Century*, January 1961.
'Lament for Archaeology': *The Irish Times*, 31 July–1 August 1979.

'Mr Pfeffer of Sarajevo': *Nonplus* (Dublin), Winter 1960.
'The Last Izmirenje': *The Irish Press*, 28 February 1947.
'The Sub-Prefect Should Have Held His Tongue': *The Twentieth Century*, June 1956.
'The Artukovitch File': Section I appeared in *New Blackfriars*, February 1971, under title 'What Became of Artukovitch? Reflections on a Croatian Crusade'.
'Peter's Window': Originally published in Robet Greacen (ed.), *Irish Harvest* (New Frontiers Press 1946) under title 'The Teaching Brigade'; now revised and expanded.

FOREWORD

Hubert Butler is old enough — if only just — to be my father. For this reason I regarded him, when I first met him over forty years ago, with the awe which young aspirant writers reserve for those who were of the time just past: in this case the time of AE, Yeats and Sir Horace Plunkett: the time I had just missed. The very first words of his that I ever read were in *The Bell* for July 1941. In an article called 'The Barriers' he said, 'A nation cannot be created negatively by elimination or strategic retreats into the past.' 'It is a strange time,' he said, 'to maintain the theory that a distinctive culture cannot exist without cultural intercourse.' At that time, when our isolation, physical and moral, was intensified by the war, here was a voice intent, in AE's words, 'Against the sceptred myth to hold The golden heresy of truth.'

Upholding the heresy of truth has been a principal part of his business ever since, sometimes at considerable personal cost, as readers of these essays will learn, if they do not already know it. Some of them were written during, and others refer back to, the 'ice-age' of the forties and fifties when Ireland seemed gripped by paralysis and when only the voices to whom *The Bell* under Sean O'Faolain and Peadar O'Donnell gave a platform spoke for freedom.

Courage, common sense and elegance: and the rarest of these is elegance. Again and again I have been struck, in reading these essays, by the felicitous phrase, the apt metaphor, and the vivid image, as though this prose had been written with the care which poets give to the writing of their verse. And why not? It is, in the end, for his style that an author is read; and what is the use of writing to persuade if you cannot charm your reader and disarm him?

Hubert Butler is a deceptive writer. Just as we find ourselves sagely nodding agreement with one of his strictures, the knife is deftly slipped between our own ribs and we are transfixed upon his point. The merciless description of Mrs A. in 'Portrait of a Minority' is no more than she deserves. But when Hubert Butler attributes his independence of mind to the possession of a few fields beside the River Nore, he is not doing himself justice. 'Privilege,' he says, 'develops the faculties and sharpens the sensibilities.' No doubt it is morally beneficial to be neither too rich nor too poor, and there is a mystique about the possession of land which sometimes — but only sometimes — serves to stiffen independence. But his evident admiration for the minor country gentry is for the most part misplaced, because, as Swift pointed out, all classes of persons are contemptible and redeemed only by the virtues of individuals. There are even just men found among academics, bureaucrats and other classes of the damned.

There is another notable category of achievers. It was long ago observed that rectories and manses produced able offspring out of all proportion to their numbers. The reason is not far to seek. In the houses of the clergy there were books, the things of the mind were held in esteem, their children enjoyed educational advantages, and they were raised to some degree above the prevailing economic level.

The one great truth which seems to underlie almost everything in these essays of Hubert Butler is this: that the magnitude of a moral issue, like that of an angle in geometry, is independent of its reach or scope. This old philosophical conundrum (Is the suffering of ten people ten times as great as the suffering of one?) is never far from his attention. 'We grieve,' he writes, 'for distant events and people with sympathy as thin and ephemeral as the newspapers in which we read about them.' But he has no difficulty in showing how easily moral issues are fudged even when they concern our relations with our next-door-neighbours ('Boycott Village' and indeed *passim*).

A wise historian has written, 'Throughout the ages there have always been hopeful politicians who believe that if only the peoples of the world could come together they would love and understand each other. It is a tragic delusion. So long as X and Y had little to do with each other their relations were friendly.' X and Y, in that particular equation (from Sir Steven Runciman), were the Byzantine Empire and the Latin West. That very quarrel, in its modern form, is still with us, and forms much of the subject of the essays in the third section.

Hubert Butler is better placed than most people, by reason of his Balkan and Russian experiences, to judge whether travel really broadens the mind or not. It depends on what kind of a mind you have to begin with. What it has done for him is to illuminate the scene at home and help him to understand it better. He is telling no more than the truth when he says in his introduction that whatever their ostensible subjects, these essays are in fact about his relationship to Ireland.

A writer without a point of view is like distilled water: pure no doubt but hopelessly insipid. There is no danger of this with Hubert Butler. His viewpoint, that of a protestant republican, is one which I share (and there are many more of us than is commonly supposed). Some of his other prejudices are less widely shared. They can be crudely overstated in some such form as this: amateur good, professional bad; rural Ireland good, Dublin bad; parish pumps good, metropolitan water boards (and all other metropolitan boards) bad; and so on to taste. Bureaucrats, academics and 'experts' are easy targets, and we have not all the good fortune — if it is good fortune — to be born country gentlemen. Some of his dislikes are, just at present, rather fashionable. But no man I know is less subject to fashion, intellectual or other. He is a living example of Ibsen's principle that great majorities, whether silent or vocal, are always wrong. 'Justum et tenacem propositi virum. . . ,' as Horace has it: but always flexibly, and always with humour. (Incidentally, though I disliked the English public school to which I was sent as much as Hubert disliked his, I do not agree with him that 'compulsory classics fester like an abscess' for the rest of our lives. My classical education is the ruins of an unfinished building: if I poke about in the long grass I find things worth digging up, and so, evidently, does he.)

In evil times he remains an optimist, one who holds 'the conviction that by foresight and ingenious contrivance men can be made happy and free without hurting each other' and the 'absolute faith that what *should* be *will* be, however long we must wait.'

How much good, we ask, can a lone man writing in minority periodicals from an obscure Co. Kilkenny retreat, how much good can such a man possibly do in the era of mass communications? Never mind about that, says Hubert Butler, and quotes approvingly Owen Skeffington's favourite dictum from (of all unfashionable people) Herbert Spencer: 'What I must realize is how infinitesimal is the importance of anything I do, and how infinitely important it is that I should do it.' (The angle with the infinitely extensible arms.) His portrait of Skeffington, that man who, tacitly evading questions of belief and profession, believed in and practised the Christian virtues, might be taken as a portrait, *mutatis mutandis,* of Hubert Butler himself. And, in parenthesis, how refreshing it is to read again (in 'Three Friends') how Skeffington dealt with that inverted Broadbent, the egregious

Muggeridge. We learn a lot about the author, all of it to his credit, from noticing who he most admires: Eoin O'Mahony, for example.

For all his elegance, Hubert Butler is no belletrist. For him an essay is a projectile, aimed at a particular target and freighted with what it needs to do its work: no more and no less. All his projectiles tend to converge on the same area of moral choice: the responsibilities of the individual to his community, and, by implication, those of the community towards him, in the special sphere where belief and conduct, dogma and decency, are so often in conflict.

'The great creeds, dissolving,' he writes in his essay on George Borrow, one of the most spirited pieces in the collection, 'have filled the air with so much shredded theology that the most fastidious can find some palatable nourishment for his soul without rudeness to any other believer. Religion, which once rampaged like a shark, devouring everything which could not escape, now feeds itself like some non-poisonous jelly-fish groping for plankton with sensitive tentacles.' That was written in 1958, before the Eastern horizon had been darkened by the resurgence of Islamic fundamentalism, or the Western by the born-again chiliasts of the Pentagon, brandishing their Bomb. There is dirty weather ahead. We shall need all the foresight and ingenious contrivance we can muster.

A good many years ago I was with Hubert Butler when he visited the cottages on the slopes of Slievenaman in which occurred the bizarre and macabre events rehearsed in 'The Eggman and the Fairies'. The cottage had been heavily modernized, perhaps even rebuilt; but we were still in pre-televison Ireland, only a short distance from the Butler stronghold of Kilcash, subject of one of the most plangent of Irish poems, and only seventy years or so, barely a man's lifetime, from the events of 1893. It was a strange conjunction, prompting reflections on mutability.

I am one of those who is apt to end on a diminuendo and a dying fall. Hubert Butler is not like that at all. Let him therefore have the last word, with one of his characteristically vivid images: 'When an incendiary sets a match to respectability, it smoulders malodorously, but piety, like patriotism, goes off like a rocket.'

Now read on.

Maurice Craig
Dublin, January 1985

INTRODUCTION

These essays are not so heterogeneous as they look. They are all skewered together by a single idea. Or perhaps I should call it an obsession, a mental necessity that turned into a physical one. When I was a boy of fourteen I decided I was going to live in the place where I was born and where my father, grandfather and great grandfather had lived before me. It seemed then an easy and obvious thing to do, since I was my father's eldest son and he had a house and farm in Kilkenny. There was also another reason, which influenced me, even when I knew how insubstantial it was. Though we have long been unimportant people, the Butlers, of whom my family is a junior branch, had ruled the neighbourhood since the fourteenth century, and there is scarcely a parish in Tipperary or Kilkenny that does not bear some trace of our sometimes arrogant, sometimes kindly interference. Could I not interfere too?

It was some time before I grasped how difficult this was going to be and noticed that not only was all my education slanted away from Ireland but that the whole island was tilted eastwards. It was very hard to stand upright unsupported on this precipitous slope, for as many people were pushing me from the west as were pulling me to the east. And ambition was tugging me vigorously the whole time towards the land of opportunity. And in fact, in a strongly centripetal world, staying at home is scarcely even respectable; certainly no one thinks it public-spirited. The man who does it can surely have no feeling for 'broad horizons' and mighty enterprises, for the unity of mankind and the exploration of the universe? Even in a manual worker it can be a discreditable thing to do, for our economists often moralize now about the need to make labour more 'mobile' so that it can be drafted to those spots where it is most needed. It is perverse and selfish to resist.

And if living in one's own neighbourhood is difficult, to write about it is harder still. Who, anyway, are our neighbours? Our real neighbours, both of the spirit and the flesh, both those we know and those we don't, seldom live near us nowadays. We keep contact with them by telephone and plane and car, or else we have one-sided commerce with them through books and television screens. In spite of that, though the familiar hills and rivers seldom now enclose a stable or self-sufficient community, I think they are only waiting to recover their plundered significance. The canals that once diverted the rivers are all choked and after five generations the railway cuttings that ravaged the hills are collapsing. Why should the great dams at Ardnacrusha and Poulaphouca, or the television mast on Mount Leinster, or the huge roads that level out villages and raths and esker ridges, prove more enduring? They are all linked with certain ways of life and thought, and ideas have never been as ephemeral as in the twentieth century.

But to look ahead like this is not very comforting to the beleaguered country-dweller. At eighty-four I am, like everybody else, very disillusioned but only averagely discontented. Fundamentally I think as I always did. The post to which I am willingly tethered still holds firm and I have grazed around it in a sufficiently wide circle. Close-cropped grass comes up again fresh and sweet, and whoever comes along next may find my patch slightly improved.

So even when these essays appear to be about Russia or Greece or Spain or Yugoslavia, they are really about Ireland. We choose some of our experiences and others are forced on us, but they have little meaning till they are related to some central focus of ideas and this focus for me has never varied. Many of the irrelevant things that have happened to me have been boring or nasty, but not all of them. For example, like many Europeans, I have exchanged a couple of dull sentences with Chou Enlai and seen the Great Wall of China, but I have no idea how to profit by this fascinating adventure, for I think we Westerners can mostly only sense the sweetness of China, we can bring nothing home with us. We are like honey bees which can get nectar from white clover but not from red, because their sucking apparatus is too short. And I do not believe that we should be spiritually impoverished if for a century or more we were excluded from all Asia and all Africa beyond the shores of the Mediterranean.

But nowadays can we exclude ourselves from anything? Can the ant ever escape from his anthill? Even the most sedentary and homebound person is obliged to roam the world in spirit ten or twenty times a day. The newspapers and the radio and television release a million images of remote places and people. They settle like butterflies on the brain till every cell is clogged with the larvae from their unwanted eggs. How can one protect oneself from the ravages of secondhand experience? Here and there perhaps one can replace this pre-digested stuff with experiences of one's own. But to most people this seems an affectation, like the quest for free-range eggs or vegetables from 'organic' farms.

While we are more or less committed to mass travel and to information that is canalized for press-conferences, the experiences that nourish us are individual, not collective. Few of us have been of use to any Indian, Negro or Chinaman, and the regard we have for them is unmixed with personal gratitude; yet many generations of vicarious involvement have caused us to think we are necessary to each other, and it will take as many more to unlearn this.

When this happens we shall recognize again that within a few square miles we should have everything which we can possibly need. Here in Kilkenny the earth is fruitful and the neighbours are intelligent, imaginative and kind; their minds are well-adapted to poetry and jokes and the propounding and solving of problems. Though it is not easy to be independent of tinned pineapples and the Dublin dailies, we could be, at a price. But even the tinkers and the retired colonial administrators are more restless and discontented than they used to be. The colonials, travelling round the earth, have lost the countryman's acquiescence in seemingly immutable things like temperature and rainfall and local prejudices. It is now easy to avoid what one cannot change, so they move about. And though our tinkers come back every summer to the same lanes and clearings, the last ones who came here had spent the winter washing dishes in the Cumberland Hotel at Marble Arch. They play the familiar tricks with a touch of urban sophistication, and it is hard to see them as neighbours whom it is one's duty to love.

All this sounds misleadingly nostalgic. In fact nothing has happened that cannot be reversed if it is accurately recorded. That is the purpose of these essays, in which I try to show that the countryside, where mean and silly things happen because energy and intelligence have been drained away, is an essential part of the world pattern which too few have studied. In 'Boycott Village', for example, I complain that no one has investigated why ordinary people with nice intentions and neighbourly instincts proved to be such incompetent guardians of freedom. I do not know what the answer is but, if we relate the facts as we see them, posterity will perhaps handle them less clumsily than we have done.

I grew up before the great emigration of the Anglo-Irish in the twenties had begun, when some of the pioneers of the Irish Literary Revival were still alive and active, and through the *Irish Statesman* AE was still confidently elaborating his plans for a co-operative Ireland. These were dreams with reality and achievement behind them but they could not stand up to the Gaelic dream of Patrick Pearse, for it had been sanctified in blood. Now that dream too has faded, though the blood sacrifice still goes on, like the fire that smoulders slowly towards the forest when the picnic is over.

Now there are no dreams left to sustain us and all we have is a rag-bag of tangled notions and prejudices, of which I have exhibited a sampling in 'Envoy and Mr Kavanagh'. I do not doubt that a new generation, with fresh ideas and the vigour to carry them through, will solve some of our problems, and yet in times of troubled peace like ours, when the old idealisms have lost their magic, the future, I believe, lies with the solitary individual of whom Chekhov used to write. I quote from one of his letters:

> I see that our salvation will come from solitary personalities, scattered here and there over Russia, sometimes educated, sometimes peasant. Power is in their hands even though there are few of them. No man is a prophet in his own country and these solitary individuals, of which I speak, play an imperceptible role in society; they do not dominate it but their work is visible.

It was in the same way that Vershinin reassured the three sisters that knowledge and intelligence were never wasted. He said there was no town so boring and dead that three people of intellect and education could not make a faint impression; they would get swallowed up, of course, by the dark masses, but not without leaving some slight influence, and after them there would be six, then twelve, till at last they would be in a majority. 'In two or three hundred years life would be unspeakably, amazingly lovely.'

Yet now something has happened to thrust this future loveliness even farther away. Vershinin had not forseen that as culture, under official patronage, became increasingly centripetal, Feeny, Meany and Sweeney, the three people of intellect and education, would fall under the irresistible, techno-cultural influence of the capital. Long before the three had propagated six and the six twelve, each nourishing his successors with the rich decay of his talents, the tempter would address himself seductively to them. Feeny and Meany would persuade themselves that they could serve their little town best from outside. Feeny would get a plum of a job as adviser to Channel 3 on South-Eastern Regional Culture, and Meany, no longer his ally but his rival, would draw a smaller income from his Friday afternoon talks on rural problems; Sweeney would stay behind, a new element, jealousy, penetrating his loneliness and distorting his judgment.

And what of the dark masses? They would be just as dark as before but with no trouble to themselves they would be given extension lectures and loan exhibitions, so that even Sweeney in his unpopular enthusiasms would seem superfluous and the task of swallowing him up would be greatly eased.

It is in fact a problem of men, not methods, and we can hope for little from the clever educational gadgets with which we try to irrigate the intellectual deserts. The soil that has been robbed of its natural creativity cannot be restored to health by fertilizing chemicals. Make it possible for Feeny, Meany and Sweeney, the 'solitary individuals', to live in their own homes, for nature has planted them there like antibodies in a diseased constitution. Only they have power to regenerate it.

This, of course, is contrary to all current notions. Everything that is seminal or germinative in the way of ideas is thought to develop in the great centres of culture, where intellectuals congregate. It is in the press, the theatres, the clubs of the metropolis that revolutionary ideas are expressed and challenged. Things are openly said that could scarcely be thought in a provincial town. Yet there is something self-destructive about these great congestions of originality. A sense of doom hangs over them as over the exuberant freedom of the Weimar Republic.

Here is one of the reasons. In a vast society like ours, 'the man of intellect and education', as Chekhov saw him, is one among several thousands, a natural solitary, in fact. His function is to be the pinch of bread-soda in the dough, and not to foregather with other ex-solitaries and form a bread-soda pudding. Yet an Irishman sees this happening every year. Feeny and Meany, drawn away from their solitude, bring with them to the city their instinct to defy. They gather together with other ex-solitaries; then they are no longer solitary and what is more they find they are no longer original. Their insights and perceptions, which surprised and often vexed their fellow-citizens, are banal and irrelevant among the exuberant heterodoxies of their new community. In place of the known neighbours whom it was their duty to challenge, there are faceless strangers who can only be met with abstractions. To get attention in such circles, the ex-solitary may have to turn in his tracks, to sacrifice the particular to the general, and to accept as valid some mass-produced consensus whose insufficiency he would quickly have detected among the familiar diversities of his native town. In this way the cities acquire fanatics at the same rate as the provinces lose their solitary individuals.

Am I exaggerating? Probably, but there is evidence from Russia and Italy and Germany that totalitarian beliefs spread from the cities to the provinces where sharp antagonisms had been held in check by a long history of neighbourly interdependence.

So I go on believing that the strength to live comes from an understanding of ourselves and our neighbours or the diaspora that has replaced them. If we could focus on them all the curiosity and wisdom that we disperse round the world, as we focus all the rays of the sun through a burning glass on a pile of dead leaves, there is no limit to the warmth and life we could generate. It is easier of course to collect the dead leaves than to make the sparks to kindle them. Yet I believe the life which Chekhov prophesied, 'unspeakably, amazingly lovely', is not out of our reach, though it may now be a century or two farther away than he calculated.

Some of this material is unpublished (the latter portion of 'The Artukovitch File'), some has been recast ('Beside the Nore', 'Divided Loyalties'), updated ('Boycott Village') or extended from the original ('Peter's Window') – sources will be found under Acknowledgments – but for the most part these essays are unaltered, though a few of them deal with problems that appear to have been solved or episodes that have long been forgotten. We have lived though two world wars and, in Ireland, rebellion and civil war. Yet the basic things remain the same. When I was a boy of ten the Ulster Unionists were saying Home Rule is Rome

Rule and civil war was threatened. Now I am eighty-four and the Ulster Unionists are saying Home Rule is Rome Rule and civil war does not seem immeasurably far away. It is as though we were on a scenic railway in a fun-fair. We pass through towering cardboard mountains and over raging torrents and come to rest in the same well-trodden field from which we got on board.

I have lived for long periods at home and my garden, with its vegetables and raspberry canes, its orchard and neglected flower-beds, has had to take the place of people and events. Thirty-three years ago my life of active involvement in enthusiasms which I shared with my neighbours ended abruptly. I have described how this came about in 'The Sub-Prefect Should Have Held His Tongue'. I shall not refer to this again as my affection for my neighbours has not changed. We were all of us victims of events beyond our control. Ireland was caught in the backwash of a tremendous religious struggle in Central and Eastern Europe, which we did not understand and for which we were unprepared. It was inevitable that there should be casualties.

Are we here in Ireland any nearer to that eighteenth-century dream 'to unite the whole people of Ireland, to abolish the memory of past dissensions, and to substitute the common name of Irishman in place of the denomination of Protestant, Catholic and Dissenter'?

The idea of a religious war is so abhorrent and disgraceful that many prefer to think that it is for loyalty to the British Crown that Ulstermen will fight. They are wrong, because Ulster loyalty is to a Protestant monarch and would not survive if the monarch became a Roman Catholic. In fact it is the old insoluble conflict between authority and private judgment. Though all of us sometimes defer to authority, sometimes judge for ourselves, the moment we cease to act as individuals and think collectively, what was a matter of choice becomes a matter of principle and a clash between Catholic and Protestant is likely.

Can ecumenism help? In Ireland 160 years ago there was a vigorous ecumenical movement. The circumstances were more favourable then than now but it ended in a deadlock. I have told the story in the following pages.

In 'The Bishop' I write of an eighteenth-century young man, agreeable and popular, who could not resist the fleshpots of an ascendancy he knew to be doomed.

In 'The Eggman and the Fairies' the Captains and the Kings

have all but gone and taken with them their sophistication and learning, their love of their home and their self-knowledge by means of which what looked irremediable might have been remedied. The Clearys in their cruel innocence and isolation could only escape from poverty and ignorance into fairyland.

Most of the other Irish pieces are self-explanatory.

When I was thirty-one and Soviet Russia was fifteen years old I taught English for a term in Leningrad. I was very happy there and would like to have stayed longer but the pull of my home and those I loved was too strong for me. I came back with as little understanding of Marxism and Communism as I went but I made many friends whom I still remember with affection. There was a multitude of small misunderstandings and difficulties but they all counted for nothing compared with the imaginative kindness with which I was welcomed. In 'Peter's Window' I tell the story of that time.

Men and women are surely more important than the systems in which they imprison themselves. Yet it is not easy to disentangle ourselves and to commit ourselves unreservedly to personal relations. Organized religion cannot liberate us for it is a system too, and there is nothing more bitter than the conflict of two religious systems, as I have found both in my own country and the foreign country I know best, Yugoslavia.

Three years after I returned from Russia I went to teach in Zagreb in the Anglo-American-Yugoslav Society. It had been founded by my friend, Dr Milan Churchin, the editor of *Nova Evropa,* the leading liberal journal of Central Europe, and by Dr Georgievitch, the Orthodox Bishop of Dalmatia. I also had a small scholarship from the School of Slavonic Studies in London.

Yugoslavia had been born in 1918 after the defeat of Austria-Hungary and the rise of the Succession States. For the southern Slavs it was the fulfilment of an ancient dream of harmony between four neighbouring and kindred peoples. I was at Oxford then and there was springtime in the air. There were Serbs, Croats and Czechs, there were Irish too, all rejoicing in their new-found freedom. We all had minority problems and I was surprised that Ireland, least scarred by war, did not identify herself with the other small new states more warmly, share experiences and take the lead for which she was qualified. The Croats knew about Ulster and some of them talked of Croatia, ruefully, as 'the Ulster of Yugoslavia'. This needed a readjustment of roles, but one knew what they meant. They were Catholics and to them Zagreb, the Croatian capital, was 'a little Vienna'. They wondered how they would fare in union with the more primitive Serbian Orthodox, who had fought for freedom while they had mostly fought for Austria-Hungary.

The day we arrived in Zagreb, 9 October 1934, news had just come that King Alexander, a Serb, had, with Barthou the French Foreign Minister, been assassinated in Marseilles by agents of the separatist Croat leader, Pavelitch. Zagreb was plunged in well-organized mourning with portraits of the king surrounded by black crape in the shop-windows and black bows on the funnels of the railway engines. Two days later the king's body arrived from Split, where it had been shipped from Marseilles on its way to Belgrade. It lay for a couple of hours, surrounded by pot-plants, in the first class waiting-room at the station, where it was visited by mile-long processions. One of those who prayed beside the royal coffin was Archbishop Bauer, the Catholic Primate, accompanied by his Auxiliary Monsignor Stepinac.

During our time in Yugoslavia the shadow of the assassination hung over the whole country. Hitler had come to power in Germany and Jewish refugees were flocking to the Dalmatian coast. In Italy and Hungary, Pavelitch and his helper, Artukovitch, were training the army of the Croat rebels, who were, in 1941, to sweep into Yugoslavia with the Nazis and proclaim the Independent State of Croatia.

And yet my recollections are of peace and beauty. There was almost no traffic in Yelachitch Trg, the central square. Fat amethyst pigeons strutted through the market stalls looking for pickings and panicking when the church bells rang. The scent of mimosa and wood-smoke, holy candles and freshly tanned leather drowned the faint whiff of petrol. On Sunday, we walked up Slijeme Mountain, where wild cyclamen and hellebore grew through the beech woods. In our room I rooted oleander cuttings in bottles between the double windows. And when my pupils were on holiday I wrote down the story of Mr Pfeffer.

Zagreb, in the thirties, was a very cultivated little town; it had an opera house and theatres, and there were still remnants of an Austrianized aristocracy in the leafy suburbs. Dalmatia was Italianate and Belgrade was still largely Turkish in character. When one went south and penetrated to Montenegro, one seemed to pass from our cruel, complicated century to an earlier one, just as cruel, where each man was responsible to his neighbours for his crimes and where organized twentieth-century barbarity had not yet emerged. Possibly in 'The Last Izmirenje' I have idealized what I saw. To know what Montenegro was really like you must read Djilas's superb autobiography, *Land Without Justice'* (1958).

The war came and Yugoslavia was carved up by Germany and her allies. Croatia, which had not resisted the Nazis, was rewarded with her Independent State under the rule of Pavelitch, King Alexander's convicted murderer.

Then in Zagreb an Aeschylean tragedy was enacted. The same young priest who had stood beside the coffin of his murdered king, reappeared before his countrymen as Archbishop at the right hand of his king's assassin, helpless in the face of Pavelitch's resolve to exterminate the Orthodox by expulsion, massacre or forced conversion. Unhappy but icily correct, Stepinac considered himself to be the servant of a power that is higher than the king or his murderer, and one that has rules for every occasion. His conscience was clear.

Violence came a second time to the city. Caring neither for king nor priest nor pope nor assassin, the Communists swept in, resolved to make all things new. I have written about this period in my two pieces, 'The Sub-Prefect Should Have Held His Tongue' and 'The Artukovitch File', yet I would like here to recall the historical background to the events I have described. There are three great sources of power and influence in Eastern and Central Europe: Roman Catholicism, Byzantine Orthodoxy and Communism. Orthodoxy, which broke away from Rome five centuries before the Protestant Reformation, was once, with its Patriarch magnificently enthroned at Constantinople, the rival of Rome in power and splendour. Now the Orthodox Church is a shadow of its former self. With Saint Sophia a secular museum, the Patriarch lives on sufferance from the Turks in a small quarter of Istanbul. Since the Russian Revolution the other Patriarchs over whom he reigns as *primus inter pares* are weak and scattered. Communist Moscow threatens them from the East and the Catholic powers from the West. Those Russian Orthodox who survived beyond the borders of Tsarist Russia and later the Soviet State, have had to fight for their faith and culture against the politico-religious scheming of Austria-Hungary and her successors, Czechoslovakia and Poland.

A powerful instrument in this little-known stuggle is the Uniat Church, devised by King Sigismund III of Poland and the Pope in the sixteenth century to attract the peasants of the eastern border-lands away from Orthodoxy. The Orthodox received into this Church retained their ritual and their married clergy but Rome, not Moscow, became the focus of their obedience.

This Uniat Church has been used many times in our century by the Western Powers for political purposes. At the beginning of the war in 1914, when the Austrians were advancing against the Russian Ukraine, a detailed memorandum about its occupation was formulated by the Uniat Archbishop, Count Szepticky of Lemberg in Austrian Galicia. Apart from the military and juridical arrangements, the Orthodox Church in the new Protectorate was to be detached from the Moscow Patriarchate and subjected to Szepticky himself, as Uniat Metropolitan. Prayers for the Tsar were to be forbidden and prayers for the Emperor substituted. The Muscovite saints were to be eliminated from the calendar. The new Prince of the Ukraine was to be Archduke Wilhelm, who had changed his name to Vasily, learnt Ukrainian and wore an embroidered Ukrainian tunic. But the Russians struck back, occupied Lemberg, arrested the Archbishop and published the Memorandum in the Petrograd papers. Soon after this the Revolution occurred.

In the Second World War the Uniat Church was active in Croatia; in 1941-2 Dr Shimrak, the Uniat Bishop, played a notable part in the campaign for the conversion of the Orthodox.

For many years the Czechs and Slovaks used the Uniats to secure and, if possible, extend their eastern frontier, where Carpatho-Russian Orthodox were settled along the Ukrainian border. They revived for themselves the old Austro-Hungarian dream of a vast Ukrainian protectorate and for this purpose rechristened Carpatho-Russian 'Carpatho-Ukraine' and supported the Uniats against the Orthodox. The story of this often violent struggle has been told month by month in *Svobodnoye Slovo (Free Word)*, the organ of the many *émigré* Carpatho-Russian Orthodox in the USA.

In Europe it is now only in Greece that a free Orthodox Church survives. When in 1964 there was a friendly meeting in the Holy Land between the Pope and the titular head of the Orthodox Church (the Patriarch in Constantinople), Chrysostom, the

Primate of Greece, and his bishops refused to participate and even asked for the dissolution of the Uniat Church. The world was shocked that when all Christendom is craving for unity the Primate of Greece could be so intransigent, yet it is intelligible enough. The Greeks are the countrymen of Aesop, who wrote so many fables about small animals to whom large ones made friendly overtures. It is natural for them to dread the Uniat embrace.

Should we involve ourselves with complex happenings in far countries? Sometimes we have to, but we misinterpret them at our peril.

On May Day 1949 a crowd of 150,000, said to be the largest ever seen in Dublin, assembled in O'Connell Street to protest against the imprisonment of Archbishop Stepinac of Yugoslavia and a Hungarian Cardinal Mindszenty. There were bands, speeches, telegrams, women fainted and a young man, wrongly suspected of distributing Communist leaflsts, was struck on the head and taken to hospital.

In America there were even greater demonstrations and many thought that with so righteous a cause, and Russia still weak after the Nazi invasion, the moment for a third world war had arrived.

I know nothing about Cardinal Mindszenty but I knew that the struggle in which Stepinac was involved was totally misconceived. It was a pre-Communist and inter-Christian one. As in Ireland, race and religion go together, Catholic Croat confronted Orthodox Serb and Hitler's war had triggered off a massacre of the Orthodox by the Catholics. Hugh Seton-Watson, the well-known historian of Central Europe, wrote in 1945: 'The Communists saved Yugoslavia from a bloody civil war on racial lines, which would have been inevitable, if Mihailovitch [the Serbian Orthodox general] had come to power.'* This is something which in Ireland we would be reluctant to believe. Who could wish a Communist solution to our own racial and religious problems?

We live and think under a nuclear cloud and stretch our brains, built for solving human problems, into thinking cosmically. If sooner or later they fail us, friend and enemy will be destroyed together. How soon can we return to being men, not human adjuncts to machines, and handle again man-sized problems? How soon can we escape from the anthill which we have built round ourselves?

* Hugh Seton-Watson, *Nationalism and Communism* (London 1945), p. 90.

PART ONE
ANGLO-IRELAND AND AFTER, 1745-1984

Like circles raised in the water by the impulse of a heavy body, our social duties, as they expand, grow fainter. . . .The love and service of our country is perhaps the widest circle in which we can hope to display an active benevolence. . . . If every man were to devote his powers to the service of his country, mankind would be universally served.

CHARLEMONT

1

HENRY AND FRANCES

One afternoon fourteen or fifteen years ago we were cataloguing the library of our neighbour, Miss Power of Kilfane. It is a long beautiful room with tall windows between the bookcases looking on to a sweep of green lawn and beyond it a classically planted park. The library with its great fire was a delightful place in which to work or shirk work and we found ourselves too often sinking into luxurious arm-chairs and reading the books we were supposed to be cataloguing. Most of them were collected in the eighteenth and early nineteenth century and the family had two ruling passions, Art and Sport. The Kilkenny Theatre and the Kilkenny Hunt were their creations but the first of their two enthusiasms evaporated when the Theatre closed its doors in 1819 and when soon afterwards its founder, Richard Power, died. John Power's hunt still flourishes but the literature of hunting is not large and only a few books appear to have been added to the shelves in Victorian times. In his day, Richard Power filled his bookshelves not only with a unique collection of plays; he had also a fine store of essays, biographies and political pamphlets. I was cataloguing these books when, on one occasion, I took down four small volumes dated 1770. They were called *A Series of Genuine Letters between Henry and Frances,* but they had no author's name and I searched the pages for a clue. Some of the letters were dated from Kilfane and some from Farmley, where Henry Flood, the orator, lived; I exclaimed aloud when I discovered that many of the letters were dated from my own home, six miles away. Maidenhall is a small unpretentious Georgian house and I knew nothing of its history in the eighteenth century for my great grandfather did not come to the district till 1800 or later, but to the best of my knowledge it was built about 1745. Then I remembered having seen the name Griffith on an old Title

Deed. I borrowed the books to compare dates and make what inferences I could from the letters themselves. I was fascinated by the supple and often witty prose and successfully placed the authors, for there were two of them, Richard Griffith (Henry), and his wife, Elizabeth (Frances), who lived here and built this house over two hundred years ago.

The letters are disappointingly meagre about the ordinary social life of Bennettsbridge and Kilkenny; they mainly deal with the complicated, uneasy love affair of Henry and Frances. The Griffiths were a learned and cultivated couple, who for some reason to which they only allude mysteriously, had first to delay then to conceal their marriage for several years. Possibly delays and dissimulations were caused by money difficulties or a disapproving relative but I think it more likely that Frances' pride was the hindrance. Henry did not consider it necessary to be faithful to her and wrote to her about his infidelities in an aloof, philosophical way. For example, he had told her how his maid Nancy had had to be dismissed because she made such a scene about being supplanted in his affections by Sally. Frances tried to reply with equal philosophy but probably her heart was not in it:

> As for the affair of Nancy and Sally, it is of no farther consequence to me than if James and the Coachman had been the Disputants. Nor did I mention my Opinion of Sally with any Design; for you may easily conceive that it is a matter of Indifference to me whether your present favourite was called Sarah or Anne; for while I am in possession of the Jewel that is lodged within I care not who holds the Casket.
>
> O free for ever be his eye,
> Whose heart to me is always true.

Her biographer, Miss Tomkins, has discovered an ingenious sentence in Frances's novel, *The History of Lady Barton,* which suggests a different outlook and may throw light on the postponement of the marriage. 'There is something extremely indelicate in professing a Passion for a virtuous Woman before we have undergone a sufficient Quarantine after the Contagion of an abandoned one, and Man in such a Situation resembles a Centaur, half-human and half-brute.'

Perhaps she was waiting till Henry had been purged by time of all those earlier contagions before she would acknowledge him as her husband.

Henry lived at Maidenhall, farming and building a flaxmill,

Frances stayed with her old aunt at Abbey Street, Dublin, and later in lodgings in Chapelizod. Now and again, heavily chaperoned, she paid visits to her husband at Maidenhall. Before they published their letters they must have pruned them drastically, because though they are certainly genuine letters they contain very few of those trivial accounts of everyday life which the originals must certainly have had and which we would today find so enthralling. In the first edition the Irish place-names had been changed to English, so that the polite eye should not be offended by our barbarous nomenclature. Though frank about his morals he is fastidiously evasive about his occupation and finances, and it is only by inference and reference to other works that we find why he paid visits to country houses round Kilkenny and what happened to his flax mills.

He was doing some electioneering work, though for whom he was canvassing I do not know; as for the flax mills, he had got a grant from parliament for starting linen-manufacture on the Nore and in the expectation of a larger one he had built his factory and the house of Maidenhall. Then to set it going he had mortgaged it all. But very soon times changed for the worse, the second grant was withheld and Henry was ruined. It was soon after this that he and his wife decided to publish their letters to see if they could earn by literature what they had lost on linen. They succeeded and she became an immensely popular novelist and the first English translator of Voltaire; he too earned a living by his novels and his philosophical reflections. Most of their original work except the *Letters* is today unreadable but it charmed their contemporaries. Fanny Burney, after she had been reading *The Letters of Henry and Frances*, took up *The Vicar of Wakefield* by a new writer, Oliver Goldsmith, but she tells us she nearly threw it aside after reading a few pages, so disgusted was she with its coarse,indelicate outlook on life and in particular on matrimony; it was a cruel contrast to the 'so elegantly natural, so unassumingly rational' tone of the Griffith *Letters*. In London the Griffiths became well known in the circle of Garrick and Johnson; their little boy, Harry, who in the days of their poverty had to be brought up by his grandmother at Portarlington, became a nabob in India. He returned to Ireland, bought the estate of Millicent in Co. Kildare and played an influential part in Grattan's Parliament. He was the father of Sir Richard John Griffith, the distinguished geologist and civil engineer.

Last year I got a letter from a lady in an American university, enquiring about the Griffiths on whom she was writing a thesis. Americans are well known for their choice of recondite subjects for theses, but I was ashamed that this learned couple should be the object of careful researches in Alabama, while I, who lived in their house, knew so little about them. I found that an excellent biographical sketch of them had been published in 1938 by the Cambridge University Press by Miss J. M. S. Tompkins, who had collected much new material from English sources. Naturally it was their late London career that interested her most; for me these few troubled years they spent in Bennettsbridge have by far the greatest appeal.

In those days it was possible for country gentlemen to see their lives in terms of classical analogy and imagery. It was easy enough for Irish landlords who left their latifundia to be administered by agents to picture their estates as 'rural retreats' to which they retired like Horace or Cicero from the cares of state to plant trees and study philosophy. They reflected on the vicissitudes of life, its inequalities and injustices, with a freedom that would have seemed to a later generation subversive and disloyal to their class. Henry Flood regarded his substantial estate nearby at Farmley, as 'Tusculum', where he relaxed from toil. He had amateur theatricals and lent his support to the revival of interest in the Celtic past. Griffith, though only an unsuccessful mill-owner with a bare 600 acres, modelled himself naturally on these philosophical grandees, calling his tours around his Bennettsbridge farm his 'Ambarvalia'.

Henry used to attend the Kilkenny assizes and watch with philosophical melancholy the procession of the condemned to the gallows. His contempt for worldly values was of a rather static and literary kind but there are many letters which show him to have been a kindly and original character. He had a peculiar variety of colic, which he treated with opium and horse radish emetic and once or twice with the 'Hygean waves of Scarborough'. When on a journey his agonies used to arouse so much exasperation and compassion in his fellow passengers that he forced himself to fast. Once at an inn he had three ginger-bread nuts and a pint of white wine and the landlord presented him with a bill for the full dinner. Griffith retaliated by going into the street and calling in an old beggar woman, to whom he insisted that the dinner which he had paid for but not eaten, should be served. 'She is my stomach,' he told the furious landlord.

Henry scarcely mentioned his employees or his factory. Before he purchased his machinery he paid a visit of inspection to Smyth's Linen Factory at Waterford and, for Frances' benefit, he tried to assimilate this revolutionary spectacle into his rational philosophy. In the mid-eighteenth century Chartism was still far off and machinery seemed capable of liberating Rational Man, a noble and exalted being, from his dependence on other living creatures. The animal nature, unlike machinery, 'through Caprice is capable of disappointing the Ends of its Creation'. Rational Man, Henry thought, would be made free to contemplate Truth and Beauty and to practise Morality and Religion. 'The Vulgar Herd, who are insensible to these advantages, I take to be more imperfect instruments than a Windmill or a Loom.'

There is no evidence that Henry and Frances were snobbish or insensitive employers. Henry at least was by no means fastidious in his intimacies. But it seemed to them that the higher pleasures were the fruits of the cultivated understanding and those to whom fortune had denied cultivation were of necessity barren and therefore uninteresting. We hear almost nothing about them.

Last autumn, watching a reaper and binder going round one of his fields with a couple of men accompanying it, I remembered how Henry used to sit among the stooks in a barley-field, writing to Frances and reading Pliny's *Letters*. Watching the binders and stackers, he counted forty-seven women and fourteen men. Yet their lives were more remote from him than the lives of the ancient Romans. When his son was born, he wrote to Frances that if it *had* to be called Pliny he would prefer it to be named after the Younger Pliny than Pliny the Elder, since he would wish it endowed with liveliness rather than learning. Frances too liked to clothe her jokes and reflections in classical dress.

They had great skill in descriptive writing. How could the following account by Henry of a painted ceiling be bettered? 'A Fricassy of Cherubims with here a Head and there a Leg or an Arm, peeping through the Clouds, which look like a good, rich, thick Sauce poured about them.'

They were wholly unpolitical people. I doubt whether it ever occurred to them that happiness could be brought about by social legislation. Happiness depended on the right ordering of life, on the enjoyment of rational delights, and the consolations afforded by wisdom and learning. In this system religion had an important function since it gave warmth to life, and Henry and Frances tinker with it experimentally like a pair of amateurs trying to coax heat out of an old-fashioned boiler. The principle on which it worked, they were aware, was Belief in God. This, Henry thought, was accessible to Protestants only. 'The popes of Rome,' he declared, 'by assuming to themselves the powers of Binding and Releasing, have long since superseded their God.' And at the request of a friend of his Henry wrote a strong letter denouncing the Errors of Rome and the Foulness of its Superstitions, its idle Forms and useless Ceremonies.

The occasion for this letter is remarkable. A Roman Catholic neighbour of Henry's had changed his religion in order to receive an estate valued at £700 per annum. He had been crushed by a letter 'all fire and brimstone' from a brother, who was a priest at Bordeaux, and he had asked Henry to compose a reply for him. Henry reproduces his reply of which he was evidently proud. It could only have been written in the Age of Reason, when a Rational Argument was a weapon which could be adapted to every circumstance. It can justify apostacy for £700 per annum and is equally formidable whether it comes from the brain of the apostate or the friend who impersonates him. Henry was too volatile to be called a humbug; he could not deceive himself for long. He was an experimentalist and would quickly have revolted against his own arguments if anyone had imposed them on him as dogma.

'Our Religion,' Henry wrote, 'is deduced from the plain Text of the Scriptures, yours from the sophistical Comments of the Priests. When a Priest once asked a Protestant, where his Religion was before Luther, he answered humorously but not less justly by asking him where was his Face before it was washed?'

He was as satisfied when his speculations led him to an orthodox conclusion as a patience player, when his patience comes out. Riding, once, towards the Castlecomer hills from Maidenhall, he saw the horizon flushed with fire so that he thought the coal seams were ablaze and that the whole earth was burning. He learnt from a passer-by that it was some natural exhalation of the heathy soil but he fell to meditating on the Last Conflagration which is prophesied in the Scriptures. At last it seemed to him that he had found a way of reconciling Religion and the Philosophy of Nature. His explanation is ingenious rather than convincing. It concerns the extra weight of the earth due to God's Creation of Living Things. Bodies attract in proportion to the weight of matter in them. The centripetal by degrees overcomes the centrifugal and the earth rushes into the sun. Hence the conflagration. About this argument Henry said rather smugly: 'As I am not quite orthodox, on some points, I own that I heartily rejoice when I can make amends on others.'

Henry believed in resurrection of the body, but he elaborated this sombre belief with private fancies of his own. He often meditated how his body could best be disposed of so that its elements could be converted into some other animate being or beings with the greatest speed and economy. Mummification he held in horror. 'I could not bear the Thought of lying a moment Idle, alive or dead.' Burning he could tolerate, provided it were not in an 'Asbesto Shroud'. But best of all, he said, 'I would chose to be devoured by Beasts, as by that means, I should more immediately become Part of Living Animals.' He preferred dogs and among dogs he chose a mastiff for its courage, a hound for its sagacity and a spaniel for its fidelity.

Even before his financial crash they were finding life in the countryside lonely and unsatisfying. When Frances was away, he now had no friend to console him for her absence at Maidenhall, save a 'low-spirited cat' called Sultana Puss. 'Her nerves,' he said, 'are so weak (which I attribute to her drinking tea in a morning without Eating), that the least loud Word sets her trembling; so that I dare not chide an awkward Housemaid for fear of putting Madam into her Hysterics.'

On his visits to country houses, Henry was continually affronted by the spectacle of 'bookless, sauntering Youth'. 'Before this century shall be closed,' he wrote, 'it is not impossible that anyone who can commit a Speech or a Sentence to Writing will pass for a Conjurer, who can paint his Thoughts on Paper.' And to Frances he wrote, 'Your Sense, your Principle and your Taste are thrown away upon the Deaf Adder and the very Seeds of them all stifled in the Growth or buried like a bad Ploughman's Grain by Clods of Earth laid over them.' In another letter he compares her writings 'to certain rich Essences which only affect the finest Capillaries'. Their neighbours were sociable enough but without fine capillaries and, thinking of their tedious visits, Henry said, 'Momus very justly found fault with the Construction of a House, because it had no Wheels to be moved by when the

Situation became uneasy.'

At last Henry gave up Maidenhall, which he had loved so much. He told Frances how riding home from Dublin, when his decision was made, his impatience to see it grew at every mile. 'The thoughts of quitting it have the more attendered me towards it. If I thought there was a Naiad or a Dryad in the Place who would lament my absence, I should sacrifice my Interests to my Superstition; but my Religion teaches me that wherever we go our Guardian Angel accompanies us. I think I but obey its Call whenever I change my Situation to my Advantage.'

The Griffiths often indulged romantic dreams but they held them under control, submitting themselves constantly to calm and ruthless examination. It is rumoured that their marriage ended in separation, but, even if this were true, I doubt whether either of them would have considered it an ill-advised marriage. Continually at every stage they had tested the flavour of their relationship and found it good. It can only have been the dregs that they jettisoned.

But his marriage was still recent and wholly satisfying when Henry left Maidenhall. He must have felt that a turning-point in his life had been reached and that a rather more solemn self analysis than he had hitherto attempted should be undertaken. On leaving the house he made a will in favour of Frances and her infant son and wrote upon the wrapper the reasons for his marriage and his theological beliefs.

> I was not overreached into this Match by Art nor hurried into it by Passion, but, from long experience of her Sense and Worth, I reasoned myself into it. . . I found that I had so engaged her Affections that no other Man could make her happy and so dallied with her Character, that only myself could repair it. . . I am in my Religion a Christian; but of the Arian heresy as it is stiled by bigotted Councils. I was for many years a Deist, till Dr. Clayton, Bishop of Clogher, his Essay on Spirit and subsequent Writings on the same Subject had reconciled the doctrine of the Trinity to human reason and metaphysical science.
>
> Humanum est errare et nescire;
> Ens Entium, miserere mei.

Last year the Nore flooded, as it so often does, and flattened out the remaining wall of Griffith's flaxmill, which has been used for some generations as a boundary fence. The mill-stream has long been choked up and it was only quite lately that poking about on the banks of the river I found traces of its stone-built sides. The cottages that housed the mill-hands as well as the sixty-one harvesters have gone without trace, but the elm trees which Henry planted are still standing. As for Maidenhall, it has not changed very much; its successive owners have always been poor and never had the money to make many of those lavish improvements which were admired in Victorian times.

[1950]

Réproduction d'une carte manuscrite du Waterford-Shire et du territoire offert aux émigrés Genevois de 1782. (Bulletin de L'Institut National Genevois, Tome XXXIX, Genève 1909.)

2

NEW GENEVA IN WATERFORD

The little fishing village of Passage lies on the west bank of the Suir, between Dunmore East and Waterford. It still retains a rather special air of antiquity and distinction, but I do not think that many of those who live around it realize how near it once was to becoming the centre of a large and flourishing city with academies of sciences and the arts and many thriving industries. The city was a dream of the late eighteenth century, but a dream that came very near to realization. In Ireland itself very little if anything has been written upon this project, but here in Geneva, the mother-city of this future town, I have found much of interest in the archives of the Hôtel de Ville, where the records of the City Council and many documents relating to its history are scrupulously preserved. There are minutes and letters and biographies; there is even a plan of the New Geneva on the Suir.

Why was the plan conceived, why did it fail? I will try to compress into a few paragraphs a complicated story which is woven out of the troubled history of two small states. In the last decade but one of the eighteenth century the City of Geneva was in ferment. It had a conservative aristocracy and also a prosperous and ambitious middle-class, which had been deeply affected by the liberal ideas of the time. Rousseau himself had been a citizen of Geneva, and Voltaire at Ferney had lived only a few miles away. Geneva was a hot-bed of humanitarian thinking, very disquieting to its rulers and also to its neighbours in the Kingdoms of France and Savoy. In 1768, at a time of similar commotion in Geneva, Rousseau had given the following advice:

> There is a last course left for you to take. Instead of staining your hands with the blood of your compatriots, you can abandon these walls, which should have been the refuge of liberty and now are to become the resort

of tyrants. All, all together, in the broad daylight, you may leave the town, your wives and your children in your midst, and, since men must wear chains, you can go and wear the chains of a great Prince, rather than the hateful and unbearable yoke of your equals (Dardier, *Esaic Gasc*).

In 1782 the troubles culminated in a small but bloodless revolution: the middle-class *représentants* overthrew and imprisoned the aristocratic council. But in a very short time the council was restored to power by a joint invasion of the armies of France, Savoy, and the canton of Berne. The disciples of Rousseau and the advocates of democratic ideas were thrown into despair. . . they decided that the only hope for their afflicted city was for the democrats to emigrate in a body bearing with them the crafts and craftsmen, chief among whom were the watchmakers. On them the prosperity of Geneva was based. In those days, in so many ways wiser than ours, refugees were welcomed, and invitations to the Genevese rebels came from many of the princes of Europe, from the Grand Duke of Tuscany, and the Elector Palatine, from the Landgrave of Hesse-Homburg, and finally, through the medium of an English republican and great friend of Geneva, Lord Mahon, from George III of England. I believe it was the Genevese themselves who pressed that their colony should be in Ireland rather than in England. In England they feared the jealousy of the English watchmakers, also the competitive claims on English sympathies of the loyalist refugees from the War of Independence in America. Moreover, Ireland was at that time also entering a period of generous idealism and enthusiasm. It was the year of the Convention of Dungannon, when the Volunteer Army was formed, which extorted from England those concessions which made Grattan's Parliament possible. On 3 October the Dublin Volunteers (commanded by Lieut.-General Henry Grattan) assembled at the Royal Exchange and passed resolutions to the effect that 'Irishmen armed for the defence of their constitution and liberties ought naturally to be attached to every country or body of men, armed for the defence of a like glorious cause. . . Therefore, the virtuous Genevese had the most lively claim on their pity . . . and should be received among them as brothers and friends.'

The Duke of Leinster, the Commander of the Southern Branch of the Volunteers, himself offered 2000 acres to the Genevese, and accommodation for 100 in Leinster Lodge till their houses had been built. Lord Ely, offering them land in Wexford, explained that he was quite disintererested.

I am already extremely rich. . . I wish to benefit the most enlightened people in the universe, the first Protestant colony on earth. When I am called to leave this earth, I shall repose with the serenity worthy of a man who knows that in giving happiness to you, he has reared a monument more durable than marble and shaped by the most able artist.

The newspapers of the time and the speeches of the Volunteers were filled with eulogies of the 'virtuous Genevese', who had 'stood up like Catos against Tyrants'. Some of them were given honorary rank in the Volunteer regiments. However, it was not the Duke of Leinster's land near Athy which was ultimately chosen, but some confiscated property near Waterford Harbour which belonged to the British Government. Lord Temple, the Viceroy, favoured the project, and a grant of £50,000 as well as 11,000 acres, including the town of Passage, was decreed. From this sum the transport of the citizens' families from Geneva was to be paid and the building of the town was to be started.

There is no need to question the sincerity of the Volunteers, but on the generous motives of the British Government Swiss writers have cast a doubt. The County of Waterford was at that time disturbed by the activities of the White Boys *(les enfants blancs)*, and the sinister John Beresford, one of the architects of the Union, was not only a large landowner in the district, but also a member of the commission of the Genevan settlement. Lord Temple himself, in a letter to a friend, explains why a southern rather than a northern site was chosen. 'I wished to remove them from the Northern Republicans and to place them where they might make an essential reform in the religion, industry and manners of the south.' The Genevans interpreted their rôle differently. 'We must not overlook the need to conciliate the poor, who cultivate the soil that is offered to us,' wrote Clavière, one of the Genevan Commissioners. 'The greed and harshness of the great landowners have made the tenants violent and irritable. That is the reason for the disorders of which you have heard. They are in revolt against treachery and abominable outrage. If we behave well we shall gain their confidence.'

A group of Genevans arrived in Ireland and rapid progress was made. An engineer visited the site and made plans for a water supply and a cotton factory and a laundry. At the start there were to be 50 houses, a communal bakery and an inn; there were to be a tannery and a paper factory. There was to be a big square in which was to stand a university which it was hoped would attract, like the Academy of Sciences at Geneva, scholars from all over Europe. It was to have 44 professors and assistants and to cost £4554 per annum. In the plan of the settlement, a dotted line runs from Passage to the base of the Creden Head, including nearly 1000 acres of tidal land described as 'sables à conquérir sur la mer'. Today the tide still sweeps in as it has always done, across the great curve of Woodstown Strand, but Swiss engineers were celebrated even then and it is possible that their ambitious project would have been realized.

One of the Genevese members of the Commission, Ami Melly, went back to rally the refugees who were assembled at Neuchâtel, and to summon the disaffected watchmakers to emigrate. Four of the principal watchmakers employed 2000 workmen, and their displacement would naturally be a serious blow to the city. Melly had taken the precaution of securing Irish citizenship, but even so he was clapped into gaol by the rulers of Geneva. He was tried, and despite the protests of the British Government and the personal support of two Irishmen – James Butler, Lord Cahir,and another – he was sentenced to a long term of imprisonment. However, he escaped on a rope of knotted sheets and rejoined the refugees at Neuchâtel. The warder who looked after Melly was arrested. It is characteristic of Swiss scrupulousness and attention to detail that he was punished, not only for conniving at Melly's escape, but also for stealing two of his shirts.

There is a long poem of the period dealing with the escape and describing how Melly was led out of prison by an angel. Though there was a 'Nouvelle Genève' printing press at Waterford, which published some French poems, I think this one is more likely to have been printed at Neuchâtel than in Ireland. The poet, not a very good one, exhorts the Genevese craftsmen and scholars to follow Melly to Waterford.

> Pour vous, pour vos enfants une ville s'éléve,
> Déjà l'on voit bâtir la Nouvelle Genève!
> C'est là que le bonheur, que la prosperité
> Vous attendent sans doute avec la liberté,
> Aux bords da Suir en Cook, Dublin vous favorise.
> Par differens moyens Georges vous est propice. (Rivoire, 2668)

Readers will be puzzled to know what Cook had to do with it till it is recalled that the old Templars' Castle of Crook was included in the land granted to the Genevese.

Melly had had a discouraging reception from the watchmakers. They were beginning to get used to the new régime, and to dread the hazards of the journey to Ireland. The outlook for New Geneva was not so promising. All the same, in July 1784, Mr Cuffe, an Irish enthusiast, laid the foundation stone of the projected city. On it was a bronze plaque inscribed with the date, and the reason for the settlement. In a large tent over the spot where a statue of Lord Temple was to be erected, a fête was given to the burgesses of Waterford.

Six weeks later both the Government and the Genevese representatives had decided to abandon the plan – New Geneva never came into being. A few Genevese settlers remained in Waterford, but the majority scattered over Europe waiting for better times to return to their city. The watchmakers never stirred.

Why did the plan collapse? The Genevans attributed it to a change of Viceroy and Government policy. The serious Lord Temple had sponsored the scheme but 'the virtuous Genevese' were not to the liking of the gay Duke of Rutland. Moreover, George III began to distrust the Genevese rebels. The aristocratic party at Geneva had a capable representative in London, M. Saladin, a connection by marriage of an English earl. He managed to persuade the Government that Melly, though he might be an Irish citizen, had a wife and family in Geneva, as well as a house and shop. His attempt to cause a widespread emigration of wealth and skill from his native town could not be overlooked. George III, recovering from his momentary sympathy with the Genevese rebels, for which Charles James Fox had been principally responsible, exchanged courtly compliments in royal Latin with their oppressors: 'Pacem tandem recuperavisse,' he wrote, 'atque sublata anarchia vestram administrationem stabilivise lubenter intelleximus.' And he signed himself, 'Vester bonus amicus, Georgius R.'

Louis XVI's agents were working hard to frustrate the emigration. As for the local magnates of Waterford, they found that the Genevans were expecting a far more liberal system of franchise than was current in Ireland. In a very short time, if it was granted, the safe seats of the landlords would be in peril. To others it appeared unwise to establish a body of foreign republicans at the mouth of the Waterford river right opposite Duncannon Fort. Could they be relied on in the event of invasion?

To add to their difficulties, the idealistic leaders in Neuchâtel and in Ireland were beginning to quarrel among themselves, and the Genevese merchants were less and less inclined to give up their comfortable homes and businesses and venture into the unknown. Some time before they had all re-opened their shops. Jean Gosse, the bookseller, had written to his son who was a refugee dreaming of Ireland: 'The troops whose drumming I could not endure do not now seem such devils after all.' Another of the *représentants,* Etienne Dumont, whose name is still borne by one of the streets in old Geneva, wrote: 'Il faudrait pour ranimer notre zêle quelques nouvelles décisions sur notre chère Irelandé.' Worse than all this, a solicitor, Richards, came back from Ireland to Geneva, 'cruelly deceived in his hopes', and begging for bread for his seven children.

Pensions and jobs were found for some of the disappointed refugees. Of the leaders, several were later to make a considerable mark in history, and it cannot be too much emphasised that they represented the real intellectual élite of Geneva. Their boast that they could transfer the intellectual life of Geneva to Ireland was not an idle one. H. A. Gosse, one of those interested, was the founder of 'The Academy of Natural Sciences', and his bust now stands outside Geneva University. Etienne Dumont played a prominent part in French politics before the revolution, and assisted Mirabeau with his speeches. Clavière, whose words I have quoted, became a Girondin leader and took his life to avoid the guillotine. D'Ivernois, the leader of the emigration, later succeeded in interesting Jefferson in the project of transferring the Genevan Academy to the USA. Here, too, he failed, but he was later, as Sir Francis d'Ivernois, to play a significant part in British diplomacy.

Ami Melly was the leader of the watchmaking, as opposed to the intellectual branch of the emigration. When Ireland failed him, he obtained the consent of the liberal Emperor Joseph II to set up a colony of Genevan watchmakers in the city of Constance. The interesting story of this refugee settlement is told in M. Chapuisat's *Figures et choses d'autrèfois* (1920). Du Roveray, Gasc, Ringler are well-known names in Genevese history, which are also associated with the emigration to Waterford. There is a list of the emigrants in the archives of the Château de Crans, near

Geneva, the home of the Saladin family, but it is not at present accessible.

Other books and papers in which the emigration is discussed are:

Sir Francis d'Ivernois by O. Kamin.
Henri-Albert Gosse by M'lle. Plan.
La Prise d'Armes de 1782 by E. Chapuisat.
Lettres de Jean Roget à Samuel Romily (1911).
Rivoire, 2530. *Pièces relatives à l'asyle offerte aux Genevois en Irlande.*

The original of the accompanying map is in the *Papiers Gosse* in the Geneva University Library.

For many years blocks of stone lay about on the abandoned site. It was proposed to colonize it with American loyalists. Finally, the New Geneva, which was to have been an example to Ireland of the triumph of freedom and democracy, became a prison for Irish patriots.

New Geneva may have dropped out of Irish history, but its name is familiar to all in the old song, 'The Croppy Boy'.

However mixed may have been the motives of the British and Irish Governments in encouraging the Genevan colony, it is hard not to regret its failure. The new city was to lie on the very edge of Wexford County, where sixteen years later, in 1798, Irish rebels were to fight a last desperate battle. Those sober and thrifty disciples of Rousseau and champions of liberty would surely have exercised a moderating influence on the fierce passion aroused by the struggle. In all their dealings they spoke and wrote with friendliness and understanding of the Irish people among whom they were to settle.

In telling this story I have used only such material as I have found in the archives at Geneva, and also the work of the eighteenth-century German traveller, Kütter, *Briefe über Irland*, in the National Library, Dublin. A closer investigation of Irish sources would certainly throw fresh light on the sad catastrophe that befell the New Geneva.

[1947]

3

THE BISHOP

In St Canice's Cathedral, Kilkenny, there is a monument to our bishop, Robert Fowler, who died in 1843, after having occupied the Palace for thirty years. All that our diocesan historian can say about him is that he appears to have been 'an excellent bishop', but he hints that despite his brilliant intelligence it was lucky for him that his father was Archbishop of Dublin. A later Archbishop of Dublin, Dr Whately, in his private memoirs is more explicit. Fowler's moral character is severely impugned and there are one or two scandalous stories. In local Roman Catholic tradition, too, an aroma of sin hangs about his name. For example, John Hogan, the Mayor of Kilkenny, who compiled seventy years ago an entertaining book of local history and anecdote, tells of Fowler's war with the Rev. Peter Roe, the rector of St Mary's, an ardent crusader for Sunday Schools and Bible Societies. Roe had rather incongruously erected three confessionals in St Mary's and the bishop in a fury had incited the local Protestants to throw them out. Hogan relates how one of Roe's parishioners tackled him about the confessionals.

> What did you put them there for? Did you expect Bishop Fowler would go to confession to you? I tell you the Bishop does not want to go to confession to anyone as everyone knows his Lordship's sins.

That was over a hundred years ago. Those sins, which everyone knew, have now been forgotten, but a diary that Robert Fowler kept during the years 1792, 1793 and 1794 has recently come to light. He was proud as well as candid and I believe that he would have preferred that posterity should examine it disapprovingly rather than not at all.

It is a solid leather-bound book of 200 pages, which he bought as a student of Christchurch. When he began it, at the age of twenty-five, he had been for four years rector of St Anne's, a fashionable Dublin church. Because of his father, his preferment had been swift and splendid. He was clearly a high-spirited and popular young man and from his easy narrative it is plain that he was quite at home with his character and had no mind to alter it. I doubt if he ever did, otherwise his revealing diary would never have gone with him from rectory to rectory and palace to palace and survived for 150 years. Fowler was the centre of an urbane and sociable society, confident in its own values. It was the collapse of that society after the Union, rather than the Evangelical movement, which moderated the manners and the morals of the Irish upper classes and their Church. To Fowler, honour was what mattered most in human relations. One's private behaviour only concerned others when it injured them in fortune or repute, and he had a fine scrupulosity about such injuries.

Clearly, for example, he did not think adultery wrong in itself, but one must be delicate and scrupulous in committing it. In the closed society in which he moved, unwritten laws could be observed and the dictates of the heart obeyed without grave repercussions. Between Right and Wrong there stretched a carefully tended enclave of It-All-Depends, from which the ill-bred and uncultivated were debarred.

Some of the Irish aristocrats – they were very rich and powerful at the end of the eighteenth century – brought ridicule on the private ethic by their abuse of it. Fowler's brother-in-law, the Earl of Kilkenny, when he felt himself to be unjustly treated in a law-suit, sent a challenge to his opponent's attorney and was wounded in the arm and thigh. His son, Somerset Butler, then challenged the leading counsel, while Lord Kilkenny, recovering from his wounds, challenged the next in rotation and his second son, Piers, challenged the third. It was only when its representatives had been badly bruised and shaken that the Law was allowed to take its course.

Robert Fowler followed his own judgment less explosively. He was robust in his tastes, liking horses, betting and balls, but he was delicate in health and prone to fits of ague, so that day after day is simply labelled 'A Fit'. They, or the inclement weather, frequently prevented him from going to church, but, though God is never mentioned in his diary, he had no prejudice against religion. He was generous in his views towards the Catholic majority and supported their emancipation, though fully aware that the Protestant ascendancy would not survive it.

Soon after the diary opened, a fervent petition from the Protestants of Belfast 'that Catholics should be admitted to every privilege' was laid before the Irish House of Commons. (This surprises us now, but the Ulster Protestants, many of them Nonconformists, felt a solidarity with the Roman Catholics, who endured disabilities comparable to their own. The Act of Union, which was to undermine Irish unity in the interests of imperial solidarity, had not yet been passed and the Ulstermen fought for their liberties within an Irish framework.) Fowler observed that, when the Catholics got the vote, they would undoubtedly use it to recover the land of Ireland from the Anglo-Irish, yet the vote could not be withheld:

> When the Numbers, the Riches and the Power of that Body are considered, tis wonderful they have submitted to the Yoke so long. For what is it but Oppression for so large a Majority of the Inhabitants of one Nation to be deprived of almost every priveledge dear to a Citizen on account of a difference of Religion, when they pay their share of the Taxes of the State?

Fowler's health did not improve, despite Purges, Leeches, James's Powder, Goat's Whey and Drawing Plaister, so finally Dr Purcell advised him to go abroad for a while to recover. He set off with plentiful introductions and a present of Irish Snuff for the Archbishop of York, who entertained him as he passed through London.

The sense of belonging to a doomed society is romantic rather than depressing, when one is twenty-five, and Fowler, reaching revolutionary France, found its calamities as stimulating as those of his native land. He was as much entertained by the passport he had to procure at Calais with its impertinent questions about his complexion and the colour of his hair as by 'the paltry treasures' of Rheims Cathedral. At Pontarlier the National Guard, convinced that he was bringing money to *émigrés* in Switzerland, rummaged through his baggage and delayed his arrival in Lausanne. Once established in his lodgings he started paying calls. Lausanne was overflowing with cultivated and fashionable foreigners and in the first few days he had visited the Duchesses of Devonshire and Ancaster, Mr Gibbon, and a multitude of *émigré* French and Polish aristocrats. There were German princes and an Irish group headed by Buck Whaley. But it was the Princess Lubomirska, former mistress of the King of Poland, who fascinated him most. Before the end of the month he had invited them all to a ball and had erected a ballroom in the garden for the occasion.

After that, every door in Lausanne was open to him, but it was the Princess's house at Cour that he visited most frequently. He and his friend O'Brien took her out on the lake, they had Bow and Arrow parties and walked in Mr Gibbon's garden. She gave him a Polish book and he noted

> That she had deeply considered the subject of the Immortality of the Soul and did not believe in it. She said it was merely Cowardice that made the World believe in it. I endeavoured to persuade her to change such dangerous opinions, but without success. She told me some curious anecdotes of some English, who had been in love with her. . . I found her more pleasant than ever and better informed than I had any idea of.

There were parties every day, at Cour, at Princess Bellossiska's, at Prince Joseph de Monaco's, at the Duchess of Devonshire's, often on the lake with a band following them by boat. He became increasingly attached.

> *July 8*. Rode out to Cour. Had some most extraordinary conversation with the Princess. She lent me the *Constitution of Poland*.
>
> *July 25*. Went to Cour and rode out with the P—; we returned to Tea. I supped there. She said she expected the Prince, her Husband, in three Weeks. After Supper a full explanation took place. I staid till past two o'clock. xxx

I should mention that after one has read a few pages, it becomes apparent that small crosses, one, two, three or four, are symbols of an amorous consummation. Yet the diary is in no way salacious. Passages are written with a greater care than one gives to a record which is intended for one's own eye alone. He must have been prepared for unsympathetic readers but too proud to present himself as different from what he was.

The diary is mostly a dry record of the name of preachers and dinner-guests, brief comments on operas, plays, meals, hotels, but of his love affairs he writes at length. Love was his principal talent, and to his diary, at least, he had to confide his successes. Of his mercenary loves small crosses are sufficient record.

He makes no excuses. The Protestant Right of Private Judgment was in those days freely practised even by the clergy. On the eve of the Union, the Irish Protestant hierarchy were more independent in their doctrines and behaviour than they have ever been before or since. The famous Bishop of Derry, the Earl of Bristol, who was to be Fowler's bishop for a time, was a Deist, indulgent to every heterodoxy, Nonconformist and Romanist, and had the lax morals and elegant taste of a Renaissance cardinal. Dressed in purple and diamonds he had driven to Dublin, escorted by a private troop of cavalry, splendid outriders and trumpeters, to demand an independent legislature for Ireland. More sober-minded bishops had followed their own judgment more gravely. Not long before, the Bishop of Clogher had assailed the doctrine of the Trinity in many publications and violently denounced St Athanasius and his creed in the Irish House of Lords. In Mayo the Bishop of Killala, despairing of converting the Catholic majority to Protestantism, was circulating among them such Catholic literature as might elevate their morals and manners. In Kilkenny, Dr O'Beirne, who was bishop before Fowler, was both zealous and fashionable. He had promoted the Association for Discountenancing Vice, and also, in collaboration with the Duchess of Devonshire, written a modish comedy for Drury Lane.

During the latter half of 1793, Fowler had almost daily encounters with Princess Lubomirska. There were more parties, more outings on the lake or on Mont Benon, many small crosses. He engaged in these improprieties with the prim formality of a Jane Austen courtship. We never learn the Christian name of any of Fowler's high-born mistresses. They were always called 'the Princess' or 'Madame'. Fluctuations of mood are recorded punctiliously as on a temperature chart. Sometimes when he rides beside the Princess or hands her out of a carriage, she is 'civil', sometimes 'low and discontented'. On August 22nd she lost his regard for some weeks by being too flirtatious with Prince Jules de Rohan. Fowler becomes 'distant', the Princess 'cool'. She tried to regain his affection by kissing his pony and telling it she loved it as much as its master. But it was no use; Mme d'Espanchal, a French *émigrée*, who lived with the Princess, and disliked Prince Jules, regularly reported her moods and movements to Fowler. The rector had had the habit, when invited to a party at Cour, of making his good-byes and then slipping back into the house and now he had reason to suspect that Prince Jules was doing this too. Prince Jules was a practised seducer, a kinsman of that

Cardinal de Rohan whose gallantries had landed him temporarily in the Bastille. Fowler was deeply hurt at being supplanted by anyone so lacking in seriousness. Riding back from church on September 2nd he passed the Princess's carriage, but when she shouted out gay banter at him, he and his friend O'Brien looked the other way with huffy dignity. The following day she met him at Buck Whaley's and, asking him back to Cour, she appeared to capitulate.

She said I had acted in the handsomest way possible by her and begged my pardon a thousand times. I was very cool to her all the Evening. The P— absolutely denied ever having had — with Prince Jules, which I knew to be false. I supped at Cour.

Two days later he saw her driving in a curricle with Prince Jules and the following day she went off with the Prince to Yverdun. Mme d'Espanchal, greatly dismayed, borrowed Fowler's horse and sent her man to urge the Princess to return. She would not and the messenger was sent off a second time to tell her that her child was seriously ill and that she must not delay. Was this a cruel trick and was Fowler a party to it? I cannot make out. When the Princess at last returned he was in bed with 'confirmed Ague' and she had startling news for him:

She said that now nothing anyone could say would hurt her in her self-esteem. She said she was with Child by me and was in great fear about her lying-in as the Prince her Husband wrote her Word he should be here in April, she said she had been blooded and thought she shd miscarry.

September 29. The P— said she was very unwell and has spit much Blood.

Meanwhile in France the King and Queen had been imprisoned and with the September Massacres the Terror had begun. The Swiss were greatly alarmed and very wary in their behaviour. But the Princess's ebullient temper would allow no breath of Public Disorder to encroach upon her private affairs. When her valet de chambre was arrested for political intrigue she stormed at the Bailiff and in return was called 'a Democrat', the worst abuse he could think of, and ordered to leave Lausanne within forty-eight hours.

Before her departure she went to Fowler, wept and gave him a ring. 'She said she had never felt such a weight on her spirits before and was sure some misfortune would happen to her.' She said her wealthy friends were avoiding her, she would go to Paris, and, if it was not 'quiet' there, to England. Soon Fowler got a letter from her. Yes, Paris was 'quiet'. Everybody was so occupied with the trial of the king.

On her departure for Paris, Fowler had reflected on her character; he commended her good-sense and boundless generosity, but regretted her impulsiveness and vanity, which had so often been exploited by designing people. 'I have,' he recalled, 'passed a great many of the pleasantest hours of my Life with her.'

There is little more about the Princess Lubomirska in the diary, but, from Buck Whaley's diary, we learn that the Princess had exaggerated the quietness of Paris. She was guillotined.*

Other friends in Lausanne were equally imprudent. Princess Joseph de Monaco insisted on returning; she too was beheaded. Mme d'Espanchal, unable to keep on the house without the Princess and resolved to go to France to claim back her estates, appealed to Fowler. He sold some lace for her, and, pretending he had found a tenant for her house, advanced the rent for it out of his own pocket. She too set off for Paris and an unknown fate.

O'Brien was an equally incompetent Scarlet Pimpernel. When a 'Ruffian', in no way apparently obstructed by the Swiss, came to take the Duchesse de Charrot to Paris, without a servant or linen at two hours notice, O'Brien accompanied her to the frontier, where they met 200 French soldiers. He assured them he was the Duchesse's brother and, drinking with them convivially, persuaded them to toast the Prince of Wales. It is not clear how this helped the Duchesse, who went on with the Ruffian to Paris.

The days when an educated man could think and act according to his own judgment were drawing to a close but the fashionable visitors to Lausanne had nothing but their ethic of honour, gallantry and high-spirits to oppose to the slogans of the revolution. Fowler drove off in a gig to Berne to see the British Ambassador, Lord Robert Fitzgerald, on behalf of a friend, who had had a duel. The Swiss had just made duelling illegal and had ordered his expulsion. Lord Robert, the brother of Lord Edward, the Irish rebel leader, agreed that this was monstrous but advised patience. He asked Fowler to christen his new baby.

* In the 'Liste des Guillotinés' the Princess is listed as No. 693 'Rosalie Chodriwick, femme d'Alexandre Louis Lubeaumesky, agée de 24 ans, née à Lucrek en Pologne, demeurant a Chaillot, çi devant princesse polanaise, ex noble.'

Buck Whaley, the wealthy Irish gallant, was also helping his friends after his fashion. He offered to free Prince Jules from Princess Lubormirska, who was writing to him too possessively from France. He would get her to write a compromising letter to himself also and then show it to Prince Jules. The Prince would then have an excuse for quarrelling with her, as he had transferred his affections to Princess Bellossiska. On all this the Rector of St Anne's commented primly: 'The more I hear of this young man – he is but 23 – the greater scoundrel I find him to be.'

Fowler's own difficulties were now beginning. His landlord sent him a huge bill for cleaning his house and garden after his ball. He left his greatcoat on a public bench and it was stolen. A London wine-merchant demanded an immediate settlement of a bill for £100. Finally, an outraged letter came from his father, the Archbishop, threatening to disinherit him for his extravagance. There was nothing for it but to leave Lausanne, so eluding the landlord, who tried to stop him, he made for Montpellier. As he passed through Lyons, to his astonishment he caught sight of Prince Jules with his hair *'en queue'*. Was this great aristocrat stalking some new mistress through the shambles of revolutionary France or was he working for the royalist insurrection, which was soon to break out in Lyons? Fowler looked the other way; 'I did not renew my acquaintance.'

When he reached Montpellier he found a 'very abusive' letter from his father:

> All the faults I had ever committed were recapitulated and my condemnation pronounced without any enquiry made. Worthy conduct from a parent to his only Child, when in a bad state of health and in another country! It has always been his Grace's practice to conceal any appearance that could be favourable to me, whereas every possible attempt to calumniate was eagerly embraced.

And he observed that though his father claimed to be paying him £1300 a year, his Grace was in fact, in his absence, receiving the emolument of his preferment, St Anne's, £700, 'so the wonderful stretch of Generosity amounts to allowing £600 for one year to his only son. Intended to go to Church but it rained. xxx.'

Montpellier was very dull after Lausanne. On his first Sunday he risked a return of ague by attending a church service, which the Protestants, singing a great deal, held in a kind of barn open on two sides outside the town. He learnt that the wine-merchant had sent on the bill to his father. He felt very ill and took an emetic, 20 grains Hippo, 2 tartar emetic and brought up a great deal of Bile. On January 21st, 1793, he wrote: 'On the conduct of my father on receipt of my reply depends my future Prospect in Life', and in a postscript he added: 'Louis XVI beheaded at Paris'.

He was lonely at Montpellier, all the small crosses were anonymous ones and having no private life he filled several pages of his diary with a recital of the astonishing public events of 1792, 'so wonderful that Posterity will hardly credit the Belief of their having happened in one year'. He noted with disgust the timidity of the leaders of society at Montpellier. When in the theatre news came of the execution of Louis XVI, the Parterre and the Nobility joined in the Marseillaise. 'The Municipality, although some of them had tears in their eyes, durst not leave the Theatre but stood up and held up their hats in sign of Approbation.'

A few days later he found himself in a similar predicament. France was now at war with England and all the foreigners in the town were expected to subscribe to the French armies. He resisted a polite morning deputation, but a more determined one arrived while he was dressing for dinner. 'Either pay in money or person!' they threatened. 'Not a sou!' he replied. But he found that in fact all the English were subscribing and an amiable French gentleman advised him *'as a friend* to give a trifle *to insure against further insults!'*

'I told him my sentiments very fully but as I would not risk my Life for 25 Livres I gave him the Money to hand over and determined to quitt the Republick immediately.'

So back again for some months to Geneva and Lausanne, where he learnt that his sister, Milley, was engaged to Mr Butler, future Earl of Kilkenny, and was to get a handsome jointure. Driving with Lord Morpeth to dine with Lord Cholmondeley, the gig overturned and he damaged his ribs. While he was recovering, he had one of those opportunities for chivalry which delighted him. M. Chauvelin (we know him from *The Scarlet Pimpernel)* was visiting the town and dining with the Comité de Sureté. As he and his escort were passing under the window of an Irishman called Knox, who was entertaining Lord Morpeth and some Irish friends, one of them 'very imprudently' poured a jug of wine down on the Frenchmen. An immense mob, angry and drunk and waving swords, instantly collected and stormed up the staircase. Morpeth and his friends rushed for their swords but they were disarmed and two Irishmen were led away to prison. Fowler, coming to the rescue, got a blow from 'that brute President Jannot' on his still aching ribs. But he escaped and next day went to the prison and breakfasted there. He got passports for the two Irishmen and an order for their release. The bridges were lined with soldiers and Fowler, crossing one, was 'most amazingly abused'. So the Irishmen escaped by boat across the lake, to the indignation of M. Chauvelin, who upbraided his hosts because they had not burnt Knox's house and hanged all the English and Irish in the town.

After this Fowler and the others decided to retreat to Italy, but his last few weeks in Switzerland were as busy and sociable as ever. He intervened to help an Irishman, who had got into trouble 'for beating a man', he rose early to avert a duel, lost some money at Pharo, went to see a glacier and was entertained several times by Mme de Chambon xx. On September 27th momentous news arrived from Ireland; the Dean of St Patrick's Cathedral, Dublin, had died. A few days later he learnt that his father had instructed the Chapter to elect him to the vacant Deanery, and he had scarcely settled in Milan when word came that he had been unanimously appointed successor to Jonathan Swift.

The new Dean was quickly a centre of life and gaiety at Milan. The friends, who had baited M. Chauvelin, were there already and Knox had a box at the Opera and many fashionable acquaintances. Robert Fowler sat for his portrait, took Physick and rented the ground floor of the Marchese Visconti's house. In a couple of weeks he had made Mme Visconti his mistress, with the sympathetic understanding of her husband. They all three went for a holiday to the Marchese's country house at Varese and visited the Madonna del Monte, 'which the most ridiculous bigotry has built on top of a very high mountain'. On their return to Milan he fell ill again and the Marchesa came to sit with him almost daily. x. Soon after his recovery the diary becomes complicated and obscure. Although the Marchese made no difficulties, all was not well. There are small crosses with no names attached and on December 11th Mme Visconti wrote a note to him: 'You do not care for me. You are attached to another. I cannot love one, who is so inconsequent.'

I was obliged to go upstairs to see the Marquesa much against my will. Madame was very distant and so was I. I remained but a very short time. I wrote an answer to her curious Note, which I ordered to be delivered in the Morning.

Dec. 12. I went and told her how much she was in the wrong. While I was in her Room her Brother-in-Law called. We partly made up her foolish Quarrel. . . We were friends again. xxxx

The New Year 1794 began with a reception and ball given by the Austrian Archduke, who was Governor of Lombardy. A fortnight later Fowler got an urgent letter from his father. If he did not take possession of his deanery before March 1st, it would lapse to the Crown. 'This determined me to set off for Ireland as soon as possible.'

He made his farewells to Mme Visconti. xxx. 'She was most wonderfully affected, so much so that I fear she will be very ill. She expressed how much she loved me and I believe she does with the most sincere affection.'

Then off post-haste to Ostend. At Cremona the gates were closed on him and he had to sleep without supper in a peasant's hut. Though his wheels broke four times in Germany and Belgium, by February 8th he and his man, François, were in Margate.

In London he only stayed to inspect the coach that was being made at Hatchetts for his sister, Lady Kilkenny; he was in Dublin by February 17th and warmly received at the Palace by his father. The same evening Dr Hastings, the Archdeacon of Dublin, died. This was providential, for the plans which his father had made for him miscarried. Though he had lost no time in being installed as Dean of St Patrick's and though his father had arranged that he could draw simultaneously a Precentor's emolument, the Crown was determined to win. It decreed that the Chapter had no authority to make the appointment and the Lord Chancellor refused to seal it with the Great Seal. However, as the Archdeaconry of Dublin was now vacant and could be held simultaneously with a good living at Urney, Co. Tyrone, matters were not so bad as they had at first appeared.

In any case, in these first few days in Dublin, he was too busy seeing old friends and paying calls on the great to spend a moment in repining. Typical of other days was February 22nd:

Called on Lord Loftus, Tom May, the Duke of Leinster, the Archbishop of Cashel and Tuam, Lord Shannon, Lord Boyle, Lord Portarlington, Lord Kingston, the Bishop of Killala.

He bought a Blood Horse and contemplated marriage with Lady Isabella Beresford. His father was much pleased and said he would make up his preferment to £3000, give him a house, furnish it and settle on him £90,000. Lady Isabella's parents were pleased too. The Marquess of Waterford told the Archbishop 'that he always had the highest opinion of me and had not the smallest objection to the terms offered'. Lady Waterford said she wished for the match above all things, only Lady Isabella demurred. 'She said she has no partiality for anybody, liked me very well but thought herself too young to marry and be taken from her mother.'

There was no ill-feeling. In a few days the Archdeacon was dancing with her at the Marchioness of Antrim's Ball and Lord Waterford has written to him: 'Your feelings and your conduct are those of a man of sense and honour.' In the end he married Lord Mountjoy's daughter and it was she who erected to him the monument in St Canice's Cathedral, Kilkenny.

The diary ends during a visit to his new parish at Urney. He was enchanted with the scenery, for it lay along the River Foyle, looking westward to the Donegal mountains. He had friendly neighbours, the Hills and Hamiltons and Lord Abercorn. He was always entertaining, for, as well as François, he had a housekeeper and a cook and a housemaid, who was dismissed for hiding stolen tea under her mattress. In addition, there is frequent mention of someone called Peppa, always with a small cross after her name. She had certainly not accompanied him from Italy, but he had written to her from Disschenbach and other places on his route home and it is possible that she had followed him to Urney from Italy. She must have been a complication in a small country neighbourhood and after a few weeks she disappears from the diary.

On his way to Urney he had called at Downhill, one of the splendid palaces of Lord Bristol, Bishop of Derry. He was instituted in the absence of the bishop, who had deserted his diocese for those sumptuous continental tours which can still be traced by all the Hotel Bristols in Europe. Downhill is now a roofless shell, but the temple on the Derry coast, from which the bishop and his guests used to contemplate the stormy sea, has survived. Fowler must have read with appreciation the famous lines from Lucretius, which the Bishop had carved on the architrave. '*Suave mari magno. . .*'

It is sweet, when on the great sea the winds are convulsing the waters, to watch another's struggle from the dry land. Not because it delights one that another should be in travail, but because it is sweet to observe what evils you have not to endure.

Educated Irishmen in Fowler's day knew that the storm would one day sweep away the refuge, from which they could look down so pleasurably on the distress of others. In fact they anticipated that ruin would come more swiftly and dramatically than it actually did and that mitred and coroneted heads would shortly dangle from gibbets. If they had not felt so guilty and so scared, they might have managed better. In a panic after the '98 they passed the Act of Union, which seemed to guarantee their safety and their property. A huge price had to be paid. Their country, so recently almost on a parity with England in regard to the splendour and independence of its leading men, dwindled to an obsequious province. When we meet rich Irishmen travelling abroad in the days of Thackeray, they are vulgar creatures aping English manners and ashamed of their provincial origins, fit subjects for the novelist's satire.

Among the clergy after the Union there was certainly more earnestness and morality; there was less laxity about doctrine and as a consequence more sectarian bitterness. In the diocese of Killala, for example, where the Protestant bishop had once circulated Catholic tracts, a vigorous campaign of proselytism was initiated. In Kilkenny the Rev. Peter Roe did his best to counteract the influence of Bishop Fowler, who had always loved opera and drama and who favoured the Kilkenny Players as much as Roe abominated them. Twice a year this famous band of amateurs performed Shakespeare, Sheridan, Goldsmith, Congreve, earning huge sums of money for charity and attracting to the town every lover of art in Ireland.

Roe as regularly denounced them. For him the Kilkenny Players symbolized all the frivolity and sin and unbelief of an age which was coming to an end:

This city presents one continued scene of riot and extravagance, the rich and great strengthening each others' hands in wickedness, reviling religion and taking pains to show their natural enmity against the Birth of God. . . In the last three years thirty-eight clergy, six Bishops, six Deans, seven Archdeacons and fifty clergy of other denominations were among the foolish votaries of riot and dissipation, who crowded into Kilkenny to drink the maddening draught from the cup of Fashionable Riot and Ungodliness. . . We may well conceive how they would have been regarded by Our Lord and His Apostles.

Needless to say the Rev. Peter Roe was much more disliked by the Roman Catholics of Kilkenny than was his lax and tolerant bishop. But making war on Shakespeare as well as Sin, Roe left a permanent mark on Irish society and on the Protestant Church of Ireland.

Yet when the life has gone out of a community it needs more than propriety to revive it. The once intoxicating doctrines of the Reformation compounded of indignation and compromise are chemically unstable. They decompose easily into bigotry and flaccid benevolence. Their integrity is as precarious in Orange Lodges and Church Bazaars as in Mr Gibbon's garden or Princess Lubomirska's curricle.

Bishop Fowler was often wise, where the Rev. Peter Roe was foolish. Men will usually respect those who have good humour, good nerves and a knowledge of human nature. They do not ask too searchingly how these virtues are nourished. Probably most of Fowler's contemporaries would have agreed with our diocesan historian that he made 'an excellent bishop'.

[1960]

4

THE COUNTRY HOUSE AFTER THE UNION

I wonder if a century ever closed with such drama and finality as marked the passing of eighteenth-century Ireland. New men, new measures, new ideas at once came on the scene and those who had spent themselves in the tragedy and intellectual turmoil that preceded the Union all at once became antiquated figures, left high and dry in a world that had little use for them. Perhaps it was in the country houses that the spirit of the eighteenth century lingered longest. One thinks of Edgeworthstown House, the most illustrious of them all, and a carriage making its way across the bog to Castlepollard one February day in 1817. In it sits an elderly much-muffled invalid, R. L. Edgeworth, and beside him his daughter Maria. They are on their way to visit Lord Longford's new bride, and Maria is reading him the first chapter of her novel *Ormond*. She is working against time for she knows that her father has not long to live and she is anxious that as he has shared in the writing of this book, he should at least see it in proof. And he too with his wide-ranging eighteenth-century mind is conscious of many other obligations to fulfil before he dies. There is a new bridge to be built and Mr Fallon, the contractor, to be seen at Longford; there is a scheme to be prepared for an interdenominational elementary school in Edgeworthstown, which he hopes that his son, Lovell, will carry into effect upon his death. And he is wondering how Maria will get on without him. He must fortify her against the importunities of her younger brothers and sisters. She is business-like and will be rich but she is generous to a fault, and though he is proud of this gifted brood, which does much credit to himself and their elder sister, Maria, all the same there are complications in their characters. . . There is Francis for example. . .

One has the fancy that as they jog along they are leaving a full century behind them and plunging deeper and deeper into an empty one. Of course that is a ridiculous way to refer to the century of the steam engine, of electoral reform and Queen Victoria, but it is terribly true for the Irish country gentleman. Old Mr Edgeworth's mind was as tightly packed with notions as Sir Jonah Barrington's with memories or as Lady Blessington's ballroom with gay and distinguished guests. He had no conception of the vacuities that yawned ahead.

For it was not only from politics that the next generations were to feel themselves excluded. From every field the gifted country gentleman was to find himself evicted by the specialist and the civil servant. His most formidable enemies were not, I think, a resentful tenantry, but the salaried professional who came to adorn the chairs and institutes which often owed their existence to the schemes hatched by the library fire, the lonely experiments in the outhouse or the observatory in the garden. Frankenstein had come to grips with his monster. I was told that when some years ago Edgeworthstown House was up for auction, strange mechancial contraptions were found in the loft. We are so apt now to smile at these lonely fancies from the provinces that it is not easy to visualize a world in which old Mr Edgeworth could have been called by the Government from his County Longford library to organize a telegraph from Dublin to Galway so that Dublin should have news of a French invasion. He spent two years at it and manned it with a telegraph corps from his yeomanry and tenants, and he refused all financial reward. A couple of years later he served as a commissioner for the Board of Education in Ireland and the Government of revolutionary France appealed for his advice about industrial development. In the meantime he was reflecting on the construction of carriages and the making of roads, to such purpose that his biographer says that the tarred MacAdam of our century should rightfully be called tarred Edgeworth. As a member of parliament, he had spoken logically and forcibly against the Union. He was also collaborating with Maria in the writing of treatises on education and, as we have seen, contributing whole chapters to her famous novels.

But my illustration would be pointless if Edgeworth had been a man of sublime genius capable of overriding all obstacles. He was merely a landlord with an experimental turn of mind, wide interests and a good education, and to such a man the eighteenth century was kindly. A remote estate and a large family were not handicaps to the gratification of ambition.

There were many other survivors besides Edgeworth but the 1820s saw most of them in their graves. You will see how abruptly provincial life fizzled out if you are lucky enough to find an old country house library whose shelves have not been combed by the dealer. You will certainly find the wide bottom shelf still occupied by the vast handsomely bound volumes of the proceedings of the Irish House of Commons, because no dealer is interested in these. They are too bulky for anything but pulping, though I have seen them used effectively as door stoppers. And above them there are probably rows of angry leather-bound pamphlets. Take one down and you will find some furious diatribe about jobbery or Arian heresies or a local election. There are equally fiery poems with significant blanks conveying to the well-informed the most appalling innuendoes. It is all very intimate and local; one of the neighbours is called Brutus and the other Beelzebub or Judas but as you cannot now guess what nobleman or country squire is hidden under this antique dress, you put the book back on the shelf. It is as mysterious as the roar of the ocean heard in an empty cockle shell. How is it possible that the ancestors of one's kind sensible neighbours were once so inflamed and eloquent?

But as you work your way round the library you will see how the change came about. Soon after the Union the pamphlets thinned out. Judas and Beelzebub had crossed to Westminster and somehow the shafts of Irish satire are only really deadly at very close range. About the 1820s the philosophy and the plays end and the sermons begin, with here and there, like an island, Walter Scott or a geological survey. And then even the sermons dry up and a very waste period begins and sometimes it never ends.

No doubt I am generalizing far too much, but in some ways we've got to account for that appalling smugness which creeps over the Irish gentry, like a paralysis, as the century advanced. At first it had quite a genial aspect; there was less abuse, less violence, less drink, less extravagance. I think it was merely that the Rakes of Mallow had taken their money and their merriment to Bath and Brighton! A great crop of charitable institutions and alms houses grew up, there were Bible classes and farming classes. In the drawing-rooms where chair covers had been embroidered to the sound of the harpsichord, acres upon acres of warm cross-over shawls were knitted, in the kitchens where rum punch had been brewed, gallons of soup and mountains of nourishing jellies were prepared for the deserving poor. It is said that Lady Elizabeth Fownes literally killed herself with woolwork; and at Piltown the four daughters of Lord Duncannon regularly taught in the village school. Hand in hand with this there was a religious revival among the Protestant gentry. How was it that these improved manners did not lead to friendlier feelings but instead the old bitterness intensified, the old divisions deepened?

I think that the answer is that the upper classes had been scared, first by the French revolution and then by the '98 rebellion. In the memoirs of Dorothea Herbert, the Tipperary clergyman's daughter, you get a wonderful picture of that wave of horror and repudiation that swept across Ireland, assisted no doubt by Castlereagh and Fitzgibbon and their kind but based also on vivid personal experiences. Dorothea's opinions were ordinary; she is only extravagant in the freedom with which she expresses herself. She gives incidentally a vivid picture of the uninhibited gaiety and gorgeousness of the Irish provinces, before the thunderbolt had fallen. Do you remember her account of the Cashel races, their new bottle-green, silver-plated coach and the glass vis-à-vis of their cousin Ned Eyre and how he attended the Assembly Ball that night in 'a pink lutestring suit blazing with brilliants from tip to toe, and covered with double paste buttons on cuffs, knees and shoes'? The dominant theme through the memoirs is of course her unrequited love for John Roe of Rockwell, but I don't think that, without the horrors of the rebellion, the anguish of the heart alone would have unhinged her reason. While they were away from Knockgrafton rectory her nurse had been riddled with bullets by the rebels and the sexton had been hacked to pieces with a chopper.

Such things had happened all over Ireland and only a handful could risk being dispassionate and try to analyse the origins of cruelty, the nemesis of injustice. Dorothea Herbert seeing the bloodstains on the rectory carpet plunged deeper into a region of horror and hallucination from which she seemed never to have returned. At the end of her memoirs it is plain that she had gone out of her mind. Though revulsion seldom took such extreme forms, the bulk of the Irish gentry did, after the rebellion, plunge into a mood of stern self-righteousness, and moral repudiation of lawlessness. One cannot call it hypocritical, because hardly anyone of any party or faith defended the rebellion, except those implicated in it. In Cruikshank's illustrations to Maxwell's *History of the Rebellion*, you see this mood of self-satisfaction at its most repulsive – small girls transfixed with pikes at the barn of Scullabogue, drunken peasants dancing jigs on grand pianos, while their blowsy wives with a bottle to their lips tear the portraits from their frames and trample on the Holy Bible.

Every respectable person was thinking along those lines, and it needed courage and independence of mind in a high degree to swim upstream against so strong a current. Naturally the British did not want to see too much cordiality between the two Irish parties. They had been scared by the *rapprochement* that had led to the Volunteer movement and to Grattan's Parliament. So everything was done to play on the fears of the Anglo-Irish.

Because of all this there was a revulsion not only against the idealism of Grattan's Volunteers but also against the easy lavish ways, the liberal speculation, the generous acknowledgment of the right to think otherwise, which had been characteristic of the movement. The educated eighteenth-century gentleman was not averse to experiment in politics, religion, morals; I don't mean that he was more irreligious or immoral than his forebears or descendants, but to a surprising degree he was uninfluenced by those two solemn considerations that weighed so heavily on a later age: 'What will the neighbours think?' and 'What would happen if my tenants got hold of these ideas?'

It appeared to the post-Union gentry that 'ideas' had much to answer for, and they began to criticize their humanist ancestors for tolerating them and even publishing books about them. 'Ideas!' that was what led to the guillotine and to Wolfe Tone, to the calamity that had fallen on the respectable Emmets, the disgrace of the noble Fitzgeralds. Down with ideas!

The result was that one had the impression of a whole generation tip-toeing round their subordinates, ready to make any concession, except the perilous liberty of independent thinking. When they erected a pillar in Sackville Street it was not Grattan they put on top of it, but Nelson, who had safeguarded Britain from the pernicious doctrines of revolutionary France, a Nelson who was made the pattern of chivalry and whose eighteenth-century morals were tactfully ignored. And as for the Duke of Wellington, an Irishman married to an Irish woman, even Maria

Edgeworth lost her head about him; monuments sprang up to him right and left and little local societies all over Ireland wrote to him asking him to be their patron. But the Duke had his feet firmly planted in the logical eighteenth century and refused all these invitations with notes which would have been offensive if they had not been personal and painstaking. 'The Duke of Wellington,' he replied to one such invitation, 'fails to see the value of joining a society, whose meetings he would be unable to attend.'

The Duke, in this way, unconsciously perhaps, challenged the delusion of the nineteenth-century Irishman that he could spread his wings in the wide imperial world, which the British laid open to him, and not lose his foothold in the small community in which he was reared but whose meetings 'he would be unable to attend'. In fact the story of the wealthy talented Wellesleys illustrates accurately what was happening all over Ireland to the indigenous gentry. When Mrs Delany, a generation earlier, had visited the family in their splendid mansion, Dangan, near Trim, the head of the house was still busy laying out artificial lakes and planting trees. They still called themselves Wesley in those days but the name was getting middle-class revivalist associations and they were anxious to be rid of it. Mr Wesley was a cultivated gentleman, who turned to the classics for entertainment. He used to give all his guests white walking sticks engraved with the names of classical deities, whom they might be supposed to resemble, and they went for stately walks in keeping with the characters they represented. The Wesleys were all very gifted, some played a part in Dublin musical societies, others in Co. Meath. They seemed perfectly established there and yet already the tide was flowing away from Ireland. It was inevitable that little Arthur's talents, displayed in those days in making miniature fortresses on the lake, should draw him away to England and that his brother should look for fame in India. Remarkably soon Dangan had been sold to a speculator. He insured it heavily and, most opportunely, it immediately took fire. You pass the ruins today between Trim and Summerhill. They stand in the remnants of a park and no one could guess that they commemorate a catastrophe a century earlier than the neighbouring Georgian ruins of the 1920s, Summerhill and others. There was no particular tragedy about the burning of Dangan. The house was only a stage in the passage to imperial glory; but obviously these voluntary departures weakened the confidence of those who remained. After the Union many of the enterprising and intelligent began to speak with the lukewarm conviction of temporary lodgers. They were not prepared to commit themselves as deeply as their ancestors had done.

But of course there were exceptions to all this. There was a small group of the Irish gentry living in the neighbourhood of Thomastown, who felt that they still had something to offer to Ireland exclusively and who did not intend to abdicate their responsibilities or be thrust aside. The best known of them was Charles Kendal Bushe, the Incorruptible, who had made the celebrated speech against the Union. One of his sons wrote a prologue for the Kilkenny Players. It is a forlorn appeal to the Irish gentry to stay in Ireland where their roots were and not follow the tide of fashion to England where they would only be patronized as remote provincials.

> The worthy Esquire sells his old estate
> Possessed with proud ambition to be great
> And what's his view of greatness? to be sent
> An independent man to Parliament.
> And truly independent, forth he goes,
> Of all the comforts his old home bestows.
> See him in London to a chop house sneak
> To famish on a solitary steak.
> Yet on each meal more substance wasting
> Than here would furnish hospitable feasting.
> Or see him round St James' purlieus straying
> With wonderous eyes that wealthy world surveying
> And half his income for a garret paying.
> Or at St Stephen's on a top bench waiting
> In fretful doze while statesman are debating,
> Unknown, unnoticed save by some pert peer,
> Who thus accosts his neighbour with a sneer,
> 'Who's that my Lord? His face I don't remember?'
> 'How could you? 'Tis a Scotch or Irish member.
> They come and go in droves but we don't know 'em.
> They should have keepers, like wild beasts, to show 'em.
> But wait a moment till he gives his vote,
> And then you'll know his nation by his note.'

The Kilkenny Theatre season scarcely lasted twenty years, yet it became a rallying-point for all those in whom the critical, conciliatory, gay and sceptical eighteenth-century spirit survived. It is sad that the most embittered opposition which it met came from the ardent but very narrow reforming element in the Protestant Church to which I have already referred. The Rev. Peter Roe of St Mary's denounced the theatre as 'a gilded bait to lure souls into Satan's net' and with execration he recorded the precise number of rectors, canons, deans, archdeacons and even bishops, who had abandoned themselves to the biennial orgies of Sheridan and Shakespeare.

I can think of many philanthrophic enterprises of this time but over most of them there broods the panic fear of democracy, of liberalism. Class distinctions were registered in Heaven but it was right to alleviate the sufferings of the poor. When Lovell Edgeworth started the schools at Edgeworthstown, which his father had planned, he decreed that during school hours linen smocks were to be worn to conceal the distinctions of rank which the boys' rags or fine clothes might betray. But after school there was to be no mixing, 'to avoid,' said Lovell, 'the alarming appearance of a democratic tendency'. Then there were a few ventures like the Merino cloth factory at Annamult on the Nore, an experiment in economic and social organization such as R. L. Edgeworth would have approved of. Some progressive local gentry sank and lost a good deal of money in it and for ten or fifteen years the fields were white with vast woolly sheep from Spain and the looms were busy; a village was built and a church for the workers whose needs and hopes were carefully studied. The Kilkenny Players said of it in their last prologue:

> There sports and toil the alternate hours beguile
> And man, poor labouring man is taught to smile.

But on the whole very little was done to realize that dream of unity, which had been an inspiration to Grattan and his colleagues.

Elizabeth Bowen in her book *Bowen's Court* says of this period that, after the Union, 'from the big lord to the small country gentleman, they were being edged back upon a tract of clouds and obsessions. . . the sense of dislocation was everywhere. Property was still there but power was going.' And she tells a story of Lord Kingston which is so illuminating that I will repeat it. He was the landlord of Mitchelstown, wealthy, far-seeing, magnificent, the very type of benevolent despot. When his despotism was threatened, not only did his benevolence disappear but even his reason. He went mad. This is how it happened. He was, I ought to have said, the creator of the broad streets of Mitchelstown, the pleasant college square, a Protestant and a Catholic church. His estates were models of humane and efficient management. But he loathed industrialism and when he saw a tall chimney go up in Mitchelstown he took a solemn farewell of the townsfolk and told them with a breaking voice that he was leaving for England the next day for there was no room in Mitchelstown for himself and the owner of the chimney. That evening the manufacturer was obliged to receive some uninvited guests and a couple of days later he had gone.

It was democracy as much as Ireland that finished Lord Kingston, or Big George as he was called. Soon after this episode there was a by-election in Limerick and Big George, confident that his tenantry would vote as he told them, organized them into a mile-long procession to the city. When he learnt a little later that to a man they had voted against his candidate, the bottom fell out of his world. For a paternal despot it was an insult beyond forgiveness. He summoned all the tenantry of three counties to the long gallery in Mitchelstown Castle. For a few moments he gazed at them in speechless stupefaction and then suddenly. . . he went mad. Jumping from his chair, he screamed, 'They are come to tear me to pieces!' A little later he was removed struggling by his servants, and that was the end of Big George's duel with democracy.

I doubt whether the era of aristocratic rule ended so dramatically in other counties. But the defeat of the Beresford candidate in Waterford through the interposition of Daniel O'Connell was a sensation of even greater magnitude. The Irish landlords of the ascendancy had loathed Wolfe Tone, but he spoke a language which they understood and abhorred, as later, in the same way, they were to loathe Parnell. Yet I think their real detestation was for Daniel O'Connell, whose powerful influence was outside their comprehension. There were qualities in him which should have warmed their hearts, if narrow self-interest alone had been consulted: his hatred of revolution, his loyalty to the young queen, his indifference to Irish culture. But I believe it was from their contact with O'Connell and the deep mass-emotion which he organized against them, that they first began to feel themselves irremediably alien. And they minded far more being called alien than being called blood-suckers or parasites. For it appears that landlordism, good or bad, is an inevitable stage in social development. Daniel O'Connell was a landlord, evicting his tenants like everybody else. Smith O'Brien was a landlord and led his tenants to challenge the British Government at the battle of the Cabbage Patch. It is a phenomenon which would run its appointed course, whatever the source of authority. But to be called an alien is far more bruising since you cannot change your blood and I think that in the early nineteenth century, many of the gentry, despairing of politics, were trying to restore in the field of letters and science and scholarship that idea of a united people, which Castlereagh had once quenched and which O'Connell was unlikely to favour. I am not thinking of the followers of Thomas Davis, whose motives were avowedly political, but of less sanguine people who decided to study the country which they could not rule.

Perhaps the times being what they were, they had chosen well, because there is scarcely any course of study relating to Ireland which you can pursue very far without running into the work of some early nineteenth-century scholar from a Big House, who has managed to prove he was Irish by being indispensable to Ireland. It is mostly conscientious, unostentatious work, often defiantly parochial and as unexciting to the general public as it was unremunerative to its author. That fine series of county surveys, organized by the RDS, was never better done then when entrusted to a local squire like William Tighe. County histories began to be written and county archaeological societies founded. If you look at the membership lists of these old societies you will see how fully they justified their claims to be impartial and representative and how often in their hands history, contrary to her usual habit, seemed, when investigated without prejudice, to heal old grievances rather than to inflame them. In the second quarter of the nineteenth century all Ireland was traversed by scholars in gigs and dog carts measuring raths, recording legends, evolving theories or even more enthusiastically refuting them. It was the age of Graves and Prim as well as of O'Donovan and O'Curry, and in almost every Irish country house you will find traces of its passage; perhaps it is some feeble antiquarian water colour on the wall; perhaps it is a pile of dusty archaeological journals in the attic.

And if you look at the minute-books of these old societies you will be astonished at the venom and the vigour with which ignorant officials and barbarian land-owners are chastised. It is as though, like their grandfathers, these country scholars saw their opponents in the guise of Judas or Beelzebub. But we owe a great deal to their ill-temper. If it had not been for these unofficial bodies with their backbone of educated country gentlemen, Newgrange would have been destroyed to make a County Meath by-road and Clonmacnois and Glendalough would have been irreparably damaged.

I dare say, through concentrating on political frustration and its antidotes, I have given a too morbid and melancholy picture of this period. I think that even in Ireland only two per cent of the human race ever worries for long about political frustrations and I should have told you more about hunting and sport and travel and gardening. But I could not have done that without also speaking of the sons and daughters who worked outside Ireland and whose visits and adventures filled the house with reflected glory and excitement. Undoubtedly Irish country houses often had and still have this kind of glamour. But I have been thinking of them as places which once generated light and diffused it. I have been voicing the discontent of the restless two per cent. Their views are not of course very representative, but to balance that you must remember they are very seldom heard.

[1957]

5

AN IRISH ECUMENICAL MOVEMENT

In 1824 there started in Ireland a brief ecumenical movement. It was the work of the learned and generous minded J. K. L., otherwise Dr James Doyle, Roman Catholic Bishop of Kildare and Leighlin, and an English collaborator, Frederick Robinson, later Earl of Ripon.

They astounded their contemporaries in both islands by proposing the union of the Roman Church and the Established Church. 'It is pride and points of honour which keep us divided on many subjects,' wrote Dr Doyle, 'not a love of Christian humility, charity and truth.' And he argued that disagreement arose mainly upon 'matters of discipline which are of human not divine arrangement. . . and these the Catholic Church has power to modify or abrogate altogether.' 'The time is favourable,' he went on, 'for the government is powerful and at peace, while the Pope is powerless and anxious to conciliate.'

One of the reasons why prominent members of the Established Church considered this extraordinary proposition was that Catholic Emancipation seemed at hand. What sort of leaders would the newly liberated choose for themselves? The Anglo-Irish still had advantages of education and since the Catholic Church is traditional and conservative, it might be assumed that in a spiritually united Ireland the old rulers of Ireland might retain their leadership. These reflections were not necessarily base. Doyle, an ardent Catholic, seemed to share them. He thought that all progress in Ireland had been arrested 'by the incessant collision and conflict of religious opinions,' and he did not think that emancipation would lessen this conflict.

> The mind of a nation, fettered and exasperated, will struggle and bound and, when a chasm is opened, will escape by it in a torrent, like lava

from the crater of a volcano. . . The ministers of the crown are educating the people without providing for their distress and thus putting the sharpest weapons into the hands of men, who, as they learn to read, will also learn to calculate their strength and to devise and meditate on schemes of retaliation and revenge. The ministers of the establishment are and will be detested by those who differ from them in religion. The Catholic clergy have been ill-treated and they may yield for a moment to the influence of nature, though it be opposed to grace. They are, with few exceptions, from the ranks of the people; they inherit their feelings; they are not, as formerly, brought up under despotic governments; they have imbibed the doctrines of Locke and Paley more deeply then those of Bellarmine or even of Bossuet on the divine right of kings; and they know much more of the principles of the constitution than they do of passive obedience.

Only through the drastic remedy proposed by him and by Mr Robinson, could Ireland be tranquillized, the union of the countries cemented, peace and prosperity diffused and the empire rendered invulnerable.

'When the schism was healed,' he went on, 'the idolatry of Rome, the heresy of England would shortly disappear.' And Mr Newenham of Gloucester, one of his Anglican supporters, argued that 'if the missionary zeal of the Irish Catholics were combined with the missionary means of the Church of England, infidelity and sectarianism would soon be confined within very narrow limits'.

In fact, the Protestant Archbishop of Dublin, Dr Magee, was in those days very much alarmed at all the spawning sects. What else could he expect, thought J. K. L., for are not heresy and schism the logical consequences of the Protestant belief in Private Judgment? He defended against Dr Magee the most radical of them, the Unitarians, who supported Catholic Emancipation more vigorously than the Trinitarians did. James Devereux, a distinguished Wexford Catholic, wrote him an interesting letter commending this diplomacy:

Better surely for us quietly to look on and see the thousand Protestant sects and the Unitarians at it ding-dong. . . When the Unitarian has cleared the green of them, it will be time enough for us to step in and give him his quietus. . . . Unitarians generally should be spoken of by us as fair and candid men. They form a rising and powerful body here, every day increasing in numbers and consequence. They are eaten up with vanity and self-conceit and none would be more gratified than they by the flummery of a complimentary notice. . . It would be no difficult matter to get their High Chief, William Smith of Norwich, to allude to such notice in praise of our liberality, though we differ from him, and contrasting that with the illiberality of the Establishment, who at heart agree with him.

But ecclesiastical cunning like this was not really to Doyle's taste; it was in complete sincerity that he prescribed his drastic remedy for the increasing estrangement, which he believed would follow upon Emancipation. He proposed a conference of twenty Protestant and Catholic clergy, who were to draw up a scheme of union and lay it before the Pope. The proposal caused much interest. A flood of letters and deputations came to J. K. L.; the Provost of Trinity, Dr Sadleir, called on the Catholic Archbishop of Dublin and discussed rather fruitlessly a compromise about the number of the sacraments. Mr Newenham secured the interest of Lord Lansdowne and his enthusiastic letters to Doyle are still full of interest. They are sad, too, for they revealed to J. K. L. that the gulf was unbridgeable. Newenham had suggested that Jebb, the Bishop of Limerick, and the Bishop of Lichfield should select 'ten learned, pious, liberal-minded and benevolent Protestant divines'; Doyle and an English Vicar Apostolic should select their ten Catholic counterparts. But Newenham made the appalling gaffe of suggesting that the Catholic divines 'should resemble Quesnel in most respects'. Quesnel was a liberal Catholic against whom a Papal Bull had been launched, and Dr Doyle exploded. 'The very mention of Baius or Quesnel would cause every Catholic to revolt from you, so odious are their names to us.'

Jebb, too, was an odd choice. He was bitterly opposed to Emancipation and he had written: 'My conviction is unalterable that the worst consequences, civil and political, to England and to Ireland must result from admitting under any modification the Roman Catholic body or any part of it to political power.'

Yet he was among the most deeply loved and conciliatory of Irishmen. He had once given an address after Mass from the altar of a Catholic church in Limerick so movingly that the congregation had wept. When his Vicar General died, the Catholic Bishop of Limerick had followed his funeral with his priests walking arm in arm with the Protestant clergy. Newenham no doubt thought that Jebb would prefer a union of the Churches to the sectarian deadlock that would follow Emancipation.

Doyle's proposals were strongly repudiated by Maynooth but welcomed by the Catholic Association, who expressed their thanks in a motion moved by Daniel O'Connell. Disillusionment followed. Doyle had pictured the dialogue as comparable to a famous one that Bossuet had once held with some Lutherans. But Bossuet had rejoiced when Louis XIV had proscribed the Huguenots and his name acted on the Protestants as explosively as the name of Quesnel did on the Catholics. Alexander Knox, an eminent Protestant theologian, said that Bossuet's object in his dialogue had simply been to exact submission from the Protestants. 'I am obliged to say after all the consideration, of which I am capable, no other union between the Church of England and that of Rome is possible but such as would involve the complete resubjugation of the former to the latter.' Lord Ripon sadly gave up his ecumenical scheme. He became Viceroy of India and a Marquis and in 1874 became a Roman Catholic.

At that time Irish Protestants and Irish Catholics, apprehensive of the storms to come, yearned for unity. Wolfe Tone had preached 'the common name of Irishman' and it had led to bloodshed. Now they were looking for some bond of union more comprehensive and more specifically Christian. When Doyle's plan failed, only two ways of spiritual unity remained: all Ireland must become Catholic or all Ireland must become Protestant. And for several years a lively ding-dong ensued which surprisingly seldom developed into rows and rancour. It was not now between the Established Church and the Sects but between the two leviathans themselves. At Carrick-on-Shannon, Carlow, Cork, Kilkenny, New Ross, Downpatrick, and Easky, Co. Sligo, great public debates took place on the Bible and whether we had a duty to circulate it, on the Articles of the Creed and the Right of Private Judgment.

The climax was a six-day debate in Dublin with Daniel O'Connell and the Protestant Admiral Oliver as joint Chairmen. Sackville Street was blocked with the crowds, but, though there was great enthusiasm and both sides usually claimed the victory, there were seldom rows. The Carlow debate was, however, followed by a riot and after a time new methods were employed. The whole of Ireland was deluged in Bibles (English and Irish) by the Scripture Readers' Society. What was called the Second Reformation began and a vast number of shortlived conversions were registered. The missionaries were earnest men and even Dr Jebb approved of them. Dr Doyle had earlier sought to counteract their influence by the help of the miracle-working Prince Hohenloe, Dean of Bamberg. Through his prayers Miss Maria Lawlor of Rosskelton recovered her speech after being dumb for six years. There was, of course, much ding-dong about this, and the Surgeon-General, Sir Philip Crampton, was an able leader of the sceptics. J. K. L. defended his miracles with much psychosomatic knowledge and was able to quote Martin Luther himself in defence of them. All this ding-dong was friendly on the whole. Dr Jebb and Dr Doyle loved each other dearly and only the timid and tepid-minded were scared at these polemics.

Has all this any present relevance? Then as now spiritual unity was encouraged by material forebodings. But, where our ancestors were passionate, we are luke-warm. Even 'the infidels' and 'the sectaries', who once terrorized the establishment are apathetic. . . In Russia atheism among the educated is becoming a word without meaning. Many dissenters have dissented right out of the Churches and have reverted to the Anglican Church, which is adjusting itself to their heterodoxies. Lately I heard a Unitarian preacher in an Irish church say that in twenty years time he believed that the Unitarians would be able to return to the Mother Church. He meant that she is already so full of crypto-Unitarians that their beliefs will become acceptable.

The 'Liberal Christians', who supported Emancipation 140 years ago, believed that both Jebb and Doyle were wrong, but that rancour and oppression are always evil. Their successors today mostly support the ecumenical movement, believing that the Churches have a future, which they wish to share. (I do not think they are frightened as William Smith of Norwich might have been that once they have 'cleared the green' of the reactionaries and fundamentalists they will be 'given their quietus'.) But they recall that when twenty years ago every Christian value was savagely attacked in Europe, the shepherds for the most part trotted after their sheep. The Church of Authority and the Churches of Private Judgment were equally helpless and even the best of pastors were forced by diplomacy or necessity to connive at hideous crime. There is no evidence that large flocks are less corruptible than small ones.

The first problem is not a unification of doctrine (more improbable now than in 1824), but to discover in what form of Christian, para-Christian or post-Christian community we can best do our duty to our neighbours and offer protection to the innocent, the just, the wise.

[1964]

6

THE EGGMAN AND THE FAIRIES

You can see Slievenaman from my fields, though it is across the Tipperary border, a pale blue hump with the soft, rounded contours of ancient hills whose roughnesses have been smoothed away by time. Starting after lunch you can climb to the tip and be back by summer daylight, though it is over 2000 feet high. It can be seen from five or six southern counties and is one of the three or four most famous of Irish hills. Finn MacCool lived there and so did Oisin and Oscar, and fifty beautiful maidens, who give it its name, 'The Mountain of Women', embroidered garments for them there, or so they say. The top of the mountain to within a couple of hundred feet of the cairn of stones is bare except for an odd patch of sphagnum moss and heather. Below it there is more heather, well grazed by sheep, and a few frochan clumps, but except for some piles of stones that might once have been a house and a rough track for carting turf, there is not much sign of human traffic. I had always supposed that the Clearys' house had been in one of these ruined stone heaps upon the mountain side, because I could not associate their uncanny story with the prosperous and populous plain below. But one day I went to look for Ballyvadlea, where they lived at the foot of the mountain. A hurling match was being broadcast from Dublin and the cottagers came reluctantly from their wireless sets to direct me to the 'fairy-house'. It was almost indistinguishable from their own, except that it was bare and without flowers or shrubs, an ugly cement building rather smaller than the county council houses of today but of the same type. It was only a couple of hundred yards from a main road and, though it suggested poverty, it did not suggest mystery, remoteness, primaeval superstition. Farmers and gentry driving past the door to Fethard or Clonmel will in 1895 have been talking of Dreyfus and Cecil

Rhodes and some of these, who took part in the Ballyvadlea tragedy, may be still alive. They belong to our age and clime. The fairies are, if not exactly at the bottom of the garden, at least only a few fields and a few years away.

It is not very easy to build up a consecutive story out of a court case, for the end is always told before the beginning, and the central episode, seen differently by different witnessses, is often blurred like a negative several times exposed. But roughly this is how it happened.

In the spring of 1895 the Clearys were living at Ballyvadlea below Slievenaman. Michael Cleary was a labourer and his young wife, Bridget, was the daughter of a neighbour, Patrick Boland. Michael and Bridget were fond of each other and never quarrelled. They were religious people believing in the mysteries of the Catholic Church. But they also believed in the fairies and Michael was persuaded that, many years before, his mother had changed her nature. A fairy had entered into her body and once she had disappeared for two nights and it was known that she had spent them on the fairy-haunted rath at Kilnagranagh. It lay above John Dunne's cottage on the low road, and when Bridget too began to talk, like his mother, of Kilnagranagh and often to walk towards it of an evening on the low road, the old dread took shape in Michael's twilit mind. And some contagion of his fears spread to all his neighbours and all his relations, the Kennedys, the Bolands, the Dunnes, the Ahearns and Burkes, paralysing their wills and dulling their sensibilities. A whole community seemed to be bound with the spells of fairyland and powerless to extricate themselves. They appealed to the priests and the peelers to save them from themselves, but no external power was stronger than their obsessions. 'It's not my wife I have,' Michael told John Dunne, 'she's too fine a woman for my wife. She's two inches taller than my wife.' And even Bridget Cleary herself talked to her cousin, Mary Kennedy, as though she were bound with spells. 'I've a pain in my head,' she said, 'he's making a fairy of me now and an emergency. He thought to burn me three months ago.' She began to suffer from nerves and her illness was to Michael yet stronger proof that she was possessed. Dr Creary, the local doctor, declared it was due to dyspepsia, but he carried no conviction, and Michael went to Denis Guiney, the herb doctor, who prescribed a decoction of herbs and milk to be cooked in a saucepan and fed to the possessed woman.

But Michael had not much faith, either, in this innocent herbal remedy. He was convinced that there was only one way in which his Bridget could be restored to him. The fairy must be burnt out of her and then he would go to Kilnagranagh, and he would find the real Bridget there. She'd come out of the rath, riding a white horse and bound by cords to the saddle. He'd have to cut the ropes and then, if he was able to keep her, she'd stay with him.

But I should have mentioned that Michael Cleary once casually told his cousin John that Bridget on her evening walks to the fairy rath sometimes met an eggman on the low road. He used to go the rounds of the Tipperary farmsteads with his cart, collecting eggs for a wholesale distributor in Clonmel. When the story was all told in the Clonmel Court House the eggman was only mentioned once and never again by judge, jury, witnesses or prisoners. For all the relevance he appeared to have to the story he and his cart might well have been swallowed up into the fairy mound. Yet these oblique and tender-hearted people had a habit of hiding their thoughts from themselves, and perhaps they sometimes thrust upon the fairies the guilt for desires and jealousies whose crudities they shrank from facing. It is possible that Michael suspected his wife of a tenderness for the eggman and just as a grain of grit will provoke an oyster to secrete a pearl, so the eggman from Clonmel unlocked the door to fairyland.

When Michael Cleary's father died he was waked in a house eleven miles from Ballyvadlea and on their way to the wake, the neighbours assembled the evening before in Michael's house. Patrick Boland, Bridget's father, was there and the Kennedy cousins including William, aged sixteen, and William Ahearn and several others. Bridget's cousin, Hannah Burke, was still washing some shirts that were needed for the wake and Mary Kennedy, young William's mother, went off to feed their hens, but when the others started to walk off for the wake, Michael Cleary stopped them. He said he would not leave his wife's sick-bed and that 'he did not care the devil about his father whether he was alive or dead'. 'No and ye won't go either,' he said to them, 'until I give her a little of the business I have to give her. Wait, boys, till you see her, till you see what I'll put out the door. I haven't Bridgie here these six weeks.'

So they did not leave for the wake, but stood about till midnight watching with mild exclamations while Michael tried to drive the fairy out of Bridget's body. Her father, Patrick Boland, raised some objections which Michael dealt with impatiently. 'Haven't you any faith?' he said. 'Don't you know it's with an old witch I'm sleeping.' 'You are not,' said Patrick Boland, 'you are sleeping with my daughter.' And telling about it later in the Clonmel courts, he, like the other witnesses, preserved a trance-like calm, as though he were watching a tragedy in which he was doomed to be a spectator, knowing the truth and yet powerless to intervene.

It is Johanna Burke who gives us the most coherent account of it all. She came back from washing the shirts about 7 p.m. on this first day of fairy exorcism, 14 March 1895. She found the Clearys' door locked and two neighbours called Simpson standing outside unable to get in. Through the window they could hear a voice saying, 'Take it, you witch or you bitch!' And when the three of them were at last let in she found the three Kennedys and John Dunne holding Bridget down on the bed, while Michael tried to give her herbs boiled in new milk from a spoon. Mary Kennedy, returned from feeding the hens, had brought some wine with her, and Michael threw it over Bridget's face and breast, exclaiming 'Are you Bridget Boland in the name of God?' while her father echoed, 'Are you Bridget Boland, in the name of God, the daughter of Patrick Boland?' But Bridget was exhausted and speechless and the liquid was pouring down her chemise. So, while the Rosary was recited, the men raised her out of the bed and put her onto the fire. It was John Dunne's suggestion. 'We raised her over it,' he explained to the courts, 'I thought it belonged to the cure.' Hannah had just been putting sticks on the fire to make them a cup of tea and when Bridget, in the men's arms, saw her, she exclaimed in a mournful voice 'Oh, Han, Han!' She was wearing, Hannah recollected, a red petticoat and navy-blue flannel dress, green stays and navy blue cashmere jacket, and Hannah, a conscientious witness, said of her later: 'When she was taken out, she looked like one that was silly, she looked wild and deranged and had not her own appearance. She looked different. She looked worse when she was taken out of bed than when I went into the room.' She was just 'tipping the bars' and her father and Michael Cleary were questioning her urgently in the name of God. It was too much for Hannah, she shouted out, 'Burn her away, but let me out and I'll go for the peelers.' She got out, but she did not go for the peelers.

That was the first night of burning; though there had been

thirteen people in the house, we do not know much else about the remaining five hours before the visitors walked off to the funeral, except for what Patrick Boland told the court. About the first night he was very reassuring. 'Indeed,' he said, 'the fire wouldn't do anything the first night, 'twas no fire I might say.' He had left with the others at midnight and returning with them from the wake the following day, he had found nothing to complain of in Bridget's condition. 'She was grand then when I came back from Michael's father's wake, and the next night after that she was grand and the night after that she was grand until we were all taking a cup of tea.' At this point the old man broke off in tears; he tried to tell what happened on the third night in a few disjointed phrases. It appeared that Michael had gone to his wife with the dish of herbs and milk and said: 'I'll make you take it, you old witch! I have herbs that there's nine cures in. It will be very hard to make her take these.' He struggled to explain what followed but failing to articulate, wound up: 'I had to run away from the smell. So 'tis all the way to make a long story short he burnt her.'

The witnesses all rambled incoherently backwards and forwards between the two nights of burning, lingering over what seems to us trivial, suppressing what appears to be relevant. They lived in a fairy-haunted world, whose thoughts and feelings can be measured by no ordinary rule. The poet is apt to overestimate its charm, the moralist its cruelty. The mere chronicler is exasperated by his powerlessness to sort out the events of the successive nights. Of all the witnesses Hannah Burke is the most easy to follow. The peelers to her were almost as real as the fairies, she had actually thought of going to fetch them, and her chronology is the same as ours. After Bridget had been on the fire the first night, Hannah Burke had returned and put on her a fresh nightdress, which she had been airing for her and she had examined her body. Like Patrick Boland, she agreed that Bridget was 'grand'. 'I saw no marks on her except the size of a pin and a little blister on her hip not the size of sixpence, and a couple of little spots of burns on her chemise and a red spot under her chin. I thought it might be from the pin in her chemise so I put a safety pin there instead.' She stayed on with Bridget after the men had left for the wake and gave her some new milk, whey and claret wine, but when she left at 2 a.m. Bridget was still awake.

Hannah came the next morning with the fresh milk and her daughter Katey for company. She laid the milk on the window, and Michael gave her a shilling for it. But he said that Bridget had taken the shilling back from Hannah and, putting it under the blanket, had rubbed it against her thigh, a fairy trick, before returning it to Hannah. But when Michael had accused her of doing this, she had denied it. 'No, I am not a pishogue.' Yet she was aware how easily one might become a fairy, and for her, too, the borderland between fact and fantasy was very ill defined. 'Your mother gave two nights with the fairies,' she argued gently, 'that's why you think I'm one.'

Michael Cleary then went to the parish priest, Father Ryan, and asked him to come and say Mass for his wife. We know that in health she was 'grand', so it was surely because she was a fairy and had rubbed the shilling on her thigh that he appealed to him. But Father Ryan, doing his duty, appeared to have no inkling of the turmoil that was going on in the hearts of his parishioners. The court seemed to think it strange that he should know so little and it is difficult not to feel that Father Ryan, depending on the time-honoured formulae and ceremonies of his Church, felt excused from those simple movements of the mind and heart which might have saved the Clearys. Michael told the courts that Bridget, when she had received the sacrament, had removed the wafer from her mouth, refusing, fairy that she was, to swallow it.

To this Father Ryan replied reproachfully: 'I wish to add that if any Catholic saw Bridget Cleary remove the Blessed Sacrament from her mouth, he would be strictly bound to tell me at once so as to enable me to save the Sacred Species from profanation.' I cannot altogether blame the Clearys if it was only the supernatural claims of Father Ryan which impressed them. They appealed to him as a magician, whose magic had world-wide power and authority to reinforce it, to stand up against a more ancient magic whose power was waning. And they were deeply disappointed in his failure. The fairy failed to come out of Bridget and they were thrown back again on their own resources.

The next evening Michael tried Bridget once more with the herbs and boiled milk. He was very resolute this time. Hannah had made them cups of tea and the fire was blazing brightly. Young William Kennedy held the candle for Michael to work by, an oil lamp stood on the dresser and Patrick Boland and all the neighbours were there as on the former night, all of them distressed and friendly and solicitous. There was bread and jam and claret wine as well as cups of tea. Bridget kept saying that she was not a pishogue and that she was not turning into a fairy like Michael's mother, and her father and husband kept appealing to her in the name of God to say whether she was Bridget Boland or not. And once she asked for Tom Smith and David Hogan, 'two honest men', and she said she'd do anything they said. Smith and Hogan appear to have come and gone without altering the situation very much. And once, shifting inexpertly to the everyday world of crime and detection, she said: 'The peelers are at the window. Let ye mind ye now!' But everyone knew they were not and the observation had no consequences.

It was midnight and young William Kennedy had gone to sleep in the back room with his brother James, but they were roused by a sudden hullaballoo in the front room. Michael had taken from under the bed what was called in the Clonmel Court House 'a certain utensil' and poured the contents over his wife, then, seizing a burning log from the grate, he had forced her to lap up the herbs and milk from the saucepan, while young William once more held the candle by the bedside. Then Michael forced bread and jam down her throat, crying out all the while: 'Are you Bridget Cleary, my wife, in the name of the Father, the Son and the Holy Ghost?' while Mary Kennedy demurred, saying: 'Leave her alone, Mike, don't you see it's Bridgie as is in it?' Then Michael locked the door so that no one could leave and put the key in his pocket. Then he put Bridget on the floor and threw the lamp on her and some oil from a half-gallon oil-can from between the table and the dresser, so that Bridget was in a blaze of fire and the house suffocated with smoke. All the neighbours stampeded to the door and tried to break it down, so great was their dismay, but Michael told them they were not to leave till he had got his wife back. 'Are you Bridget Boland in the name of the Father, and Son and the Holy Ghost?' shouted Michael once more. 'Hold her over the fire and she'll soon answer!' Someone seemed then to have found the key in Michael's pocket and Patrick Boland escaped. William, a delicate boy, dropped the candle and fell down 'in a weakness' and his mother threw Easter water over him. There were signs of renewed disapproval from the neighbours, but Michael silenced them, saying: 'Hold your tongues! It isn't Bridget I'm burning. You'll soon see her go up the chimney!' Reassured by this, some of the neighbours came forward to help him and, in the words of Hannah Burke, 'They placed Mrs Cleary in a kind of sitting position on the kitchen fire, her body resting on the bars. The fire was a slow one. Mrs Cleary's appearance was greatly changed.'

After that there is mention of a large sack-bag with a dirty sheet in it, which Michael laid on the floor. Knowing what he had to do, he laid what was left of Bridget on it, on her back with her feet bent up. 'It's not Bridget,' he repeated. 'As I couldn't drive the devil out through the chimney, I'll drive her through the door.' He asked Pat Kennedy to help bury her somewhere till she could be put by her mother's side. At first he said 'No', but then he agreed and at 2 a.m. Michael and Pat went out and buried the body. Michael had lost his confidence now: 'She's burned now,' he said, 'and God knows I didn't intend to do it. It's Jack Dunne I may thank for it all.'

Mary Kennedy went round to the Clearys' cottage the next morning and found a little group of neighbours already assembled. Hannah was there and old Pat Boland, Bridget's father, was on his knees, lamenting. 'Now that my child is dead,' he said, 'there is no use in saying anything about it, but God help me in the latter end of my days!' Michael was wearing the same light suit of clothes he had worn when Bridget was being burnt and it was badly marked. He had stayed back from work to clean it. 'I saw him,' said Hannah, 'scraping the stains like of grease off the ends of his trousers, and says he to me, "Oh, God, Hannah, there is the substance of poor Bridget's body".' But he still considered that it was her body only, for he told them again that his wife had gone to Kilnagranagh to see the fairies and that they were to come there that evening and help him lift her from the white horse and cut the ropes that bound her to it and persuade her to stay with him. And in fact that evening and later evenings, till he was arrested, a crowd of people did go with him to the rath. He carried a bread-knife in his hand to cut the ropes. But fewer and fewer went and John Dunne, declaring now that it was 'all moonshine', urged him to go to the priest.

Michael's mother, she who had given two nights to the fairies, also gave evidence. When she reached his cottage she had found him, she said, still scraping himself, 'scraping the juice of the poor creature off his clothes.' 'Mike,' said I to him, 'if you were scraping your clothes for ever and if you cut them off you, God would never let the stains go out of your clothes, the stains of your poor wife.' And then she had said: 'Acorrah, go down to the police barracks and tell them what you have done.'

'No, mother,' he had answered, 'because people would be calling you a prosecutor.'

Michael asked them then to come and help him bury Bridget and one of the Kennedys said he'd come and help if she was to be buried in consecrated ground, but Michael had gone away, and without him to direct them, the neighbours wandered round the kitchen garden, hunting for the body.

Michael Cleary was at confession. Kneeling at the altar, he had torn his hair and cried would he ever be forgiven?

When the priest came out into the chapel yard, John Dunne, he who had helped to lift Bridget on to the fire, because he thought it 'belonged to the cure', accosted him. 'They burnt her to death last night, Father,' he said, 'and I have been asking them all the morning to take her up and give her a Christian burial.'

Hannah Burke ended her evidence abruptly: 'That's all I have to say and sorry I am.'

Michael from the dock said, 'You did that well, Han.'

'I did so, Mick.'

'I hope you will do it in Heaven as well as that.'

'I will with the help of God, Mick.'

When the nine prisoners from Ballyvadlea were taken for trial in Clonmel, there were demonstrations in the streets and in particular against Denis Guiney, the herb doctor. They received, however, a merciful sentence and commentators on the case in the Dublin and London periodicals were on the whole more tolerant than the Clonmel neighbours. The reaction against Victorian rationalism had started and there was a new reverence for the supernatural when it had a respectable ancient tradition behind it. Folklore had become a science, and in Ireland Standish O'Grady, by his poetical reconstruction of the Irish past, had prepared the way for Yeats and AE and the Celtic Twilight. I do not think that the fairies suffered any serious set-back by the happenings at Ballyvadlea.

In *The Nineteenth Century* E. F. Benson wrote an essay on the trial, which was typical of the period in that he covered a great deal of ground with very thin speculation. He drew analogies from the Hottentots, who try to shake out the spirit of disease from the dying, and the Zulus, who believe in Amatongos or ancestor-spirits, and he offered the Clearys a respectable place in the *Encyclopaedia of Primitive Superstition*. But to those who live around Slievenaman such a diagnosis seems as inadequate as it is pretentious. There is no need to call in the Zulus and Hottentots. A woman had been burnt to death for witchcraft in Kilkenny in 1324 on the instigation of the bishop, an English Franciscan, the only known instance of such burning in Ireland. Such catastrophes often happen when reason is in bondage to Fear of the Unknown, even when such Fear calls itself Faith.

In fact the Ballyvadlea tragedy had quite a sophisticated and civilized background. Everyone was perfectly familiar with priests and peelers, doctors and prosecutors, and for many centuries they had been subject to the laws of England and the faith of Rome. Nor were they altogether outside the current of world affairs. Some years before in the little village of Mullinahone, where the Clearys did their shopping, twenty-eight volunteers had set off to defend the Papal States against Garibaldi and had returned from Sardinian prisons to a welcome with bonfires on the mountain and triumphal arches.

All the Clearys and their neighbours lived in that perilous region of half-belief which the sophisticated find charming because they are more acquainted with its tenderness than its cruelty. It is a no-man's land of the imagination, in which fantasy, running wild, easily turns into falsehood and ruthlessness. It has still in the twentieth century its appeal and highly civilized people, as well as simple ones, claim access to it.

In the past in Ireland both the Churches and the Anglo-Normans often tried to harness the fairies to their ecclesiastical and political designs, and the results were often so delightful that the guard upon the frontiers of fairyland has sometimes been unwisely relaxed.

In an old Irish poem about Slievenaman, St Patrick raised Oisin, the famous hunter, from the dead and said to him:

> Oisin, sweet is thy voice.
> Tell us how many deer fell upon Slievenaman?

And Oisin answered:

> We killed six thousand deer
> In the glen which lay in the mountain,
> O cleric of the clerks and bells!

A thousand hounds with their collars of gold
Fell before noon by one hundred hogs.

In fact St Patrick did not dispel the spirits of the mountain but became one of them himself. The fairy goldsmiths made chalices and fonts for Patrick and the saints as readily as they made collars for the hounds of the Fianna. The result is that cultivated Irishmen will often have the same ironical, indulgent smile for the mysteries of their faith as for the legends of Fionn. And simple people, like the Clearys, not so skilled at walking the tight rope between belief and disbelief, are at the mercy of some temporary spasm of credulity. None of them consistently believed that Bridget was a fairy. Every now and then the voice of reason insisted: 'Don't you see it's Bridgie as is in it?' but reason could make no headway against Michael's passionate conviction, whose origins Michael himself maybe did not rightly understand.

The great Norman castles on the flanks of Slievenaman, Kilcash and Kiltinan and the others, have long ago fallen into ruin or decay, and the noble lords whose horses and hounds evoked memories of the Fianna have vanished. Life has been drab and poor for many generations and poets like to transfigure it with the myth and magic of fairyland. A couple of centuries ago a native of Slievenaman, Father Lalor, wrote a charming and sophisticated elegy in Irish on the death of his friend Archdeacon Kavanagh. He saw the Archdeacon, like St Patrick, among the fairies on Slievenaman and the fact that these two solitary priests did not believe in the fairies makes their need of them more poignant. The poem starts gaily:

As I one time was travelling the province
Airily, cheerfully spending my youth;
Some time to gamble I bestowed and to drinking,
And a small, short time I devoted to knowledge.

Then Father Lalor describes his visit to the fairy palace on Slievenaman, the wines and the clothes and the servants, and how he asked the fairy queen why the mist had swept up from the Nore enveloping Dunane and Barnan-Ely, 'What makes the side of Carnduff impenetrable to the sun?' And the fairy queen had replied that it was because

A steady pillar of the church has died
Who was the friend of the poor and needy. . .
The friend of idiots without reason's light,
Who in the Lord's vineyard laboriously toiled.
He was an example to the whole diocese,
He never spent his time on lands or flocks,
He never raised the price of land by bidding against the labouring
classes.
Now the white hand which distributed the sacrament
Is stretched without the power of motion by his side, alas!

Then the damsel had vanished and the splendid palace with her and there was nothing left on the mountain side but the mist, the gorse and the heather.

I doubt whether Archdeacon Kavanagh was quite as good as they thought him on Slievenaman, or Bridget Cleary so bad, or Oisin so splendid a hunter. A great deal of Irish poetry and romance is born of isolation and the nostalgia of those who escape it. Eyes that are dim with tears are not particularly perceptive; focused on the fairies they never give the eggman his due. Indeed I have read through hundreds of verses about Slievenaman without finding a single reference to him. And as for the Clearys, nobody, of course, since E. F. Benson, has mentioned them at all; though they were poetical people, they are out of harmony with what the poets tell us of that fairy-haunted mountain.

In purple robes old Slievenaman
Towers monarch of the mountains,
The first to catch the smiles of dawn
With all his woods and fountains. . .
There gallant men, for freedom born,
With friendly grasp will meet you;
There lovely maids as bright as morn
With sunny smiles will greet you
And there they strove the Red above
To raise Green Ireland's banner –
There yet its fold they'll see unrolled
Upon the banks of Anner.

[1960]

7

ANGLO-IRISH TWILIGHT

Lately, an exhibition, organized by the National Museum, paused for a short spell in Kilkenny Castle. It was called 'the Landed Gentry' and in Dublin it was advertised by a poster of a smart lady in a top hat and hunting kit* jumping over a bill of eviction. The show was full of fascinating items, orders for footmen's livery and for the stocking of wine-cellars and imperious instructions to farm labourers and tenants on the great estates. In order to be fair, reports of Clothing Funds were included and a note that Daniel O'Connell was also a land-owner with an estate of 30,000 acres. Yet the general impression was created that the Anglo-Irish had been, contrary to what Yeats had said, a Petty People , whose main concern had been horses and rents.

There were a few mistakes (e.g. Sheestown, a small estate near Kilkenny, where Otway Cuffe had lived, was wrongly located in Co. Waterford), but it represented well enough the skeletal structure of a civilization outwardly as dead in Ireland as that of the Hapsburgs in Bohemia. If there had been more than a spark of life left today, surely some voice of protest would have spoken of the Grattans, Floods, Edgeworths, Parnells, Plunketts and a thousand others, who had built that Anglo-Irish civilization, which is still, battered and hiding behind a Eurocratic façade with neo-Gaelic trimmings, unchangingly ours. It is only the heirs of those who created it who are doomed. J. C. Beckett in his fine book, *The Anglo-Irish Tradition*, declared that in the Anglo-Irish community even the will to survive appeared to be fading and predicted that, before the end of the century, Protestantism, their

* In fact, a photograph of Lady Clonbrock, best known as organizer of the Clonbrock and Castlegar Poultry Co-operative, which with associated home industries and crafts, outlasted all similar rural cooperatives and only died in 1952. See Patrick Bolger, *Irish Co-operative Movement*, p. 287, for a different photograph of her.

prevailing religion, would be virtually extinct in the Republic.

In the exhibition there was a photograph of the fourth Earl of Desart and his Countess who lived at Desart Court near Kilkenny. It was taken from a London illustrated paper and the caption under Lady Desart's picture explained that she had 'a good seat on a horse' and tackled 'Pat's fences' with the same grace with which she rode in Rotten Row. There followed a humorous story of how she tricked 'Land-Leaguer Pat', who had thrown stones at the fox-hounds, into playing 'God Save the Queen' on his harmonica.

I knew Lady Desart when I was young and she was old and she was not in the least like that. She was a plump and plain little Jewess with high intelligence and spirit, a guttural voice and very strong pince-nez. She would have looked ridiculous on a horse, though she may have pretended to like them because her husband, whom she loved, was MFH and had even written a novel called *The Honourable Ella of Foxshire*. He died in 1898 and was succeeded by his brother, a distinguished London barrister and there was then no longer any need for his widow to model herself on the Honourable Ella. As she was very rich, she felt free to follow her own ideas or rather those of her youngest brother-in-law, Otway Cuffe, who was a disciple of a well-known writer, Standish O'Grady. Cuffe had led a wandering life outside Ireland, but when he realized that he was likely to succeed his brother as sixth Earl of Desart, he had, under O'Grady's influence, begun to take very seriously his responsibility to his country.

Of O'Grady, whom the Cuffes had brought to Kilkenny, W. B. Yeats was later to write: 'Whatever should come out of Ireland in the future will owe itself to two books. O'Grady's *Bardic History of Ireland* and Ferguson's *Poems*.' The *Bardic History*, in George Dangerfield's words,

> released Cuchullain and the other heroes of the Ulster Cycle from the grip of a scholarship, which had preserved the Irish myth, like a splendid fly in a kind of philological amber.
>
> 'In O'Grady's writings,' said AE, 'the submerged river of national culture rose up again, a shining torrent. It was he who made me conscious and proud of my country. . . He was the last champion of the Irish aristocracy and spoke to them of their duty to the nation as a fearless prophet might speak to a council of degenerate princes.'

When in 1898 Cuffe urged O'Grady to take over *The Kilkenny*

Moderator, the Unionist and Protestant weekly, from Mr Lawlor, the Editor, who had to look after a sick brother in Bournemouth, nobody but he could guess the storms this dynamic character might precipitate in a stagnant community. All that Mr Lawlor knew of O'Grady was reassuring. He wrote in his valedictory editorial:

> Mr O'Grady is among the first rank of the Irish gentry; he is first cousin to Lord Gort, second cousin to the present Viscount Guillamore and near relation to the Persses of Roxborough, the Wallers of Castletown Waller. . .

Then followed more names of distinguished families all of which have long disappeared and a list of medals and other distinctions he had won at Trinity.

> Furthermore, Professor Lecky of Trinity and Lord Castletown of Upper Ossory have subscribed to bring over an eminent artist from England to paint his picture.

What could be more reassuring than this? In fact, the portrait was by an Irishman, John Butler Yeats, W. B.'s father, and O'Grady, though a fervent champion of the 'Landed Gentry', was also one of their most savage critics.

In one of his books which few in Ireland could have read, he had addressed the leaders of Anglo-Ireland in the manner of Carlyle.

> Your ancestors who raised the noble classical buildings of Dublin loved a classical quotation, but could one in twenty of you translate the most hackneyed Latin tag in a newspaper? Christ save us all! You read nothing, you know nothing. You are totally resourceless and stupid. . . England has kept you like Strasburg geese which are kept until they can hardly stand without support and so slow and sleepy that they are scarcely aware when they are killed. As I write, the Protestant Anglo-Irish, who once owned all Ireland from the centre to the sea, is rotting from the land in the most dismal farce-tragedy of all time, without one brave deed, without one brave word.

He predicted that unless they could

> reshape themselves in a heroic mould there would be anarchy and civil war, which might end in a shabby, sordid Irish Republic, ruled by corrupt politicians and the ignoble rich,

and he told them that they gibed at Ireland and everything Irish:

What native, I ask you, with the spirit of a rabbit would bear forever such an aristocracy as ours?. . . Yet bad as you are you are still the best class we have. You are individually brave and honourable men and do not deserve the doom which even the blindest can see approaching.

You are hated to an extent you can only dimly conceive. The nation is united against you. In your hands the Irish nation once lay like soft wax ready to take any impression you chose and out of it you have moulded a Frankenstein which will destroy you.

As Editor of *The Kilkenny Moderator*, with Otway Cuffe and Lady Desart behind him, he maintained for two years a highly original provincial newspaper. Mr Lawlor, like most provincial editors, had flattered his readers. O'Grady challenged them.

He looked to the Ormondes for a lead, for in one of his books he had recalled the centuries of struggle during which they had built up their princedom.

Love, labour, sorrow and fighting, consultations many with the wise, close intense study of the characters of men, recruitments and dismissals innumerable before a Butler could write the proud title 'Capitanus Suae Nationis', have a nation of which to be captain and a territory on which to sustain his nation.

And he asserted that only by dedication like this could the Anglo-Irish recover the authority which was their due. Only under their guidance could Ireland be true to her history, part Gaelic, part Norse, part Norman, part Scottish, part English, but distinctively Irish and united. He was supported by all those writers, most of them Anglo-Irish, who had created the Abbey Theatre and the Literary Revival and by the Gaelic League, at that time a non-political and non-sectarian body, whose president and founder, Douglas Hyde, was, like Standish O'Grady, a rector's son. Many of them wrote for *The Moderator*.

When O'Grady came to Kilkenny the landed gentry were still outwardly at least immensely influential. The Ormonde supremacy was securely based on history. In the muniment-room of Kilkenny Castle one of the greatest collections of historical documents in the British Isles still survived. In drawers and pigeon holes were charters heavy with the wax seals of the Plantagenets, the title-deeds of monasteries that had long been dissolved and of kindred families that had been dispossessed by Cromwell or William of Orange. There were still Van Dycks, Lelys and Knellers in the Gallery.

The Ormondes had never seemed more splendid. The third Marquess and his wife had just been visited by the Duke and Duchess of York (later George V and Mary), and were shortly to receive Edward VII and Alexandra; they had been to Potsdam and the Kaiser had given Lord Ormonde the Order of the Crown of Prussia, First Class. Socially the Desarts ran them close, for the fifth Countess was later to be sister-in-law to the Princess Royal. They were all good landlords and because of the Irish love of sport they seemed to be very popular, and even though the genius of the first Duke (1610-88) and his capable son may have trickled away in Hanoverian times down obscure branches, the Ormondes still brought a breath of majesty and feudalism to puppy shows and agricultural gatherings. They had it in their power to drape ordinariness, even their own, with some of the glamour of the Middle Ages. It is unlikely that any of these people had ever heard of O'Grady.

His first year in Kilkenny was the centenary of the '98 rebellion and there were processions to commemorate a Wexford man called Hammond who had been executed in the town for manufacturing pikes. In demolishing an old house a pike was found in the wainscoting. It was regarded as an omen and it was urged that it be put in the Tholsel (town-hall) in place of Gladstone's bust. But O'Grady maintained, in *The Moderator*, that the date to celebrate was not 1798 but 1782, for it was then that the Volunteers had assembled at Dungannon in Ulster and had extorted from England those concessions which had made Grattan's Parliament possible. The Commander-in-Chief of the Volunteers had been an Ulsterman, 'the Good Lord Charlemont', and Irishmen of all creeds and classes had, for the first time, been united for a single purpose.

Now, O'Grady maintained, an analogous situation had developed. In 1782 the Volunteers had seized their opportunity, because England was at war with France and welcomed their offer to defend the Irish shores. In 1898 England was at war with the Boers. O'Grady, in *The Moderator*, refused to speak on the moral aspect of this war; all he saw in it was an opportunity for raising a new national army. If such a force were mustered now, the two opposing factions in Ireland could unite for the defence of Ireland, and Dublin would quickly take the lead from Kilkenny as once it had taken it from Dungannon. Thirty thousand British troops, which were garrisoning Ireland, could be relieved for service in the Cape.*

O'Grady, looking round Kilkenny for some military potential uncommitted to Boer or Briton, had to overlook the Kilkenny Militia and the local branch of the Irish Brigade, who were drilling to fight each other in the Transvaal; he could see nothing but those two embryonic armies, the Catholic Boys Brigade and the Protestant Church Lads Brigade and that phantom of a cavalry force, the Kilkenny Foxhounds. He managed to collect recruits from the two boys brigades and got Otway Cuffe, a former army officer and equerry to the king, to drill them. He said prophetically, 'If we do not act now, a very dangerous class of men will take over the drill financed from the other side of the Atlantic. Our natural leaders, the Irish Gentry, must step forward and lead.'

O'Grady saw another way in which the Irish people could rally round those whom they had formerly revered. The Childers Report had revealed that since 1880 Ireland had been overtaxed by £250,000,000 and it was calculated that of this sum Kilkenny County had been annually overtaxed by £135,000. A Financial Relations Committee had been formed with a Kilkenny branch under the leadership of Lord Ormonde. They had met in the Courthouse and O'Grady had declared that if the Anglo-Irish headed the crusade for financial justice, they could once more become the legitimate representatives of the people. Men of education and breeding could still, as in the past, influence the destinies of their country. There must be no delay.

But the committee members had other things to attend to and in the autumn O'Grady wrote,

> Of the sixty Kilkenny gentlemen, who trotted down High Street en route for Knockroe last Monday, every man is a member of the Financial Relations Committee, yet it has never met since its appointment 11 months ago. What artillery can ever penetrate our subterhuman torpor?†

* On the eve of the First World War, Sir Horace Plunkett made a similar proposal for the conversion of the two private armies of the North and South into units of a Territorial Army.

† Yeats in this way, explained in his autobiography their strange apathy: 'Landlord committees were formed in every county and Lord Castletown made a famous speech declaring that Ireland must imitate the Colonists, who flung the tea into Boston Harbour. Protestant Ireland had immense prestige, almost every name sung in modern song had been Protestant. Yet they lacked hereditary passion and whatever corporate action was attempted, the show however gallant it seemed, was soon over.'

Yet O'Grady and Cuffe were not discouraged. To advertise and pay for their new volunteers they started a gymnasium and club, and there were frequent concerts at which Irish songs and dances alternated with gymnastic displays.

O'Grady believed in reviving in each county all the old cultural societies and industrial enterprises, which had been killed by the centralizing policy that had followed the Union. He was proud that *The Kilkenny Moderator*, Protestant, Conservative, Anglo-Irish, was the first significant Irish paper to print a weekly Irish lesson. Soon they started in Kilkenny a branch of the Gaelic League with Cuffe as President.* Douglas Hyde, invited down to address the Gaelic League, told his audience that no Act of Parliament could bring them a national identity. They themselves must create a cultural uniqueness strong enough to resist the pull of sectarian and political fanaticism and to rescue them from the ocean of vulgarity in which the English press was submerging them.

Lady Desart here interposed that her own people, the Jews, had revived a forgotten language and were using it to bind together the disparate branches of her race.

Cuffe referred to the ancient Irish system, which was patriarchal, regional, communal. Though primitive, it contained in itself the germ of a society happier than ours. To help our neighbour should not be a duty but a love: 'As for myself, if I devoted all my thoughts and hopes to my near surroundings the field would still be far larger than I could cover. Yet I could do more for my country if I kept to this field than spread myself over the universe.'

It was a time of excitement and hope, which was suddenly arrested by what was called the County Scandal, a war between the Ormondes and the Desarts. This became of more interest to the Kilkenny citizens than the Boer War itself and, maybe, it had

* They were following in an old local tradition, for Henry Flood of Farmley, near Desart Court, the great orator of Grattan's Parliament, had in his will left most of his fortune for the foundation at Trinity College of a chair in Irish history and language and the purchase of all Irish manuscripts. The Kilkenny Archaeological Society, whose aims were even broader, was founded in 1848 and rapidly became the most famous provincial archaeological society in the British Isles. The founders were the Rector of Ennisnag, a Kilkenny parish priest and a predecessor of O'Grady's as editor of the local Unionist paper. It was a disaster for Ireland that Flood's relations successfully contested his will.

more significance for them.

Here is the story: The Colonel of the Kilkenny Militia, the popular and sporting Charlie Gore (this is not his real name), had been the fourth Earl of Desart's agent and it had been discovered on Lord Desart's death that he had appropriated £6000 belonging to the family. Charlie Gore's family, a much respected one, had paid what was owing and Charlie, though dismissed, was not taken to court. Then, as time passed, he saw an opportunity of clearing his name. The missing money, he said, had really been owed to him by Lord Desart, an unpaid racing debt. To save Lord Desart's reputation he had adjusted the matter himself.

Lady Desart and her two brothers-in-law reacted strongly. Not being litigious people, they persuaded their friend, O'Grady, to print a letter telling the true facts in *The Moderator*. In this letter Ellen, Lady Desart, called the Colonel a 'thief' and challenged him to sue her for libel. The Colonel, after a long delay, had contemptuously replied that the matter had been settled up long ago by reference to the Lord Chancellor, the Commander of the Forces and the Marquess of Ormonde. The fifth Lord Desart had then replied that the Lord Chancellor had assured him that he had made no enquiry at all and, if the Marquess and the Commander of the Forces had given a decision, they had done so without reference to a single member of the family against whom the offence had been committed. The Cuffes demanded that the Colonel be relieved of his responsibilities as a magistrate and the command of the Kilkenny Militia.

O'Grady accompanied the letter with an angry editorial and Lord Ormonde, already enraged that this upstart journalist had dared to reprove him and his friends for their neglect of the Financial Relations Committee, decided to reinstate the Colonel as publicly as he could.

When the Bishop, Dr Crozier, asked Lord Ormonde as Lieutenant of the County to review the Church Lads Brigade in the large grounds behind the Palace, he had brought the Colonel with him as ADC and at a suitable moment asked the Colonel to step forward and address the boys. The Colonel spoke and the Bishop replied, 'in terms', wrote O'Grady, 'of eulogy and approbation'. (The Bishop was later to say that he was not addressing the Man but the Office and that he had not invited the Colonel to the Palace.)

O'Grady was beside himself. All the pillars of society, which he had hoped to strengthen, the Church, the aristocracy, the army and, worst of all, the Butlers, appeared to be collapsing. He rushed to his desk and wrote a scorching editorial. He concluded:

> Now for this blazing scandal I do not blame the poor Colonel, whose weak good nature may have led him into these courses. I blame the bad and dishonourable men, who, out of sheer perversity and worse motives, backed him up in the maintenance of his commission and have undertaken to see him safely through this affair. Those men who have betrayed the honour of the county are the Marquess of Ormonde, the Protestant Bishop of Ossory and the Master of the Kilkenny Hounds.

How the third of them, Sir Hercules Langrishe, comes into the story I do not know. But in the next editorial O'Grady focused all his fury on Lord Ormonde, who had disappointed him most. He began:

> We are not at war with the Bishop, but with the great and dominant social power in our midst, reaching up to the Throne and down to the smallest Kilkenny huxter, a power which has almost obliterated a sense of honour and public morality in the minds of the few and dulled and paralysed the conscience of the community [and he referred less explicitly to others] who had weakly followed the line of least resistance and afforded support to a stained reputation.

After that he printed a detailed summary of what had happened and sent copies of *The Moderator* to the colonels of all the regiments on Salisbury Plain and one to the Duke of Connaught. The Kilkenny Militia was at that time on manoeuvres in North Kilkenny and it is said that he urged them to mutiny.

In a very short time a writ for libel came from the Bishop. He asked for £2000 and had engaged 'six eminent counsels'. Further writs were reported to be on the way from the Marquess of Ormonde and Sir Hercules Langrishe, who were yachting at Cowes, and from others, whom O'Grady had accused of shielding the Colonel. At a special meeting of the Kilkenny Club, of which Lord Ormonde was President, O'Grady was asked to resign.

It would take too much space to carry on this story to the end of the Boer War, to O'Grady's departure from Kilkenny, saddened, but not discouraged. Yet there were many fascinating incidents. I should like to tell how the Kilkenny Militia, in their red tunics, spiked helmets and snowy bandoliers, set off a thousand strong, to embark at Waterford for training on Salisbury Plain. At their head was Colonel Charlie, on their heels a straggling Kilkenny mob, screaming: 'Hurrah for Kruger and Lady Desart!' and throwing stones and bits of coal. 'Nature abhors a vacuum,' O'Grady wrote. 'If the leaders of society betray their trust, new centres of influence will arise.'

O'Grady left and Mr M. W. Lawlor returned from Bournemouth and took over *The Moderator* again. For many months he wooed back its affronted subscribers among the gentry with philippics against O'Grady and his 'wanton, wicked and libellous attacks against one of the most exalted, popular and esteemed Peers of the Realm, whose popularity in the hunting fields of Kilkenny and in yachting circles in England and America is so well known. He brought about a state of things', he declared, 'which should bring a blush of shame to the face of even a strolling play-actor, if such a person were capable of blushing.' He spoke of his 'slanderous wagging tongue' and his 'Silly-Billy publication, the vehicle of idiotic drivel.' He revealed that O'Grady was only 'collaterally' related to the Gorts and Guillamores and that a lot of kitchen utensils had been sold at his auction, which had never been paid for, 'A man of failure,' he summed it all up, 'at everything he touched.' Finally he sent him a bill for printer's ink and another writ.

It was the Cuffes' letter to *The Moderator* that destroyed O'Grady's paper and so I have no doubt that it was Ellen, Lady Desart, who rescued him from financial disaster. She and Otway Cuffe continued vigorously the work which he had inspired and started. The list of their enterprises is scarcely believable. They built a theatre, a hospital, a model village with a Woodworkers Factory at Talbot's Inch, a public library, a recreation hall, a woollen mills, a tobacco farm and many other small co-operative ventures. There was a little bridge across the Nore to link Talbot's Inch with the Woollen Mills. Cuffe became Mayor of Kilkenny and you will see his name carved on John's Bridge, which was rebuilt in his Mayoralty, underneath that of his forbear the Earl of Desart, who was Mayor when the previous bridge was erected. They were trying to domesticate and regionalize the dragon of international industrialism, at a time when almost everyone was directly or indirectly in the pay of the dragon.

The story of the slow decay of all these enterprises, one by one, through strikes, fraud, arson and under the unchanging pressure of politics, religion and social jealousy, would have value as a small-scale model of a universal phenomenon. Trouble started almost immediately.

In the Kilkenny Woodworkers they needed a cabinet-maker and Cuffe after long advertisement had to accept a non-trade union worker from Glasgow. Thereupon 18 men out of 100 went on strike. The Glasgow man was a Jew and this incensed the strikers still more. They struck him and chanted in chorus, 'Clear out, Ikie!'

None of the strikers, the Kilkenny papers defiantly declared, were Kilkennymen and they underlined the mean ingratitude to Cuffe and Ellen Desart, the Jewess, who had poured money into the Kilkenny industries, regardless of profit. The English trade union officials backed up the strikers. There came a sharp letter from Alexander Gossip, General Secretary of the National Amalgamated Furnishing Trades Association of Finsbury Pavement. He said he was 'not prepared to tolerate unnecessary grievances of kind indicated'. He trusted that Cuffe 'would at once see that end was put to same'. Representatives were sent to Kilkenny but Cuffe refused to see them, and answered all their letters with haughtiness. The interference from England, the flare-up of anti-Semitism and the threat to that community, which Cuffe was trying to build up, not upon impersonal officialism and scheduled rights, but on personal relations, all this cut him to the quick. He refused all mediation and started to replace the strikers with men from outside. He knew they might be stopped by picketers at Kilkenny station, so he had them met at the station before it, Gowran. One morning a little man called Flanagan got out of the train at Gowran with his trunk and found the draughtsman there with a jennet trap. They set off together, when suddenly a side-car loaded with strikers lurched down on them. 'That's your game, is it?' they screamed. 'Get out, you white-livered little scamp!' 'I'm only doing my duty,' said little Flanagan, but he was dragged out of the trap and the box flung on the road. Finally box and Flanagan were hoisted onto the side-car and cantered off to Kilkenny. A procession of tradesmen and a piper met them in John Street and with the piper playing a victory march and the tradesmen cheering, they drove their bewildered captive and his trunk through the town. That was the first of a series of disasters.

When after years of disappointment, Cuffe died in Australia, all the shops in Kilkenny were closed and the flag on the Tholsel was flown at half-mast. He had seen the doom that was approaching and had tried to reverse it, but it was too late. Meanwhile O'Grady in Dublin continued a journal, *The All-Ireland Review*, which he had started in Kilkenny and in which, as always, he tried to reconcile the old ascendancy with those who were groping towards the recovery of a national identity. He never retreated from his Anglo-Irish and Protestant background. In one of his novels his hero was an Irish Protestant, who fought for William of Orange. From its legendary past to its confused present, Irish history was to be seen as a unity based on diversity.

Few of his disciples understood this. He had brought a new theme to Anglo-Irish literature, and new ideas, like sparks in a time of drought, can purge or destroy. Patrick Pearse and Thomas MacDonagh, who were executed in 1916, produced at their school, St Enda's, one of O'Grady's Ulster plays. Cuffe organized another at Sheestown; it was acted by the Cave Hill players from Belfast. Both were well attended.

Could anyone have guessed at the explosive force of poetry and ideas? Why does it so rarely happen that those who lay the fire are allowed to light it? Yeats had said 'O'Grady's *History of Ireland* had been the start of it all', and George Dangerfield observed that the book was 'somewhere at the heart of the Easter Rising in 1916. Cuchullain was one of the shadowy heroes who fought side by side with the living in the General Post Office.' Yeats in his old age never ceased to wonder at the effect of his own poetry.

> Did that play of mine send out
> Certain men the English shot?

O'Grady's health broke down soon after the Rebellion and he left Ireland to join his son in an English rectory. Then came the Black and Tans and the Treaty and early in 1922 the British Army left Kilkenny in trains with 'Back to Blighty' chalked on them, as the crowds cheered and the church-bells rang. The soldiers added to the noise by ringing from the carriage windows the large bells, which they had used on the Crossley tenders.

Many of the Anglo-Irish, who accepted the new Government, as did Ellen, Lady Desart, took office in the new Senate and, when the civil war broke out, they became the target for the Republicans, who rejected the compromise of a Free State from which most of Ulster was excluded. The houses of 37 Senators were burnt and one night in February masked men broke into Desart Court, hacked the furniture and the doors with axes and, making a huge pile, sprinkled it with petrol. Some furniture survived in an untouched wing. It was sent by van to Kilkenny, but it too was stopped on the way and burnt. Presumably this was to punish Senator Lady Desart, who was not in fact the owner. Between January 1922 and March of the following year 139 country houses were destroyed, many of them treasure-houses of great beauty, with fine libraries, whose owners had shaped Irish history. When on 28 June, the Four Courts, where the archives of centuries had been stored, was bombed, it was like the end of a civilization. In May 1922 Kilkenny Castle was taken by the Republicans* and relieved after a few days by the Free Staters. Thirteen years later all the contents were sold and for thirty years the dry-rot invaded room after empty room.

But no purely cultural impoverishment could matter so much as the withdrawal of a whole historic class. Though O'Grady had called them degenerate, outworn and effete, and had prophesied with accuracy what would happen to them, they were stupid and defenceless simply because since the Union they had exported all their brightest and their bravest to England. They had generalled her armies, governed her provinces, dominated her newspapers and her theatres, written her plays. Many of those who remained behind had been educated in England and knew nothing of Ireland's problems.† Waterloo may or may not have been won on the playing fields of Eton, but Ireland was certainly lost there.

AE wrote of O'Grady:

> When a man is in advance of his age, a generation, unborn when he speaks, is born in due time and finds in him its inspiration. O'Grady may have failed in his appeal to the aristocracy of his own time but he may yet create an aristocracy of intellect and character in Ireland.

[1978]

* The fifth Marquess of Ormonde has told the story in the *Journal of the Butler Society*, Vol. 1 No. 4.

† Characteristically those who defended Anglo-Irish values most vigorously after the Treaty were those who had previously criticized them most severely. When a bill was brought in to repeal the right of divorce, which England had introduced, Yeats in the Senate gave his famous No Petty People speech and Lady Desart supported him.

8

BESIDE THE NORE

I have lived for most of my life on the Nore and own three fields upon its banks, some miles before it turns to the south-east and forces its way under Brandon Hill to join the Barrow above New Ross. In sixty years it has changed remarkably little. From a top window, looking across the river towards Blackstairs and Mount Leinster, I can still see the same stretch of cornfields, nut groves and mountain slopes. Beside the woods of Summerhill and Kilfane I can spot the round tower of Tullaherin and Kilbline, the sixteenth-century castle of the Shortalls. There is only one new cottage in sight.

This does not mean that we stagnate. The landscape is domestic and life is mainly prosperous but it has edged away from the rivers. The Nore, which traverses the county of Kilkenny, and passes through the city, and the Barrow, which skirts its eastern border, and all their tributaries gave up work and took to an easy life about a century ago. The mill wheels stopped turning and the roofs fell in on the millworkers' cottages, flags and duck-weed and king-cups choked the mill race and there is so much tranquil beauty around that some hope and many fear that the tourist agencies will soon discover us.

A century ago there were twenty-two flour mills, three large distilleries and four breweries on the Nore between Durrow and Inistioge. But industry had left the rivers long before I was born and as children we were constantly driving donkey carts down little lanes to riverside ruins beside which we bathed and fished and picnicked. And every ruin had its story and the tradition that these stories are worth recording, correcting, analysing has never died out.

Our riverside ruins are mostly not depressing, for many of their founders were original and complex men, whose lives gave evidence that vision and ingenuity can flourish here. Some of their industries did not survive them for long. They subsided gracefully after a generation or two but, like the flowers of summer, were fertile in their decay. Various economic causes can be alleged for their failure but often there is nothing to be said except that men grow old and have bored or stupid sons and that today there are many prosperous industries which would be more admirable as ruins covered with valerian and wild wall flowers.

One of our favourite picnic places was Annamult Woollen Factory, a very stylish and spacious ruin on the King's river just before it joins the Nore. Before the king-cups and the bullocks took over, it was in 1814 one of the most progressive factories in the British Isles. Its owners, Messrs Shaw and Nowlan, rivalled Robert Owen, the Utopian industrialist, in their concern for their 400 work people. The children all had free schooling and lesson books, their fathers and mothers had health insurance cards, and every Sunday they danced to the fiddle in the large courtyard. George Shaw and Timothy Nowlan were stern but just, and rather quizzical. (Shaw was, I believe, a great great uncle to George Bernard.) Employees who misbehaved were punished but not sacked. Sometimes the offender, dressed in a yellow jacket, was obliged to roll a stone round the courtyard in full view of the Sunday merrymakers. The factory, while it lasted, was hugely successful. The Prince Regent and all the employees of the Royal Dublin Society dressed themselves in its woollens and the fields around Annamult were white with a flock of 600 Merino sheep, vast bundles of wool with tiny faces, which the Prims, a famous Kilkenny family with Spanish relations, had imported from Spain.

The Marble Works at Maddoxtown, below Kilkenny, is another beautiful spot with proud memories. Children still hunt about among the loose strife and the willow herb for polished slabs, green Connemara, pink Midleton, and Kilkenny which is black with white flecks. William Colles, who invented special machinery for cutting and polishing by water power, was so clever that his neighbours thought him a necromancer. He almost succeeded in making dogs weave linen by turning wheels, and he invented an instrument, like an Aeolian harp, which played tunes as it floated down the Nore. His house and his manager's house, which face each other across the Bennettsbridge road, are still among the pleasantest of the old houses that decorate the banks of the Nore. Colles was a philosophical man; he wrote tragedies and to remind himself of the 'lapse of time' he had his portrait painted every seven years. His business had prospered in adversity for it was during the Napoleonic Wars, when foreign marble ceased to be imported, that he was able to flood the English market with his chimney pieces, punch bowls, buffets and vases. Then metal mantelpieces arrived and a few years ago all the blocks of marble that littered the river bank were bought by a firm which pounded them into a variegated paste, from which ten chimney pieces could be made as easily as Colles made one.

Maidenhall lies between Annamult and the Marble Works and the Griffiths, who lived there 230 years ago, were such an original couple that I have written of them separately. There are many beautiful little towns along the Nore, but since 'each man kills the thing he loves' it is perhaps unsafe to admire them. Their beauty depends on hump-backed bridges and winding streets and large trees, all of which obstruct the motorist in his race to progress. The curves of the bridge are now being straightened with cement but often you can see the great stone slabs of the parapet jutting out of the stream below the bridge.

All these little towns should have had their chroniclers, for one chronicler attracts another and a village, conscious of its history, can resist the tyranny of the government official. The Nore has not been as lucky as the Barrow. I am sure that it was the O'Learys, hereditary scribes and bakers of Graiguenamanagh on the Barrow, who attracted Sean O'Faolain to the village in 1945. As editor of *The Bell* he stayed there for a week and studied the town as a good teacher studies a child. How did it begin, how was it going to develop? He found that it had been started by Wiltshire monks, planted there by the Normans. For generations they had adhered to their English ways, but had finally become assimilated. At the time of the Reformation the last Abbot was one of the Kavanaghs and their descendants still own the beautiful woods along the river bank at Borris. O'Faolain made a transparent map of the town, marking all its shops and dwellings and offices and laid it over an outline map of the old Cistercian Abbey. You can see how O'Leary's Bakery crept over the cloisters, how the refectory became a Corn Store, and Denny's Pig Scales took over the monks' cemetery. Everything changes, yet there is a core of continuity. O'Faolain traces how the very same processes which eliminated typhus in Graig and gave fresh water, sanitation and medical care, also almost destroyed the town. When the railways brought 'civilization', the bargees, the canal workers and the local craftsmen all became superfluous and got on the trains themselves. In 1841 there were 2248 inhabitants, and in 1945 there were 844. And now? Are charabancs likely to be more beneficent than the railways?

If Inistioge on the Nore is one of the loveliest of Irish villages, much of the credit is due to William Tighe of Woodstock, the large house, whose ruins lay till recently on the hill above it. For anyone who wants to know about the Nore and the Barrow, his work, *A Statistical Survey of the County Kilkenny, 1802*, is still indispensable. It has never been surpassed and never will be, because the tribe to which he and Colles and Griffith belonged, the rural polymaths, is now extinct. Tighe was a classical scholar, an archaeologist, an economist, a sociologist, a politician (a passionate opponent of the Union). He knew the names of all the flowers and all the fish of the two valleys of the Nore and the Barrow, in English, Irish and Latin, and the price of potatoes in Goresbridge in 1798 and how many 'unlicensed tippling houses' there were in Inistioge in 1800 (twenty-eight). He was a humane man and soberly recalls how melons and pineapples could be bought in Kilkenny while the poor children of Iverk went to school 'almost naked'.

He wrote a poem in four cantos called 'The Plants' about the Oak, the Rose, the Palm and the Vine. In the manner of Virgil's *Georgics* it is intended to be diverting as well as instructive. There are 150 pages of notes in Greek, Latin, Hebrew, French and Italian, and he lists 39 species of oak. He was specially interested in the oaks of Mamre, where Abraham, Isaac and Jacob were buried, and he built a small house near Woodstock in an oak grove and called it Mamre, the name by which it is still known.

His eighteenth-century archaeology once collided sensationally with the less adventurous kind which grew out of it. On Tory Hill, in south Kilkenny, there was a large stone slab inscribed with words which he copied scrupulously on a page of his *Statistical Survey* and interpreted as BELI DIVOSE.

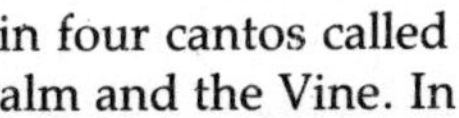

He deduced from this that Baal and Dionysus were worshipped in Early Ireland. Nearly a generation later John O'Donovan, who was working on the Ordnance Survey, came up with a different explanation. He found people alive in Mullinavat who remembered hearing of Ned Connick, the carpenter, and how he had climbed up Tory Hill and carved his name on an ancient block of stone which had later been turned over.

Tighe had copied the inscription so conscientiously that it is only necessary to turn his page upside down and, making allowances for the roughness of the stone and Ned Connick's illiteracy, you can easily read:

ECONIC 1731

William Tighe's sister-in-law, Mary Tighe, whose effigy by Flaxman is housed behind the church at Inistioge, wrote a long poem called 'Psyche', or the Legend of Love. She died young but, published after her death, 'Psyche' received considerable critical admiration. It is based on the story of Apuleius about the love of Cupid and Psyche.

The burning of Woodstock House, the home of poetry and learning, in 1922, was one of the saddest of Ireland's tragedies. But the beautiful plantations survived and there is scarcely in all Ireland a more charming walk than that which runs below the ruins along the Nore. On one side the river with its swans and water lilies, on the other the wooded cliffs and mossy glades sprinkled with ferns and frochans and foxgloves.

When I was young there were plenty of river picnics and neighbours visited each other by cot (long flat-bottomed boats which were used for net-fishing). It was every boy and girl's dream to take a cot to Inistioge, where the river becomes tidal. My brother and I once got as far as Thomastown and then our patience ran out and we walked to Inistioge and spent the night at a small hotel. There was a large stuffed white rabbit on a chest of drawers and at dawn we awoke scratching and observed two columns of insects advancing on us from the rabbit.

The hotel turned into a pub and small shops have come and gone but Inistioge is still the most beautiful and peaceful of villages. Not long ago I was sitting on a bench beside the bridge waiting for my grandchildren to come down the river by canoe from Maidenhall. I remember the red valerian, a broad bank of colour reflected on the dappled current. In such a place time stands still. The past comes close in disconnected fragments and

I was thinking of the days when we were children and had dancing classes with the young Tighes at the Noreview Hotel in Thomastown; their mother, with my Aunt Harriet, used to run a Christian Science Reading Room opposite the Castle in Kilkenny, two spiders into whose web no fly ever came, and I remember when we went to Woodstock a side-car used to meet us at Thomastown station and the branches of the trees brushed our faces as we drove along.

The Tighes were friendly charming people who did not deserve the misfortunes that happened to them. When the war broke out Captain Tighe took his family to London, where he met his death in an accident that has never fully been explained. I do not believe they ever returned. In the spring of 1920 the Black and Tans took over Woodstock and patrolled the country at breakneck speed in their Crossley tenders. Then the Treaty came and they left as rapidly as they had come. It was an empty, undefended house that was finally destroyed.

Later in the afternoon an old man came and sat beside me, and I asked him what it was like when the Tans were in Woodstock. He was very ready to talk and afterwards I wrote down what he told me.

They were in the village too [he said] and we had them in the house next door to us. They weren't too bad. They made us have a notice on all the doors with the names of the people in the house. I remember there was a young chap, Ned Brennan, maybe eight or nine, and they stuck him up on the pub counter and asked him to sing, and he sang 'Wrap the Green Flag Around Me'! He was a young chap, you see, and it was one of the songs he'd learnt. But the Tans just laughed and filled his pockets with pennies. When he came home his mother was very angry and said it was 'blood money' and wouldn't let him keep it.

The Tans had two spies going round the village [he went on] and didn't fourteen of our chaps chase after them so that the two jumped into the river. And our chaps shot one of them and the other got out and ran back to Woodstock to tell the Tans. And after that didn't the Tans burn O'Hanrahans' farm, oh, a big place with cow-sheds and barns and hay ricks. And they did nothing to save old Mrs Hanrahan from burning, till Mrs Newport of Ballygallon – she was an Englishwoman – came and blamed them for not getting her out, and they got her out and she took her to her own place.

I have always believed that local history is more important than national history. There should be an archive in every village, where stories such as the old man told me are recorded. Where life is fully and consciously lived in our own neighbourhood, we are cushioned a little from the impact of great far-off events which should be of only marginal concern to us.

[1984]

9

DIVIDED LOYALTIES

In 1984 Ireland is so deeply divided that few now talk of a *modus vivendi* between Unionist and Nationalist, between Catholic and Protestant. You never read that ancient newspaper cliché about a 'Union of Hearts', or think as I did when I was a boy, and read AE's *Irish Statesman,* that Ireland might become the central focus of our love and loyalty.

Nobody ever investigates how these ethnic and religious love-affairs, which occasionally occur, are conducted. It is obvious though that while they can be easily frustrated, they can only very warily and deviously be promoted.

Opposites often attract each other but the attraction seldom lasts if the full extent of the opposition is ignored. It is as neighbours, full of ineradicable prejudices, that we must love each other, not as fortuitously 'separated brethren'.

I became an Irish nationalist when I was very young. I had to return to school at Charterhouse some days after the Easter week rebellion and to pass barricades near O'Connell Bridge. I had to show a pass signed by the sergeant of the RIC in Kilkenny. There were still wisps of smoke coming from Sackville Street, the names of Pearse and Connolly meant nothing to me but I felt it was my war in a way that the war in which I was being prepared to fight in the Charterhouse OTC was not. When I came home for the holidays I argued ignorantly with my parents about it. Most of our Protestant neighbours, diminished in numbers and in spirit by the everlasting brain-drain to England, were solidly Unionist. They got their little jokes about Ireland from *Punch* and *The Morning Post*.

As far as I was concerned, the first crucial discussion occurred when my slightly older cousin, Theobald Butler, came to stay. He had been head boy at Charterhouse but had become an Irish nationalist and, refusing to fight in an imperialist war, had taken a job in a school in Co. Down. He had first done relief work in Serbia with a friend, Eric Dodds, who, for the same reason, was teaching at Kilkenny College. Dodds had won the famous Craven Scholarship at Oxford. There were heated arguments when they came to lunch. Sometimes after this, if I made a nationalist remark, my mother said, 'Oh, you got that off Theo and Dodds. They'll scuttle back to England the moment the war is over.' And that indeed is what they did, for England has a magnetism for the Anglo-Irish intellectual that very few can resist. Sometimes even a few acres of Irish soil can give us an unreasoning obstinacy and the illusion of security, but Theo and Dodds had not an acre between them. Before he died Theo had a full inch of London legal achievements after his name in *Burke's Peerage,* and Dodds became Regius Professor of Greek at Oxford. In his autobiography, *Missing Persons* (1977), he has described the missing person, the Irish nationalist he once was, and the disillusionment endured by all Anglo-Irishmen who had given their first love to Ireland. 'The birth of a terrible beauty has ended with the establishment of a grocers' republic,' he wrote.

But, if you are heir to some trees and fields and buildings and a river bank, your love for your country can be more enduring. It is a not too blameworthy extension of self-love; you feel qualified to influence its destiny on a small scale and you are not content, as so many of the Irish are, to radiate goodwill to Ireland from across the sea. We were minor gentry and our activities were all minor, but my father had brought the village creamery to Bennettsbridge and was the committee's president, and my mother ran a Boot-and-Coal Fund and a committee connected with tuberculosis, both subsidized by annual jumble sales and concerts. My aunt had founded the Kilkenny Horticultural Society and used to drive a fat pony round the country judging cottage gardens; I used to think she judged the cottagers as well as their gardens. She had a bossy manner and this seemed to me suitable enough.

AE had believed that, as the co-operative movement developed in Ireland, a real village community would grow round every creamery and that the principle of sharing would extend into every branch of life, spiritual, economic, cultural. The communal marketing of eggs and butter would lead to more intimate and domestic forms of sharing. AE saw the hedges planted with apple trees and gooseberry bushes, as in Germany, and gymnasiums and libraries, picture galleries and village halls, to which each man or woman made his contribution according to his powers, so that each village became a focus of activity and debate. Sixty years ago, an ingenuous young person could really believe this would happen. There, anyway, was the new creamery on the edge of the village and it stood till 1983 when it was bulldozed away. To make all these creameries AE had travelled hundreds of miles on his bicycle and Plunkett, a sick man kept alive by his burning zeal, had made these long journeys which he records in his diaries: 'A two hours crawl in the Major's brougham to Longford. Did good I think but, oh, how boring and tiring! Two long speeches to two small meetings. My thoughts germinate in other brains and when the brains are attached to the proper physique the enthusiasm works.'

When I told my mother about the gooseberry bushes, she said, 'Stuff and nonsense! Those trees that the Kilkenny Corporation planted along the canal-walk were all slashed down in a week. When O'Grady and Otway Cuffe gave that Irish play at Sheestown the crowds all strolled out from Kilkenny and pulled up all the shrubs and broke the tea cups.'

When I suggested to my sister, who organized the village concerts, that they should do a Synge play or a Lady Gregory or at least a George Shiels, she said, 'Oh they'd hate that sentimental Irish stuff,' and as usual, she sent for a bunch of one-act farces from Messrs French in London, and she was quite right. They vastly preferred them.

And it always happened like that. When it was rumoured in the Kildare Street Club that the creameries had become social centres where the farmers discussed sedition over their milk-churns, and when the Black and Tans started burning them, many members congratulated themselves on the hostility they had shown to Plunkett. The rest of the story runs along familiar lines.

AE and Plunkett died disillusioned, in England. Kilteragh, Plunkett's house in Foxrock, which had been the meeting-place for the Anglo-Irish who were concerned about their country, was burned to the ground in the civil war, because he had become a Senator.

I was young at the time and did not realize that I was living at the end of a relatively humane and sensible era and at the beginning of a cruel and chaotic one. Ireland had her freedom and Europe had her League of Nations. I enjoyed my holidays at home, the raids and rumours, the 'battle of Kilkenny' and the three-day siege of Kilkenny Castle, and I believe there were many young people as silly as myself.

Compared to other counties, Kilkenny was peaceful and gentle. Apart from the burning of three famous and beautiful houses, Woodstock, Desart Court and Bessborough, life went on as usual with rare interruptions.

One night, at 3 a.m., we were woken by loud knocking at the front door. My sister and I went down and found two unknown men there. We were elated rather than scared. Here was real life at last. One of the men said they wanted money for the 'dependents of the Irish Republic'. I said, 'We've no guns in the house; if you're just common thieves we can't stop you taking what you want.' He replied, 'Ah we're not that sort of chap at all,' and they went away.

Another afternoon two of them came again, asking as before for money. My mother and I were in the porch and she danced about with fury. 'I know who you are,' she said to one of them. 'You're Jim Connell. Take your cigarette out of your mouth when you're talking to me.' He took it out and I began to scold my mother for interrupting what might have been a revealing conversation. It was only the second time I had seen a Republican, and when I went back to Oxford I wanted at least to say what they were like and what their plans were. My mother answered me sharply and we started an angry argument. The two men looked at each other in embarrassment and slunk politely away.

The third occasion was an episode that found its way into J. G. Farrell's *Troubles*. My sisters and I were on our way with two friends to the St Georges' dance at Kilrush, seven or eight miles beyond Kilkenny. It was a period when everyone had to have a permit signed by the police for his car, and all those who were legally on the road could be thought of as the enemy. When we got to Troyeswood, a mile outside Kilkenny, we found a wall built across the road. In front of it stood two men with long white beards, which proved, when we got closer, to be white scarves veiling their faces; they had revolvers. Behind them lay three or four cars turned upside down in the middle of the road. They turned us out of the car and led us across the hedge into the field where already a dozen of our friends were grouped with another muffled figure guarding them. When three or four more cars had been turned over and their occupants ushered into the field, we were told: 'At the expiration of half an hour you may proceed to your destinations.'

We walked back in our evening clothes across Kilkenny. Some stayed at the Club House Hotel. I tramped back home to tell my family.

Far worse things happened in Tipperary. One night in March 1923 Graiguenoe Park, my mother's home at Holycross, was burnt. We shared her sadness for we had spent many happy days with our cousins there. It was between thirty and forty miles away, but when we were children we thought of it as in another country,much wilder, less ordinary. My sister and I used to get up early and start off with our night things on our bicycle carriers and the dew still on the grass. As soon as we crossed the Tipperary border the smell of turf, unknown to us in Kilkenny, prepared us to expect everything strange and new. Leaving behind us the familiar woods of Farmley and Desart Court, we crossed Slieveardagh and turning aside after Littleton bog, we made for Killough hill and, when it came in sight, we knew we had arrived.

The little bridge across the Suir at the approach to Holycross had been rebuilt by an ancestor of my father, James Butler, twelfth Baron Dunboyne, and his wife, Lady Margaret O'Brien, in 1624. There is a Latin inscription on it and an appeal in verse to the passer-by:

Dic, precor, ante abitum,
verbo non amplius uno,
evadat Stygios
auctor uterque lacus.

Pray, traveller, before you pass, offer one prayer only,
that the two builders may escape the Stygian lakes.

This interesting pagan fancy has been christianized in the Tourist Board translation into 'Hell'.

James Butler had given a miraculous statue of the Virgin Mary to the Abbot of Holycross. It had come from a wrecked Spanish galleon and was said to cure toothache and keep rats from the grain.

Even Graiguenoe itself, a large early Victorian house built by my great grandfather beyond the ruins of Holycross Abbey, had romance and mystery for us. My uncle had been boycotted in 1910 and there was a police barracks on his property and for a time a general store. His farm workers had stood by him and could buy their food there when the shopkeepers in Thurles, intimidated by the Land Leaguers, refused to supply them.

Some years ago there was a dramatic dynamiting of the ruins of Graiguenoe in the presence of a photographer from *The Tipperary Star*, and the stones were used in the reconstruction of Holycross Abbey. When I went there soon after, there was no trace of the house except for a broad band of daisies that wound through the field where the avenue had been. Tom Nolan, the coachman's grandson, still lived in the lodge and I found that the new proprietor farmed a thousand acres more than Uncle Charlie had done.

Some twenty houses of the Anglo-Irish were burnt at this time in Tipperary. Most of them vanished without record, but many letters must have been written like the one which follows. It is from the housekeeper at Graiguenoe to my aunt, who was in London at the time.

March 31. 1923

From Mrs A. Good, Housekeeper, Graiguenoe Park, Holycross, Co. Tipperary, to Mrs Charles Clarke.

Madam,

By now you know the bad news how Graiguenoe is burned down. Oh it was terrible to see it blazing away!

Just at 5 past 12 on Wednesday night the bell was rung. I was only just in bed, so I jumped up and called the girls and went to Nolan; but he was up. They never stopped ringing till Nolan and I went to the hall-door; and there were two men with revolvers and demanded to know why we did not open before and come out; so I said, 'Surely you will give us time to get our things.' He said 'Yes, If we were not too long.' He wanted to know how many there were in the house. I said 'Three girls more.' He wanted to know who were all those inside there. I said, 'That is yourself in the mirror.' He thought (when he saw our reflections in the glass) that a lot of people were there. So we all got our things put together as quick as we could, but all of us had to leave a lot of things as they kept asking, 'Are ye ready, as we are in a hurry', so we got out. Nolan saved three pictures out of the dining room and your dressing case and a small case under the bed and Mr Clarke's dressing bag, but they did not want him to take anything only his own things. He also saved the harness; he worked like a nigger but he could do nothing more. He also tried to save the harness room by throwing buckets of water on the inside and the roof; but no use. The fire got too firm a hold on everything before those demons left. They had petrol, straw and hay so they made a good job of it. The only place not burned out is the scullery and Mrs Curtin's room. We were in the coach house watching it blazing. The flames were very high but the wind was in our favour, or the outhouses would also be in flames.

The Laundry Basket (Dublin) was in the passage and the man asked us was it ours and I said Yes, so he let us take it; also there is a basket at Thurles laundry, which I expect will come back on Monday. Will the things be sent to you? They could be packed in a box. Also we managed to grab some coats off the rack in the dark. They turned out to be your grey coat and the brown. Will I send them on also? There were about seven or eight men through the house but they told us not to stir from where we were for at least half an hour as the house was surrounded and we may be shot. They left before one o'clock so you see we got no time. We stayed all night.

It was heartbreaking to see the house burning where we were living so long. But we were thankful Mr Clarke was not there for the story was bad enough and he may be shot. They asked several times where was the Boss. We all came up to Mrs Hilton's at 7 o'clock in the morning. Bridget has gone home, also Maggie and Josie. I am staying here with Mrs Hilton for the present. I will never forget the sight and experiences of Wednesday night. I feel sorry for you and Mr Clarke, but I'm thinking there will be no gentlemen's places soon.

Hoping you and Mr Clarke are well,
I am, Madam, yours respectfully,

A. Good

I can't find a pen so please excuse pencil.

Did the Anglo-Irish deserve the fate which was so often predicted for them? Wolfe Tone had written, 'They have disdained to occupy the station they might have held among the people and which the people would have been glad to see them fill. They see Ireland only in their rent-rolls, their places, their patronage, their pensions. They shall perish like their own dung. Those that have seen them will say, "Where are they?"'

The Anglo-Irish could have dodged their fate if their interest in Ireland, let alone their love, had been more than marginal. They recognized a duty certainly to their neighbourhood and this duty was usually intelligently fulfilled, but it only rarely happened that, like Plunkett and a few of their contemporaries, they could give their first love to their country. I believe that in a generation or two, had there been no 1914 war, no rebellion and no civil war, this duty might have turned itself into love as it often had in the eighteenth century.

Then, for a brief period, they had been able to represent something very precious. Only they could give Irishmen a sense of historical continuity and of identity. It was to be found in their bookshelves, when those who remained no longer read books, in their estate maps when they no longer had estates, in their memories when they no longer had the leisure or literary skill to write them down. The Irishmen who burnt down those Tipperary houses were sawing away the branch on which they were sitting. Clamouring that they were a distinctive people, they obliterated much of the heritage that distinguished them. The burning of the Four Courts, which swept away the records of eight centuries, was only one episode in this tale of self-destruction.

A new and more suffocating ascendancy, that of international commerce, was on the way; many of those ruined houses would have been strongholds of resistance to it, and the Anglo-Irish, with their easy-going pragmatic Christianity, would certainly have tempered the religious and political passions of our northern countrymen.

[1984]

10

THE INVADER WORE SLIPPERS

During the war, we in Ireland heard much of the jackboot and how we should be trampled beneath it, if Britain's protection failed us. We thought we could meet this challenge as well as any other small nation, and looking into the future, our imagination, fed on the daily press, showed us a technicolour picture of barbarity and heroism.

It never occurred to us that for ninety per cent of the population the moral problems of an occupation would be small and squalid. Acting under pressure we should often have to choose between two courses of action, both inglorious. And, if there was moral integrity about our choice, it certainly would not get into the headlines.

We did not ask ourselves: 'Supposing the invader wears not jackboots but carpet slippers or patent leather pumps, how will I behave, and the respectable Xs, the patriotic Ys and the pious Zs?' How could we? The newspapers only told us about the jackboots.

The newspapers have by this time worked the subject of resistance to the Nazis to death. They have passed on to livelier issues, so it is possible to anatomize this now dessicated topic in a quite callous way. We can forget about the heroic or villainous minority or those other irreconcilables who adhered to some uncompromising political or religious creed. We can look at the ordinary people, the Xs, the Ys and the Zs, about whom there is a mass of documentation. By a little careful analogy and substitution we can see ourselves, and a picture of our home under occupation emerges with moderate clarity. It is more like an X-ray photo than a war film. It is quite unglamourous and perhaps it is only by the trained mind that the darker shadows can be interpreted.

In totalitarian war human nature is reduced to its simplest

terms and a skilled invader can predict with fair accuracy the behaviour of the respectable Xs, the patriotic Ys, the pious Zs. Of course there are innumerable divagations but in an avalanche it is the valleys and the riverbeds that count, the hundred thousand cart tracks can be disregarded.

I know that we Irish were not more complex than anyone else and that our percentages of Xs, Ys, and Zs were about average and known to every likely invader. And I dismissed as inapplicable to us the propaganda stories of the jackboot with which the allies tried to shake our neutrality. We did not, I thought, like most of the Slav regions, belong to the area of German colonization in which extermination and spiritual enslavement would be practised. And it seemed to me that the respectable Xs who told us the reverse were speaking either without reflection or with concealed motives. It was surprising when the inevitable volte-face came after the war. The people who had been threatening us with the jackboot in places where no sensible invader would dream of using it, began to applaud his restraint. Indulgent things were said of generals, even jackbooted ones like von Manstein, 'who simply did their duty', and Rommel's biography was widely read in those pleasant Dublin suburbs where the Xs live.

It seems to me that we civilian Irish, finding indulgence where we had been led to expect violence, might easily have been tricked into easy-going collaboration. Yet small peoples should become specialists in the art of non-cooperation with tyranny. It is the only role we can play when the great powers clash, and we are hopelessly untrained in it.

Careful observation of precedent and analogy is the first need. This can be done best in small circumscribed regions, whose characters are fairly homogeneous. I found three such occupied zones within my reach, where the tactics of the invader with the Xs, Ys and Zs severally were displayed as on a small diagram which could be indefinitely enlarged. There were the Channel Islands where the respectable Xs were in the majority, Brittany, where the influence of the romantically patriotic Ys was strong, Croatia, where the Ys were reinforced by the fervently pious Zs.

The policy of the invader in all these places, and the response it met, is best studied in the newspapers of the occupation. Reminiscences of course are helpful but they are usually written by men who are exceptional either for their independence of mind or their complacency. They are edited to flatter the vanity of their compatriots, seldom to chasten it. But the newspapers show the invader at his highly skilled task of manipulating the Xs and Ys and Zs. Reading between the lines you can judge of his success.

I think it was only in Zagreb that I found easy access to the files, though even there I was met with some suspicion and surprise. The reason was that in Zagreb a revolution had taken place which had, temporarily at least, undermined the natural desire of every nation to conceal its weaknesses from itself, or in the smooth phraseology of self-deception, to 'let bygones be bygones'. Somebody before me had been over the files in the university library with faint pencil marks and an incriminating collection of the acta and dicta of the Xs, Ys and Zs had been published.

This had certainly not been done in Rennes, the capital of Brittany. In Jersey there is an excellent museum of the occupation but it deals with the behaviour of the Germans and not with that of the Jersey people themselves. And in the newspaper room of the British Museum I searched in vain for the Jersey newspapers which were published all through the war, and had to be content with the incomplete Guernsey file, the personal gift of a Guernsey man. This indifference of the British archivist to the history of the Channel Islands under occupation struck me as curious and significant. Has the national mind, like its individual prototype, some Freudian censor, which automatically suppresses what is shameful or embarrassing?

The public does not want a truthful account of occupation. It prefers to switch over from extremes of reprobation to extremes of condonation. You will see what I mean if you read the most authoritative book on the occupation of Jersey by R. C. Maugham. The publisher appears to be about four years behind the author. On the dust-cover the title, 'Jersey under the Jackboot', is illustrated by a big cruel boot crashing down on a helpless little green island and the blurb talks of the 'courage and fortitude of the islanders' and 'the misery, ignominy and privations that marked the trail of the Nazi hordes across the face of Europe'. But the author makes it plain that the islanders were subjected to a more subtle instrument of pressure than the jackboot. They were very liberally treated indeed. The small island parliaments and courts continued to function, provided all their measures were submitted to German sanction. It was by an ordinance of the Guernsey

Royal Court that all talk against the Germans was made punishable; thus when the manager of the Rich's stores was cheeky to a German customer, it was before the Guernsey Court that he appeared. He got off by explaining that it was all a mistake, that the German officers had all been charming and his son-in-law was taking German lessons. Divine service with prayers for the Royal family and the Empire were permitted. So were cinemas and newspapers.

In an organized society our dependence on the newspapers is abject. The readers of the *Guernsey Evening Post* were shocked and repelled no doubt to see articles by Goebbels and Lord Haw-Haw, but not to the pitch of stopping their subscriptions. How else could they advertise their cocker spaniels and their lawn mowers or learn about the cricket results? Ultimately Haw-Haw became an accepted feature like the testimonials for digestive pills, and an edge of horror and revulsion was blunted. Here is the printed summary of events for an October day in the first year of the occupation.

'Dog-biscuits made locally. Table-tennis League of Six Teams formed. German orders relating to measures against Jews published. Silver Wedding anniversary of Mr and Mrs W. J. Bird.' The news of the deportation and torture of the local shopkeepers is made more palatable by being sandwiched between sport and domestic pets and society gossip. 'Lady Ozanne had passed a fairly good night.' 'Mr Stephen Candon is as comfortable as can be expected.' There was Roller Skating at St George's Hall and 'Laugh it Off' was still retained at The Regal and 'the bride looked charming in a white georgette frock'. Lubricated by familiar trivialities, the mind glided over what was barbarous and terrible.

The *Herrenvolk* philosophy judiciously applied, as it was in the Channel Islands, can be swallowed easily enough if you have not too sensitive a digestion and belong to a ruling race yourself. Flowerbeds were trampled, housemaids whistled to, garden tools unceremoniously borrowed, but formal apologies, printed receipts were often forthcoming if applied for. 'I must record,' wrote Mr Maugham, of the German soldiers in his garage, 'they did their best to give us as little trouble as possible, were perfectly polite and grateful for any slight help which they received from us,' and the Procurator of Guernsey officially declared: 'The Germans behaved as good soldiers, sans peur et sans reproche.'

Such behaviour is plainly more formidable than the jackboot, we are hypnotized by the correctness of the invader into accepting invasion itself as correct. The solidarity of our resistance is undermined by carefully graded civilities, our social and racial hierarchies are respected. For example in Jersey there were Irish tomato pickers and Russian prisoners at whose expense German prestige was adroitly raised in British eyes. When wireless sets were confiscated the Irish, with disdainful correctness, were paid for theirs as they were neutrals. This punctiliousness was more repaying than jackboots since it drove a wedge of jealousy between English and Irish. When later on a feud broke out between the 'correct' occupation troops and some 'incorrect' naval ratings who daubed the shop fronts of St Helier with swastikas, the authorities blamed this breach of etiquette upon the Irish, and there were some gentlemanly headshakings between the German and English officials over these vulgar antics of an inferior breed.

I don't think the Germans on the island had a difficult task in making the Russians in Jersey detested. Some of the Russians, who were employed in the fortification of the island, were convicts liberated from prison in the German advance into Russia. They were worked hard, fed little and flogged. A whip that was used on them can be seen in the Jersey Museum. They were inadequately guarded. Almost mad with hunger, they broke loose and pillaged the neat holdings of the Jersey farmers, taking hens, pigs, cabbages, clothes from the line. These raids began through the carelessness of the guards, continued through their connivance and finally had their active encouragement. The guards indicated the eligible premises and exacted a huge percentage of the plunder. When the Jersey people asked for protection they were met with a humorous shrug from the officials. 'Well, they are your allies. Must *we* protect you from them?'

It is hard for the Xs to keep a balanced judgment in such circumstances. Other problems too arise. Should they acknowledge the salute of the aimiable Rittmeister, who had known their cousins at Weybridge? Should they turn the other cheek when a degenerate Mongol ally robs the hen-roost? These problems are more disintegrating to the resistance of the Xs than bombs or jackboots, and a competent invader will make them inescapable.

In a Zagreb newspaper of 1942, *Deutsche Zeitung in Kroatien,* I read that Ireland, with Croatia and Slovakia, was to be one of the three model 'allied' states in German Europe. In other papers too there was much of flattering intent about the common loyalty of Croats and Irish to Faith and Fatherland, our similar histories, romantic temperaments and literary gifts. Irish plays continued to be played in Zagreb, when English were tabu.

All the same I think that Brittany under the Nazis offers more profitable analogies for us in Ireland than does Croatia. In Brittany the German attempt to exploit the patriotism of the Ys and the piety of the Zs, which in Croatia had been triumphantly successful, was only half-hearted. The Nazis had no doubt of the need to disintegrate Yugoslavia, they were undecided about France. Perhaps, after defeat, France might be won over more easily if her unity was not impaired, perhaps a separatist and Celtic Brittany might slip out of German influence and look westward to Celtic Wales. Also in Brittany the Catholic Church did not support the separatist movement, as it did in Croatia. There was no wide-scale convergence of patriotism and piety. By conciliating the patriotic Ys, the Germans might risk offending the pious Zs.

For all these reasons Nazi policy in Brittany was very inconsistent. The Germans sheltered the Breton rebel leaders, Mordrel and Debauvais, as they had once sheltered Roger Casement and they too were invited to recruit a rebel army to fight for independence among the prisoners of war. The Breton prisoners responded in the same half-hearted way as the Irish had once done. The Germans, however, continued to support the Breton movement till France had been brought to her knees. Then they made terms with Vichy, withdrew all aid from the Breton separatists and allowed them to operate only against the Maquis. They led the Bretons the sort of dance that cannot be done in jackboots.

I think the Nazi policy in regard to Ireland would have been equally agile and ambiguous. The Celtic nationalist would, as in Brittany, have been regarded as a valuable tool for undermining a non-German hegemony, but of decidedly less value for the reconstruction of a German one. The nationalist would have been manoeuvred, not kicked, out of his privileged position.

Judging by the Breton analogy, I think the first impact of the changed policy might have been borne by the handful of single-minded German Celtophiles, who would have been entrusted with the early stages of the programme. A successfully double-faced policy requires at the start the complicity of many single-minded idealists, native and foreign

I think when the success of the invasion had been assured, it would have emerged that the respectable Xs, the Anglo-Irish *Herrenvolk* of Ulster and the Dublin suburbs, would prove the more satisfactory accomplices in establishing the German hegemony. The Jersey treatment would have been applied to them, insofar as they were civilians. There would have been a dazzling display of 'correctness'. It is probable that at Greystones and Newtownards, as at St Helier and at Peterport, divine service with prayers for the King and the British Empire would continue to be permitted in the Protestant churches. Certainly the inevitable bias of German correctness would have been towards the Anglo-Saxon, towards bridge and fox hunting, and away from the Irish, from ceilidhes and hurley matches and language festivals. A master race will be at times indulgent to these regional enthusiasms but will not participate in them. Ultimately this bias would have led to a complete reversal of policy, more in keeping with the *Herrenvolk* philosophy. Lord Haw-Haw, an Irishman himself, seems to have been in closer sympathy with the Mosleyites than with the Irish republicans. The British Naziphiles were romantic, traditional, imperialist. Irish separatism would have been incompatible with their Kiplingesque ideal of a merry, beer-drinking 'old' England, allied with Germany, grasping once more in her strong right hand the reins of empire and dealing out firm justice to the lesser breeds. I do not see how the Irish could have raised themselves permanently into the *Herrenvolk* class from which Czechs and Poles had been excluded. Of course the Croats had arrived there. But they must have felt their position precarious, because two well-known Croatian scholars, Father Shegitch and Professor Butch, developed the theory that the Croats were really Goths who had slipped into a Slav language by some accident. Pavelitch, the 'Leader' of Croatia, who had a private passion for philology, favoured the theory and brought out a Croat lexicon in which all words of Serbian origin were eliminated, a work of great ingenuity because the Serbian and Croatian languages are all but identical. We Irish would inevitably have felt uneasy. There had been in Ireland eminent German Celtic scholars who had not managed to conceal their contempt for the modern representatives of those Celtic peoples whose early history enthralled them. Nazi philosophy was permeated with race snobbery and we are outwardly a rustic and unpretentious people. When a Nazi leader, Ribbentrop, visited Ireland, it was with a Unionist leader, Lord Londonderry, at Newtownards that he stayed. In the Nazi hierarchy of races the Irish would not I think have ranked high.

It is likely that ultimately more attention would have been paid to our piety than to our patriotism. Its pattern is universal and familiar and so more easily faked, whereas patriotism has so many regional variations that no ready-made formula could be devised to fit them all. Many of the pious Zs would have responded to skilful handling. The other day I read in an Irish newspaper the sermon of a well-known preacher. 'The world', he said, 'may one day come to be grateful to Hitler.' He was thinking, of course, of Communism and it was the constant pre-occupation of the Nazis that the minds of the pious should always be inflamed with the fear of it. In that way charity and humanity, where they were only superficial, could be skinned away like paint under a blow-lamp. But in the technique of perverting piety it was in the Independent State of Croatia that the Nazis first showed their consummate skill. Pavelitch's Croatia deserves the closest study.

When an incendiary sets a match to respectability, it smoulders malodorously, but piety, like patriotism, goes off like a rocket. The jackboot was worn by the Croats themselves and used so vigorously against the schismatic Serbs that the Germans and the Italians, who had established the little state, were amazed. Pavelitch, the regicide ruler of Croatia, was himself the epitome, the personification, of the extraordinary alliance of religion and crime, which for four years made Croatia the model for all satellite states in German Europe. He was extremely devout, attending Mass every morning with his family in a private chapel built onto his house. He received expressions of devoted loyalty from the leaders of the Churches, including the Orthodox, whose murdered metropolitan had been replaced by a subservient nominee. He gave them medals and enriched their parishes with the plundered property of the schismatics, and he applied the simple creed of One Faith, One Fatherland, with a literalness that makes the heart stand still. It was an equation which had to be solved in blood. Nearly two million Orthodox were offered the alternatives of death or conversion to the faith of the majority. The protests of the Xs, Ys and Zs were scarcely audible.

Yet, as I read the newspaper files in Zagreb, I felt that it was not the human disaster but the damage done to honoured words and thoughts that was most irreparable. The letter and the spirit had been wrested violently apart and a whole vocabulary of Christian goodness had blown inside out like an umbrella in a thunderstorm.

It is easy to illustrate this from the newspapers of a single week in spring 1941. In one Zagreb paper, for example, the king's speech on the bombing of Belgrade was published with appropriate comments on April 10.

'On the morning of Palm Sunday,' he said, 'while children slept their innocent sleep and the church bells were ringing for prayer to God, the German aeroplanes without warning let fall a rain of bombs on this historic town. . .' and the king went on to describe the terror of the women and children, who were machine-gunned as they fled from their homes, by low-flying planes.

The following day the Germans in Panzer divisions arrived in Zagreb. Flags were out in the streets to welcome them and the same paper wrote in solemn phrases: 'God's providence in concord with the resolve of our allies has brought it about that today on the eve of the resurrection of the Son of God our Independent Croatian State is also resurrected. . . all that is right and true in Christianity stands on the side of the Germans'!

When Pavelitch fell, the Zs had to take a third somersault. Words had by then lost all relation to fact and thereafter there was something schizophrenic about the exaggerations of the Croatian Zs and their sympathizers. Rather than admit their horrible inadequacy, they plunged about in contrary directions, sometimes whitewashing Pavelitch, sometimes making him blacker than life.

Many were able to turn head over heels in a quiet, gentlemanly way. For example the Bishop of Djakovo, Dr Akshamovitch, who received the Delegation from the National Peace Council, of which I was a member, in a very friendly way, was a kind old man of whom we already knew a little. Under Pavelitch circulars flowed from his diocesan printing press headed 'Friendly Advice', reminding the Serbs that Jesus had said there was to be one flock and one shepherd and that, as Catholics, they could stay in their homes, improve their properties and educate their children.

When Tito came to power the bishop is said to have invited the Central Committee of the Croatian Communist Party to lunch. He certainly attended a Peace Meeting in Belgrade. His photograph was printed in the press, as was his speech, in which warm praise was given to Tito. Should one charge him with opportunism? At this range one cannot judge him, but what is clear is that both governments valued his support and profited by it.

In future wars, if there are any, the formulae of corruption will be a little different but the principle will be the same. It may be said that the respectable Xs will only be wooed by the invader if he comes from a capitalist country, but that, if he is Communist, no dangerous flirtations need be feared. I am not so sure. Acquisitive, tenacious, timidly orthodox people are not confined to any class or creed. It is a matter of temperament rather than of social standing or of politics. They have the force of inertia, which all invaders will wish to have on their side. As for piety and patriotism, whether they are deep or superficial, they are ineradicable from the human race. In the long run the modern state, east or west, will try to assimilate the Xs, Ys and Zs, not to exterminate them.

Horace once wrote that the honest man, innocent of crime, could protect himself without Moorish javelins, without his bow or his quiver full of poisoned arrows. But is ordinary innocence enough nowadays or must he cultivate the unseeing eye? Must he not 'mind his own business' like the professional man, or 'simply do his duty and carry out orders' like the soldier, or like the tradesman 'just get on with the job?' (The Channel Island papers are full of cheery synonyms for connivance!) Are we really obliged to admire the armour-plated innocence and respectability of General Rommel, that 'preux chevalier' of the subscription libraries? He concentrated so fiercely on his professional duties that ten years after Hitler came to power he was still able to be ignorant of, and shocked by, the Jewish extermination policy, by gas-chambers and the destruction of Warsaw. I don't think these questions can be answered unless we isolate them and study them in a small more or less homogeneous area. It is clear that small peoples are used as guinea pigs by the great powers. Experiments are tried out on them which are later applied on a wider scale. Their suffering and their reaction to suffering are studied but only for selfish, imperialistic ends. Should not the results of these experiments be recorded now while the memory is still fresh and accuracy and candour are available? For though such knowledge will not of itself bring us the will or the courage to resist tyranny, it will prevent us from dispersing our strength in fighting against shadows. By learning from which direction the most insidious attacks are likely to come, we may acquire the skill to forestall them.

[1950]

11

PORTRAIT OF A MINORITY

We Protestants of the Irish Republic are no longer very interesting to anyone but ourselves. A generation ago we were regarded dramatically as imperialistic blood-suckers, or, by our admirers, as the last champions of civilization in an abandoned island. That is the way the Roman settler may have appeared to himself and others when the legions had departed from Britain and he was left alone with the tribes he had dispossessed. Our brothers north of the border are still discussed in such colourful terms; as for ourselves, we merely exist and even that we do with increasing unobtrusiveness.

So we are flattered, when, as recently, an American writer like Mr Blanshard investigates our problems.* No Irish Protestant has hitherto questioned Mr Blanshard's facts or could easily do so, for he has taken pains with his documentation. But facts, by themselves, are dispiriting things and it would be wrong if we appeared as a depressed or resentful community. A stranger would find us cheerful enough and on excellent terms with our Catholic neighbours.

Inevitably, the more conscientious foreign investigator prefers newspaper files and libraries to human beings as a source of evidence. Mr Blanshard tried both and I am not surprised if he found us appallingly unsatisfactory in the witness-box. Take Mrs A., whose husband is an impoverished country gentleman; she is chatty and genial about our relations with the Catholic majority, but all her comments are marginal. Mr B., the accountant, obviously feels more deeply involved and, as a result, his replies are unconvincingly soapy and safe. On the other hand, Mr C., the plasterer, has nothing to lose by candour, for he can always get a job in England. As a result his denunciations of Ireland and

* Paul Blanshard, *The Irish and Catholic Power* (London 1954).

the Irish are frivolous and self-centred. So I do not blame our investigator if in despair he rushes to the reference library in Kildare Street and feeds for the rest of his stay on statistics as dry and impersonal as he can find them.

Useful books usually result but we Irish, who had been posing for our picture, invariably belittle them. We consider our problems too personal for charts and diagrams. And I am afraid we are mostly shockingly vague about those abstract issues which Mr Blanshard discusses.

There is a criticism, too, which many Protestants as well as Catholics might level at Mr Blanshard. It was well expressed in a letter I got from a Catholic neighbour. 'We Irish are, whatever they say, a spiritual people. Has Mr Blanshard never heard of "grace"?' There is in fact in Ireland an undertone of spirituality about our most sordid sectarian wrangles. Mr Blanshard, like most Americans, believes in the panacea of good government, but our deepest discord appears to us to lie beyond the reach of legislation. It concerns impalpable things, sentiments so delicate that they seem betrayed when they are defined, loyalties which are only vulgarized by oaths and protestations. There is no orderly conflict of principle, but there are sudden gusts of noise and fury, which end as mysteriously as they began.

Mr Blanshard has made a record of these violent irruptions, but should not some Irishman also chronicle the long periods of rather hazardous calm and contentment that intervene? Discord roars through the newspapers like an express train, blotting out the fields with dust and smoke, but in a minute or two everything looks exactly as before. There was the Tilson case, for example, in which Catholic and Protestant views about the legality of premarital *Ne Temere* pledges met with a prodigious impact; there was the case of the Master of the Galway Foxhounds, where Catholic disapproval of divorce collided with the more neutral Protestant attitude. There was Dr Noel Browne and his Health bill, when it appeared to the Protestants that the Government, responsible to the electorate only, was taking its orders from the Catholic hierarchy. There are innumerable *causes célèbres* where the children of mixed marriages and their religious upbringing are involved.

I should not underestimate the importance of these issues or their long-term effect, but they seldom interrupt the friendly relations of neighbours and there is in Ireland such a very strong tradition of 'live and let live' that in the country at least these ideological collisions are quickly forgotten. Can we congratulate ourselves on our Christian charity or is it merely that country people are slow to grasp the significance of abstract issues? Or is it that rural neighbours are not easily organized into solid blocks of opinion on religious issues?

That is so with Irish Protestants anyway. I do not like solid blocks of opinion but, in fact, there is nothing very reassuring about our Southern Protestant incapacity for congealing into aggressive or defensive blocks. It merely means that the Ulster Protestant, a more fanatical and bitter champion of the Reformation, assumes the leadership of Irish Protestant opinion. And that leadership really belongs by tradition to the Protestants of the South, the people of Swift and Berkeley, Lord Edward Fitzgerald, Smith O'Brien, Parnell, men who often jeopardized their careers and even sacrificed their lives in the cause of an Ireland, free and united. So now our amiable inertia, our refusal to express grievances or cherish hopes about Ireland, are really delaying our ultimate unity and the reconciliation of our two diverging communities.

I can imagine how exasperating we must appear to any American investigator. Let us picture him asking leading questions of that typical Irish Protestant lady, Mrs A. Though she is impecunious, she has an air of assurance based on a long inheritance of privilege of which only the tradition now remains. She is quite likely to be met in the town selling peaches to the greengrocer. She has parked her car on the wrong place but one must admire the humour and determination with which she handles the civic guard who comes to protest, and the easy pleasantries with which she enlists the greengrocer on her side. She will be ready for a talk as soon as she has delivered a large parcel of cast-off clothes at the diocesan jumble sale. She is flattered at being consulted but a bit wary and inclined to think it would be better to ask the dean: 'Look why not *you*, take him the jumbles for me? That will save me the climb up the deanery steps and give you an opening.' But in the end she agrees to answer some questions herself. For instance, the American has been reading an article by Mr Frank O'Connor in which the Irish censorship of books is ferociously denounced. 'What do Irish Protestants think of this violation of their sacred right to judge for themselves?'

'Well, you see, my husband and I subscribe to the London

Library and no one interferes with what comes by post. He's reading *Kon-Tiki* at present and I've got *Lord Ironside's Memoirs*. And my naval nephew sent me *The Cruel Sea*, though I believe it's banned. I only read one of O'Connell's books. I thought it rather morbid.' (I regret to say that Mrs A. is very vague about the names of our leading Irish writers. Though Yeats, our greatest Irish poet, was a Protestant, she is not sure how many 'e's' there are in his name.) 'So the censorship doesn't really affect us.'

'And then about divorce, don't you think. . .?'

'Oh, really,' she interrupts, 'what horrible people you must think us Irish Protestants, always hankering after divorce and nasty books! Why I don't know a single Protestant family in the whole diocese where there has been a divorce. . . Oh, yes, there's Colonel Johnson's eldest boy, poor Eric, he got caught by a horror in a military hospital after Dunkirk. He got a DSO you know. We were all so on his side.'

'But surely he didn't manage to get a divorce *here*, did he?'

'Oh, dear me, no! In England, of course! And now he's very happy on an orange farm in South Africa and the Johnsons are charmed with the new Mrs Eric.'

'Then you do approve of divorce?'

'Well, what I say is where there are no children in the case, far better make a fresh start than lead a cat and dog life for ever after. . . but, look here, you'd much better ask the dean, not me. He'll tell you it all *theologically*.'

'The first Mrs Eric didn't have any children then?'

'No, mercifully not. Poor Eric couldn't afford it on his pay, but now he's got two darling little boys.'

'Then, um. . . er. . . ' The American sees an opening for an embarrassing but necessary question about family restriction and a Catholic government's veto on it, but he just cannot bring himself to ask it. Yet no one could call Mrs A. evasive. She is as frank as a blackbird which hops onto a different tree when the cat approaches, with scarcely a pause in its cheerful twitter. Obviously, if the Irish Protestants get their divorces and their banned books from England, then they won't be worried by Catholic legislation on family restriction or anything else. Only the very disinterested will even attempt to oppose it. Otherwise one just hops across the sea with a merry twitter when a difficulty arises.

So instead he asks about jobs. Do Irish Protestants feel themselves discriminated against in the Republic?

'Well, my two are very well placed, I'm thankful to say. Amy is in the Brussels branch of Thomas Cooks and Arthur is in the British Consulate in Cuba. Denis is still at school in Dublin and would like to find work in Ireland but the pensions are so poor and not knowing Irish would militate against him.' Then follows a long diatribe against compulsory Irish, which I must be excused from repeating for I have heard it once a month for the past twenty years; usually it pivots on the cook, who spells jelly with a 'g', because she has been taught through the medium. It's all perfectly true, but, recalling that Mrs A. doesn't know how to spell Yeats, I find it arrogant. Yet compulsory Irish *has* become a cynical travesty of a once noble ideal. It plays right into the hands of those who deride the Irish as a nation of self-deceivers. And now Mrs A. is launched on another equally beloved theme, the attempt to suppress the coronation film in Ireland. 'The manager of the Mayfair said he'd show it but then he got a threatening letter and the wretched creature got cold feet and refunded all the tickets. But thank goodness dear old Archdeacon Potts had a bit of pluck! He showed the film at the Diocesan Rooms. They were packed twice over and I even saw Catholics there and we took enough at the door to get a new bathroom for the rectory. It's such *nonsense*. Why *they* would give their eyes to see it too, I know. My cook has stuck up a photograph of the Queen in her bedroom.'

All quite true doubtless but misleading. And so too are Mrs A.'s other views. Though all the cooks in Ireland plastered their walls with pictures of the royal family, the dominant sentiment of the Irish people is anti-monarchist, anti-imperialist. Also, though Mrs A. is so little perturbed by the censorship and the other violations of what Protestants call 'the right of private judgment', there is an abiding Protestant resentment against much that is enshrined in our laws. And yet very few are sufficiently articulate to express it. There is a very real clash of philosophies and our present preoccupation with queens and empires merely distracts us from the realities of our disagreement. Supposing the Queen of England became a Catholic and appealed to the Irish for support, like her predecessor James II, or supposing England became a republic (and odder things have happened in our time), there would be some confusion, no doubt, but I suspect that in the end the creeds of authority and the creeds of private judgment would run roughly along the same frontiers. Across a reconstituted barrier Irish Protestants and Irish Catholics would confront each other as before.

Mrs A. will not be very helpful on the subject of mixed marriages and *Ne Temere*. As usual she sees only the trees and no wood. 'Fortunately the two Catholic husbands in our parish are both charming. It might have been rather embarrassing for all concerned if they had to settle down here but one is in Imperial Chemicals and the other in Shell, and everything is so much easier *over there*. And *both* wives send me their subscriptions just the same for the Protestant Orphans. Even Colonel Johnson, who is on the synod, but very broadminded, says that every club has a right to make its own rules and that non-members must lump it.'

These who argue like Colonel Johnson, are usually bachelors with plenty of loopholes by which to escape from the pressure of their own arguments. Colonel Johnson has Eric but Eric has been safely remarried and, for the rest, his broadmindedness is nourished on a small house at Camberley and some queer beliefs about the Secret of the Pyramids.

But in the parish, which I know best, there are few loopholes and many children with the result that most of the families have now given one or two hostages to the community from which some centuries ago they seceded. Before the application of *Ne Temere* to Ireland hostages were exchanged *pari passu* and the two communities shared in each other's lives on equal terms. Now there is no reciprocity and in those who have given all and received nothing there is often a feeling of slow strangulation which they are forced to dissemble in case they do injury to those they love. A whole community can die without drama as though it had been struck by one of those instruments of 're-education', which leaves no external bruises.

I had hoped to say something constructive, but here I am dodging just like Mrs A. And there is no time to talk about Mr B., the accountant, or Mr C., the plasterer, though they are as Irish as she is. But, undoubtedly, Mrs A. sets the tone of Protestantism in her small local community, so that dodging and hoping for the best is no merely personal creed. It is a highly infectious habit of mind, which nothing but the reunion of Ireland is likely to cure.

There is no doubt that Salvation, if it ever comes to the As, can only now come from across the Boyne. The whole character of Irish life might well be changed by a strong Ulster contingent in the Dáil. But the saviours are reluctant and the doomed are resigned. When questioned about Partition Mrs A. advises letting sleeping dogs lie. She has some very entertaining stories about smuggling from her married sister, who lives on the border, and she doesn't believe 'They' really *want* the border abolished 'in spite of all their shouting'. But she has no really dynamic hatred of Partition, smuggling or humbug that cannot be anaesthetized by a funny anecdote. And if you were to remind her that in a United Ireland, many of the ideals, which she cherishes, would once more find a vigorous echo in the Dáil, she would only look bothered and begin to quote her naval nephew about submarine bases in Loch Swilly. Her intellect, like a barrage balloon that has lost its moorings, hovers uncertainly between Fishguard and Rosslare. She is really more concerned that England should get the ports than that the Anglo-Irish should be able to raise their voices again in Ireland. And, while she approves of Colonel Topping (the Chief Whip of the Northern Parliament) and knows cousins of his in Sussex, and (with reservations) of Mr Blanshard, she does not think the Colonel should ever have been invited to the Kilkenny Debate, 'It only stirs things up.'*

For thirty years and more she has grown used to the Cassandra-like mournings of her hybrid race; gradually they have become less shrill and have the familiar monotony of a lullaby. They save thinking. It would only upset her to reflect that the doom which threatens the House of Atreus might be averted and all the dearly loved dirges have to be rewritten.

'The fact is,' she branches off, 'I don't really like Ulster people, though nothing could exceed the kindness of the Ballymena people to Arthur when he was stationed there. But let them mind

* The Kilkenny Debate was initiated by the author and his friends on 23 April 1954. We invited the Stormont Government to send speakers to Kilkenny, and Colonel Topping and William Douglas, Secretary to the Unionist Council, were chosen to speak on Partition against Sean MacBride, former Minister for External Affairs, and Eoin O'Mahony. Professor Miles Dillon chaired the meeting. There had been no such encounter before. *The Kilkenny People* said it was 'an insult to our patriot dead'. In Belfast there were fiery appeals to the Government to resign or 'seal the border' rather than sanction the visit of the Orange leaders to discuss partition 'with murderers and traitors'. Disturbances were anticipated and the Garda Siochána were reinforced.

In fact nothing could have been more serene and friendly than the atmosphere of the debate, which was continued annually – always on controversial subjects – until 1962, when televised discussions in Dublin made our local efforts seem redundant.

their own business and we'll mind ours. And that's what Colonel Topping wants too!'

[1954]

12

A HOUSE OF GOD

REMEMBER DONERAILE. BOYCOTT ENGLISH PAPERS. KEEP OUT FOREIGN FILTH. I read this on a tattered poster in a village street the other day. Of course I remembered Doneraile and the celebrated libel action. Libel actions are sordid in repute but often they are intellectually exciting in their development. Nursed by a clever counsel, some trivial personal insult will often expand and pullulate so that it appears that not an individual only but a class, a nation or a creed has been outraged. Some sacred principle has been violated, some great truth has to be vindicated. The Doneraile libel case was no exception.

It was the second of two such actions in Ireland in 1954, both of them highly stimulating. When Patrick Kavanagh, the poet, sued an Irish literary paper for libel, the rights of the critic and the rights of the creator were squarely confronted. Many stupid and some wise views were advanced, there was pathos as well as wit. But in Ireland both poets and papers have such a hard struggle to survive that, when they assail each other, it is no ordinary conflict. It is more like a suicide pact between two old cronies, unhinged by despair and at the end of their tether. It was a libel action that destroyed the best of all our papers, the *Irish Statesman*, edited by AE, financed by Sir Horace Plunkett. This paper was a bridge between the old traditional world of Yeats and Lady Gregory and the young experimentalists and firebrands of the Republic. When it collapsed, the sense of isolation, against which the Irish writer has to struggle, was enormously intensified.

Miss Honor Tracy's recent action was also against a newspaper, but a great organ of Fleet Street, *The Sunday Times*, not a precarious and idealistic Irish weekly. Her victory seemed to establish two principles: firstly, in certain circumstances, an unmerited apology can be as damaging as an unmerited insult; it is wrong, for example, whatever the pressure, to apologize publicly for the statements of a contributor, without ascertaining first whether what he wrote was in fact false or unjustifiable. Secondly, there is no section of the community raised by Grace or Divine Appointment above the need to give an account of itself, if challenged.

It was this second principle on which Irish attention was so passionately focused last year. In England its validity is surely seldom questioned, but in Ireland it is a relatively new conception. Those of us who value it must ask whether Miss Tracy's triumph will seem in Ireland, as it certainly was in England, a resounding victory for free speech and free enquiry. The answer is by no means self-evident.

It all started with Miss Tracy's graceful sketch of an Irish village in *The Sunday Times*, and her delicately ironical description of the canon's efforts to build himself a new house with a view. What a to-do there was to collect the funds, little girls went scampering round with raffle tickets, the church dues went up and up, and in the chapel itself the canon's voice, though rather dim and confused when preaching the gospel, was 'clear as Shandon bells' when it came to 'pricking on the faithful to fresh endeavour'! And what excitement and gossip there was about the size and splendour of the canon's new house! But here and there, Miss Tracy said, the reverential awe was tinged with dismay and there were quite audible grumbles. It was the first house that had been built in the village since the war and many of the villagers were without light and water. 'O Lord!' they exclaimed, 'O Lord! It's the size of a ship! And they rolled upon their tongues the incredible figure of £9000. 'But mind you I've said nothing!' they added, cautiously.

The staff of *The Sunday Times* later maintained that they had printed all this under the impression that the village, the canon and his parishioners had no existence outside Miss Tracy's imagination and they were aghast when a real Irish canon loomed up out of the bizarre half-light in which Miss Tracy sees us as immersed, an angry canon, Canon O'Connell of Doneraile, Co. Cork, brandishing a writ and clamouring for £5000 damages. There were many complicated manoeuvres which Miss Tracy has alluded to in her book, *Mind You I've Said Nothing!* but the climax came when Miss Tracy was in Italy on an assignment for the BBC. *The Sunday Times* in her absence printed an apology to the canon in its pages and gave him £750, which he handed over to charity. A draft apology had also been prepared for Miss Tracy to present. When Miss Tracy heard of all this she indignantly dissociated herself from every apology and, in due course, started proceedings against *The Sunday Times*. The apology, she claimed, was a reflection on her integrity as a journalist, and a threat to her livelihood. A commission went off fromLondon to Doneraile. They saw the canon and the schoolmaster and the bishop, the Protestant clergyman and many other notables of the village. For five days in the Queen's Bench Division the spiritual, cultural and economic welfare of Doneraile was debated by English lawyers, pondered by an English jury. At the end of it the jury brought in a verdict for Miss Tracy and she was awarded £3000 and costs which were very large indeed.

The villagers of Doneraile had a fresh series of staggering figures to roll on their tongues, but if they thought they were nearer to getting sanitation and light in their cottages they were careful not to say so. Miss Tracy had felt she was crusading on their behalf but they showed as emphatically as they could that they repudiated her solicitude for them. When news of her victory over *The Sunday Times* reached Doneraile, they saw it as a victory over their canon and a tremendous ovation was prepared for him. The village was decked with flags and a procession of 3000 marched to the canon's house from the Presentation Convent. It was headed by the Buttevant Boys' Brass Band. There were civic guards at all the entrances to the town to regulate the cars that came from all north Cork to watch the celebrations. The Children of Mary were there and the Gaelic League and the parish choir, there were labour organizations and pious confraternities. And banners were held aloft, inscribed with loyal slogans: 'We revere and honour our Canon!' 'We stand for God and our priests!' And then in a field behind the parochial house, there were anthems and 'Faith of our Fathers!' and speeches from a solicitor, a parliamentary deputy, and the insulted canon himself. Such heat was generated that had Miss Tracy herself been present would she have needed faggots? Would she not have evaporated by spontaneous combustion? While I was asking myself this question, a friend showed me a poem by Cavafy, translated by E. M. Forster. 'Of course,' he said, 'I know Doneraile isn't really very like ancient Alexandria but can't you catch an echo from the age of the Ptolemies? Don't they have the same swift loves and hates, the same ardour, easy to kindle, hard to sustain?' and he read me:

An Alexandrian crowd collected
To see the sons of Cleopatra,
Cæsarion and his little brothers,
Amid a splendid display of troops.
Cæsarion stood a little in front,
Clad in silk the colour of roses.
Him they acclaimed more than his brothers,
Whom they called the kings of Armenia, Media, the Persians,
Of Cilicia, Syria, Phœnicia.
Him they named King of Kings.
The Alexandrians knew perfectly well
That all this was words and empty pomp.
But the day was warm and exquisite,
The sky clear and blue,
And the Alexandrians ran to see the show
And grew enthusiastic and applauded
In Greek, in Egyptian and some in Hebrew,
Bewitched with the beautiful spectacle,
Though they knew perfectly well how worthless,
What empty words were these king-makings!

No, I don't think that would be very fair to us and our sad dreams nursed under cloudy skies. But I think I was wrong in supposing that the ardour against Miss Tracy would ever have reached burning-point. I have a notion that had Miss Tracy been there, under quite a thin disguise, no one would have wished to force the issue by penetrating it; she would have met with the same courtesy that she found before, and, had she questioned them again privately, even the Children of Mary themselves, she would have found that they surpassed the Alexandrians in their terrible self-knowledge, their ruthless contempt for each other, for their dreams and pretensions. But let an outsider show the same perspicacity at their expense, and he had better run for his life.

This is surely normal enough. Probably we are all Alexandrians at heart. The veils of self-deception in which we clothe ourselves have to be peeled off tenderly by our own loving hands. We won't stand it when an outsider does it. Independent judgment, a sensitive growth, had showed its nose above the parched soil of County Cork and Miss Tracy, who had observed it, instead of nursing it through the weary months, as only a native can do, had, with the best of intentions, smothered it with a pail of nurseryman's chemicals and made off for Italy, where she had an assignment with the BBC or something of the kind. One cannot blame Miss Tracy; a journalist with wit and style is everywhere in demand and our claim, advanced by an angry Irish critic, to consider her, on the strength of her name and her faith, as a crypto-Celt, an Irish Catholic with permanent responsibilities to Ireland, is a very slender one. She was born, she told the courts, in Ipswich.

The episode illustrates the altered role which the liberal journalist now finds himself playing. Formerly in Ireland he was the champion of the exploited and disfranchised. He clamoured for Catholic Emancipation, for Repeal, for Agrarian Reform. He roused the conscience of the British electorate with stories of eviction and coffin-ships, of famine and political corruption. Now everybody has been emancipated and the liberated and their Church have no more use for the liberal than the spider has for her mate, once his generative task has been performed. He is simply to be gobbled up. A consequence of this is that the intelligent liberal is less ready than he was to idealize the victims of barbarity or to dramatize their sufferings. If you want to hear the hair-raising details about the torture of the innocent, you must go to the Sunday papers, whose modern machinery for wringing the heart and raising the hair on a nation-wide scale requires a cruder fuel than the liberal can command. A sensitive journalist is more intrigued by connivance than by crime, the small equivocations and reticences of respectable people, who 'don't like to be mixed up in things' and who persuade themselves that the murderous noises in the flat below are the result of spring cleaning and the clouds of oily smoke that hang over Auschwitz mean only that a refuse dump is being destroyed and 'anyway one so often makes things *worse* by butting in'. Many women journalists excel in their investigation of these genteel suburbs of sin, and Miss Tracy's portraits of humbug in Japan and in Germany, and, unforgettably, among the Oxford groupers at Caux, are often unsurpassed. But in her book on Ireland, she is like a miniaturist trying her hand at murals. Her generalizations are often so lacking in background knowledge and experience as to be ridiculous. Had she realized the limitations of her art as well as its power, the battle of Doneraile would have had more fruitful results; Free Speech, assailed in Doneraile, rehabilitated in England, would not finally have been extinguished by the martial strains of the Buttevant Boys' Brass Band.

I think you will see how Miss Tracy mismanaged her crusade and alienated potential allies if you subject some of her statements to the same severe analysis to which she exposes our Irish pretensions. She commends an English friend, who had settled in Doneraile, for 'getting Ireland's number' faster than anyone else and 'enjoying all the nonsense'. 'Coming from outside,' Miss Tracy remarks, 'and thus having no responsibility for the general state of affairs, she could freely give herself up to the pleasure of contemplating it.' Miss Tracy obviously based her article, her libel action and her book on the conviction of a like unaccountability. But is it right for anyone to be so detached? Is she not like a doctor, who knocks at our door when we are ill, checks up on our heart-beats and pulse-beats, takes samples of our blood and urine, and then without a word or a pill makes off to win a gold medal for a thesis on our disease? Of course the world is the gainer and we have not lost very much, but some imponderable element of trustfulness and good fellowship is missing. An Irishman, who went to (say) Chipping Norton and 'getting England's number' there, studied in their regional dress the equivocations, doubts and hypocrisies with which today religion is everywhere beset, would not be granted complete unaccountability. Perhaps I am saddling Miss Tracy with a guilt which belongs not to her but to her craft. Journalists were probably never more perspicacious than they are today, but the extent and the variety of their assignments force them to be predatory as well as perceptive. For a moment or two they come incredibly close to the subject of their investigation. But often it seems like the closeness of the pickpocket breathing down our necks at a race meeting. It is an intimacy that excludes affection. The result is that there is less mutual understanding, though more mutual knowledge, among neighbours than ever before.

I was led into this homily by the acute distress of an Irish Catholic friend who attended the hearings of the Tracy case in London. She is no Anglophobe and would not defend the extravagance of Irish sacerdotalism, but she was saddened to the verge of tears by the evidence of an English notion that a gulf between two neighbouring peoples could be bridged by knowing, indulgent guffaws about 'the magnificent dottiness of the Irish' (the phrase comes from Miss Tracy's publishers). So much of this dottiness is subjective. A literal translation from the idiom of one people into the idiom of another always diverts some and dismays others. I was dismayed, for example, when Miss Tracy's counsel called the Protestant clergyman of Doneraile 'an Anglican priest', an expression unheard of in Ireland, for, dressed up in this ill-fitted English magnificence, how could we fail to look dotty?

Nor, as an Irish Protestant, could I take much pleasure in Miss Tracy's tribute to our superior 'truth-telling, word-keeping, fair-dealing', because she seemed to be using us as a stick, which she did not greatly esteem, to beat the Irish of her own faith whom she esteemed even less. And, as a Catholic herself, was she not perhaps using the Irish as convenient scapegoats for Catholic elements in her own environment which she disliked but feared to attack in home waters? It is true that Derek and Nigel, her cultured English converts, are seen as ludicrous in their horror at the smells and stupidities of an Irish village service. But why does she find their Irish Protestant cousins more ludicrous still, when they deplore the influence of Derek and Nigel on the Foreign Office and the BBC? Eminent Englishmen have also seen this bogey and are not we, who pass our lives, a small group of heretics in a Catholic state, better equipped than most to comment on it?

Not long ago H. G. Wells wrote of the

> systematic and impudent attempts to subjugate this easy-going and profoundly sceptical country to the Roman Catholic Church. . . Great Britain has been officially behaving like a Catholic country determined to emerge from a deplorable past. . . The Rev. So-and-so, S.J., and the Very Venerable So-and-so have had a disproportionately large share of our broadcasting time.

That H. G. Wells is statistically correct about this disproportion, even those, who defend it, would concede. To an outsider it certainly seems as though an attempt was being made to hold the balance 'fairly' between Catholic and Protestant apologetics, while the unorthodox, who undoubtedly, as H. G. Wells claimed, represent the English majority, broadcast almost as little propaganda for their beliefs as do the Protestants on Radio Éireann. But surely H. G. Wells had no right to talk of Catholic 'impudence'. There is nothing 'impudent' in using every opportunity that is offered to propagate a belief that is ardently and sincerely held, and most of these Catholic propagandists are as sincere as they are courteous. The fault lies with the English sceptic and humanist who, like his Anglo-Irish cousins, has raised upon his half-belief or non-belief an ethic nobler and saner than any ever followed in the 'Ages of Faith'. For they have captured our minds for this ethic but not our hearts or our senses. It is without warmth or poetry or brotherhood. The wasteland of the emotions is uncultivated and, when the evicted tenants return or the evangelists of some crude, new gospel stake out a claim, the humanist, in terms of his own ethic, has no grounds for excluding them.

If the truth-telling, fair-dealing Protestantism, which Miss Tracy found in Ireland, had its analogies in England, so too has the lack of 'deep religious conviction', which she sees as its concomitant, and the hazy, class-bound loyalties focused on the Crown, the Bible, and the Reformation. I do not see how our kind of haze is more 'magnificently dotty' than the religious haze which she finds admirable in England, where in her words, there is 'a large body of people vaguely agnostic and yet vaguely following the Christian ethic'. She contrasts to our disadvantage the 'easy secular atmosphere of Europe' with our 'doctrinaire little society', where everybody wants to know who is a 'Prod' and who is a 'Cat'. (Miss Tracy must have got the word 'Cat' from some facetious friend. I have never heard it used. If we want to be humorous about RCs we call them 'Papists'.) But the easy secular atmosphere of Europe is not easy at all, outside a tiny enclave of liberal intellectuals; it is aglow with passionate beliefs, more bloodthirsty and intolerant than any Irish creed. And even in the still smaller enclave, which Miss Tracy mistakes for England, how defenceless is that vaguely agnostic, vaguely Christian ethic which she finds congenial! Lately we saw Mr Billy Graham bringing back the God of the Israelites from the Pentateuch and with a couple of blasts on his trumpet the walls of the citadel of 'easy secularism' were breached. His message, like a tropical hurricane, tore through the chaste and chilly corridors which the Arnolds and Huxleys had swept and Bishop Barnes had sparsely garnished.

Miss Tracy does not judge us unheard, for, whether it was for the good of her soul or the *The Sunday Times*, she appears to have attended some of our heretic services in Ireland. She describes the reedy harmonium, the broken stove and the Protestant gentleman, growling out the General Confession but thinking all the time of his neglected fencing. His theology is 'God Save the Queen' and, as to the Catholics, who are plotting against Britain, his counsel is 'Turn 'em out! Turn 'em out!' She sees little in the former ascendancy but dilapidated Blimps, still able to give the same old lecture on Burma to bored inferiors, but the bitch is pupping on the library sofa and the chandelier is due to crash down any moment from the ceiling. Their faces, male and female, are the regulation purple; Miss Tracy compares them at various times to 'wine', to 'boiled lobster', to 'scarlet lanterns'. I do not entirely disbelieve in these people, and Miss Tracy, peeping through her fingers in the General Confession, may have guessed correctly that their minds were wandering less intelligently than hers, but, as always, a mural is being made out of a miniature. Her talent for detail becomes a handicap if more than a square foot of surface has to be covered.

Ours is a broken world, as Sean O'Faolain has called it in a beautiful story, and, if the rest of Europe were harmonious and intact, we should be legitimate objects of pity or ridicule. But in fact the cracks that Miss Tracy sees in our society can be traced back to her own and are local symptoms of a universal disharmony, a rift between the real and the ideal. For centuries the Irish were schooled and drilled to a pattern that was not their own. They struggled and all at once they were free, but their own pattern had irreparably faded from their minds and they were forced to shape their ideals upon negation. Lecky once wrote: 'When every other northern nation had abandoned Catholicism, the Irish retained it out of antipathy to their oppressors.' The tenacity with which the Irish cling to Catholicism is merely the obverse of the violence with which the English settlers came to reject it. The Catholic Church had been in its time to the Anglo-Norman as efficient an instrument for the oppression of the Irish as Puritanism later became to the Cromwellians. To take an average county, Kilkenny, for two centuries after Strongbow's invasion no Irishman was admitted to the principal monasteries, no Irish bishop was appointed to a diocese.

Then the Reformation came, but there is very little evidence that the reformers wished to share among the Irish the spiritual liberties which they claimed for themselves. Provided the natives were docile and did not indulge in foreign intrigue, they might wear to their heart's content the ancient, moth-eaten livery which their masters had rejected from their wardrobes. Down to our own day the British have seldom scrupled to use an Irishman's docility as a Catholic against his recalcitrance as a subject. They appealed to the Vatican against Parnell and against agrarian outrage and met with friendly attention. And imperial diplomats still consider it clever to use the Papacy against the papists. But now and again a true Christian has appeared in the ascendancy Church and, like the famous Bishop Bedell, eliminated all racial arrogance from his heart and straight away his heresies were forgiven him. When all the Protestants around him were being massacred in the rebellion of 1641, Bedell was protected affectionately by his neighbours. Yet he was the founder of Protestant proselytism in Ireland.

The Bedell way is better than the Tracy way. Miss Tracy is amazingly perceptive but she is always, in the old, old way, scolding us for not being English and for belonging to 'a small, empty country where everything has been chewed over and over to the point of nausea'. She chastizes the 'arrogance, greed, pride, and vindictiveness' of the Irish Catholic clergy, their 'preoccupation with power and authority', the moral servitude of their flock. She writes:

> I believe I could name a dozen Irishmen, perhaps, who, if goaded sufficiently far, might be capable of saying 'Boo!' to a goose; and half of them, I suspect, would treat the goose simultaneously to a furtive and reassuring wink. 'Don't mind me,' that deft, conspiratorial closing of an eye would say, 'I'm only codding!'

That needed saying and no one could say it better than Miss Tracy but, if only she would cast off that shabby genteel cloak of Apartheid and tell us just how Irish she is herself, we would listen more readily. It is true she dared to say 'Boo!' to her goose, but would she have done so had she not been able to put the whole width of the Irish Sea between herself and it? Every time she says anything that is highly provocative she seems to take out her British passport and to give it a menacing wave; this is surely a second-rate substitute for courage, like repelling the devil with Holy Water instead of virtue.

An Irishman, following the procedure of this London court, must have been aware of a keen solicitude on the part of everybody on both sides to isolate this Doneraile conflict so that it revolved upon the 'magnificent dottiness' of the Irish rather than on the claims of a universal and authoritarian Church over its members. How lucky it was for the English that they fought their last battle for spiritual freedom upon the Boyne rather than the

Thames! If tempers are to be strained or blood to be shed to keep the heretic flag flying, for God's sake, they might urge, let it be on the Liffey and the Lagan and the Lee! And so the major issue of the inviolability of the Catholic clergy was only raised by implication, yet it was fundamental. It was the principal reason why the case was ever brought. Miss Tracy's counsel, Neville Faulks, argued vehemently that *The Sunday Times* had apologized to the canon, not because he deserved an apology, but because they thought that, with a Catholic jury, they would have no chance against a Catholic priest. The editor said 'That isn't true!' But, as a matter of fact he had written to Miss Tracy earlier: 'It was not a matter of the justice of our cause but of the probable views of the jury, which made us act as we did.' In fact a great English newspaper showed the same coyness about 'Boo' for which Miss Tracy reprimands the Irish so severely. But Mr Faulks did not follow this up. He, too, as he said, was anxious to avoid 'a wretched religious dispute'.

Everybody knows that the infallibility which the Vatican claims for itself casts a reflection upon the least of its ministers. The Bishop of Cloyne made the matter clear to the commission which visited Cork. A Catholic priest, he explained, is considered 'the spiritual lord' of his community. And at the anti-Tracy celebrations in Doneraile the TD, Mr McAuliffe, made the position clearer still. 'The priest,' he said, 'is God's minister and his house is the House of God and it is right that it should be the best in the village.' And when the bishop was asked: 'What would you say if someone suggested that the canon was not a sincere Christian?' he replied, 'God bless us! That would be blasphemy!' On this Mr Faulks later commented: Blasphemy is an expression usually used about our creator, you know – not about the clergy.' And he suggested that none of the people who believed that what Miss Tracy said was true would dare to come and say so, and that the schoolmaster, who gave evidence for the canon, depended on him for his appointment.

But all this is very thin ice and with one accord they made for safety. Is it not more Christian to have a cement floor than a tiled one in the scullery? And though admittedly it is unsuitable for a curate to lodge next door to a public house, could not the two curates share with the canon and so economize in dwelling space and attendance? But it was pointed out that the curates' housekeeper might gossip about the guests which the canon's housekeeper might admit; and so on the safe inter-denominational field of the proprieties the contest went briskly on.

And certainly the evidence did not show the canon as either greedy or self-interested. The house had been built at the bishop's orders and by no means for his own gratification. And yet a sad situation was revealed for which no easy cure is apparent. When the canon was asked by the commission whether he had consulted his parishioners about the building of his house, he replied that ninety-eight per cent of the working classes of Doneraile could read and write and little more, and that it was pointless consulting them. This candid remark must have slipped out of him in the stress of litigation for he retracted it publicly before the crowds who came to pay their respects to him in Doneraile after the conclusion of the Tracy case. He is quoted as saying then that 'the standard of education of the working people in Ireland is higher than in Britain and in most European countries'. Had they not a community of Presentation Nuns in Doneraile as well as the Christian Brothers? We must draw what comfort we can from these conflicting diagnoses.

But an Irish Protestant would hesitate to accuse the Catholic clergy of either greed or arrogance. For scattered over all the provinces are large, half-empty Protestant rectories, deaneries, palaces, for whose maintenance Catholics and Non-Conformists once paid tithes. There is scarcely one of them into which Canon O'Connell's little house would not fit several times over. Burdensome as they are today, they make it hard for us to assert that we, too, were never grasping or domineering.

Our defence must be that Berkeley lived in one of these mansions, Swift in another, and that, though privilege was often based on plunder, it was not always abused. Our scholars had an amplitude of vision which could not be called disreputable simply because they lived in easy circumstances. They could indulge a passion for accuracy and truth and even democracy, which would have been thought subversive if they had lived more meanly. They could even get away with heresy – we had an Arian bishop once or twice – and dogma was seldom allowed to become oppressive. Above all we critized our clergy and their doctrines as sharply as they criticized us. It is, I think, the absence of that healthy and open mutual criticism, which has given good cause to remember Doneraile.

[1955]

13

BOYCOTT VILLAGE

Fethard-on-Sea is a small village of about a hundred houses on the Wexford coast. It is not a seaside resort, for the muddy creek, which brings the houses to an end, can surely only be called 'the sea' to distinguish the village from the less notorious Fethard in Tipperary. The ancient hotel near the creek is now Mr Leslie Gardiner's General Stores, but neither he nor Miss Betty Cooper, who sells cornflakes, sweets and newspapers on the opposite side of the street, expect much from the seaside visitors. Tourists, of course, pass through, but they are mainly the self-sufficient kind with picnic-baskets in the boot. They are bound for Baginbun, a short distance away, where there is a charming secluded shore, rock-pools lined with emerald seaweed and, on most days, no one else. It was at Baginbun that the Normans first landed in Ireland eight centuries ago. They had been invited by Dermot Mac Morrogh, the great chieftain to whom all Wexford belonged. He had stolen another chieftain's wife. There had been unpleasantness and reprisals as a result and so he had asked for English help. The English came and they stayed. So much so that today men of English blood predominate in Wexford.

And now there has been turmoil there again about another truant wife and things have happened that have shocked all Ireland, north and south, and made the hope of unity recede still further. It is not a parochial squabble; it is not exclusively an Irish one. It is a collision between human nature and the 'immutable' principles of the Roman Catholic Church. Such collisions happen somewhere every day, but this one has been watched with such breathless interest, because in Ireland we still have the primitive power of focusing our minds like burning-glasses on tiny patches. Just as bird-watchers go to the Saltees, those three uninhabited islands which lie off Baginbun, so men-watchers should come to

Ireland to see how men, not yet trapped in the mental zoo of the television set and the Sunday press, still think and act in a natural untamed state.

In the spring of 1957 Eileen Cloney had reached the age of six. She lived with her parents and her baby sister in a bald grey castle just outside Fethard. It is 600 years old but it has been liberally renovated with concrete and has rather new-looking battlements and a turret. There is a huge barn beside it, whose corrugated iron roof has grown rusty in the salty air. There are elm trees and sprawling hedges, where in late June, when I first saw Dungulph, the blackberries were beginning to flower, the last bells were still clinging to the tips of the foxgloves and the first ones climbing up some stray mulleins. It seemed an enchanted place in which to be six years old. But Eileen Cloney had reached school age and Father Allen and his curate, Father Stafford, were insistent that there must be no further delay. She must go to school. They were emphatic about this, because Mrs Cloney, a strong-minded women, showed signs of wanting to send Eileen to the small Protestant school, where there were twelve other pupils, children of local farmers and of Leslie Gardiner. Though her husband was a Catholic, Mrs Cloney was the daughter of a Protestant stockbreeder of Fethard. I have never met Sean Cloney or his wife, Sheila, but they seem to be a likeable pair and their marriage appeared to be a happy one. The sudden split, which occurred in the middle of April, arose out of Eileen's schooling. It is disagreeable to discuss the characters and lives of quiet modest people like the Cloneys, who have never courted publicity, but circumstances and, in particular, Father Allen and Father Stafford, have decreed that their private lives are no longer their own. Sean Cloney, in his press photographs, looks a pleasant, good-looking, easy-going young man. He has that amused, cynical, shoulder-shrugging appearance that is common enough in Ireland. Sheila Cloney, who has hitherto escaped the press photographer, seems to have been more vigorous and dominating. Immedately after her marriage she started to make the 116-acre farm at Dungulph pay, wrestling herself with the tractor and the accounts and achieving such success that last year they bought a combine harvester. She was as devoted to her own Church as to her home and, when she came in from the fields, she often went with broom and scrubbing brush to the Protestant church of Fethard. It was being redecorated this spring and she was among the most tireless of the volunteers, who every night tidied away the builders' débris.

It was on May 13th that the squabble became public property, but it is not yet clear who was squabbling with whom. Was Sheila at war with Sean or was she warring with Father Allen and Father Stafford, while Sean, shrugging his shoulders, looked on? Certain it is that Sheila on April 27th took the car and the children to Wexford, where later it was found abandoned in the street. Three days later a barrister came from Belfast with 'terms of settlement'. They were drastic terms, suggesting an extreme state of feminine exasperation. Sean was to sell Dungulph Castle and they were to emigrate together to Canada or Australia, where the children were to be brought up as Protestants. 'No one influenced her in her decision,' Sean declared to a reporter. 'Once Sheila gets an idea into her head, a regiment of soldiers wouldn't change her.'

The news was received with consternation in Fethard. There was a thunderous pronouncement from the altar, and the next day a boycott started of all the Protestants in the neighbourhood. There was a Catholic teacher in the Protestant school, a Catholic sexton in the Protestant church; they both resigned. The elderly music teacher, Miss Knipe, lost eleven of her twelve pupils, Mr Gardiner's General Store and Miss Cooper's more modest emporium were rigorously boycotted. So were the Protestant farmers who sold milk, and from one of them a Catholic farmhand walked away. The boycott, the priests declared, would continue till Mrs Cloney brought back the children.

For the first week the better-disciplined Catholics refused to greet or to look at their Protestant neighbours, but here and there a rebellious one gave a furtive smile when no one was looking. At the end of the week, either because a breath of Christian charity forced its way through some crack in the united front or because it was better to abate the rigour of the boycott rather than betray any lack of unanimity, the boycotters began to smile and nod. But there was no relaxation of economic pressure.

By this time the newspapers of Dublin and Belfast were headlining the news from Fethard. It was anticipated that very soon a word from the local Catholic bishop, the Bishop of Ferns, would put an end to what was becoming a national scandal. But the ecclesiastical intervention, when it came, was more astounding than what had preceded. On Saturday, June 30th, the Annual

Congress of the Catholic Truth Society was being held in Wexford, and at the Church of the Immaculate Conception Cardinal D'Alton was received by the Bishop of Ferns. In front of them and five other bishops of the Roman Church, including the Archbishop of Dublin, the Bishop of Galway preached a sermon defending the boycott.

There seems [he said] to be a concerted campaign to entice or kidnap Catholic children and deprive them of their faith. Non-Catholics with one or two honourable exceptions do not protest against the crime of conspiring to steal the children of a Catholic father. But they try to make political capital, when a Catholic people make a peaceful and moderate protest.

In the same newspaper which reported this apology for a 'peaceful and moderate protest', we read that two of Mrs Cloney's brothers in Fethard had been obliged to seek police protection, because a shot had been fired at one of them near his home. At the same time a young Protestant teacher from Trinity College arrived to take charge of the Protestant school, which had been closed since the teacher had abandoned her pupils. He found a warning nailed onto the school-door:

SCABS! BEWARE OF THE LEAD IN BOYCOTT-VILLAGE!

No prominent Catholic had come forward to condemn the boycott except a barrister, Mr Donal Barrington, who in his address to a Catholic Social Study Conference in Dublin, said that the boycott was doing damage to the cause of Catholicism. 'It is', he said, 'the most terrible thing that has happened in this part of the country since the Civil War,' and he went on to say that he was only echoing the opinion of all the intelligent Catholics, laymen and priests, with whom he had discussed the matter. But their opinion had been given in private and he felt it his duty to speak publicly. 'There is a time in the affairs of people, when nothing is necessary for the triumph of evil but that good men should maintain what is called a discreet silence.'

No other Catholic made so bold a comment, till a week later Mr de Valera himself declared in the Dáil:

If, as head of the Government, I must speak, I can only say from what has appeared in public that I regard this boycott as ill-conceived, ill-considered and futile for the achievement of the purpose for which it seems to have been intended, that I regard it as unjust and cruel to confound the innocent with the guilty, that I repudiate any suggestion that this boycott is typical of the attitude or conduct of our people, that I am convinced that ninety per cent of them look on this matter as I do and that I beg of all, who have regard for the fair name, good repute and well-being of our nation, to use their influence to bring this deplorable affair to a speedy end.

Mr de Valera was right. The Irish are not by nature bullying or ungenerous; they are indulgent to human weaknesses and disinclined to totalitarian judgments. This essay, therefore, is not about bigotry, but about the ineffectuality of ordinary people with nice intentions and neighbourly instincts. This has often been demonstrated before in totalitarian countries, but only the last stage in the suppression of the amiable, when they are being finished off by threats and violence, has been closely observed. The earlier stages of coercion by 'peaceful and moderate protest' have never had the same attention, yet they are more important. For the handful of free spirits, who in any community are the last-ditch guardians of freedom, are not defenceless till the amiable majority, which forms an inert but not easily negotiable obstacle in the path of tyranny, has first been neutralized. How is this done? It is not difficult. The events in Fethard show how eagerly the amiable will cooperate in their own extinction.

It is now fifty years since the *Ne Temere* decree, which condemns the Irish nation to live in two mutually distrustful camps, was first applied to Ireland. It has broken up many homes besides the Cloneys' and brought an element of hypocrisy or perjury into every marriage between Irish people of different faith. Yet never till now did the whole Irish nation observe and deplore the cruel tensions which it has created. It is doubtful whether de Valera lost a single vote by championing the boycotted. For the Church of Ireland is much more than a vast complex of emptying palaces, rectories, cathedrals. In Ireland it is still the spearhead of the Reformation and few people are ready to renounce the liberties won at the Reformation, even when they repudiate the reformers. Father Stafford and his anathemas are as much an anachronism in Ireland as the Anglo-Irish ascendancy.

Yet this time the Protestant hierarchy made a scapegoat of Mrs Cloney and did not reiterate those protests against *Ne Temere*, which our primate made long ago and more recently republished. He and others had denied the validity of a promise 'extorted under pressure', and such denials undoubtedly influenced Mrs

Cloney in her decision. Weakened perhaps by the emigration of vigour and intelligence, our clergy counselled appeasement and that 'discreet silence', which Mr Barrington saw as the prelude to the triumph of evil. By inference they accepted the *Ne Temere* promises as valid; they deprecated excessive newspaper publicity, condemned any lay attempt to organize aid for the boycotted Protestants as 'senseless retaliation' and, in our diocesan magazine, gave retrospective approval to a strange undertaking given by Mrs Cloney's father, Mr Kelly. Speaking 'on behalf of the Church of Ireland community', he had pledged it to do all it could to bring back his grandchildren to Fethard, and published this promise in the Irish papers. Tactfully he said nothing about the boycott, which is known locally as 'Parish Co-operation' and was described by Father Stafford in the press as 'this grand, dignified, legal profession of our Faith'. By implication Protestants were committed to act as watchdogs for the observance of a decree directed against themselves. It was assumed that, as a *quid pro quo,* the boycott would be called off, but the Church of Ireland bit the dust in vain. The boycott continued and our clergy, returning from their Munich, gave themselves over to exhortation against mixed marriages, and the social intercourse that might lead to them. Canute, rebuking the waves, was not less profitably engaged. In the countryside we have dwindled to two or three per cent of the population (the rector of Fethard controls five amalgamated parishes); if we are to mix exclusively with ourselves, we are condemned to social isolation, to celibacy, inbreeding or dreary marriages of convenience. But can we really believe that our duty to our neighbour is to avoid him socially, lest we love him as ourselves and forget the dangerous contagion of his faith? For that is the way in which the gospel precepts appear to have been revised.

This ecclesiastical advice will not of course be followed, but nor will it be repudiated for, as in the early days of the Brown Shirts in Germany, respectable people put their faith in the healing properties of time. We like to think that, left to themselves, our difficulties will all 'blow over', 'peter out', 'die down'. There is a rich range of synonyms for the spontaneous disappearance of evil and we seldom commit the folly of sticking out our necks or poking in our noses. And, in fact, if we only have patience, the victim of injustice will probably emigrate and cease to embarrass us with his tedious lamentations.

Irish Protestants are generally 'broad minded' about belief. They tend to judge other religions as they judge their own, by its social consequences. Having sometimes a hereditary interest in property, they are impressed by the Catholic defence of property. A true instinct also informs them that the Catholic Church is basically as unsympathetic to Irish nationalism as is the average Irish Protestant and might at any moment barter its support of the Irish Republic for a favoured position in the Commonwealth. This emerged clearly at Fethard. The Bishop of Galway, in his Wexford address, deliberately gave arguments to the Northerners against the abolition of Partition and cannot have been dismayed by the repercussions in Belfast. A united Ireland, in which there would be a twenty-five per cent heretical minority, might seem to present the Church of Rome with problems insoluble, except in the vast dilution of the Commonwealth. But to declaim against Irish unity would be unpopular; the Orangemen could safely be left to do all the declaiming, for Ulster eyes are dim with gazing on far-off imperial horizons and cannot focus clearly on what goes on under the nose. A fund was raised for the boycotted Protestants and a Northern MP sent to distribute it. On July 12th not a single Orange orator failed to mention Fethard, but, as interest on the large 'political capital' derived from the boycott, the dividend that went to Fethard was small.

Some weeks ago Father Allen bought some cigarettes at Gardiner's. This momentous act did not mean the end of the boycott, but it has cast a rose-pink veil over its origins and the responsibility for its continuance. An irreverent person, peering through the veil, would see that the boycott can never now end. The lost customers have found other tradesmen, eager to supply their needs, a new newsagent bicycles round with the papers to Miss Cooper's former clients, a new milkman goes the rounds and the old schoolteacher and the old sextoness will never return. Nor will Miss Knipe's pupils. To end the boycott more unpleasantness and fresh dislocations would be necessary, and these are things which in Ireland we always avoid if we possibly can.

[1958]

POSTSCRIPT I (1978)

In the past years there have been some verbal concessions about the *Ne Temere* decree but very little effective change. Yet I am confident that had Protestants listened to Primate Gregg's 'Resistance in God's Name is the Duty of us all' and acted with courage and unity, they would have caused the total abolition of the decree in 1958.

At that time we were doing up our house in Co. Kilkenny, which was fifty miles away, and we bought all our putty, paint and as much else as we could at Gardiner's Stores and Miss Cooper's Fancy Goods Shop. In two journeys we spent twenty or thirty pounds and I wrote to *The Irish Times* suggesting that if all the Protestants within fifty miles of Fethard did all their shopping there, the boycott would be over in a week. I wrote anonymously, as one often did in the fifties.

However, our bishop, Dr Phair, wrote in reply that this would be 'senseless provocation' and that was the end of my campaign. As he had always been friendly to me I might have forestalled this, had I the wit to sign my name.

Ne Temere came up in *The Irish Times* fifteen years later, when the Rev. R. C. Johnston declared that Fethard had been a turning-point in our history and that Protestants in their spinelessness had left the defence of their liberties to liberal Catholics like Noel Browne and humanists like Owen Skeffington. In reply I recalled Gregg's words and insisted that had Dr Phair encouraged us rather than the reverse, there would have been such an avalanche of Protestants from Wexford, Waterford and Kilkenny as would have kept all the boycotted in plenty for the rest of their lives and secured the repeal of *Ne Temere.*

Dr Phair was dead but his widow was much hurt; she wrote to me privately and said that those who suffered were aware of their prayers and that £1754.10.4 had been subscribed to the Fethard Relief Fund in the Bank of Ireland and that his behaviour had met with general approval. I am sure it did but it seemed to me as though the Protestant leaders were trying to buy us off our duty with cheques and as though the welfare of some shopkeepers and dairy farmers was at stake and not our children's freedom and the Protestant right of private judgment.

A great common gesture would have given us courage and confidence and arrested the sad slow Protestant decline. It would have reminded the northern Protestants that we belong together and that they belong to Ireland.

Success would have been inevitable, for the decree, only imposed on England and Ireland in 1908 and not extended to Germany, was in no way infallible. It could, in Gregg's words, be 'withdrawn at any time or thrust into the capacious waste paper basket kept at Rome for the reception of Papal utterances that have miscarried'.

Here is the conclusion of the statement made by the House of Bishops of the Church of Ireland soon after the application of *Ne Temere* to Ireland in 1908: 'We, the archbishops and bishops of the Church of Ireland, appeal on behalf of the oppressed and helpless to all lovers of justice and liberty to do their utmost by all lawful means for the redressing of a grevious wrong.'

POSTSCRIPT II (1984)

In the past six years Irish Protestants, faced with a real possibility of extinction before the end of the century, have reacted more vigorously than before to the demands of the dominant majority.

In November 1983 the Irish Catholic Hierarchy issued a new 'directory' about mixed marriages. Couched in conciliatory terms, it left the situation much as it was before, except that the promises made by the Catholic parent to bring up the children as Catholics could be oral and not written. The House of Bishops of the Church of Ireland was deeply dissatisfied; in their view a promise is a promise, whether written or spoken. The Protestant bishops also complained that 'God's Law' was being invoked to support the Catholic claim: 'We do not know where in God's Law there is support for a promise to ensure the Roman Catholic upbringing of all the children.' The directory claimed that in some areas of Ireland the Protestant spouse was frequently only nominally so and therefore had no difficulty in agreeing to the Catholic ruling. The Church of Ireland reply was that in other areas the reverse was true. They were surprised, too, that whereas the directory regarded the Protestant attitude to divorce as an impediment to mixed marriages, an exception was made for the Orthodox

Church, which also recognized divorce. I would suggest that the reason for this is practical not spiritual; since the Russian Revolution the Orthodox Church has been so weakened and divided that it presents a tempting mission field. There was every reason to be conciliatory.

There had been an earlier confrontation on a different issue. The Constitutional Amendment of September 1983, whose intention was to guarantee beyond all possibility of change the existing law against abortion, was passed by a majority, which was deceptive, as only half the electorate voted. It split the country as it had seldom been split before. The Protestant Churches, galvanized by Dean Griffin of St Patrick's Cathedral, took a prominent part in the resistance. Accepting that abortion is an evil, they still saw no necessity of copper-fastening a law whose observation it was impossible to guarantee. Many felt that the publicity given to the Amendment would be counter-productive. The evidence that between 3000 and 5000 women were going annually to England to have abortions revealed how easily the law could be defied. Many, too, asked themselves what advice they would give if someone dear to them was raped or told by her doctor that she would bear a hopelessly handicapped child or was forced by circumstances to give her fatherless child to others to rear. To them it seemed that the Amendment was the negation of the Protestant right of private judgment.

There is some truth in the directory's argument about nominal Protestantism. Although there is far less vocal 'unbelief' today than a century ago, when it was based on biblical criticism and caused heart-break and alienation, there is wide-spread indifference in both Churches. On the other hand there are many who long for spiritual guidance but cannot accept it in the form in which it is offered. They see how in our materialistic and deeply divided society the Churches have lost their mediatory power. There are sectarian murders, which have nothing to do with a conflict of principle. Great blocks of hereditary conformities, which owe nothing to the movement of the individual mind, jostle each other in inflexible hostility. The arguments of the ecumenists at no point touch these embattled certainties. The leaders of rival Churches have come together and, forgetting their differences, have preached against violence. Their united voices have had no effect. They are addressing themselves to a small but powerful body of men, superbly armed and subsidized from many sources, who are confident that, if they crush their adversaries, and win, they will ultimately be accepted. History, they know, is on their side; in country after country *coups d'état*, brought about by violence, have later received ecclesiastical sanction.

The only future for the Churches in a time of mounting violence is to forget all their dogmatic differences and the supernatural claims with which mass unanimity is cemented and to concentrate on the Christian teaching of brotherly love, which applies to all our neighbours and all our countrymen, whatever their faith. This is the only catalyst that can break down every consensus, which has outlived its day, and free that teaching from sectarian overtones.

Christianity was born in a small community and it was to small communities, no bigger for the most part than Fethard-on-Sea, that St Paul wrote his epistles. The New Testament precept, 'Thou shalt love thy neighbour as thyself', was not purely allegorical. It was not impossible then to identify oneself with those with whom one associated and to feel a deep concern for them.

Today the idea of neighbourly love has been diluted till it covers all humanity. We grieve for distant events and people with sympathy as thin and ephemeral as the newspaper in which we read about them. We suffer from a disease so widespread as to seem incurable. Yet where the diagnosis is obvious, the cure cannot be for ever beyond our reach.

Is it possible that in some far-off day Christian society, responding to human needs, will gradually be structurally transformed?

PART TWO
STUDIES LITERARY AND SPECULATIVE

14

THE BELL: AN ANGLO-IRISH VIEW

In my generation we have had several good Irish journals, but two whose influence surpassed that of all the others. When I was growing up, there was the *Irish Statesman*, which led me and many others out of the Anglo-Irish ghetto in which we had been brought up and reminded us that we were Irishmen. For our parents of the ascendancy it was easy and obvious to live in Ireland, but we of the 'descendancy' were surrounded in the twenties by the burnt houses of our friends and relations. England beckoned us and only an odd obstinate young person would wish to stay at home.

In fact, we who stayed were rather odd. I had met AE and Sir Horace Plunkett and had been enchanted by them. I had seen W. B. Yeats prancing up and down the floor of the Oxford Union, declaiming against English politicians. Empires were crashing all round us and Oxford was full of scheming young students from the new resurgent nations. I was proud that I belonged to one of them. I was, however, too young and inexperienced to know that Plunkett and AE, and the other older men who ran the *Irish Statesman*, were already tired and disillusioned, although the final insult to Plunkett – the burning of Kilteragh – had not yet happened. But many of their creameries had already been destroyed by the Black and Tans, who believed that the farmers hatched sedition over their milk churns. It was round the creameries that AE's new Ireland was supposed to develop: a community of spirit was to grow organically from the co-operative marketing of eggs, beef and butter.

In 1923 Plunkett persuaded me to join the Irish county libraries and in them I found many like-minded people, such as Lennox Robinson, Thomas McGreevy, Geoffrey Taylor, Robert Wilson, the poet, Frank O'Connor and Helen Roe. It was the writers who brought calamity on the libraries, as one can read in Lady Gregory's journals, when they collided with Irish piety and prudery. The result was that the central organization moved to Dunfermline in Scotland and we all dispersed. In 1927 I went off as a teacher to Egypt, then to Russia and to Yugoslavia, and only returned to Ireland in 1938. The *Irish Statesman* was gone. Plunkett and AE had left for England, with the result that we remnants of the Anglo-Irish 'intelligentsia' would have been nobody's children, had Sean O'Faolain's *The Bell* not taken us under its wing.

There were in fact quite a few of us. There were survivors from the days when Irish writing had been focused on Coole Park: Joseph Hone, Lennox Robinson and the Yeats brothers; there were those who had made their name in England: Cecil Day Lewis, L. A. G. Strong, Elizabeth Bowen; there were Northerners: Louis MacNeice and W. R. Rodgers; and there were my own contemporaries: Geoffrey Taylor, Arland Ussher, Denis Johnston, Monk Gibbon, Harry Craig, Arthur Power, all of us rather odd and not finding it easy to put Ireland first.

Taylor became literary editor of *The Bell*, later on I became its review editor. We both knew the country as a whole. We had organized new libraries in the north, in Derry and Antrim, and knew the truth of what O'Faolain had written in an editorial for one of his Ulster numbers. Partition, he declared, had resulted from the stupid rivalry between the 'hypernationalism' of the south and the 'hyperinternationalism' of the north. The Ulsterman, cut off from his roots, was being suffocated by the indiscriminate flood of news and views that poured in on him from overseas, as we were in the south by our intense introversion. In my Coleraine library I had also learnt a little about Ulster intransigence, although I met more Anglo-Irish nationalists there than in Kilkenny.

O'Faolain's attitude to Ulster was generous and imaginative and he met with a generous response. In the pages of *The Bell* the Dean of Belfast defended the Ulster Protestant with firmness and courtesy, as did Frederick Leahy, a northern clergyman. Others took part in the dialogue. Leahy maintained that the Ulsterman fears 'principles' not people, that his Protestant faith is very dear to him, that his loyalty to the English monarch is dependent on the Protestant succession and that his religion is rooted in Ulster, whereas the creed of the south is international and must be judged not in Ireland alone, but by what happened all over the world, in Spain, South America and Canada. Yet, he ended as follows: 'North and South we both love Ireland. May God yet unite us peaceably and securely!' Thomas Carnduff, an Ulster poet, wrote in the same way: 'We Belfastmen love Ireland. Every sod and stone and mountain and lake is part of us. . . Yet the Orange movement began with the people, it has remained with the people. . . The sneers and gibes at Orangeism have only strengthened its hold upon the Ulstermen.'

A symposium of 'the five strains', which omitted the Scottish strain, provoked a memorable letter from James Auchmuty, which possibly has relevance today. He said, just as Leahy had, that the northern Presbyterian looks to Scotland as his spiritual home. 'He is sprung from the same Gaelic granite as his fellow-countrymen and moulded to a different pattern.' I believe that for the truth about Ulster you must still look to *The Bell* and not to the sensationalism of the contemporary press. But as I reread Auchmuty, I remember a prophecy which I read not long ago in a Dublin daily by a Belfast sociologist, A. E. Spencer: that, after many vicissitudes and much bloodshed, Ulster might become a part of a new self-governing Scotland, enriched by oil and federated with England. Ulster had once been the bridgehead between two branches of the Gael; in this way history would only be repeating itself. That indeed would be the end of a dream that many of us believed in, but I can conceive of worse endings.

The Bell pealed out its invitation to all those who loved the Irish language and loathed the way that the politicians, the pedagogues, the urbanized peasants had sucked the life and beauty from it. Those who inherited it as a mother tongue used it to pass examinations and get jobs in Dublin. The East Gael used it to oust the West Briton who here and there still administered the institutions his ancestors had built up.

The true lovers of the language, O'Faolain himself, Daniel Binchy or Myles Dillon, bitterly turned on those who by compulsion had made it something to be shirked and scorned. To Arland Ussher, an Anglo-Irishman, it had been 'his first love in languages, abounding in a beauty and expression of phrase of which the Irish-English of Synge alone could give some idea.' 'It was', he wrote,

> the great language of conversation, of quips, hyperboles, cajoleries,

lamentations, blessings, cursings, endearments, tirades. Its unsuspected rhythm had even given an intimate and personal quality to the great Irish writers of English. It was the winged word in its flight that was beautiful. Stuffed and mounted on the page of a school book, it stank.

I have quoted Ussher more fully than others, because the Irish National Movement, like the Gaelic League and the 'Literary Revival', has often been attributed to a rebel faction of the Anglo-Irish who, like Ussher, were tired of 'broad horizons' and empire building but found at home a promise of warmth, stability and intimacy in which the shyer, more complex talents might expand. Once in 1941 O'Faolain looked back forty years and thought of those who 'had kept the air vibrant with their patronage, curiosity, optimism and width of interest'. Now that Anglo-Ireland seems all but dead and the defence of Protestantism left to the northerners, there can be no chauvinism in recalling that more than half of those he mentioned were Anglo-Irish Protestants. As O'Faolain said, they were national, not 'nationalistic', and in the pages of *The Bell* you will observe how difficult was the task that confronted them. The old strands of affection and loyalty had to be unravelled and woven tenderly into a new pattern. There was British imperialism and Catholic universalism; there was Irish and English racialism; and there was the many-sided dissent of Protestantism.

Michael Lennon described in two articles how, years before, Douglas Hyde steered the Gaelic League past all these rocks and shoals and whirlpools. For example, because Lord Castletown, who was proud of his Gaelic ancestry, was serving in South Africa, Hyde discouraged pro-Boer demonstrations.

In the very first number of *The Bell* Elizabeth Bowen, still tethered to Ireland by her home and many family ties, considered what role, if any, the Big House could still play. It no longer carried privilege with it, but loneliness, isolation, expense. Yet one held on. Old houses crumble, but the vigour and resolution that built them takes a long time to die. Elizabeth Bowen mentioned the strength that these houses impart, the great feeling of independence:

One lives by one's own standards, makes one's own laws and does not care within fairly wide limits what anybody outside the demesne wall thinks. . . . The purpose of our big rooms was social. 'Cannot we,' they seem to ask, 'be as never before social? Cannot we scrap the past with its bitterness and barriers and all meet, throwing in what we have?'. . . The doors of the big houses stand open all day. The stranger is welcome just as much as the friend. . . in fact he is the friend, if he does not show himself otherwise. But who ever walks in? Is it suspicion, hostility, irony, that keeps so much of Ireland away from the big house door? If this lasts, we impoverish life all round.

She wrote and reviewed fairly frequently for *The Bell* and it was there, I think, rather than at her own front door that she met Catholic Nationalist Ireland. Yet her book, *Bowen's Court*, which, celebrating one Anglo-Irish family and one dearly loved region, in effect celebrated them all, was written behind demesne walls and by its rare independence of spirit might seem to justify them. Yet her grandmother's house in Tipperary, which was my grandfather's, kindly but traditional people, had been burnt in 1923 and Elizabeth Bowen well knew that the ghosts of the ascendancy haunted these long avenues and scared away all but those realists to whom O'Faolain appealed. She filled Bowen's Court for many summers with English writers and the few Irish ones that sought her out. But then her husband died and *The Bell* died and finally she allowed Bowen's Court itself to die. When I last met her in County Kilkenny, just before her own death, she spoke of Ireland with such bitterness that I have tried to persuade myself that it was her last illness that was speaking and not her utter disillusionment.

A few years after O'Faolain had left *The Bell*, something happened which brought him to my defence in its pages and earned him my deep gratitude. I had given great offence by supporting the Serbian Orthodox against the Croat Catholics and was publicly denounced in Dublin and Kilkenny. I had long before published the relevant facts in *The Church of Ireland Gazette* but, apart from Elizabeth and my brother-in-law, Tyrone Guthrie, who wrote a letter to *The Irish Times* which was not printed, the only prominent people who dared suggest that there might be truth in what I had said and that I was right to say it, were Sean O'Casey in *Sunset and Evening Star* and Sean O'Faolain, who wrote at length in the February 1953 issue of *The Bell*.

The Bell had a special quality about which I have not spoken. No doubt they used rejection slips in plenty, but in its early days Frank O'Connor, as poetry editor, and Geoffrey Taylor treated their contributors as friends, explaining their refusals with comments and advice and sometimes in a friendly foreword criticising what they printed. O'Faolain too worked as though he were not merely making a magazine but shaping a literature or calling it into being. Given time, that is what *The Bell* might have done. Peadar O'Donnell carried on worthily for six or seven years after O'Faolain retired; then he too found the strain too much and increasingly withdrew from it. I never learnt why *The Bell* died. Slowly it began to sag like a balloon from which the air is escaping. Some strong puff of passionate conviction might have inflated it again, but none came. For a while it had kept hope alive; for a while O'Faolain's enthusiastic vision kept it going. 'When the will of Ireland,' he wrote, 'becomes intense again, Romantic Ireland will return. When the will of the world, now barely hanging by its finger nails, becomes intense again, romance will warm life all over the globe.'

[1976]

15

ENVOY AND MR KAVANAGH

A Frenchman who was asked why a number of French writers and artists had collaborated with the Germans, replied with an indulgent smile: 'Writers and artists are children when it comes to politics. What can you expect?'

Perhaps that is specially true of poets and in an over-stable society maybe their childishness has value. It is like a window pane being broken in a stuffy room. Shelley in Dublin inciting the poor against their oppressors or in Oxford scandalizing the dons with revolutionary pamphlets is dear to us because he trusted the impulses of the heart and was indifferent to consequences. Swinburne, a little later, threw his stones with greater effect. Though society still stood four square, a good many windows had been broken in the meantime and what had been a pleasant freshness became an ominous draught. The more settled shivered apprehensively, in the deep Victorian afternoon.

Then came d'Annunzio, who strutted and declaimed like Swinburne, but by this time society was shattered and rocking and the child poet with his toy state of Fiume, his flags and flamboyant rhetoric, needed more than a spanking. Poetry, like a neglected adolescent, had become vicious and self-willed. It had met with bad companions. After that chaos followed, a few heads bob up, posturing and ranting, Pound, Montherlant, Roy Campbell, and in the east the former *enfant terrible* became not only a tolerated but a subsidized figure. For a moment or two the Shelleys sat in judgment on the dons. Then a new donnishness, more anti-poetical than anything before conceived, overwhelmed them.

What has happened to the rebel writers in Ireland? Fifty years ago their focus was Irish nationalism. It gave them unity and direction and the power of collective creation. They created the Abbey Theatre and the *Irish Statesman,* which was a bridge between literature and social endeavour, between Coole and Kilteragh.

Then something happened to this idea of an Irish Nation, which was fastidious but generous. It collapsed and by degrees everything else collapsed with it. What becomes of the ivy when the tree falls down? It doesn't die immediately. For a time it seems freer than before, thrusting out tendrils in all directions, choking some undergrowth, being choked by others. It is some time before it is finally suffocated.

Many Irish writers today seem pleased that nationalism is in decay. They think that art is liberated from a restricting preoccupation and can range like the ivy over the whole earth, not over a single tree. But does this happen? Has it happened anywhere? Is is possible that a rotten tree is better than no tree at all? What is the truth?

It might be helpful to conduct a post-mortem on the defunct monthly *Envoy*, for this was the organ of Ireland's rebellious writers. We might learn what they were rebelling against, and if and why the rebellion failed. It was a well-produced magazine with many brilliant writers. I don't think we can argue pessimistically from its death, which even its critics deplored. An Irish journal is like a sortie from a besieged city. Its effects cannot be measured by its duration.

As for the campaign of rebellion, *Envoy*'s objectives must be guessed at principally from the editorials and from Patrick Kavanagh's monthly diary. For the editor in his final issue claimed that one of the great achievements of *Envoy* was to have given Kavanagh the opportunity of serving the cause of truth in Ireland and of scourging the untalented, who are bringing Irish writing into disrepute beyond our shores. This scourging was plainly an important part of the programme and in the valedictory number the editor and Mr Kavanagh complimented each other on having done a good job! Apart from several living writers, who had to take their trousers down in almost every issue, all the major figures of the Irish Renaissance came in for a severe beating. Matthew Arnold was told he was a 'well-meaning bore', and disciplinary measures were taken against the *Irish Times*, Radio Éireann, and the Protestants (whose 'coarseness' was the 'loutish superiority of a mediocre ruling class'). Somebody suggested to me that these were ritual flagellations, symbolic and without malice. It was like an initiation ceremony from the South

Sea Islands, slightly humanized by the Church, and all it meant was that the young were ready to take over from the old. 'We shouldn't worry,' he said, 'that's life and it shows there's good stuff in them. The grandfather gorilla would only get seriously worried about his posterity if he didn't get beaten up by his children.'

But I don't think an anthropological or zoological explanation will really do. *Envoy* was a serious paper engaged on a real campaign against the Philistine and it was bad management that all the violence went on in the guard-room behind the lines, while the Philistines looked on and laughed. Compared to Patrick Kavanagh, a dashing guerrilla captain, Matthew Arnold was a great general, a tried campaigner against the Philistines, trained in all the academies of war. Rivalry was inevitable. Yet if Mr Kavanagh enjoys today a certain freedom to express himself, Arnold was one of those who guaranteed it.

Envoy had something serious to say. Perhaps it was the very urgency of the message that made the messenger so breathless. His end in the twentieth issue was tragic. It was as though he raced through the enemy's lines, bearing some tremendous news, and at last collapsed raving among his friends, whom in his delirium he mistakes for the Philistines. His lips are frothing, his pulse racing but he can only stammer out a few baleful familiar syllables, 'Mr Smyllie', 'Austin Clarke', 'Radio Éireann', 'Faugh!' He gives a last belch and dies pillowed in his own vomit, his message undelivered.

I am afraid some of the bystanders tittered at his death-bed scene. But laughter, even indulgent laughter, is out of place. *Envoy* was a good and gallant paper and its death is a tragedy. Moreover, Mr Kavanagh can be a very good writer indeed.

Envoy had been seriously schizophrenic from the start. Confronted by the fact that our best writers of a generation ago had had 'microcosmic' tendencies, the editor and Mr Kavanagh began to tug in different directions. Here is an editorial manifesto, once or twice re-echoed: 'For fifty years Dublin has been the scene of the major literary Renaissance in Western civilization.' Now let's look at the hind legs of the horse, but stand well clear! It's Mr Kavanagh: 'One of the things it would be necessary to teach in this country is that the pygmy literature which was produced by the so-called Irish literary Renaissance is quite worthless.'

And then, midway in *Envoy*'s career, Mr Hogan, the Dramatic

Critic, who had also been using his hooves rather wildly right and left, started to exchange kicks with Mr Kavanagh, and it was he who finally pranced on the dead body of *Envoy* in *The Irish Times*.

Yet conflict, even editorial conflict, inside a paper can be very wholesome; it is the conflict within the writer's own mind which is demoralizing. Mr Kavanagh's mind, when he abandons poetry and fiction, is like a monkey house at feeding time. It is worthy of a careful examination because in an exaggerated form he is suffering from the same disorder as many other Irish writers. *Ex uno disce omnes.* Mr Kavanagh is highly gifted and the fact that he has to tell us so himself is in our grudging society no proof of the contrary. There is much excuse for his antics.

The perversion of the national ideal has forced Irish writers into spiritual and intellectual acrobatics for which there are few parallels outside central Europe. Many of those who thirty years ago encouraged or condoned the expulsion of the Anglo-Irish are today talking for the BBC and would not shrink from doing propaganda for the British way of life through the British Council.

Nor can we moralize about this. AE and the Anglo-Irish nationalists of a generation ago were not subjected to the same trials and temptations, and it is scarcely fair to claim that they were more consistent in their loyalties. Under stress the artist has to make the strangest recantations (they never appear as recantations since the adjustment is by stages). Our minds run a little ahead of our gross material needs and, when the economic pressure comes, it finds us spiritually conditioned. Alas! Is not Chekhov's widow, the greatest of Russian actresses, quite proud of her Stalin prize? But adjustments, though they are inevitable and gradual, may still be painful. They may shake the whole machinery of the mind so that it shrieks and rattles like an abrupt and clumsy change of gear. All the shrieking and rattling that goes on in Irish literature today is surely the result of these psychological adjustments. Compare the wise and equable tone of the *Irish Statesman* under AE with the neurotic tantrums of *Envoy*.

The Anglo-Irish contribution to letters is today, as I have suggested, a chief focus of psychological disturbance. The Anglo-Irish writers who surrounded Yeats deliberately left the big world for the small one. They were more afraid of being culturally submerged in a big empire than of being stranded in sterile isolation in a small island. Time has justified them. Work of European significance was done under the stimulus of what might be considered parochial enthusiasms, and their fame is even today one of the strongest of the links that bind Ireland to the outer world. In fact while the parochialism of 1951 is sterile, the parochialism of 1901 was richly creative.

Envoy would have done good work by facing this anomaly and tracing its causes. But Mr Kavanagh refuses to face it; he will not see that the Abbey Theatre group not only nursed Irish talent at home but also created abroad a favourable atmosphere for its reception. Every Irish writer who travels to London is in their debt. Mr Kavanagh wants to repudiate this debt in order to make his case that genius always works its own passage. Confusing universalism with megalopolitanism, which the Anglo-Irish writers repudiated, he blames them for being parochial. Then he attacks their 'pygmy literature' front and rear. In an essay on F. R. Higgins he accuses Irish Protestants of trying to 'by-pass Rome on the way to the heart of Ireland', and several times he argues with different degrees of candour that you cannot be Irish if you are not Catholic. This is a light-hearted argument without arrogance and it can be answered without arrogance by a *tu quoque*. What Mr Kavanagh is trying to do is to by-pass Anglo-Ireland on the way to the heart of London. And it is sure that while Anglo-Ireland, north and south, may ultimately be assimilated (a very slow process of reciprocal adjustment), it cannot conceivably be by-passed. The Anglo-Irish were not only the cruel stepmothers of Gaelic civilization, they were also the indulgent nurses and governesses of Irish literature in the English language. They have been the mediators between England and Ireland for centuries. Mr Kavanagh suspects them also with some reason of having been the authors of Irish Nationalism. Yet he would sooner repudiate Irish Nationalism than acknowledge any cultural indebtedness to Anglo-Ireland. Watch him at work in *Envoy*.

Synge is 'a vulgarian'. 'The predominant note of his writings is hate.' 'Yeats showed his minor microcosmic mind by advising him to study the people of his own country.' 'Yeats' material was a very parochial thing, Irish Nationalism.' 'Had he been really great he would have abandoned the anaemic world of petty nationalism and followed his stomach's leanings.' 'Hyde and Davis, Butt, Parnell and Erskine Childers were all Cromwellians.'

'Shaw is tedious' and 'all lies', and so on.

Mr Kavanagh is not a bigot. He attacks his own Church roundly, its 'anti-intellectualism' and 'barbarous pietisms', and I think his attack on Protestantism is directed against the Anglo-Irish cultural incubus rather than against the Reformation. I think he really prefers O'Casey when he assails the Church of Rome from a Communist standpoint ('the real Protestantism of our time', he calls it) to F. R. Higgins when he writes sympathetically but with an outsider's clumsiness of the Mass. He sees a good counter-blast to a certain kind of Irish clericalism in 'O'Casey's genuine Protestant bigotry', but is angry with him when he writes with friendliness of the unorthodox Father Walter Macdonald, of whom, says Mr Kavanagh, he knows 'sweet damn all'. He argues that you cannot be Irish and not a Catholic, because (I do not quite follow his reasoning here) 'Catholicism is a universal concept of mankind and Protestantism was here an attempt to by-pass this universalism and to concentrate the light on a minor detail.' But does he not see that by excluding nationalism as a Protestant Anglo-Irish heresy and equating Irishness and Catholicism, he is in danger of the far worse heresy of racialism? He toys significantly with the theory that Higgins' name was really Huggins, a Saxon masquerading as an Irishman. This is a very slippery slope indeed.

These arguments are, of course, no longer very inflammatory, and Mr Kavanagh doesn't mean any harm. We use the old coloured counters to score points in a multitude of different games, social, economic, political; they are faded and paper thin, and they have different values for different games. It is not Mr Kavanagh's disparagement of Anglo-Ireland and its prevailing faith which is so disruptive; it is his loose unserious reasoning. His own faith seems to be nostalgic and atmospheric: it is by no means fanatical or precise; 'Christianity is the only frame for Pagan freedom. . . there is an outside ring of ethical abnegations and professional priests, but inside the old human life dancing like children and drinking wine like men.' 'We want to go down prostrate and cry out our belief but our reason refuses'. . . and so on. This does not sound very straight-laced and maybe he feels he has to establish his orthodoxy by an occasional good-humoured wallop at the Protestants. In a good cause few Protestants would grudge their backsides. But as the real menace nowadays is not theological rigorism but sloppy thinking, we cannot afford to be too indulgent. We cannot, for example, accept this alleged bond, intimate, indissoluble, between Catholicism and Ireland. What are the grounds for it? Racial? Temperamental? But the Welsh Celts adjusted themselves well enough to Methodism, the Reformation took strong root among the Breton Celts and had to be eradicated by the French. Historical grounds? Why everybody knows that Catholic Universalism was enforced in Ireland, as never before, by the Normans and the English. In the south-east, for example, the Butlers frequently used it against the Kavanaghs as a means of breaking down their strong tribal loyalties. In the Kavanagh country, as elsewhere, there was often a Pope in every parish. Their spiritual leaders, St Maedoc, St Moling, St Munnu, were all, with the doubtful exception of the last, fanatically tribal in their loyalties. Catholic Universalism was in Ireland, as in many other countries, enforced on the invaded by the invader. When at the beginning of the nineteenth century Irish Protestantism was a proselytizing creed, the missionaries often saw that they could not censure Catholicism without also censuring the English ascendancy, which had used it so profitably. That is one of the reasons why Irish nationalism has often been closely linked with Protestantism.

These are dead or dying controversies, only revived to prove that Irishmen are as free to choose their beliefs as any other people. Nor is nationalism, in so far as it is only neighbourliness grown a bit inflated and unwieldy, the pernicious force that Mr Kavanagh suspects. On this point he contradicts himself often. At one stage he says that only minor poets like Rupert Brooke care about their country, but later he concedes that 'an Irish writer is lost when he is detached from his native roots' and that 'although the real roots are in the mind and not in geography, yet the fact is we sometimes find it hard to get at our minds through the screen of a strange symbol. But this can be got over if one has a truly creative faculty.' And elsewhere he writes: 'A writer cannot come across with nonsense to an audience of his own people. The false note rings out loudly.'

But I think the proof that we are tied in some degree to geography is given in Kavanagh's last essay. Has anything more parochial ever been written in Ireland? Would a man who was not inextricably involved in a small society bother to insult it in such detail? Obviously there is love there as well as hate.

In fact Mr Kavanagh's anti-nationalism is probably a necessary antidote to some emotional excesses of his. Most of the Anglo-Irish writers whom he would like to have dosed had a surfeit of this medicine from childhood.

I don't think writers should tie themselves in knots with these words 'nationalism', 'universalism'. A writer in 1951 will want the same thing as in 1901, even though the formula for obtaining it may have altered slightly. He will want to write about the community he knows, with detachment and with love. He will want to be a free individual integrated into a stable group, not a unit in a herd. Such groups are hard to find. Do they exist? Probably not. Yet they are more likely to be foreshadowed in County Monaghan than in Fleet Street. That is the explanation of the 'microcosmic' tendencies of the Yeats circle, and perhaps also of Mr Kavanagh's own fine creative achievements.

Or is Mr Kavanagh perhaps merely thinking of 'opportunities', 'publishers, literary lunches, stimulating conversations and contacts'? These are of great though secondary importance but have nothing to do with anti-nationalism. The BBC, which is a fairy godmother to so many Irish writers, is a strongly national organization and its ramifications extend through the whole of English literary society. Mr Kavanagh has nothing but scorn for an organization such as the Pen Club, which aims, however ineffectually, at by-passing nationalism. In fact, Mr Kavanagh's universalism is all a cod.

No artist need be a nationalist or a universalist, concerned with the drawing or effacing of political frontiers. But cultural frontiers exist, and a good artist will respect them whether or not they are drawn on the map. Most of them are not and could not be, since the social and economic groups which they define are widely scattered and segmented. Kavanagh says that O'Casey, like Higgins, is incompetent on a Catholic theme, yet he is worse on an English one. Irish Catholics who write about the Anglo-Irish are also at sea, though they are their next-door neighbours. O'Faolain's book on Countess Markievicz is only justifiable as a revenge for Mrs Conyers and G. A. Birmingham. In one of O'Connor's books I recollect an Irish Protestant welfare worker who might have been described by an intelligent Chinaman. The more sensitive, the better an artist is, the more he betrays himself when he ventures outside the tiny zone in which he is at ease. To take a great writer, E. M. Forster, how bad the 'inside' view of Italy is in *Where Angels Fear to Tread* compared with the outside view in *A Room With a View*. *A Passage To India* is a great work because the Indians are almost always depicted two-dimensionally, as they appear to the English eye. They and their country are little more than a backcloth against which an English middle-class drama is staged.

Of course there are writers like Koestler who have inherited a 'universalist' outlook, but their books are not novels but Baedekers of contemporary life. Mr Kavanagh writes more permanently himself. And as for Catholic Universalism in art, I have been hoping that Mr Waugh or Mr Greene would write a book about Catholic Ireland, because then their true stature as writers would become apparent here. Mr Waugh has, I am glad to say, written a story about Anglo-Ireland. Short and slight as it was, it was more than sufficient as an index of his universalism. In his practical advice to the Irish writer Mr Kavanagh contradicts himself again. In the last instalment of his diary he urged them not to write at all if they had not genius. 'Genius alone counts.' 'The rest of the world must accept its own sterile fate. . . Better not write at all than write mediocre verse.' 'The rest of the world should be satisfied by loving God, by praising his works and the greatest work of God on this earth is the dancing flame of the poet's imagination.' And he tells us that there are only about twenty of these dancing flames in Europe.

But elsewhere in his diary he says just the opposite. He tells us that the 'worst frustration is intellectual and artistic' and that 'deaf mutes go mad'. 'We *must* express ourselves' and 'nobody need be a mediocrity, if he is himself'.

One might accept these contradictions as half-baked poetical aphorisms shortly to be fused together over a dancing flame, if so much solid material, denunciations of Radio Éireann and the like, had not been flung into Mr Kavanagh's crucible. Clearly his advice is meant to be practical, and the ordinary Irishman of literary inclinations is faced with the dilemma of either going mad in silence or else becoming the twenty-first genius in Europe. This cannot be.

These diaries were meant for speech, not print. At their best they are paradoxical challenges flung out to stimulate thought, but in a monthly the challenge cannot be met, and the effect is chaotic.

There were many good stories and poems and constructive essays in *Envoy*, and it always gave a generous hearing to its own critics. A memorable letter was published from Matthew Horgan in which he urged that 'the work to be done here is not by the angry men but by the quiet voices which drone on behind the animal cries', and he was not afraid to appeal for 'minor works of literary value'. This modest claim is more likely to be answered than Mr Kavanagh's, who is so sure that genius will flourish in the desert like a rose, that he wishes to sterilize the soil of minor talents, or so he said. On the contrary, a long and laborious task of irrigation confronts us and a whole forest of minor talents may have to flourish and die before our soil is rich enough to sustain a single genius.

[1954]

16

GRAHAM GREENE AND STEPHEN SPENDER: THE SENSE OF EVIL AND THE SENSE OF GUILT

I

Graham Greene and Stephen Spender are like two explorers who leave the same outpost in opposite directions and travelling in a wide circle, converge on each other again. They have seen all the familiar features from opposite angles, but when their experiences are collated, the sense of contradiction disappears. Greene is a traditionalist with some wayward inclinations, Spender is a rather hesitant experimentalist. I wish it were possible to confront Spender's autobiography, *World Within World*, with something more revealing and exhaustive than Greene's short personal memoir in his volume of critical sketches, *The Lost Childhood*.* But perhaps the bleakness of this memoir is in itself an autobiographical comment. Greene is buttoned up securely into his close-fitting philosophy, while Spender is always unbuttoning his looser one. Yet I would say that their obsession with buttons brings them curiously near to each other and makes them fit representatives of their age. They are both constantly concerned with life and society and the restraints that men should and should not impose on each other. They are inseparable in their dissent, like two sisters quarrelling in the family home. The one wants the front door locked in case there's a burglar, the other wants it ajar, in case there's a fire. Or so they say. But they are arguing not from objective probabilities but from personal phobias.

* Graham Greene, *The Lost Childhood and Other Essays* (London 1951); Kenneth Allott and Miriam Farris, *The Art of Graham Greene* (London 1951); Stephen Spender, *World Within World (London 1951).*

Greene's autobiographical essay, short as it is, is an invaluable commentary and corrective to his astute critical essays. It is plain that he had good reason for his belief in bolts and buttons, in social restraints and categorical imperatives. As a child all manner of strange thoughts and desires, the birth pangs perhaps of his great talents, made themselves felt and had to be suppressed. As an established writer he has not liberated himself from this fear of monstrous and seemingly supernatural intrusions. There is nothing discreditable about his idiosyncrasies or Mr Spender's but those who do not share them must dread any attempt to base on them a universally applicable philosophy. As a boy Graham Greene experimented nine or ten times with suicide. After he had run away from school his parents sent him to be psychoanalysed. His months at the psychoanalyst were, he said, perhaps the happiest in his life. He emerged 'correctly orientated' once more and yet 'wrung dry' and incapable of taking an aesthetic interest in anything. His boredom seems to have brought him to a quiet despair, from which, in a zestless way, he tried several times to rescue himself with a revolver which was kept in the corner cupboard, using it more as a stimulant (it was a six-chambered revolver with only one charge and there was an exciting risk) than a gateway to everlasting peace.

Readers of his novels may feel that this conviction that life is flat and grey has never left him and, like the fox without a tail, he has persuaded many beside himself that the only true normality is abnormality. But if we accept his philosophy as a mere mechanism of personal adjustment, it is not contagious. Like a foreign language it obscures but cannot neutralize his excellent craftmanship.

The Greene world is stricken with an induced paralysis, as though to make it more amenable to his skilful dissection. Hope is dead unregretted, like a nagging nerve that had to be killed. Boredom and torpor are surgically guaranteed like a eunuch's passivity. They are proof against life's infinite variety and can only be dissipated by an explosive from the corner cupboard. For the catastrophes that build up the plot are irruptions from outside, they are contrived and inorganic. Mr Greene's Remorseless Destiny is a mechanized scarecrow more impressive than the old broom-handle contraptions of the Hardy school but not more true to life.

In Mr Greene's last collection of critical essays we can see this technique of self adjustment and literary craftmanship doing duty as a philosophy. Like most makeshifts it seems to me clumsy and destructive and it is applied irresponsibly for the discrediting of Havelock Ellis and Samuel Butler, and, for some rather odd reasons, for the exaltation of Henry James. Mr Greene is often a generous and sensitive critic of those whose philosophy is alien to his own, of Herbert Read, for example, and Walter de la Mare. But on the whole his generosity is rationed rather primly, and he gives the impression of a bruised soul searching for soul-mates and resentful of those who are unbruised or have found a balm for their bruises which is not his own.

Mr Greene's scepticism about the possibility of human happiness seems to derive from an unhappy childhood. How many uncompromising and intolerant philosophies are based on childish misery! The scales are weighted then so heavily against rebellion and unconventionality that our wretchedness seems predestined and to resist it sacrilege. Sometimes we carry with us to the end of our days a quite artificial resignation to the system of oppressor and oppressed. Dickens, as Greene observes in his very penetrating essay, 'The Burden of Childhood', was one of those, a minority I think, who learnt sympathy and understanding for the whole human race from his years of defenceless unhappiness. But Kipling's Auntie Rosa and Saki (H. H. Munro)'s Aunt Augusta had a different effect on their victims to Dickens's blacking factory, filling them with indignation and hate, which boiled over in their writings. Greene compares Munro very justly to 'a chivalrous highwayman'. Behind all his stories he discovers 'an exacting sense of justice'. On the one hand 'with Kipling revenge rather than justice seems to be the motive (Auntie Rosa had established herself in the mind of her victim and corrupted it)'. He protected himself 'with manliness, knowingness, imaginary adventures of soldiers and empire builders'. Kipling had sensibility without judgment and for the most part it was on harmless people that he discharged this immense burden of resentment which he carried about with him.

One would naturally look for an Auntie Rosa in Mr Greene's childhood, but I expect that his resentment was not focused on any single human figure, or, as with Dickens, on any social injustice. Mr Greene was miserable in a middle-class, privileged way in a liberal humanitarian democracy and he is forced to condemn, not the abuses of society, but society itself. I think that, as with

Kipling, his sweeping damnations are a measure of his shortcomings as well as of his sensibility. Outside his craft, let us admit it, he is not very intelligent. His essay on Havelock Ellis, for example, is written with the same assured stupidity with which Kipling wrote of the Church of Rome.

In Gothic Art you will occasionally find the serpent entwined with more Christian symbols and adapted to ecclesiastical decoration by the cross on his tail. In Mr Greene's work you will sometimes find, as in this essay, a secular malice converted by a turn of phrase to Christian usage. Havelock Ellis, who had explored the recesses of the human mind in a spirit of enquiry not of condemnation, is reproached for his lack of religion and compared to 'a Father Christmas from Selfridge's with a fake prophet's air'; his work is dismissed as 'full of case histories and invincible ignorance'. Greene's essay purports to be a review of Mr Ellis's autobiography and the fact that he had dared to reprint it is sure proof of the sickness of English criticism today. For Greene has ignored or misunderstood Ellis's account of his wife's nature, which is so lovingly and faithfully described, and attempts to charge him with having driven his wife 'to the last breakdown of health and sanity' by his 'advanced' ideas. (One recalls E. M. Forster's the Rev. Cuthbert Eager, who said that old Emerson 'murdered his wife', adding hastily 'in the sight of God'!) When we reflect that Greene declared that perhaps the happiest months of his life were spent in the care of a psycholanalyst, it is plain that the writer's attitude to 'advanced ideas' might well be the subject of a case history, a complicated tangle of love and hate, devotion and betrayal. In *The Ministry of Fear* he makes the arch-villain, who is a cowardly murderer and a Nazi spy, into the head of a psychological nursing home. Even his very admiring critics, Mr Allott and Miss Farris, detect here 'a flavour of wartime highbrow baiting'. They complain that though Greene's heroes are solitaries, he dislikes the isolation of the intellectual and in the portrayal of Dr Forester, the psychologist, 'prejudice seems to have stampeded him into accepting herd warmth at almost any price'.

But I would suspect that Mr Greene's anti-intellectual bias is a mere idiosyncrasy, a distaste for the pursuit of knowledge, which has escaped challenge and insinuated itself into respectable company because of the cross on its tail. The Greene hero is permanently out of reach of the grapes; he has wearied of intellectual independence before he has striven for it. He is the type of solitary who snarls suspiciously if he is caressed. He is like a pariah dog who has lost his pack but refuses to become domesticated. The pack, invisible and unreachable, remains the focus of yearning and mystical devotion. Mr Greene's pity for the excluded is balanced precisely by his resentment of the emancipated. It is a negative kind of pity and he sees it in others as an occupational affliction of the just and the gentle, 'the horrible and horrifying emotion of pity'. He sees it as horrible because often it leads its victim, its Rowes and Scobies, to compassionate mercy-killings, adulteries, suicides. And Havelock Ellis is to Mr Greene an ignoramus and a fake Father Christmas and he has a Selfridge beard simply because of his tendency to see these disasters as sorrows rather than sins.

Greene's speculations about sin are as esoteric as the speculations of a Jew about a pork-pie. Is it really sin? Is it really pork? There is little moral censure about the enquiry. Sin is to violate a tabu, not to deceive or to be cruel. Mr Greene only once, I think, in these very Christian essays uses the word 'goodness', and then in connection with its tendency to 'wilt' into philanthropy and kindness. He sneers at Samuel Butler and his admirers for their determination to be Honest Men (ironical capitals), 'with an inability to tell polite untruths', and he shudders fastidiously at the Victorian progressives almost as the two Miss Allens shuddered at old Mr Emerson. The Emersons and their like stand by 'small and dingy shops' in 'scrubby stained and smelly clothes', reading 'ugly, cheap reprints from the Rationalist Press'. They suggest to Mr Greene a crippled childhood, attics, blackbeetles, a grim grammar school. Mr Greene shows such a refined and wincing sensibility when confronted with the scrubby, the smelly, the cheap, that one wonders why as an artist he is so irresistibly attracted to them. There is no warmth of love about his researches, no curiosity, no hope. What is this fastidious person looking for as he pokes the garbage over with the ferrule of his rolled umbrella? Only treasure trove or the consciousness of a mission would draw so exclusive a person so constantly to squalor and misery. These essays show plainly enough that he is looking for a Sense of Sin, which he seems to connect with a Sense of Evil. Samuel Butler had not a trace, Dickens scarcely a trace, but in the repugnant home-life of Havelock Ellis, which he explores with the toe of his boot, he seems to divine, despite the absence of dogmatic belief, a 'buried religious feeling'. He finds tenderness and love and nostalgic regret and Mr Greene has decided that these are the prerogatives of the religious but that the 'advanced' leave out of account 'all natural un-eugenic feelings'.

Mr Greene is the modern kind of Luddite. Those of the last century rejected the mechanical inventions of the age. But the modern Luddite has accommodated himself to the industrial revolution, to telephones, to the wireless and the cinema. He merely rejects those intellectual conceptions and attitudes which are the spiritual counterpart of material invention. Havelock Ellis, whom Mr Greene in his Luddite mood has charged with 'invincible ignorance', introduced into the world an engine of reform as irresistible as Stephenson's Rocket. Mr Greene is heavily committed to the modern world: he has not only endured that his books should be filmed, but he has also been successfully psychoanalysed. Yet he rushes at Mr Havelock Ellis's collected works like a Luddite at a lace machine. Surely he is trying to stir up among us the same schizophrenic conflict which rages in his own mind. Yet his problem, how to eat your cake and yet reject it with scorn, is one of his own making and he seems to solve it in the usual way, deluding himself that the next best thing to renouncing a pleasure or a privilege is to accept it ungraciously.

It is probable that we have entered a phase of history in which personal relations will at first be complicated, not eased, by new discovery and experiment. Often the old ignorance will seem preferable to the new enlightenment, which illuminates suffering and conflict but cannot yet show us how to cure them. The Churches once said that we should not tamper with the body, not even the bodies of the dead, and anatomy was long forbidden (not only Christians but Arabs and Indians have shared these intelligible misgivings), and perhaps if we could avoid violating these ancient pre-Christian tabus we should be none the worse. But we cannot. We should not waste our time trying. Only a minute fraction of the mental and physical suffering of our time could be cured by Mr Greene's revival of moribund dogma about sin.

Mr Greene's essays on Henry James reveal clearly how personal is his philosophy. He is like a refugee in a sanctuary whose inviolability depends on its repute rather than its defences. Its holiness is thrown into relief by the sinfulness of the world that surrounds it, so that those outside who see evil everywhere must be regarded as allies and viewed with special favour by the guardians and patrons of the precincts. I cannot see how otherwise Mr Greene should feel this curious sense of solidarity with Henry James, who, if we are to judge him as Greene does, by his letters and the moods of his characters, never ventured inside a Christian church without a frisson of disloyalty. And obviously James's interest in colourful rites and vestments derive more from the collectomania of the well-to-do American than from the Christian renunciation of the world. The most one can say is that the frisson was sometimes half-pleasurable as frissons so often are.

Excavating for 'buried religious feeling' in Henry James's work, Mr Greene puts his finds on the table. They are pathetically meagre. Henry James took a pleasure in a visit to St Peter's and Mr Greene draws satisfaction from the following account of the experience.

> To crown my day, on my way home, I met His Holiness in person driving in prodigious purple state – sitting dim within the shadow of his coach with two uplifted benedictory figures – like some dusky Hindoo idol in the depths of its shrine. . . From the high tribune of a great chapel of St Peter's I have heard in the Papal choir a strange old man sing in a shrill unpleasant soprano. I've seen troops of little tortured neophytes clad in scarlet, marching and counter-marching, ducking and flopping, like poor little raw recruits for the heavenly host.

Then what other traces have we of buried religion? Strether in *The Ambassadors* used to go into Notre Dame, yielding to some impulse, 'which he amused himself by thinking of as a private concession to cowardice'. He went so that for a moment the things of the world 'could fall into abeyance'. 'That was the cowardice, probably – to dodge them, to beg the question, not to deal with it in the hard outer light; but his own oblivions were too brief, too vain to hurt anyone but himself.'

Rowland Mallet, another character, in 1875, found in St Peter's 'relief from most contrarieties. . . from a heartache to a Roman rain', and Mr Greene finds in 'The Altar of the Dead' a promising, though ill-informed interest in prayers for the deceased.

And that is almost all. In the last analysis it is on Henry James's Sense of Evil that Mr Greene bases his tottering hypothesis. And to convince us of this sense of evil Mr Greene uses paradoxical interpretations that he would censure surely as over-intellectual in a Marxist or a Freudian. For example Mr Greene is fascinated by broad hints of an obsession with evil in 'The Turn of the Screw'. Unfortunately James has explicitly stated of this story that it was 'a fairy tale pure and simple. . . an amusette to catch those not easily caught', and Mr Greene admits, 'So a valuable ally must be relinquished.' But *can* Mr Greene relinquish this ally? Not he! In two other articles he uses 'The Turn of the Screw' as evidence of his theory. James was 'blinding his reader with a bold sleight of hand'. He was not being frank. 'One cannot avoid a conviction that here he (James) touched and recoiled from an important inhibition.' Mr Greene worries away at it like a dog with a rubber bone, picking it up and dropping it in an ecstasy of self-deception. Yet I cannot believe that he wishes others to be tormented by his unhappy obsessions. I am sure he is looking for comrades in misfortune rather than converts. The proof of that is that he is reassured rather than discomfited to find that the sense of evil which he detects in Henry James can be traced in other members of the James family but definitely allied to psychological and mental peculiarity. Henry's father 'was intermittently attacked by a sense of perfectly insane and abject terror' and his sister Alice was a prey to suicidal tendencies. To clinch the matter Mr Greene quotes a horrifying daytime hallucination of William James, who saw an epileptic idiot, which left him for months a prey to irrational terror. An ordinary student would be convinced by these instances that the Jamesian 'sense of evil' was a family misfortune like consumption or weak sight. But to Mr Greene the hereditary recurrence of these horrible obsessions is a guarantee of their validity. And by succumbing to these visions the gifted James family gave to them a horrible authenticity and importance. 'If ever a man's imagination was clouded by the Pit,' says Mr Greene, approvingly, 'it was James!'

But Greene tries to prove that not only had Henry James a hereditary addiction to the sense of evil, but it received a morbid confirmation in his youth, when he evaded military service in the American Civil War on an insufficient plea of ill-health. For, according to Mr Greene, with James 'the idea of treachery. . . was always attached to his sense of evil'. Next we note that Greene's very able and industrious biographers, Allott and Farris, detect the same twin obsessions in his work. So it is less curious to find that Mr Greene, having identified to his satisfaction these two obsessions in James's writings, next argues that they were leading James to the same goal to which they led himself. He declares that James came very close to a direct statement of his belief in Hell and Purgatory. In fact of course Mr Desmond MacCarthy was correct in claiming that James had not a trace of religious feeling. Greene's argument remains interesting, though, because it reveals how a superficial and inconsequent philosophy will give an adequate foundation to an impressive artistic effort. How can Mr Greene continue to cherish so tenderly and proudly his sense of evil, after he has shown to us how in others it can develop out of mental aberration and cowardice? I can only suppose that he reveres it as the source of his art, the pea in the shoe that provoked him into creativity, and that he would feel lonely and disloyal without it like a Moslem lady without her veil.

He stresses elsewhere this fancied connection between art and the sense of supernatural evil, when he quotes with approval Mr T. S. Eliot, 'with the disappearance of the idea of Original Sin, with the disappearance of the idea of intense moral struggle, the human beings presented to us both in poetry and in prose fiction. . . tend to become less real'. And Greene considers that without the chiaroscuro of black and white (he absurdly attributes to Henry James the view that men were either 'of God's or the Devil's party'), the characters of later distinguished novelists, like Mrs Woolf and E. M. Forster, 'wandered like cardboard symbols through a world that was paper-thin'.

Have we here a prophet rebuking sin or a black-and-white artist decrying water colours? Mr Greene, like some other writers, mounts the pulpit in order to chastise Mrs Woolf and Mr Forster and to advance some questionable opinions about literature. It is hard to fight back at these opinions without appearing to show disrespect to the venerable vestments in which they are clothed. Some time ago Miss Stevie Smith flung a brickbat or two at a group of neo-Christian essayists, accusing them, if I remember rightly, of a repellent blend of 'gaiety, cruelty and knowingness'. Those who have been cowed by Mr Greene's cleverness and learning into tolerating his sombre philosophy will draw from the evidence of his cruelty the courage to rebel. Beverley Nichols is fair game for the highbrow critic, but Mr Greene's chastisement of him is impermissible. Nichols, the man, who is as God made him, is taunted as unmasculine boys are taunted in grammar schools, while Nichols the writer, who has substituted for his real self a bestselling one, is allowed to escape.

I do not know what lies beneath all this débris in Mr Greene's mind but something that is not properly dead has been interred there. It would be justice to call up Havelock Ellis from 'the Pit' to excavate but I doubt if he would find much in his line there. Nor do I think it is some Auntie Rosa who is still giving trouble. A mere family tyrant would long ago have decomposed among Mr Greene's caustic thoughts. I think it is not a person, but an entire institution, perhaps Berkhamsted School. The ferment of his mind has acted on the place and modified it but there is a hard core of tyranny and tedium which no acid will dissolve. Mr Greene has at last had to come to terms with it and to call it the Sense of Evil, and to say that it is eternal and inevitable and to find for it analogies and apologists in the external world. But the rest of us cannot be expected to base our philosophies on Mr Greene's unhappy adolescence.

II

Stephen Spender and Graham Greene ought to be valuable correctives to each other, but the idea of mutual admonition has not I think occurred to either of them. Spender's solitary reference to Greene in his autobiography is polite and Greene says not a word about Spender. Certainly Greene would find *World Within World,* as he found Havelock Ellis's *My Life,* 'far too intimate for general reading', yet I doubt whether he will ever say so. I think they are both of them conscientious members of the artists' trade union, whose senior representatives do not attack each other, till they are dead. Is there nobility in this mutual tolerance or is there collusion? Why does one think of those French and German armament factories, which were said to guarantee protection for each other in Franco-German wars? If Mr Greene and Mr Spender were serious about their philosophies they would know they were handling explosive as lethal to society as we know it as anything produced by Krupp or Hotchkiss. The supporters of the Liberal society, as Spender conceives it, are the deadly enemies of the Catholic society championed by Mr Greene. Readers of the two books I have quoted cannot be unaware of this implacable opposition. Yet I doubt whether either Greene or Spender have committed themselves with more than a fraction of their minds or that the armaments, which they have been piling up, were ever meant for war. Like Krupps and Hotchkiss they may find tension more rewarding than conflict. Their art and their reputation would not, I think, survive a real *kulturkampf* in which first principles were not only invoked but applied.

In the meantime Spender, a representative of what he calls the 'Divided Generation', is rather a drooping figure to oppose to the more dogmatic Greene with his nicely tailored moralities and his upright carriage assisted by ethical corsets. I think that Spender reveals the liberal creed most clearly in an admirable reference to the philosophy of E. M. Forster, 'his almost pagan amorality combined with his minute preoccupation with moral issues, his love of freedom combined with his impressive self-discipline'. It is surely true to say that the liberal is always engaged on this expert dovetailing of freedom and discipline. He is always paring and splicing, taking in a bit here, letting out a bit there; he has no plan of campaign beyond day-to-day solicitude and the conviction that by foresight and ingenious contrivance men can be made happy and free without hurting each other. I doubt if Spender, though, has ever been a liberal in this meticulous way. He seems to have practised very conscientiously the pagan amorality but he does not appear to have studied how to integrate his philosophy of self-expression into society as it is or might be.

Sometimes idealism is more like a physiological phase than an intellectual conviction. It is time-conditioned and starts to flag when the hair grows thin and the dentist begins to talk of a plate. The very attractive portrait of himself which Mr Spender uses as a frontispiece, an open collar, a sun-beam on his ruffled hair, and the shy side glance of a fawn, is dated 1932 and gives a misleading period air to what would seem to be his deepest convictions. It made me revolt against the modern practice of illustrating seductively the story of our heart as though it was a packet of seeds. The search for lost time, if it is serious, begins well below camera level. Like Proust and Joyce and the great ones, we should leave our faces behind, as we leave our overcoats when we go down a coal mine. Mr Spender is a serious investigator but I think that in *World Within World* he makes the mistake of supposing that the inner and the outer world overlap and merge, whereas as a general rule they alternate and cannot be contemplated together. If in a train journey at night we wish to watch the flying fields outside, we must totally exclude the bright static images of ourselves upon the window pane. Mr Spender tries by a trick of the eye to see the two worlds at once and, though he often achieves it, it is at the cost of clarity and sense.

I think we diminish writers by our habit of classifying them, but Mr Spender is ready to be considered as a spokesman of the Divided Generation, a sad and yet somehow romantic group like the Wild Geese or the Mohicans. He and his friends take a bitter-sweet satisfaction in the thought that a certain phase of human hope and endeavour exactly synchronized with the progress and passing of their youth. The illusion is pardonable, for in 1932 for some reason (it may have been because of the death or disillusionment of an earlier generation in the 1914-18 war) the belief in a changed world had linked itself provisionally with youth, with open collars, with bronze bodies and forest camps and hazardous applications of revolutionary theories of sex. The young people thought of themselves as pioneers in a new world but in fact most of them were only the luxury tourists who follow in the wake of the explorer when the ground has been cleared and the routes marked. The Divided Generation contributed extraordinarily little beyond some well-written poems and stories to the emancipation of the human spirit; the youth movement itself, which had centred on Germany, ended in appalling catastrophe. The pioneer work had been done by a previous generation, the bearded philosophers and the crusty eccentrics with 'scrubby, stained and smelly clothes', in whom with such sound intuition Mr Greene recognized his enemies. So that Mr Spender's belief that an important epoch ended with his youth is only partially true. The age of emotional tourism had yielded disappointing results, but the findings of the explorers, who preceded it, have not been seriously challenged.

The Divided Generation was cliquey and in love with itself. It fell from the heights of over-confidence to the depths of despair. Now Narcissus has scrambled out of the pool and stands, damp and discouraged, looking at the muddied water. But instead of saying, 'I am vain,' he says, 'All is vanity!' Indeed otherworldliness is popular with many writers today simply because a collective avowal of original sin is less bruising and intellectually exacting to the individual than a sober consideration of avoidable follies.

I think that Mr Spender, even when he was expressing his individuality most abundantly, was still anxious to keep open this loophole of escape into collective guilt and atonement. The philosophy of Mr T. S. Eliot is a curious link between Spender and Greene. When he was young Spender rebelled tentatively against Eliot's 'escapism into the past', as he dared to consider it, but he repented of this and came ultimately to admire Eliot's notion that the past was in some way 'integrated', while the present is 'fragmentary'. He considered that Eliot was one of those happy few, who had secured his survival by detaching himself from liberalism and resisting 'the imprisoned preoccupation of his age with its own time'. The pivot of Eliot's philosophy, which Spender does not now find repulsive, was despair about the material world, somewhat relieved by backward glances at history. Eliot confessed to him once that for the future of mankind, he saw nothing but 'internecine conflict' and that 'what matters is whether I believe in original sin'. That is to say, acquiescence in the incurable nature of human ills is a necessary stage towards that Eliot resignation which Mr Spender seems to commend.

Pessimism has become a virtue, but it is pessimism of a rather recondite sort. 'However much the individual might be committed to social tasks, he belonged to an eternal order of events, where he was not the product and victim of his time.' This seems a mere juggling with the dimensions of time and place in the interests of equanimity. Of course we do know that against the background of prehistory our best and foulest deeds dwindle into insignificance. But equally, looking through the other end of the telescope, we can see our most trivial act or thought setting up an infinite chain of repercussions. Every sneeze is weighted with consequence. These ideas are valuable in certain circumstances, as drugs and stimulants, but a wise man will not become an addict to either. Mr Spender, an impressionable person, is strongly susceptible to both forms of auto-intoxication. He ends the book in a trance of solipsism, induced by an overdose of these ideas of the 'smallness of human life compared to the infinitude of time'. All that remains is the 'desire to love and be loved', just because we are 'ignorant and miserable and surrounded by unknowns of time and space'. And 'like shipwrecked people upon a sea. . . the only sanity must lie in helping one another'. So we are back where we began. The book is rounded off with an admirably written description of the author's schooldays. There is no doubt a parable here, but I don't quite know how to read it. Has Odysseus come back to Ithaca and the domestic pieties? Has Narcissus come back to the pool with a new suit of clothes on? Will some Daddy-figure, some Auntie Rosa in the form of a categorical imperative, slip back on to the empty throne where the Liberal Ethic once reigned?

Mr Spender sees that 'sense of social guilt' as one of the mainsprings of the revolutionary impulse in the bourgeoisie, and no doubt he is right. But it is an unreliable emotion, misdirecting the goodwill which it calls to its aid. The knowledge that he had £300 a year and that he was raised above 'those marginal existences, whose lives registered as delicately as the needle of an instrument booms and slumps', drove him into politics, yet made him 'unable to criticize a thief or a blackmailer'. 'I could never,' he explains rather foggily, 'feel within myself the rightness of a social system which would rebuke the wrongness in others.' And he reproaches himself with this attitude: 'I should have been tougher and more cynical, accepting my own position in the world and expecting others to accept theirs.'

If he can reject in this way the sense of social guilt without any feeling of intellectual recantation, he must acknowledge that it is purely subjective. What is its origin then in the mind and the reason of its great influence? Only a handful of the possessing classes is ever seriously incommoded by this sense of guilt, yet it has always been an important phenomenon. In one generation a few youthful writers affected by it, headed by Auden and Isherwood and Spender, managed to give its special character to the 'Pink Decade'. Why do such people so often love the proletariat, when the proletariat so seldom loves them? Those who gibe at 'parlour pinks' usually attribute their pinkness to ignorance and affectation. Yet Spender, like the others, was exceptionally clear-sighted and straightforward; he knew quite well that the proletariat bored him though his description of his war-time associates is the reverse of boring. I think too that he would have agreed that privilege develops the faculties and sharpens the sensibilities and that therefore the rule of the unprivileged for the first generation of its establishment would be crude and insensitive. But the heart has its reasons. Many of the Pinks felt a bitter dislike of their own class and milieu and the proletariat had at least done them no harm. We judge people by the injury they have done us, not by their capacity to injure our descendants. The English bourgeois intellectual has often an abiding and legitimate grievance against the society in which he grew up. Otherwise it is hard to explain the passionate recoil (in opposite direction) of Greene and Spender from bourgeois traditions. Greene is the more bitter of the two, since he sees the whole world as evil not merely the section of it that bred him. The sense of evil and the sense of social guilt show us two publicly approved methods of discharging a burden of private resentment and shame. To the conventionally progressive an orgy of social guilt may be as comforting as an abject general confession can be to the conventionally devout. On the surface this collective contrition seems respectable enough, but does it not often require a closer analysis?

Mr Spender is so honest, observant and uninhibited that we have abundance of evidence here for judging the Divided Generation if we knew how to use it. The question arises, were they ever liberals in the sense that Stephen's father and his uncle were? Had he or his friends ever bothered themselves as the elder Spenders did with the problem of extending to wider and wider circles the privileges of the higher classes? I think they were mostly in rebellion against these alleged social advantages, their education for example. The revolutionary changes they wished could not be effected by any political party. As this book reveals they made, in the name of the free individual, far more sweeping demands on society than the elder Spenders would have made even for themselves. When they elected for Communism, as Stephen Spender and others of them did, it was the destructive negative side of it which appealed to them, the overthrow of the bourgeoisie and the cruel régimes in Italy, Germany and Spain, which had been reared in its defence. I don't think the positive Communist programme attracted them in the least and when later it was forced on their attention they repudiated it. They were really passive anarchists, hoping, in a mystical way, that the liberties they wished for would grow up in the fissures of a shattered society, like ferns in a crumbling wall. That was why dissolving Weimar Germany held such an appeal for them and why their political activities disquieted Virginia Woolf and the leaders of the Bloomsbury circle.

The Bloomsbury group had in fact lodged itself satisfactorily in a crevice of the still intact fabric of society, against many of whose canons it was in revolt. Ethically it was like a self-governing republic within the framework of an empire. Its members enjoyed already some of the privileges of self-expression, which the Divided Generation desired, but its authority, its security, depended on a certain exclusiveness. As Spender says, it was rather snobbish. The crevice could not be indefinitely enlarged without imperilling the structure of society and alarming its guardians. That is to say the exacting Bloomsbury ethic operated in a more or less closed circle, focused on two or three distinguished households. It drew its sanctions from the mutual trust and affection which united its members, who had freed themselves from many of the social conventions, not by a social struggle but by their assurance that they were an aristocracy sometimes of birth and wealth, always of intellect. They were too self-sufficient to crusade for their convictions. For example, it is hard to imagine Virginia Woolf campaigning very confidently on behalf of the legalisation of suicide or euthanasia, yet when she found herself faced with the decay of her intellect, she consulted her own sense of what was right and took her life.

This Bloomsbury way of life was not, as Mr R. F. Harrod shows in his recent life of J. M. Keynes, for export. Divorced from personal solicitude, the intimate analysis of feelings and motives to which the group subjected each other would become cruel and gossiping; its unflinching vocabulary would become a weapon of malice. Inevitably there would be a recoil towards Victorian reticence and suppression.

The Divided Generation inherited from Bloomsbury its belief in persons rather than in principles, its difficult code of moral freedom tempered by self-discipline, yet it has less focus and friendly solidarity, less faith. I suppose their leaders were insubstantial figures, compared with the Woolfs, Keynes, Stracheys and Russells, not so intellectually confident or materially established. Perhaps too the spectacle of social collapse tempted them to think that the barriers were everywhere breaking down and that a whole new world would enter into relations with them. They need not be satisfied with a tolerated enclave in the old one.

To Communist critics, like Christopher Caudwell, these left-wing poets seemed to be Lone Wolves, whose chief value to the party lay in their destructive hatred of bourgeois restraints. It was plain that they would reject Communist discipline with equal defiance. In a previous century they might have formed their own sect or school, but they lacked even the cohesion of Bloomsbury, not recognizing themselves for what they were, a minority group, whose strength lay in concentration and not in diffusion. They preached their gospel of individualism and self-realization round all the Messianic communities but without success. A few of them became Communists or Churchmen or members of mystical communities, most of them were deflected in some degree from their individualism by the mass movements which they tried to influence.

The Bloomsbury group were sensitive interpreters of foreign cultures. Their successors, more consciously European, seemed happiest on the crumbling margins. Berlin in the Weimar days was rather like Corinth in early Christian time, a cosmopolitan dunghill, in which delicate flowers and rank weeds could flourish side by side. The artist prospered there as he did in Russia in the first chaotic years of Bolshevism. Mr Spender says of it: 'When I was living a life dangerous to myself and impossible to justify to others I was writing my best early poems', and he says that he and others used Germany 'as a kind of a cure for our personal problems'. Referring to the same period, he says: 'I sought to discover my real self by behaviour, which outraged my ideal self. The result of this was a series of relationships undertaken in a spirit of opportunism. Yet I was too much an idealist to maintain a cynical attitude.'

I think these quotations show that, if any of the reformist spirit of his liberal forbears had descended to Mr Spender, it would have expressed itself more naturally in the ethical than in the political sphere. For the Divided Generation felt indulgently towards many ethical heresies. When, as in the Spanish Civil War, Spender's revolutionary ethics came in conflict with his revolutionary politics, it was the rebel of the outer world who capitulated to the rebel of the inner one. Yet Spender has done all his public crusading in the, to him, less important sphere of politics. (This displacement of ardour is not usual. How many secret streams flow into the broad river of political discontent?) But now his inability to justify to others his way of life, to relate it to society or to a rebel group within society, makes him as defenceless as an alien without a passport. His candour and his scruples will not by themselves establish the innocence of which he feels assured. That is the tragedy of the individualist; some niggling fastidiousness, some pride in his uniqueness, will often prevent him from co-operating in the construction of an impressive dogmatism behind which to shelter his non-conformities.

In the case of Mr Spender a more reasoned apologia is needed to raise his autobiography from the level of the curious to the significant, from the case history to the critique of contemporary ethic. As it is, he will not even succeed in annoying Mr Graham Greene, as Havelock Ellis did, for the authoritarian is always indulgent to amorality of an individualistic cast. What rouses his wrath is the moral person who flaunts a private code of ethics. To be wise without paying tribute to the source of all wisdom is worse than folly. It is a graver offence against society to own an illicit still and be sober than to be drunk in the streets. Mr Spender will be scolded and then forgiven for the lesser sin of intemperance. Will he ever, like Auden, lump together his ethical with his political heresies and renounce them both?

Mr Spender tells an anecdote which shows perhaps that he prides himself on his romantic inability to fit his emotional impulses into a social framework. At his wedding in a burst of spontaneous generosity he thrust some silver toast-racks, trays 'and so forth', the gifts of his wealthier friends, on the poorer wedding guests, as they left. That is the act of a large-hearted Caliph, not of a middle-aged liberal. If you are conventional enough to have a wedding, you must observe the rules of weddings. Presents are tokens of regard and to give them away is to rebuff a gesture which you appear to have solicited. Mr Spender's assault on the proprieties often has a loud echo, because it is contained by the four walls of conventions which he has failed to breach. We are all of us tethered to our past, or, if you like, to our social background, but it is only the more adventurous who find this out by straining the tether till it is taut. The others believe themselves free. Mr Spender's frolics, abandoned as they may seem, never took him far enough from the tethering post for a real test of strength.

None the less this book is of great importance, because it shows how very feeble were the attempts which the Divided Generation made to co-ordinate the inner and the outer world. Their incursions into politics were more like plundering raids than serious attempts at engagements and in ethics they were emotional buccaneers, not reformers.

What is the wider significance of the collapse of the Divided Generation? Does it mean the bankruptcy of the liberal revolutionary spirit? I think it means merely that the intellectual cliques which have so long been the standard bearers of liberal thought, have lost their *raison d'être.* As a clique the Divided Generation had a clear heredity through the Bloomsbury group to Leslie Stephen and the Victorian Rationalists and through them to their immediate predecessors, Wilberforce and the Clapham Evangelicals. Each stage in the descent marked an evaporation of influence as the state closed its ranks more solidly against the intellectual and as the clique became more heterodox and more loosely knit.

The modern bureaucratic state is as impervious to minority enthusiasms as any autocratic régime of the seventeenth century. In those days the sect rather than the clique was the vehicle of revolutionary liberalism. Its members repudiated society because they despaired of reforming it. The sects offered a refuge from the inhumanity of the state, not, as later, an armed camp for its subjugation. Sometimes it looks as if those days might return. Freedom, the freedom of the inner world, might seem to have its best guarantee, not in legislation extorted from the government, but in pledges of mutual support and tolerance exchanged between individuals in the shadow of the state.

[1951]

17

TWO CRITICS: E. M. FORSTER AND EDMUND WILSON

E. M. Forster is rather an isolated figure in English letters, whose high standards of intellectual integrity have resisted the assaults of the modern world better than anyone else's. Edmund Wilson's recent collection of essays, a literary chronicle of the forties, show him to be an American counterpart of the great English writer.*

Superficially they are poles apart. Wilson is robust and pugnacious as a reviewer; the shoddy, the sentimental, the commercial come in for very rough handling and as a writer of fiction he has no inhibitions; all that is human is material for his art. Forster is very different in temperament and tactics. His hatred of the second-rate and the fraudulent is as deadly and his claims for the writer are as sweeping but his blows are aimed with shrewdness rather than force. Even obtuse people will be on the alert to man the defences of Philistia when Wilson thunders by, but Forster is more likely to slip past the frontier guards and plant his time-bomb in the citadel.

But no less than temperament, history and geography have influenced their tactics. As a novelist, Mr Forster's claims on posterity are evident to us in these islands, where the classics are still re-read and quiet voices are resonant beyond the grave. He can afford to wait; in America Mr Wilson has to hurry. Ignorance brays louder and more confidently, and every new mechanical invention widens her range. In England the worst that Forster can say of science is that she has renounced her right to rule and 'plays the subservient pimp', but in America she has a far greater power to override and distort the creative instinct in man. Wilson's indictment is incidental to his criticism, but it recurs again

* E. M. Forster, *Two Cheers for Democracy* (London 1951); Edmund Wilson, *Classics and Commercials* (London 1951).

and again in casual epitaphs on murdered talents. In Hollywood he sees 'an intractable magnetic mountain, which twists American fiction askew'. Of Scott Fitzgerald and Nathanial West he says, 'Their failure to get the best out of their best years may certainly be laid partly on Hollywood with its already appalling record of talent depraved and wasted.' Of another once-promising writer, Louis Bromfield, he synopsizes an appalling story. What can he say of it, he asks, since it is sub-literary, it is proto-film. In a postscript he quotes a gushing review of it from *The New York Herald Tribune.* The weeds are all watered, the flowers left to die. He finds proto-films also in Steinbeck and Hemingway and Kay Boyle. His characters, he says of one reputable novelist, are blank spaces like the figures on bill boards before the faces have been painted in. When their features are finally supplied, they will be the features of popular actors.

In the better-class newspapers he finds 'ineptitude and cynicism masked by competence of presentation'. The writer has been reduced by the speed and volume of communication to the sub-human role of digestion and abridgement. Speaking of *Time* he says that the thoughts of the men, who put it together, 'appear to have been mashed down and to figure in what they print only as blurred streaks of coloration that blot the machine-finished surface'.

In revenge these poor human-appendages of the printing-press tinge everything they touch 'with a peculiar kind of jeering rancour. . . which makes the whole human race hateful'.

In 1943 he wrote:

> The Socialists are now, for the most part, simply patriots as they inevitably become in time of war; the Communists are Russian nationalists, who would not recognize a thought of Lenin if they happened by some mistake to see one; the liberal weeklies are not merely dull shades of the luminous spirits they once were but false phantoms, whose non-incandescence is partly due to an alien mixture of the gases of propaganda, injected by the Stalinists and the British.

This appalling position of the writer in the USA is masked by the huge apparatus of learning, the academies and the libraries, which to Wilson often appear as more subtle agencies of talent-wrecking. *Finnegans Wake,* he mourns, is not a literary issue but a subject of academic research. It went straight from the hands of Joyce to the hands of the college professor. Young men, who should be challenging and appraising what is new and unfamiliar, have been diverted by the universities to the safer work of exposition and research. Wilson reverts several times to this academic blight. The scholar sees the writer not as a comrade or a teacher, but as the raw material for a thesis, 'a means of raising his status in the hierarchy of the academic world'.

It is evidence of the vigour and vitality of the liberal tradition in letters that Forster and Wilson can record such melancholy facts and yet produce books that are stimulating and combative and without despair. After all, misunderstanding has always been the lot of the genuine writer, who is often a provocative person. Wilson angrily challenges a professor who argued that Dr Johnson had exaggerated the hardships of his youth. Nonsense, Johnson knew what he was talking about when he recited the miseries of the writer's life: 'Toil, envy, want, the patron and the jail.' Society changes its methods of redress and the critic's task is to reconnoitre on behalf of literature, finding out from which direction the counter-attack is coming and giving the alarm. The writer of integrity does not suffer more today than before, but the instruments of seduction have been so perfected that the uglier forms of coercion have been discarded except in the more backward countries. This makes the critic's task more complex; he must look for danger and hope in unlikely quarters by devious routes.

Mr Wilson has even to be gratified by the huge popularity (seven and a half million readers in the USA) of a badly written, pietistic novel, called *The Robe*, 'an almost unrivalled fabric of old clichés'. For the book has a certain purity of intention and differs from the usual frankly faked, specially flavoured publisher's goods in being long and tedious. 'It demonstrates that the ordinary reader, even in our ghastly time, does long for moral light and that he cannot live by bilge alone.'

Edmund Wilson's is a noble, lonely head bobbing above the bilge water and only occasionally subsiding beneath it. He is a stern critic of prose style and sometimes appears to look on literary precision as one of the guarantees of freedom. I think he would agree with Forster and George Orwell that 'bureaucrats, who want to destroy liberty, tend to write and speak badly'. They hide their meaning in woolly or portmanteau phrases. Wilson is deadly serious, slashing at Faulkner for his syntax and his indifference to the dictionary. 'This is no coining but groping,' he says.

justly of 'regurg', 'dismatchment' and 'perspicuant'. He chastises Maugham for his becliched obscurity and he offers appalling samples of slop from his best-selling American contemporaries. Few distinguished critics can have read so much bad literature with such well-disciplined revulsion. Though his patient précis of best sellers, which intellectuals are supposed to ignore, the detective stories to which they are supposed to be indulgent, is very entertaining, entertainment is not his aim. There is permanent value in these conscientious essays, small test-tubes, sealed and labelled, containing samples of the bilge water in which the American genius is drowning.

Yet Wilson has his own dreadful lapses, which show how hard it is to think clearly in a land where muddle is mechanized. In his affectionately commemorative essay on Paul Rosenfeld, a victim of American philistinism, one reads: 'The first time I ever saw him I had not yet met him', and 'His taking the Andersons to Europe is an example that happened to be known of the kind of thing he liked to do', and of Katherine Porter he writes: 'Somewhere behind her stories there is a conception of a natural human spirit in terms of their bearing on which all the other forces are appraised.' And every now and then his possessives and relatives coagulate in diseased bunches. It is not mere human carelessness, it is how a top-quality robot would write if his plugs needed cleaning. But can you blame him? To write clearly in America is like trying to take a country walk on an autostrada.

Reading these essays one is grateful for all the cultural rifts in the English-speaking world. American and British writers can scrutinize each other with a detachment that would be embarrassing between intimates. I don't mean, of course, that a critic such as E. M. Forster would ever be tempted to the grosser forms of partiality, but there are friendly reticences and decencies of intercourse among British writers which sometimes act as a windbreak to the salutary breeze of criticism. For example, Mr Wilson's assault on Harold Nicolson has a barbarian effrontery that is refreshing and without malice. He reminds me of the Gaul who tweaked the beard of the musing Senator, perhaps some bland, accomplished precursor of Atticus or Maecenas. Nicolson is one of the most civilized people in England. He is more polished and witty than Wilson, he writes better and has a more ordered and agile mind. E. M. Forster, who deals so trenchantly with Mrs Miniver, locating her in the top drawer but one, 'moral masquerading as social distinction', is too close to Nicolson to focus him. Even if they are unknown to each other, a hundred shared ideals and inhibitions will deter Forster from a cold-blooded analysis of top-drawer Miniverism. (Nicolson, like the celebrated lady, has learnt 'the defensive value of honesty', they are both disarmingly truthful and modest about little things.) If Anglo-Irish writers had not been starved out by the Gael so that they had to sell themselves to the English for porridge, they could have dealt with every grade of Miniverism from here. It is not an Irish vice, and it is at the right range for pot-shots. Curiously enough it is on an Anglo-Irish theme, his *Life of Hamilton Rowan*, that Wilson first engages Nicolson.

Nicolson to Wilson is the 'good little governing-class boy, whose real country is neither England nor Europe but the British Foreign Office', whose 'coy and sly humour. . . almost always works in the conventional direction'. In literature he feels a fascination for 'the more scandalous type of poet. . . but he is forced in a reflex action to detach himself socially from their company by a quiet but well-placed accent of amusement, disapproval and disdain'. Wilson points out how Nicolson talks of Hamilton Rowan's 'really deplorable career', and is 'fascinated, indulgent, alarmed, disapproving'. Nicolson does, in fact, betray towards revolutionary enthusiasm that kiss-and-tell attitude which is common to so many of the children of light, to the scores of subtle intellects which have been governessed by the British Foreign Office and her flighty nurse maids, the BBC and the British Council.

I think that Wilson, with his transatlantic detachment, is right in general about official England, though often wrong in detail. He works from American analogies of copy-book clarity. American ambassadorial prose is archetypal in its awfulness, its mindlessness and pomposity, if we are to judge from Wilson's essay on Joseph E. Davis ('the greatest master of official bad English, since the late President Harding'), who through the filming of his *Mission to Moscow* by Warner Brothers, has become the symbol of the plain, rugged American businessman. On a more intellectual plane there is Archibald MacLeish, the librarian of Congress, who in a sermon to writers in 1940 warned them that 'perhaps writers, having so great a responsibility to the future, must not weaken the validity of the Word, even when the deceptions of the Word have injured them'. Mr Wilson interprets this (correctly, one judges from the context) as a reminder to writers never to weaken authority by exposing the falsity of its official propaganda.

E. M. Forster is a more urbane critic than Edmund Wilson; the iron hand is seldom out of the velvet glove and sometimes it seems unnecessarily well upholstered. I like him best when he is being serious rather than playful, least, when, as in his war-time broadcasts, he becomes a public figure and talks of 'what we are fighting for', and so on. All the recognizable features are there, but the picture is dwarfed and distorted by its frame, as though he had been snapped on the pier with his mild, serious face sticking up above the plywood torso of an alderman. All that he says is true enough, but the best truths are home-made, and here with what I suppose is loyal self-effacement we find him handing out high quality factory stuff.

Contrast a pre-war (1939) point of view with a war-time utterance of 1940. First 1939:

> I hate the idea of causes and, if I had to choose between betraying my country and betraying my friend, I hope I should have the guts to betray my country. . . There is a terror and a hardness in this creed of personal relationships, urbane and mild though it sounds. Love and loyalty to an individual can run counter to the claims of the State. When they do, 'Down with the state!' say I, which means that the State would down me.

Then 1940:

> This being so, I think we have got to go on with this hideous fight. I cannot see how we are to make terms with Hitler, much as I long for peace. For one thing, he never keeps his word, for another he tolerates no way of looking at life but his own way.

Maybe there is nothing in practice irreconcilable in these two statements, because for one who is not a German it can only rarely happen that absolute resistance to Hitler runs counter to absolute loyalty to one's friends. Yet, to a German, such a conflict of loyalties must often have occurred and Forster in 1939 was trying to speak as a human being, not as an Englishman. He was surely going too fast in 1939, too slow in 1940. It would be better never to have divulged his belief in a creed of personal relations *á l'outrance,* if he was going to repudiate it a few months later. What is the use of professing a faith which in time of war splinters along the familiar fissures of race or class? Forster in 1939 simplified the issue for himself artificially by talking of 'betraying my country'. For 'our duty to our country' now says less than it did to subtle minds. Imperialism has stretched it till it is flimsy and transparent as gauze, and science has frayed its once sharp edges, making distinctions of culture and blood appear arbitrary and unreal. Some have seen the mirage of world-unity, so we are prepared to sacrifice our country on a number of different altars, but they are usually very private altars and when we tell about them, as Mr Forster does, it is in a tone of bravado or jesting. And till we catch some approving eyes (there must be a quorum of them) we don't admit we are serious. If Forster had got his quorum I don't think he would have moved to the microphone and spoken as if he accepted the BBC alignment of loyalties, the 'we's' and the 'they's'. He would not have said 'we,' knowing that 'we' meant the Turtons and Pembertons, as well as the negligible handful who accepted his creed of personal relations, and that 'they' meant the German equivalents of Turtons and Pembertons, and also the small handful of German independents. He would have recognized that Hitlerism is only a wild German fantasia on the theme of complacency and self-deception. There is also a Russian variation. All the respectable Germans of the Turton-Pemberton class accepted Hitlerism with mental reservations that counted for little. The same class in England would have adjusted its conscience to something equally cruel. How otherwise would they feel so tolerantly now towards Rommel and Manstein and Weizäcker and all the other respectable people, who travelled so far in fellowship with the Nazis?

As I read on, I reflected that these are Mr Forster's thoughts all right, but triturated and put through a sieve so that the muscle and bone of his thinking are no longer there. How limp is his prophecy that in regard to English culture the Germans, if victorious, would use the methods adopted in Poland and Czechoslovakia. . . and with the maximum of brutality! The statement is not exactly false. On the lips of a stupid person it would even be true, for the imperceptive can only judge from the evidence they observe, and it was not apparent to everybody that the Westerners were to be bribed and the Slavs to be bullied. But Mr Forster could only have accepted a simplification of the truth if his mind had been processed in some way, not violently distorted by a magnetic mountain, but conditioned, like Nicolson's, to respond to varying temperatures. For brains can be retarded or forced nowadays just like bulbs (it is a matter of moving them at the right moment from obscurity to sunlight). And these war-time broadcasts have, in fact, the fragrance and colour we should expect from Mr Forster, but it is as though he had been kept in a cupboard for a long time, then given a drink and taken to decorate a political platform.

Forster's articles on war and the arts raise many questions that can only be touched on here. To what extent should writers associate themselves, as writers, with programmes of national defence? As men, they have the normal responsibilities to their neighbours and their consciences. But are they not falsifying facts if they claim that creative art, man's power to express himself about the world, is linked inextricably with libraries and publishing houses, and all the institutions which dictators love to pervert? Learned establishments have crushed as much originality as they have liberated and are often more fecundating in their decay. We are tired of hearing how Constantinople, when it fell, fertilized Europe for the Renaissance with its débris. Forster, who has often acknowledged his debt to Cambridge, suggests that today it would be better to raze her to the ground than turn her into a technical finishing school. (He will not get his quorum of approving eyes here so he is resolutely playful.) 'She would survive as a memory then. And a memory can do more than either a mummy or a travesty towards civilizing the world.' It would be rash, of course, to invoke Moslems and dynamite on behalf of the Arts, but writers should not be bamboozled into laying down their lives for libraries or for law and order. How many masterpieces have been produced in the interstices of chaos when there were no professors to liquidate, or printing presses to enslave! If we must die altruistically, let us follow Forster's 1939 advice, and die for our friends.

Alternating Wilson's essays with Forster's we can observe how rich and varied is the liberal, individualistic spirit. Forster, who often makes donnish little jokes and is fastidious in speech to the point of primness, is, perhaps, the more subversive of the two. We are misled by his cosy, tea-and-crumpets vocabulary, 'plucky', 'perky', 'mushy', 'stodgy', 'stuffy', 'Sunday-schoolish', 'a bit of a rip', phrases which are the printed equivalents of 'mischievous' twinkles. Nor does he handle very skilfully those dangerous weapons, paradox and overstatement. To the Americans he suggested in a lecture that man's best chance of harmony. . . might lie in 'apathy, uninventiveness and inertia'. I have extracted this remark unfairly from its context, but it has already been still more ruthlessly excised and misrepresented in print. Plainly, it is as unwise to use the language of personal relations on a public platform as to leave one's purse on the dressing-table of a hotel bedroom, as one does at home. Forster surely meant that the energy and zest and taste, which should have gone to the study and ennoblement of human relations, is being wasted on harmful inventions and mechanized enthusiasms. 'The more highly public life is organized, the lower does its morality sink.'

What is the source of the optimism which is still vigorous and tonic in both these writers? It does not lie in religion, though they are both traditionalists, often tracing back American and English culture to the Christian faith, which was once its principal nourishment. In Forster's eyes Christianity has little left of its old spiritual force and, if it is still a power to be reckoned with, it is on a material plane of money and political influence. 'The indwelling spirit will have to be restated, if it is to calm the waters again, and probably restated in a non-Christian form.' But he finds scattered through all the nations and classes, political and religious communities, 'an aristocracy of the sensitive, the considerate and the plucky', between whom there is a secret understanding, whenever they meet. No new gospel is required, but a new technique to make effective the good will and the good temper, which are already existing. And individualism is unconquerable. 'The dictator can order men to merge, he can incite them to mass-antics, but they are obliged to be born separately and to die separately and, owing to these unavoidable termini, will always be running off the totalitarian rails.'

It is for 'Love, the Beloved Republic' that Forster reserved these three cheers for which democracy is unworthy. If Wilson used a battle-slogan, I think it would be intellectual integrity. He would classify Communism with institutional Christianity among 'the dogmatisms of unsure people'. His essay on the Soviet writer, Leonid Leonov, is perceptive. He recognizes the talent, the subtlety, the apparent liberalism, but I think he diagnoses incorrectly the paralysis of orthodoxy in which Leonov's ingenious plots subside. Direct coercion over literature exists, of course, in Russia, but in the main literature is shaped, as in the USA, by popular taste, for corruption has for some time made coercion superfluous. Leonov writes like that because he thinks like that, not because Zhdanov ordered him. Why does he think like that? That is a harder question, but I believe the best answer could be given in cultural and social terms, by-passing politics.

Wilson deals firmly with a characteristic attempt to treat Baudelaire as a Christian penitent, a move in that withdrawal towards traditional religion which is habitual in times of political disillusionment. He follows Anatole France in his diagnosis: 'In his arrogance Baudelaire wished to believe that everything he did was important, even his little impurities, so that he wanted them all to be sins that would interest heaven and hell.'

'Are Baudelaire's angels religion?' he asks. 'Aren't they rather the literary devices of uncomfortable Rationalists, who, disgusted by the dullness of democracy, the vulgarity of revolution, have resorted for protection against them to the mythology and animism of childhood?'

Wilson's 'Dissenting View about Kafka' is another admirable antidote to the higher defeatism. Kafka has been given a cosmic significance which his great talents do not deserve. 'The plights of his abject heroes' are taken to be 'parables of the human condition'. Wilson recalls with common sense that Kafka was psychologically crippled. At the age of thirty-six (he died at forty-one) he wrote a long letter to his father, a bustling Jew in the wholesale women's wear trade, blaming him for his failure in life, and all his life he was wrestling with the concrete banalities and squalor of his private destiny. Too feeble to throw off his father's well-intentioned dictatorship, he chose to see his fate symbolically: Man, submitting to endless frustration from a mysterious, bureaucratic Being, unpetitionable (this nasty word is Wilson's) and inscrutable. Under Wilson's analysis, Kafka, a superb chronicler of realistic nightmares, of the comedy and pathos of futile effort, survives, but Kafka the moral guide, the interpreter of God's ways to men, is expertly demolished.

Wilson had no piety but much pietas, the sense of continuity with the past. Some of his essays commemorate forgotten authors, like Octave Mirbeau, a warm-hearted, quixotic playwright of second rank, who was overshadowed by successful imitators; others are tributes to contemporaries of his own, Whipple and Rosenberg and Eastman, who seem through some uncompromising individuality of temperament to have eluded the recognition that was their due. Here he seems very close to

Forster, who writes of obscure people not from a love of the recondite or to placate the shades of the neglected dead, but from a deeper understanding of the sources of creation. Literature is not an orderly march-past of great writers but a procession of waves, whose crests have no existence, apart from the deep disturbed waters on which they appear to ride.

[1952]

18

THREE FRIENDS: EOIN O'MAHONY OWEN SHEEHY-SKEFFINGTON AND ELIZABETH BOWEN

I. EOIN 'POPE' O'MAHONY

There is still every year a commemorative service and a dinner in Dublin for Eoin O'Mahony. He was known to everyone from his schooldays onward as 'the Pope', but why this was so no one knew. He was a great Irishman whose greatness lay in a field that he had made peculiarly his own.

When he died in 1970 I wrote an appreciation of him in *The Irish Times* and, as he is still remembered, I will repeat it here. I had a special reason for admiring him which I did not express at the time. He had seen in the extended family a blueprint for what life might one day be like. Perhaps some generations or centuries from now groups of people, linked together maybe as kinsmen, maybe as neighbours, will feel a special responsibility for each other, based on a closer knowledge and affection than is possible in our faceless and centralized society.

In forming the O'Mahony Society, Eoin was following an ancient pattern. The O'Mahonys had been a closely knit Irish clan, which history had dispersed. In contrast the Butlers were merely a group of families, sometimes closely, sometimes remotely, sometimes not at all related. Yet when the Butler Society was formed we discovered for ourselves French and German cousins, and there were intermarriages. We had the advantage of the O'Mahonys in the abundance of our historic records, which reach back to the first coming of the Normans. The Butler Society started when the sixth Marquess of Ormonde gave Kilkenny Castle to the Irish nation, the O'Mahony Society much earlier. Yet despite all their differences the two societies developed along parallel lines. We felt we were exploring the past in order to illuminate the future. Eoin wanted to restore richness and variety and friendship to lives that our civilization has sterilized and, within the compass of one man's powers, he succeeded.

Eoin never had any great triumphs or disasters and yet he liked pomp and ceremony and relished life's vicissitudes. But he kept his celebrations small and personal and on a do-it-yourself scale, and he used pomp and ceremony not to magnify the great but to make ordinary people interesting. If one went to one of his gatherings or one of those dead parties which he brought to life by attending, nobody was a spectator, everyone was a participant. Nobody came away feeling he had surrendered to mass banality, as can happen at those public functions where everything proceeds smoothly towards a well-regulated climax. At any event that Eoin organized, the Organization Man, whom American sociologists rightly regarded as the Satan of the sixties, was sure to be routed ignominiously, and the Natural Man would take over. Eoin had such faith in him that he could make the sketchiest of plans, change them at the last moment and sweep on, not to the anticipated conclusion, but to an even better one.

I only attended one O'Mahony rally, but it had a wild spontaneity, a happy, confident chaos that must have had years of practice, megatons of spiritual buoyancy, behind it. Only a great artist in social intercourse could have brought it off.

Eoin had issued hundreds of gold-embossed invitations to the O'Mahony rally at Dunmanus Castle in the name of the Vicomte and Vicomtesse de O'Mahony, a nice young barrister and his wife, who live at Orleans. The Vicomte was the elected Chieftain of the Clan, and probably owed his election to Eoin, who did not bother to tell him about the invitations.

A shower of them fell on Fleet Street and a reporter from the *Daily Express*, attracted by the idea of an invitation from a vicomtesse to dance in an ancient castle on a remote promontory in West Cork (he swore that the word 'Dancing' was written in the left-hand bottom corner), had packed his white tie and tails and, taking a day off his holidays and a ticket to Cork, had arrived at Dunmanus at the same time as ourselves. An English family with a tent and a caravan were encamped within the castle ruins and had just before been astounded by the arrival of an advance detachment of clansmen, bearing on long staves the banners of the O'Mahonys, and of all the nations that had given them refuge in the days of their exile.

They had planted their flags all around the caravan, and very soon a thousand other O'Mahonys had followed them and the small alien encampment, amazed but entertained, had been politely and totally submerged. Soon Eoin was in the thick of it all, booming eloquently in three languages, kissing continental hands, explaining and introducing. The O'Mahony rank-and-file and their friends were then planted on one side of a broken-down moat and the Vicomte stood on the other with Eoin beside him to interpret.

'I have to apologize,' began the Vicomte in high good humour and in French, 'that this is not my castle, and that it has not any roof, and that we are not able to dance in it, and that it wasn't I sent out that invitation.' Eoin translated all this jovially, and then we quickly passed on to serious matters, the long history of the O'Mahonys of Carbery and Kinelmeaky, their kinship and rivalries with the O'Sullivans and MacCarthys. Only the journalist sulked. When there was a pause in the narrative, he went up to Eoin and said: 'I understood there was to be a dance.'

'Well,' said Eoin, 'there's an excellent hotel in Skibbereen. Very nice people indeed, and, if you tell them you want to dance, I am sure they'll be delighted.' Eoin was then swept away by his kinsmen, and the journalist went and sulked on a lump of fallen masonry. He grumbled to some bystanders that he had been brought to West Cork on false pretences, that this was his holiday, not a job. But soon he observed that the O'Mahonys were entertained rather then touched by his misadventure. They were pointing him out to each other – 'Do you see that fella? Did you hear what he has in his suitcase?' – and he saw that he was becoming a stock character in a new version of a traditional Irish story, the innocent Englishman, who had never heard of Pope O'Mahony.

So he moved off to Skibbereen and, drinking himself into a good humour in the hotel, wrote a charming account of the rally for the London daily.

That was a typical O'Mahony occasion. It was an everyday setting, the ruined castle, the rocky shore, the drifts of bog asphodel, the gorse, the pools of water lilies, white as well as orange. And there were everyday people there. There were solicitors from Cork and a garage proprietor from Killarney and hospital nurses and a camp counsellor from Massachusetts. More notable was Rev. Jeremiah O'Mahony from Palm Beach, who was President Kennedy's chaplain and pronounced his name O'Mahóney. The most surprising clansman from America was coal-black. Or could he have been like myself a mere O'Mahonyphile?

Without the magic of Pope O'Mahony to fuse us and transmute us, it would have been the dullest of sea-side outings. But like a watchful cook stirring the jam, Eoin was introducing them all to each other the whole time. He could glamorize even the dullest. This one's aunt had swum the Channel, that one's brother had been in the San Francisco earthquake or as a girl she had known Fanny Parnell. Sometimes a stray sentence expanded into an immense anecdote, breeding other anecdotes, startling and complex but never malicious. If one of them were to end sadly like 'then the poor fellow took to drink and fell down a lift shaft in Las Vegas', it was like a wreath laid on a tomb. To be remembered by Eoin was to be honoured.

His great genius was to use the splendid in the service of the simple. Once I made myself hugely unpopular by flouting received opinion and became a local pariah. My friends rallied to me, but Eoin's support was the warmest and characteristic of him. He packed a shirt the next day (I think it was a shirt, not pyjamas, in that small, odd brown paper parcel), bussed to Naas, and hitch-hiked the rest of the way. He came out from Kilkenny on a creamery lorry, whose driver, he found, was a distant cousin of his. I do not think that we talked about the row at all. He was not much interested whether I was right or wrong. As with the prisoners, whom he was always trying to release, he had his own way of judging matters and always liked official verdicts to be reversed, and personal ones substituted. The next morning he spent at a table in the porch writing about thirty letters on notepaper headed with the address of a smart Dublin hotel, at which he often entertained his friends. For even if it meant starving himself later he liked to be hospitable in the grand manner.

One, I observed, was to a Cardinal, one to Her Serene Highness Somebody. He was asking them no doubt to use their influence, either for the prisoners or for building a bridge to Valentia Island, and some may have been letters of introduction for friends going abroad. (He once gave me a package of eleven.) Then he put the letters in the brown paper parcel and hitch-hiked back to Dublin.

A day or two later an announcement appeared at the very top of the Social and Personal section of *The Irish Times:* 'Mr Eoin O'Mahony, B.L. K.M., has been staying with Mr Hubert Butler, B.A., in Kilkenny.' He probably sent it to the London *Times* as well. I have never before or since appeared in that illustrious column, and I have always made a special thing of *not* being a B.A. But I immediately saw the point. Eoin was showing his solidarity, not with my opinions, but with me, in the most public and ceremonious way he could contrive.

I have just been listening to the Radio Éireann recording of an earlier O'Mahony rally at Castlemore Castle. It was so clear and characteristic, it was almost as though Eoin and his wonderful personality had been embalmed for eternity. But ten years from now, how would it sound to those who never knew him? I think, though he left so little published writing, Eoin may wear better than most of us. For the Faceless Organization Man, whom Eoin combated, though he looks so vigorous, is really already a deader. Very soon we shall be searching for the scraps of the human personalities which he has pounded juggernaut-wise into the dust, and trying to piece them together. That is where Eoin and those he influenced will come into their own again. The seeds he sowed will begin to germinate in the vast and mouldering technological rubbish heap.

Being proud of him, we can be proud of Ireland too, for it is one of the few countries in which so eccentric a genius could be so warmly appreciated and so deeply regretted.

[1970]

II. OWEN SHEEHY-SKEFFINGTON

AT A MEMORIAL MEETING IN THE EXAMINATION HALL, TRINITY COLLEGE, DUBLIN, 11 JUNE 1971

I have known Owen for thirty years and more. Dublin, of course, was the main focus of his activities but his influence was nation-wide. Much has been written about his work in the Senate and in Trinity and elsewhere, but living in the country I and many others have admired him chiefly as the champion not of lost causes but of causes that are bound to be won long after those who made victory certain are dead. Such causes don't attract the impatient or the self-seeking; they owe everything to the dedicated lives of a few, who have a clear vision of the future and know how we can shape it. Owen had absolute faith that what *should* be finally *will* be, however long we must wait. He had a buoyancy of spirit that made him the most inspiring friend and teacher.

And of course he was a great teacher, not only in the scholastic sense, for he was loved and respected by thousands of unacademic people whom he first taught to think for themselves. Inevitably we in the country know him best through the reports of his speeches in the press, through his letters and articles, and we may have got a rather unbalanced view of Owen as primarily a superb and fearless controversialist. But, in fact, those newspaper battles were his way of defending his life's work, much of which, though known to his friends, neighbours, colleagues, was of that disinterested kind that never gets into the press.

There was nothing pedantic or doctrinaire about Owen's great campaigns. They arose out of deep feeling. For example, when he fought for the abolition of corporal punishment in schools he was well aware of the difficult lives of Irish school-teachers, their over-crowded classes, out-of-date curricula and all the things that strain the nerves and spoil the temper. But even if cruelty and stupidity derived from defects in our social system, they had to be noted and denounced; or that system would never be altered. Owen had the law of the land as well as the evidence of a thousand books, educational, medical, psychological, behind him. But the books had never got off the bookshelves into the classroom and the infiltration of any new idea is extraordinarily slow. One man with strong enlightened convictions is worth many books. And in Ireland that man was Owen.

Owen, of course, followed a star, but it would be hard to give that star a name. He was a humanist, as we know, and he once engaged in what must have been the longest newspaper war ever waged in Ireland in defence of the Liberal Ethic, but liberalism and humanism are too narrow, almost sectarian, words in which to describe what Owen did and was. I think he was one of the greatest of Tone's men, for he gave to others what he claimed for himself, 'the Common Name of Irishman'.

I don't believe Owen ever expressed himself more forcibly than in that celebrated after-dinner speech which he gave a few months before he died. Malcolm Muggeridge, who might be considered the leading crusader against the Liberal Ethic in England, had come over for the launching of his new book. He had had an intellectual background not unlike Owen's, but had arrived at diametrically opposite conclusions. Muggeridge had been born of humanist parents but had lost all faith in the socialist future for which they had been working. He had not been able to shake off their disbelief in the Christian story but had allied his total scepticism with a social despair, which he and his followers considered to be Christian. Owen quoted him: 'All human hopes are fraudulent and their realization in purely human terms must always prove deceptive. . . A passion to change the world and make it nearer the heart's desire automatically excludes God.'

He has propagated these views with great wit and charm and a superb mastery of all the mass-media, so that in sceptical, agnostic England he has made thousands of disciples. You can easily see how. What can be more soothing for an easy-going people, who are often visited by pangs of social conscience, than to be told that the world is *a priori* evil and that it is almost blasphemy to try to change it?

We can see how Owen was likely to react to such a creed.

I have read Mr Muggeridge quite a lot [he said]. I am reminded how Zola, talking to the Youth of his day, says that one of the precepts he would suggest to them is that 'they should not be able to read a newspaper without growing pale with anger'. Well, I find that the reading of what Malcolm Muggeridge says as a rule enables me to live up to this precept. Not that he is not at times extremely witty and, though somewhat sourly, amusing and entertaining, contemptuous of all who try here below to lessen unnecessary misery and to improve the lot of man. A favourite sneer-word of his is the adjective Utopian. He forgets that the word Utopia was first used by a saint of the Church, St Thomas, referring not to something immediately, or perhaps ever, realizable but to a better state towards which humanity might legitimately aspire.

Mr Muggeridge derides the Welfare State and Oxfam also, which endeavours to ease the lot of many on this earth and he talks of

> That earnest open Oxfam face shining like a morning sun
> with all the glories flesh is heir to.

He reminds me of a character in a fine novel by Romain Gary. The character, Orsini, has a deep contempt for himself and his aim is to convince himself and others that all his fellow-humans are as contemptible as he is or even more so. I believe that the searing contempt that Mr Muggeridge keeps displaying for the rest of humanity and, in particular, for anybody who tries to do any good here below, derives from a deep inner contempt for himself.

Owen was criticized later for attacking the guest of honour at a dinner, which Muggeridge's publishers had given to celebrate the launching of his new book, *Jesus Rediscovered*. Yet Owen was always courteous and fair. He was attacking not a clever journalist but a noisome and contagious way of thinking. It must have astonished the publisher that, in Ireland of all places, the fashionable new devotion should meet its fiercest challenge. Owen's speech was printed in *Hibernia* and Muggeridge replied to it in the following issue, 5 December 1969.

Was Owen anti-Christian? I think his life gave the answer. If he now and then dissociated himself from Christianity, it was because the word was being made disgraceful. He believed in, and practised, all the Christian virtues; he was a great fighter but he was also humble. He liked to quote Herbert Spencer: 'What I must realize is how infinitesimal is the importance of anything I do, and how infinitely important it is that I should do it.'

Owen never wrote any books, so he is not well-known outside Ireland, but here we all know him. The purpose of these annual lectures is to ensure that he will be remembered in perpetuity by the community for which he spent himself so selflessly.*

[1971]

III. ELIZABETH BOWEN

ON THE ERECTION OF A MEMORIAL TABLET TO ELIZABETH BOWEN IN FARAHY CHURCH, 18 OCTOBER 1979

I know that our posterity will be grateful to those who helped keep this little church alive. Many will say that it is neither notable nor beautiful and that Elizabeth Bowen's real monument is her books. I wonder about this. Her books are brilliantly perceptive,

* Sadly, owing to some confusion, the lectures were not continued, but the Scholarship for French Studies founded in Owen's memory is still regularly awarded.

witty and, despite an underlying sadness, full of happiness, as she was. Are they, though, *'aere perennius'*, more enduring than bronze? The Roman poet who made this proud and justified claim for his works over two thousand years ago lived in times that he thought disturbed, but they were calm and peaceful compared to ours. In our day, events succeed each other very rapidly, books are often out of date before they are published and whole epochs of history can end, as in Eastern Europe, and leave scarcely a trace behind. People and places are far easier to expunge than they ever were before. And Elizabeth's talent (perhaps one could call it genius) was gentle, secretive, undemonstrative and closely linked to a way of life, a class, a community that is quickly disappearing. I have heard her described as the last of the Anglo-Irish novelists, though I do not think she herself would have accepted that. At the end of *Bowen's Court*, that wonderful book of social and family history, she reflects that the Anglo-Irish are tougher than they appear; they have, she thought, an independence of mind, which though it is sometimes based on 'isolation, egotism and lack of culture' (she was thinking in particular of her own Cromwellian ancestors), may help them to survive.

Also, too, I think we underestimate the extent to which our remembrance of people, families, classes and even races is linked with bricks and mortar. It ought not to be so, but it is. It is impossible not still to be moved by the sight of Voltaire's house at Ferney, Tolstoy's home at Yasnaya Polyana, though history has swept past them both in violent revolution. It is hard for an Anglo-Irishman not to regret the virtual destruction of Edgeworthstown, the total destruction of Moore Hall and Coole Park and, finally, just beside this church, of Bowen's Court itself, and not to suspect that our indifference was a foretaste of the neglect and distortion that whole centuries of Anglo-Irish history may have to suffer in the future. These four houses had all, in their day, given shelter to an attempt to blend two traditions, the imagination and poetry of the Gael, with the intellectual vitality and administrative ability of the colonist. And though this mingling of loyalties frequently did happen, each generation found it not easier but harder to create for Ireland some common culture which all its citizens could share.

In Elizabeth's day the whole weight of Ireland's long resentment against England fell upon the Anglo-Irish, the very people who, at different periods, and in different places, had eagerly awaited this mingling and worked for it. Elizabeth was aware of all the difficulties. Since she was twenty she had constantly thought of the burning of Bowen's Court. My grandfather's house in Tipperary, which was the home of her grandmother, Elizabeth Jane Clarke whose memorial tablet you see there on the wall, had been burnt to the ground in the early twenties and so had the houses of many of her neighbours, some fellow-worshippers in this church. Yet when she inherited Bowen's Court from her father, she set herself to keep the house going though it was against all the dictates of commonsense and self-interest and even her own English upbringing.

She had to forge an Irish literary personality for herself, for though her father and all his brothers and sisters were superficially more Irish than herself, warm-hearted people with Irish voices and long humorous Irish anecdotes about relations and County Cork neighbours, they were mostly unliterary and unintellectual, and when they had lived in Dublin even her father, a learned man, was unaware of the Abbey Theatre and the cultural revival which had accompanied it. Yet Elizabeth, knowing well the debt she owed to England, felt passionately Irish and often explored what this Irish feeling was. Was it sometimes, perhaps, little more than the imaginative understanding, the empathy which a sensitive writer has for those whom circumstances or the craft of letters has brought within her orbit? Possibly, yet she felt that her three-hundred-year-old Irishness was as good as anyone else's and committed her to her country.

She had a special feeling for James Joyce, though she described him as a Catholic-born city-bred man, everything in fact that *she* was not. 'In Ireland,' she wrote, 'we breed the finest natures and then by our ignorance, our prejudice and our cruelty, we drive them from our shores. . . We have given to Europe and lost to Europe her greatest writer of prose.'

We had all assumed that because she was so hospitable, so generous and so celebrated a writer, she must be rich. She was too proud to admit to prolonged financial worries. Surely, if all those to whom Bowen's Court had been an oasis of friendliness and lively thinking in a dreary world had known the truth, they would have done something to assure its future.*

* In 1960 when Elizabeth sold Bowen's Court, a large grey eighteenth-century house under the Ballyhoura Hills, she was persuaded that the new owners would live there and preserve it, but hardly a year later it was

The purpose of this tablet is not only to honour a great writer and a friend, it is also to honour the probing mind, the scrupulous observation and the truthful vision of which we stand in such desperate need today.

[1979]

---

demolished and today it is difficult to find even where it stood. Farahy Church, whose services Elizabeth and Alan, her husband, used to attend, lies on a small steep hill just inside the gates of Bowen's Court on the road between Mitchelstown and Mallow, and is the last physical reminder of the Bowens in Ireland. It was in a state of disrepair and there was talk of pulling it down, but it was saved by the efforts of the Rev. Robert McCarthy and Derek Hill, the painter, an old friend of Elizabeth. An annual service of commemoration is held there and the church is maintained by contributions from its congregation and donations from the many summer visitors, who sign their names in the visitor's book and are welcomed to Farahy by Mrs Hannon, occupant of the Bowen's Court gate lodge.

19

A VISIT TO HESSE AND SOME THOUGHTS ABOUT PRINCES

The Butler Society started in 1967 when the sixth Marquess of Ormonde entrusted Kilkenny Castle to a local committee for its preservation. Ours was an attempt to isolate out of world history one small corner, a family, its kinsmen, its neighbours. It soon became clear that the Butlers were no better than any other family, but their records had been well-kept, and it was possible to find kinsmen in France and Germany, in America and Australasia.

Our test-tube approach to the study of the human family has not, perhaps, come up with any startling discoveries. The mere problem of survival of a voluntary community in a world, which has become increasingly regimented and officialized, has absorbed much of our energies. Yet our Society is still young and we know that our approach is the right one. All round us men are rebelling against the civilization of the anthill and wish to be individuals, not units, humans not machines, and are juggling in different ways with the old human constants which are under threat, neighbourhoods, kinships, beliefs, skills, traditions.

This is an old story in Ireland. When I was young I was a disciple of Sir Horace Plunkett, who with George Russell (AE) covered Ireland with creameries which were to be the nuclei of a new society, co-operative and regional. AE recalled how all the Arts and Sciences had started in small Greek city states the size of an Irish county. But he was an Ulsterman and his visions were anchored pragmatically to Agricultural Credit Banks, and the marketing of butter and eggs. Then Patrick Pearse, a visionary without the ballast of dairy products, translated AE's dream into Gaelic and taught his pupils at St Enda's about an Irish society that was patriarchal, aristocratic, and heroic. His nationalism tottered on the brink of racism.

Douglas Hyde, our first president, tried to mediate between the two groups. He had started the Gaelic League as a sort of purge by which the Irish could be freed from their worship of the second-hand and from that 'ocean of vulgarity with which the British Press is submerging us'. He was non-political and said that no Act of Parliament could recover our nationality for us. 'Ours is the least reading and most unlettered of peoples, our art is distinguished above all others by its hideousness. Unless we can act as Irishmen we shall become the Japanese of Europe, capable only of imitation.'

There is nothing sadder than the failure of a dream, but few have capsized so totally as the Sinn Féin dream of the 1916 Rebellion. Sinn Féin means 'Ourselves' and implied that, if necessary by blood sacrifice, our Irish cultural identity must be preserved. Now, as I write, seventy-eight Japanese businessmen are in Dublin to teach us how to imitate their imitations and as an earnest of their concern for us have bought a million pound's worth of pork.

Sadly I move from Ireland to Germany, where the Butler Society spent one of its happiest and most successful rallies in August 1968. To me it was deeply interesting, for here was a family society that had gone on for eighty years and still showed no signs of failing, where old families, despite wars and revolution, still live in family homes. I observed how all these German houses seemed to reach out towards posterity with an assurance which we have mostly lost. It is this that gives to the least pretentious of them a dignity combined with domesticity that is becoming everywhere rarer. I believe that the continuity of a country's culture rests with families not with governments and county councils and that it is Ireland's loss that of all the many hundreds of Butler castles (to mention one historic family alone), all but one are ruins, waiting patiently for the bulldozer.

Could one reason for Anglo-Irish apathy be that great empires act centripetally on their subjects and that the German empire was not old enough to overcome those family and regional loyalties, which keep a national identity alive?

I was in the archives room of several castles and mansions of the von Buttlars of Hesse who claim kinship with the Irish and English Butlers. At Markershausen they have a unique portrait of the fifth Earl of Ormonde, who was beheaded in the Wars of the Roses, and Horst von Buttlar-Brandenfels had made a small museum to illustrate family history, German, English and Irish. In Schloss Elberberg there are trunks full of letters, diaries, records of the part played by the von Buttlars in the Thirty Years' War.

The von Buttlars, a large and once-powerful family, who since the thirteenth century have lived in the wooded hills that border Thuringia and East Germany, have had their regular *Familientag* for several generations and they still keep in touch with members of their family now divided from them by political barriers. One day they took us to Oberkaufungern where we saw the council chamber, church and administrative offices of the Althessische Ritterschaft. When the Landgrave of Hesse still reigned in Cassel, there must have been here a busy centre of authority; thirty of the noble families of Hesse still survive and I believe that, like the von Buttlars, they still have their own *Familientag* and a sense of family solidarity that has long since died out in Ireland and England.

In the church, Vetter Adolf von Buttlar-Stiedenrode laid a wreath on the war memorial in memory of all the Butlers who died on either side in two world wars. The Ritterschaft, though politically powerless, still owns corporately the medieval settlement with its assembly rooms, stables, coach houses and vast surrounding forests of Oberkaufungen. There is a well-preserved skeleton here of an organization that was once active and powerful. What was it like in its prime?

Now that everywhere power has passed to oil companies and steel corporations, and that the Volkswagen factory at Cassel could no doubt buy out the Landgrave of Hesse and all his nobility, one can consider objectively the German principalities and their courts. Is there anything at all to be said for small-scale paternalism (a neutral word, for fathers can be bad as well as good)?

Liberal historians would agree with H. A. L. Fisher, who called the German princes 'the idlest and most selfish aristocracy in Europe'. They were powerful, too. When the Landgrave Philip of Hesse espoused Protestantism, all his subjects had to follow suit and, when he divorced his wife, Luther himself was obliged to find in the Bible a justification for polygamy.

A later Landgrave sold Hessian soldiers to the British Government to fight against the American rebels in 1780 and the Irish rebels in 1798. About half of them were killed and he spent the sale-price of three million pounds on science, literature, the arts and the adornment of his capital. I am told that the large Hercules building in Wilhelms Hohe with its maze of fountains and terraces and its *Wasservexierungsportplatz* (you invite your friends into a grotto and put ten pfennigs into a slot machine and they are 'water-vexed' from many little jets in the rock) was paid for by selling tall Hessians to Frederick the Great, who collected them for a special regiment.

How very wicked! But the arts thrived in Cassel. The Landgraves bought nineteen Rembrandts for the gallery and took pride in those clever citizens who invented the first logarithmic tables, the first theodolite, the first German commercial bank, the first herbarium, steam engine and chime of bells. The brothers Grimm initiated there the science of philology, and their famous fairy tales laid the foundations of folklore. And now when a prosperous city of 200,000 inhabitants has been erected on the ruins left by Hitler's war, it is to the surviving achievements of the Landgraves and their nobility that the sightseer and foreign tourist are almost exclusively directed.

Could one say that, as nurseries of talent and the arts, these tiny states surpassed the great ones that gobbled them up? About this, German genius is divided. Schiller constantly satirized their pompous little courts, but he judged them by his own experiences, which by our standards were not very terrible at all. The Duke of Würtemberg arrested him because he gave up his medical studies to write plays and left Stuttgart without permission. But he escaped to another duke, got a pension from a third, and ended his life with Goethe and Herder at the court of Weimar.

In Weimar, Karl August the duke had put Goethe in charge of the mines, the roads, the treasury, the university of the little state; he directed its theatre. His life overflowed with rich and varied small-scale experiences, and it was in these years that he wrote his greatest works, made his remarkable discoveries in botany and anatomy, and became a European figure.

There is reason in this. An independent mind is always feared and detested, but the stupider princes were too capricious and jealous of each other to gang up effectively against it. If some gifted rebel like Luther or Schiller fell out with his prince, there were a dozen other rival states in which he could find asylum; he did not, like Einstein or Thomas Mann, have to leave Germany altogether. If censorship is to be effective, a high degree of social co-ordination and a loyal civil service is necessary. These were nineteenth-century achievements and because of them, German genius, which stagnated under Bismarck and Kaiser Wilhelm, was extinguished in the days of *Ein Volk, Ein Reich, Ein Führer*.

The princes were, of course, very ordinary people, operating in a familiar social cycle. Were the petty princes of Italy during the Renaissance very different? Robbers became robber-barons, who became barons, who became victims of robbers, who became. . . Irish history makes the process well known to us. There was in the nineteenth century a delusion that the amalgamation of robber-families into robber-states would arrest the cycle or make it more humane, civilized, creative. The reverse has happened.

In the days when genius flourished in Hesse the most publicized event was when the coopers of Cassel made an enormous barrel upon the surface of the frozen Fulda river and brought it in a gay procession as a present for the Landgrave. Much later, Bismarck, in the process of unifying Germany, deposed the Landgrave and annexed Hesse to Prussia. Everyone, including the Hessians, thought this was progress. Cassel became a vast railway and road junction; then a huge factory for the making of machine tools appeared. The Volkswagen factory and Henschel works followed. Cassel grew and grew till in the late war it became an obvious target for the British Air Force, which by persistent bombing over many weeks destroyed the entire city, old and new.

The huge fires could be seen at Göttingen, fifty miles away, and did worse then expunge the city. They seem to have sterilized the soil in which it was built. Anyone who has made a bonfire in a field knows that for a long time only nettles and thistles will thrive where the grass-roots have been scorched.

The new Cassel, though prosperous, is like any other big modern city. Everything in its shops, its theatres, its cinemas, is mass-produced, derivative. It is a faceless, joyless place. Apart from its German shop-signs, it might be in Kansas or Lancashire. When it attracts another bomb, bigger and better, there will, apart from men and women, be only a vast and smothered spiritual potential to regret. Or is it possible that before then, by the study of the past, some new way of realizing the great and generous German genius will be discovered?

[1968]

20

WITHOUT THE BIBLE IN SPAIN

One evening long ago I was walking through a London square when a man thrust a tract into my hands. A glance showed that his God was not my God, but it was a chilly evening for missionary endeavour and perhaps his message might have a meaning for someone else. So I held the tract in my hand till I reached a stationary taxi, then I laid it down on the taximeter and went on. I had not gone far when I heard a voice calling me and saw an elderly taxi driver trotting stiffly after me. He reached out his arm and warmly pressed my hand. 'Thank you!' he said, 'thank you from the bottom of my heart! I'm one myself. Remember you are not alone in the world!' I have forgotten how I disentangled myself from this awkward little scene; clumsily I expect, but not penitently. After all, we are always warming hearts with fuel that is not our own, assisting in the circulation of ideas in which we do not quite believe and simulating a solidarity we do not quite feel. In our huge complex society, in which so many people are alone, we hesitate to attack any belief or fiction which gives an illusion of brotherliness. I was glad I had not thrown the tract over the park railings.

It is not a matter of tracts and taxi drivers only. You will find the same diffidence about giving offence in wireless talks and intellectual periodicals. Negative words like 'unbeliever' and aggressive one like 'rationalist' are cautiously used and, to some sensitive ears, even 'Protestant' has come to have an unbrotherly sound. The great creeds, dissolving, have filled the air with so much shredded theology that the most fastidious can find some palatable nourishment for his soul without rudeness to any other believer. Religion, which once rampaged like a shark, devouring everything which could not escape, now feeds itself like some non-poisonous jelly-fish groping for plankton with sensitive tentacles.

Yet I have only half-acclimatized myself to these ways. I come from one of the outlying parts of Europe, where the old shark-and-minnow view of religion survives, and it is in another such place, Spain, that I am writing this. It is easy for an Irishman to be fifty years behind the times, a Spaniard could be even more; but the archaisms of our countries have not for us the distracting charm of unfamiliarity. We are either for or against. So I do not quite know what to say to an English friend, who is rector of the English church in the neighbouring city. He is a man of courage, humanity, scholarship, but he is also up to date and he practises the jelly-fish approach in these shark-haunted waters. The little church is in a garden belonging to the English Crown, and two stone lions with devout but vigilant expressions guard the gateway from either side. Along well-kept paths, mimosa, poinsettia and swathes of bougainvillea garnish the carefully tended tombs of consuls and colonels, governesses and tourists, who died in exile, mostly about fifty or a hundred years ago. For that was the period when the English colony, untrammelled by currency restrictions, prospered and multiplied. In the centre, towering above the German Lutherans, is the Celtic cross of a country woman of mine, Miss Stewart of Gortleitreach, who died in 1870.

There are plenty of English and Americans in the town, but I doubt whether more than one in twenty visits the church. More might come if the rector was allowed to advertise his services – but he is not. Occasionally he persuades a hall-porter to stick up a notice in a hotel, but after a few days someone tears it down. Not wishing to be aggressive, he has, on the advice of his Anglican bishop, whose spiritual empire stretches rather spottily to the Caspian Sea, explained to the Catholic bishop of the diocese that his community is Anglican and not really Protestant at all, seeing that it does not protest against the Established Church of the State. In this way – and it can scarcely please him – he dissociates it from the indigenous and unpopular heretics of Spain, as well as from Miss Stewart and her neighbours behind the bougainvilleas. Generals Franco and Eisenhower are prayed for in church, as well as the Queen and the heads of the dominions. (The head of my state and Miss Stewart's and our right governance are not prayed for, but we Irish Protestants, like the Spanish Protestants, are ambiguous and unimportant people and

I am not surprised. By a large majority our last General Synod rejected a proposal that we should officially describe ourselves as Anglican. While in Spain it is politic to present our religion as a specially English and therefore non-contagious idiosyncrasy, in Ireland it is wiser to advertise its non-English, universal character.) In his courteous adaptability, this rector in Spain is merely conforming to an agreed pattern. For example, on the staff of the British Council in Spain, whose mission it is to represent English culture, cultivated English Catholics have played a disproportionate rôle. Looking at the month's programme from Barcelona, I observed that the only public lecture was on Ronald Knox – the son of a bishop – who turned his back on the Reformation and joined the Church of Rome.

If you would argue from this the decline of the Anglo-Saxon race, you would argue wrongly; six American helicopters have just roared overhead and every now and then waves of American sailors distribute largesse among the toddlers in the coastal towns; we were due a visit here from the American navy last week, but rumour said it was postponed because the principal Spanish hostesses had not yet recovered from an unpleasant disease. There are five American air bases. The Anglo-Saxons are well on top, and in a temporal sphere they are as bossy and interfering as ever. It is only in the spiritual sphere, in which they were once so arrogant, that they have become self-effacing. The only explanation I can find for this is that Anglo-Saxon Churchmen are now mostly agnostic on matters about which they formerly dogmatized. What appeared to them once as absolute and universal truth is now only relatively true. Certain beliefs are adapted to certain people and places and have no validity beyond them. In fact they are not really true at all, but appropriate symbols for the unknowable, sanctioned by tradition and use. To the people outside the bougainvillea hedge other symbols might well be more appropriate.

This will be apparent if you contrast 'the gospel of Inglaterra' as preached by George Borrow in Spain a hundred years ago with its contemporary counterpart. To Borrow, the Bible was the unchallenged repository of truth, it was the impregnable fortress from which he made his audacious sallies against 'priestcraft', Popery, and superstition. It was the stake to which he tethered his lively, sceptical and observant mind. It was the reason and the consecration of one of the great travel-books of the world, beside which all other interpretations of Spain appear desultory, unmotivated, dilettante. But what is hardest to grasp is that in his aggression against the established faith of Spain, Borrow counted on and received the support of the representatives of Britain. The lion was prepared to roar on behalf of the gospel of Inglaterra and the humblest of its missioners. The ambassador, Lord Clarendon and his first secretary, Mr Southern, were tireless in rescuing Borrow from prison and the Word of God from the customs officers. They secured him an interview with the anti-clerical prime minister and ordered consignments of Bibles to be sent to all the British consuls in Spain with instructions about circulating them. They considered Borrow's efforts 'extremely well calculated to operate beneficially on the political and moral state of the country'. None of them had any of our modern scruples about 'tampering with the faith of others', and when the Mayor of Madrid asked Borrow: 'What would you say if the Spaniards were to go to England and attempt to overthrow the Lutheranism established there?' Borrow replied: 'Your Excellency is perhaps not aware that the Pope has a fair field and fair play in England and is permitted to make as many converts from Lutheranism as are disposed to go over to him.' The Mayor was convinced and answered: 'In my private opinion it is highly advisable in all countries to allow full and perfect tolerance in religious matters and to permit every religious system to stand or fall according to its merits.'

There were many unbelievers at that time in Spain, but Borrow, who liked chatting with everybody, never tried to convert them. 'The believer has no carnal arguments to address to carnal reason. . . Faith is the free gift of God and I do not believe that ever yet was an infidel converted by after-dinner polemics.'

It was with the unquestioning faith of the simple that Borrow preferred to 'tamper'. When at Evora, he went every day to a well outside the town, where the muleteers watered their beasts. Here he sat and talked of the Bible to all who came. He told them that they were not Christians and would not become so, so long as they placed their hope of salvation in outward forms and superstitious observances. 'I said repeatedly that the Pope, whom they revered, was an arch-deceiver and the head minister of Satan here on earth and that the monks and friars, to whom they had been accustomed to confess themselves, were his subordinate agents.'

He believed that the Spanish peasants were not the dark and bigoted fanatics which their leaders tried to make them. He thought they were craving for truth and that, if they were not given it, Satan might seduce them into the Pit of Infidelity, which lay upon the other side of the road. With this Pit in mind, he helped a young girl burn Volney's *Ruins of Empire* upon the kitchen-fire, while she told her beads. He warned her that the author (a steadfast champion of freedom, whom Robespierre had imprisoned) was 'an emissary of Satan, who inculcated the doctrine that there was no future state nor reward for the righteous nor punishment for the wicked'.

Borrow's straight and narrow path had been defined for him by Satan with the broad, black margins of Infidelity and Superstition on either side. It was impossible to miss it. Yet soon the more sophisticated children of the Reformation were beginning to think it more suitable to preach the Gospel of Inglaterra to pagans, Buddhists and Confucians than to fellow-Christians. Perhaps the opening up of Africa and Asia influenced this decision, but it may have come about because many of the more ardent and uncompromising of the Protestant heretics were sliding out of the Church altogether, and those that remained, seeing all around them in their new mission fields not Popery, but hunger, barbarity, disease, persuaded themselves that the example of their lives, assisted by hospitals and schools, testified sufficiently to the truth of their faith. They were able to forget that its fervour and its doctrines derived from a long and bitter dispute with rich and civilized followers of Christ: they could not anticipate that hospitals and schools and welfare might one day serve as weapons which the materialist would turn against the believer.

But even among the orthodox Borrow still had a few followers. Lord Plunket, Archbishop of Dublin, can be considered the founder of the small Reformed Episcopalian Church of Spain, since, after a long struggle with Lambeth and the Synod of the Irish Church, he consecrated its first bishop in 1892. This Spanish Church still depends for its dogma and its episcopal consecrations on a council of four, of whom three are bishops of the Church of Ireland. The Archbishop was as pugnaciously Protestant as Borrow. He wrote a hymn on behalf of the Spanish Protestants ('to be sung to the tune of "There is a Happy Land"'). One verse runs:

Shall these our brethren sink
  And we so near?
Can we from danger shrink
And they so dear?
Haste! e'er it be too late!
  Souls are drifting to their fate.
Dare we still idly wait
And give no ear?

Many, including the Bishop of Gibraltar and the British Embassy chaplain in Madrid, were disposed to answer all these three questions affirmatively. There was a strong feeling already against 'tampering', and Plunket's old-fashioned obstinacy would hardly have prevailed had he not been rich and influential and able to subsidize the Spanish Protestants from his own pockets and those of his friends. He was among the last of these Protestant warriors. Their extravagant hopes and aggressive schemes find no echo now behind the bougainvilleas. Borrow's Bible is no longer a serviceable weapon. In the generation after Darwin footnotes and qualifications had begun to grow upon the Old Testament like rust upon a rapier. Only Bible-Christians, simple people like Jehovah's Witnesses, can see our world in terms of Gideon and the Amalekites and would venture to present it as Borrow did to the muleteers as the undiluted Word of God. And now even the New Testament has become unserviceable. Borrow had in some ways preferred it to the Old Testament because it was lighter and more portable along mule-tracks. But against that he had found that it needed more interpretation for the illiterate. In our day the most zealous of consuls would shrink from negotiating through the Spanish customs all the wagon loads of 'necessary explanations'. These complications had been developing long before Bishop Barnes had summarized a century of criticism and before the Dead Sea Scrolls suggested that a creed of Christian form may have preceded the birth of Christ.

Borrow was a benevolent man, not cherishing hatred for its own sake, but can it be denied that hatred of 'Popery' was the fuel which turned the wheels of Protestantism for him and many of his co-religionists? If that particular fuel is exhausted, the dying fires must be stoked with something else. With what? Broadmindedness is not the answer, for our minds seem to have a fixed cubic capacity. If we broaden them in one direction, there must be compensations elsewhere. Borrow, for example, balanced his strenuous anti-Popery by taking a broad view of Moslems. Did they not worship one uncreated, eternal God and declare that Christ was a Mighty Prophet, whereas 'according to others, He is either a piece of bread or a helpless infant. Nor do they have graven images.' Like many devout people, Borrow was watchful for little coincidences, in which the Hand of God, blessing His Servant and endorsing his opinions, could be observed. Once in a mosque, observing the absence of graven images, he exclaimed (in these soliloquies it is never quite clear whether he speaks as himself or as the mouthpiece of his Maker):

> Come here, Papist, and take a lesson! Thy walls are stuck with idols: thou callest a stone thy Father and a piece of rotting wood the Queen of Heaven. Fool, thou knowest not even the Ancient of Days and the very Moor can instruct thee. He at least knows the Ancient of Days, who has said: Thou shalt have no other Gods but me.

'and, as I said these words I heard a cry like the roaring of a lion and an awful voice in the distance exclaiming "KAPUL UDBAGH"' (there is no God but one!)

Borrow does not often cheat as badly as this. In fact, compared with many religious people today, he seldom juggles unfairly with facts and symbols, with inner voices, external signs and national shibboleths. He was very little of a preacher and scarcely aimed at making converts. He counted his achievements not by the souls he saved but by the number of testaments he was able to sell. His agents were booksellers, mayors, Greek adventurers, sometimes even Catholic priests. He was a sower of seed, not a harvester of souls. He was that formidable being, a complicated soul with a very simple creed.

Much of the seed sown by Borrow and his colleagues sprouted, but bore crops very different from what they expected. The soil was favourable to anticlericalism during the Carlist wars, when the Church was divided against itself and an Archbishop of Toledo (unrecognized by the Pope) was able to give the Bible Society some equivocal encouragement. To a certain extent Spanish anarchism, that gentle creed, which in the confusion of the times became the nursemaid of arson and assassination, was born of the Bible Society. Gerald Brenan has pictured the excitement of simple peasants reading for the first time without ecclesiastical commentary the words of the Mother of God: 'He hath thrown the Mighty from their seats and hath exalted the humble and meek.' There has always been in Protestantism a rebellious anarchic streak which the Protestant defenders of the established order acknowledge with reluctance – the anarchists themselves less grudgingly. In the Civil War very few Protestant churches were destroyed in Spain; once, when a Baptist church was burnt in Barcelona, the anarchists discovering their mistake, tried vainly to extinguish the flames with buckets of water.

In fact the Anglicans have in Spain a good many near relations whom it is politic to disavow, even though it means disavowing their own grandparents. To our ears, Lord Plunket's stormy hymn seems more appropriate to a lower middle-class 'hot-gospeller' than to a great aristocrat and a scholar. Nowadays Anglo-Saxon heretics will eagerly make broadminded excuses for the pressure which is exercised on all our heresies in Spain. They have forgotten that it is only a few generations since they used gun-boats to persuade the Emperor of China to permit Protestant missionaries to 'tamper' with the faith of his Buddhist and Confucian subjects. They have not reckoned how much easier it would be to secure liberty for Protestantism in Spain from a Church to which Anglo-Saxons have for long allowed the utmost missionary freedom. It would be a just cause, not as it was in China, an unjust one. No gun-boats would be needed, because in such a cause the pressure of moral indignation, spontaneously exerted, is irresistible.

But the fact is we are not interested. My friend the Anglican chaplain was not even aware that there was a Spanish Protestant Church only a few streets away from his own. Few Anglo-Saxons, in Spain or outside it, know that conversion to Protestantism or any other heresy is not recognized by the law and that no marriage except a Catholic one is legal for those who have been baptized into the Catholic Church, even though they have repudiated it violently for the whole of their lives. There are thousands of Americans in Spain, technical advisers and members of the forces, but the heirs of the Pilgrim Fathers have been forbidden to associate with the Spanish heretics or to attend their places of worship. If a Spanish Protestant strays into a St George's Chapel at Madrid or Barcelona or Malaga, the Anglo-Saxon worshipper, to avoid provocation, has been advised to look the other way.

Is our new deference to the religious views of others the result of a revival of faith and religious feeling? Just the opposite. Most of us would seem to Borrow to be 'infidels', ordering our lives according to 'carnal reason', or 'sneering Saducees', or 'excrescences of overwrought refinement'. Our books, more insidious than Volney's, should all be burnt on the kitchen fire. Yet we are conscious of the political, social and even therapeutic importance of religion. The educated classes, who no longer find Truth in the Churches, often give them a new respectability as repositories of Tradition, Beauty or Symbolism. And since one symbol is as valid as another, liberally minded infidels come to think of religion as a matter of personal taste and seldom wish to form communities to defend or impart to others their own complicated heresies. Here is a passage from Sacheverell Sitwell's book on Spain which will appeal to many other 'excrescences of overwrought refinement':

> Now Poblet has recently been given back to the Cistercian monks, a decision which is extremely right, historically and from the point of view of sentiment and aesthetics. The Cistercian monks in their white robes and pointed hoods, so subtly differenced from the White Carthusians – and so much resembling the Moors of Fez, for theirs too is a costume that has come down unaltered from the twelfth century – are in entire harmony with the pointed arches of the Abbey Church. To its full beauty they are appropriate, indispensable indeed.

Few will be shocked by this sartorial, architectural view of religion, nor are we outraged by the psycho-therapeutic or the practical-good-sense approach, which is even more usual:

> Sybil is absolutely selfless. It was really for the children's sake she became a Rosicrucian, as religion never meant much to her one way or the other, while it meant everything to Harold. She felt she oughtn't to let her own personal feelings stand in the light, because what children *need* above all is security. And how could they get that with their parents in opposite camps?

And how generous-minded we feel when we acknowledge the restored health, the tranquillity, that comes to our friends, when they begin to believe something which we know to be untrue! Gestures that Borrow would have regarded as treacherous or hypocritical, seem to us simple acts of courtesy and tact, suitable for people with broad minds and wide imperial horizons. Did not the Roman emperors, before imperial policy demanded its destruction, send weekly offerings to the Temple of Jehovah? In return they only asked that their own divinity be recognized. Are not such small civilities the everyday currency of co-existence?

There is spiritual content in all religions and under pressure from Communist materialists, it is seemly to recognize it. It is a question of tact, not of treachery; a gesture, a few words, that is all that is necessary. This kind of thing:

> It was characteristically imaginative of the Governor to consult Sir A. Ngumbi about an auspicious date for the reception at Government House during the Princess's visit. Hepatoscopy, divination by bird's intestines, is one of the most ancient religious practices, patronized by Julius Caesar himself! Sir A. Ngumbi is no mere 'medicine man'. He is a far-sighted patriot who has used his great spiritual influence against the Communist-inspired terrorists of the interior.

A couple of generations ago many clung to the Churches in whose doctines they had ceased to believe, hoping that by the weight of their numbers and the logic of their 'carnal reason', they could draw their Church after them. But most of their fellow-unbelievers shrank from this arduous tug-of-war and considered that they could shed, without loss to themselves, the fellowship and the responsibilities which would be theirs through membership of that ancient community, which their heresies could have rejuvenated. They were wrong, and I think it is the heirs of these self-sufficient infidels of the all-or-nothing school who are our new religious authoritarians. Finding it unsatisfactory to have nothing, they grasp again impetuously at all.

As the gulf between what we believe and what we profess to believe widens, tact and diplomacy take the place of truth. Taking his seat by the well of Evora, an Anglican clergyman would have nothing to say to a Spanish muleteer, and, if he had, he would consider it politically unwise to say it.

Never was there so much sophisticated admiration for the 'simple faith' of common people or so strong a disinclination to bridge the gulf between our sophistication and their simplicities. It is often not love but fear of explosive ideas that kindles us to this admiration. While the learned world prepares vessels to reach the moon and arms the ignorant with new weapons to express their hatred, the Church of Inglaterra, which might have been able to unite learning and love, moulders away behind her bougainvilleas. She is ready to change her name and to cut all her rebellious children out of her will. She is almost prepared to offer atonement for the rebellion of her fathers. She is hurt and bewildered that so conciliatory a spirit has not met the understanding it deserves. She is surprised to find that she is not being loved. She is being ignored.

[1958]

21

RETURN TO HELLAS

When I was young, but not young enough, I walked through the Peloponnese with a mule. It took, I think, thirteen hours from Andritsaena to the ferry across the Alphaeus. I had never enjoyed anything so much, but I felt very angry that my education had been back to front. Here was the jam at last after I had stuffed myself to repletion with dry bread. Had I known of all this before, the fragrance of myrtle and mule-droppings, the memory of roast sucking-pig and retsina, would have reconciled me to knowledge, which till then had flowed in a contrary direction to my curiosity. Why, for instance, had I never grasped that the cistus, on which the mule trampled, that showy nurseryman's plant with pink flowers and dark sticky leaves (catalogue price 7*s.* 6*d.*), was a commonplace to Herodotus. The Greeks, he said, made incense from it by combing the beards of billy-goats. Why did I never guess that in a meadow at Olympia, ringed with asphodel and narcissus, the Hermes of Praxiteles would shed like the scab of an old wound its frowsy kinship with a plaster cast in the Science Buildings at Charterhouse?

Travel to Greece is now so easy and cheap that only a very unenterprising or underprivileged boy or girl would study *The Agamemnon* without going to Mycenae, or the Persian Wars without a visit to Salamis. But the more ambitious examinees will not go by mule now. The mules and the muleteers are still there, but, just as the peasant costumes of the Balkans are moving from the backs of peasants to the tourist shops, so, though more deliberately, the mules are shifting away from nature towards art, towards those unnatural animals which carry giggling metropolitans across the Gap of Dunloe, insulated from the present by a strict tabu upon tourists with cars.

Indeed, one might say that everything is too easy now,

information too accessible, and in a different way the Greek world has got out of focus again. We now know more than the average Greek knew about the development of his pots and trade routes, his dialect and his racial descent. The scholar's approach is no longer humanist but clinical. I have heard of a French doctor who failed to recognize an old acquaintance till he had seen his bottom, which he had treated for boils. 'Ah, mon camarade, c'est toi!' he exclaimed, as he embraced him. This backside intimacy with Greece is now the only kind of which we dare boast.

Is it because too many banalities have been uttered about 'the Greek spirit' that the scholar now buries his head in potsherds and paradigms? As we boarded our plane in the early fifties with twenty-eight other middle-aged unprofessional phil-Hellenes, we knew well how banal we were. Yet we were conscious of our power. It is for us that a trunk-road sweeps between Helicon and Parnassus and that six thousand new bedrooms (bathrooms attached) and thirty-three new hotels have been decreed. From now on the mariner, as he rounds Cape Sunium, will not see the Temple of Poseidon, as Byron saw it, lonely and abandoned, but flanked by a Tourist Pavilion and a Hilton Hotel. An avenue lined with cypress and eucalyptus leads right up to the tumulus at Marathon, so that the front bumpers of our charabanc could actually graze the green sod beneath which the 192 Greek warriors were laid.

Well, and why not? The Greeks, a vulgar and gregarious people, loved tours and tourists and international gatherings and painted each garment of the Caryatids a different colour. The Temple of Poseidon once was more expensively gorgeous with gold and ivory than the lounge of the Hilton Hotel, not yet completed, will ever be. The flutings of its Doric columns were red and yellow; its present admired colour is the work of time, which turns all our bones to apricot and ivory.

Obviously group travel by chartered plane is revolutionizing Hellenic travel and, to judge by our experience, the first revolutionaries are conscious of what they are doing and doing it well. On our Wings Tour in less than a fortnight we saw more of the Greek world than Strabo and Pausanias could have seen in five times the time; collectively we could have compiled a patchy but not contemptible epilogue about its flora and fauna and surviving antiquities. For sophisticated travellers it used to be a point of honour to dodge their compatriots, except those in embassies, but we found through our companions an enlargement of our senses. X saw and shared the eagle resting on a rock at Cameirus, the vultures gliding over the Doric Code of Laws at Gortyna, two hoopoes and a stonechat. Y observed how as we went southward the pink anemones faded and gave place to white, the golden camomiles of Crete replaced the white ones of Rhodes, the lemons grew smaller. Z identified for us Ithaca and Delos and the mouth of the Acheron. Above the clouds and below, our perambulating city-state was well governed by two intelligent and amiable archons and those who had no special knowledge to share cemented its solidarity with maps and aspirins, field-glasses and Penguins. It was only on the subject of Ancient Greece that I observed a competitiveness that was not shown about the best seats on the plane, the best beds in the hotel. I attribute this to compulsory classics, which fester like an abscess under the skin of so many middle-aged men. A century ago it could erupt in parliament or the Law Courts, when rolling periods were decorated with quotations. A generation ago it could still exude through the competition page of the *Saturday Westminster*, when a poem by Herrick would be 'neatly rendered' into Alcaics. But now, except for conferring Honorary Degrees in a witty way, what public use can one make of it all? If it does not earn you a salary, it is often just a focus of irritation. When at Marathon Mrs N. mused, as she pointed at Mount Parnes, 'I love to think of Xenophon sitting on a throne up there and watching the battle', there was a febrile pounce from two middle-aged public schoolmen. 'Xerxes!' gasped the first. 'Salamis!' chided the second. 'A spur of Mount Aegaleos,' said a third, a near-professional, in a competitively uncompetitive murmur, thereby winning trick, game and rubber. After that Mrs N. kept all her loving thoughts about antiquity to herself.

Nobody wants to hear about what we saw in Greece and its islands, for now they are so accessible that everyone can see them for himself. So I shall confine myself to two digressions, expounding two out-of-date heresies in terms of Attica, the Argolid, Rhodes and Crete.

First, there is the question of Mrs N. and cannibalism among amateur and professional phil-Hellenes, who, except on cruises and bus-tours and chartered planes, at conferences and in common rooms, are a scattered and insignificant community. Ethel Smyth, in an admirable Greek travel-book (not un-scholarly but anti-scholarly), indicates that archaeologists are even bigger prigs than classical scholars. 'Most workers,' she writes, 'perhaps most humans, are prone to secret jealousy, but for undisguised scorn of all other workers in his own field of business, commend me to the archaeologist.' And she describes a meeting between 'two frigid and lordly ones of the orthodox type' who were looking down their noses at each other but ran together like twin dewdrops in implied disdain of a third, who was unorthodox. 'His buoyancy of spirit was greatly against him.'

One explanation of this might be that archaeology is now largely financed by the public and not by private wealth or voluntary subscription. The paid professional, slightly askew to reality, is sheltered from the freezing indifference which unsubsidized enthusiasm would meet from 99 per cent of his fellow citizens. A century ago Mrs N.'s eager little advances might have meant a 5s. subscription to a struggling archaeological society. Now she is probably paying the state more than this towards the discovery of the past, but her enforced benevolence is hidden even from herself in the labyrinth of the budget. It does not have to be solicited or gratefully acknowledged.

Great reappraisals are often chaotic, experimental and vulnerable to ridicule. They are seldom conducted in the trim laboratories where reputations are nursed. At Mycenae and Cnossos one cannot forget that the great archaeological revolutions of recent times were carried through by amateurs in the teeth of bitter professional opposition. Schliemann, Evans and Ventris all had 'buoyancy of spirit'. Now the 'Treasure of Priam', which Schliemann had presented to the German nation, has disappeared, removed by the Russians. But who knows or cares? The apathy of the average man, which the amateur tried to ruffle, is not so burdensome to the professional.

It was inevitable that nationalism should creep in with state-supported archaeology, and its ravages could be observed in Greece. It was obvious that the superb excavations at Cameiros and Lindos in Rhodes caused acute schizophrenia in many scholarly Greeks. If you ask who carried them out, they will say in a rapid undertone: 'The Italians had that privilege', and then will explain how no proper report of the work done has yet been published and so no one knows how many treasures were transported to Italy. Yet no one can deny that these graceful columns, these ranks of tombs and votive monuments, woven out of fragments of imagination and cement, are highly magnetic and that it is not only the spirit which they enrich. One is told that the money brought in by tourists, added to that which is sent home by emigrants, is more important to Greece than all her exports of olives and oranges. Even so, there are certain debts which one ought to be excused from acknowledging. Go for instance to the most ambitious of all the Italian restorations on Rhodes, the Palace of the Grand Master of the Knights of St John. Though its medievalism is more convincing in the twilight, there is a dollar-compelling majesty about its mighty walls, clad in roses and bougainvillea, its vast courtyards and lordly stairways. Inside you must crawl crab-wise round the saloons, because the floors are covered with rich Byzantine mosaics. You may hear a whisper that the Italian governor of the Dodecanese (the guide-books call him 'the tyrant de Vecchi') looted them from the island of Cos to decorate the palace for himself, that he walked across them without even carpet slippers and that the Muse of History is mocked by his bathrooms and his alabaster lifts. Yet the Greeks are a thrifty as well as a proud people. The tyrant's palace will remain. But so too will the long Italian inscription in the hall-way which reveals that Rhodes was once one of the fairest jewels in the Fascist crown and that, reviving its ancient glories, the Italians were trying to revive also the patronage which Hadrian and others had once bestowed on the subject Hellenes. The marble plaque relates how Cesare Maria de Vecchi, Conte di, etc., in the reign of Victor Emmanuel II, King of Italy, King of Albania, Emperor of Abyssinia, etc., under the leadership of Benito Mussolini, etc., did cause to be reconstructed, etc., in defence of the Law and Faith of Rome, etc.

There is a notion that archaeology is a grave, objective science and that it can accept the patronage of governments without being defiled. But in fact it is neutral coloured and highly absorbent and can be dyed black or brown or red with the greatest of ease. Because of Schliemann and the Aryan theory Mycenae was dyed brown during the German occupation and the names of Göring, Goebbels and Himmler and scores of officers of the *Panzerdivisionen* were written in the visitors' book at La Belle Hélène, once Schliemann's headquarters. The offending page was torn out, possibly because 'learning being above politics' Greek scholars had signed their names beside Himmler's. Himmler, like Mussolini, was an ardent patron of archaeology, believing that confirmation of his Aryan theories lay beneath the sod. Many of the frigid and lordly ones believed that they could smile at his views and accept his subsidies. Distinguished German scholars went to Norway for Himmler to excavate under the aegis of Vidkun Quisling. Was learning advanced by what they discovered? We carry the past about with us in its entirety and nothing is gained if to illuminate what is remote we must wear blinkers to blot out the present. It is possible that German and Italian leaders deliberately switched the searchlight of scholarship onto ancient times, so that the darkness which veiled their own manoeuvres might be deepened.

Aristotle, now over eighty, an assistant of Professor Wace, spends much of his time sunning himself outside the Belle Hélène. He loves to talk of the Professor, of Mrs Wace and Miss Helen and of all that happened since they left. Wave after wave of foreign warriors visited Mycenae, but the Nazi officers surpassed all the others by their ability to quote long passages of Homer by heart; after them came the English and the Italians; at the bottom the Americans.

Does this mean some affinity between Himmler and Homer? I think that all it signifies is that when a state is sufficiently vast, its wartime needs are so varied that all but impossible people can accept a portion of its policy with a portion of their minds. It is a matter of bringing matching pieces together. Many who in cruder days would have had to be expensively court-martialled or imprisoned can be drafted to some zone of co-operation which does not offend their consciences. Dedicated to departmental virtue, they feed the hungry and homeless, they diffuse culture. Everybody contributes according to his gifts. While unfastidious Germans were sent to exterminate and enslave the peoples of eastern Europe, a polished and humane élite, who played French cricket with the kids in their billets and made small safe *Witze* about Göring's medals, were sent to charm the Channel Islanders. In Ireland it was well known that our cultural gauleiter was to be a competent Celtic archaeologist, who, though a German, had been till just before the outbreak of the war Director of our National Museum. It is not, therefore, surprising that genuine Homeric scholars have appeared at Mycenae with Himmler, flattering themselves that they were diverting him temporarily from his wickedness to the patronage of learning. Possibly, as the Supreme Commander of the SS and the Gestapo bent over a shaft grave, some irresponsible amateur may have been tempted for liberty's sake to push him in and crack his skull open with an inscribed stele (*c.* 1550 BC). Then he will have recollected that 'scholarship is above politics' and that one should do nothing that would discredit archaeology and check the flow of subsidies to research.

In small communities on the Greek model, self-deception was not so easy as now. There were few humane or learned side-shows in which dissenters could bury their scruples, so there was an abundance of uninhibited traitors. At Marathon there was an Athenian traitor with the Persian fleet and another signalling to it from Pentelicus.

Surely Greek art and letters owed their crystalline clarity in part to this small-scale simplicity. Traitors were traitors and there were no multiple loyalties to muddy the mind. Could one say that in the city-state men could not escape from each other except by open secession? The constant friction and fusion of diverse personalities in a confined space caused some creative combustion and sparked off explosions of genius, which could not have happened in those large loose federations, which the Greeks despised.

Here I am in the middle of my second digression. If my explanation sounded nonsensical, why has no better one been offered for the prodigious flowering of genius in the city-states? Why has no sociologist given them the same attention that he gives to more trivial and nebulous problems – the effects of television on the sex-life of miners, the devaluation of the piano as an index of social prestige and so on? Are they scared of the professors, who have been oddly fallacious in their assessments? The great Hellenizers of a generation ago (I mean those who believed that the Greeks offered to students 'a message' and not merely some interesting linguistic and ethnological puzzles), Zimmern, Murray, Lowes Dickinson, were all deluded by their enthusiasm for the League of Nations and that 'wider citizenship' in which the old Greek ideals were to be merged. They buried the city-state honourably but the epitaphs they wrote are so odd that surely the corpse ought to be exhumed for more detailed analysis?

Lowes Dickinson considered that 'the good citizen' of the Greek type could now only survive on the county council level, concerning himself with sewage and parks. More aspiring men would be liberated by the administrative machinery of a huge multiracial state for wider, freer speculations and experiences. Zimmern thought that 'the state in these days of large-scale government does not expose its citizens to the daily falsehoods and hypocrisies which seem inevitable in the life of the smaller groupings of men and women'. Writing in the year that Hitler was elected president of a small dining-club in Munich, he said that Germany, 'her population relieved from military duty and available for productive tasks, has the advantage over the most ideal construction of ancient Greece'. With all this Gilbert Murray would surely have agreed. With Nazism, Stalinism, and McCarthyism just ahead, could they have been more wrong?

The small Greek community has had many strange and fruitful reincarnations in free principalities, republics, cities. Today when all the sober orthodoxies are harnessed to apocalyptic beliefs of the most bizarre character, the Decay of the State, the Conversion of Russia, the final triumph of Communism or Democracy or Mahomet or the White or Black Races, I see nothing grotesque in believing that in some unforeseeable society of the future the function of a man and a citizen will again converge.

Who knows how? When it first happened it was an accident. It seems that many millennia ago Poseidon shook the Aegean continent into scattered fragments and imposed upon Greek exuberance a consistently small and sober pattern, which appeared to later Greek thinkers to be that best suited to man's social and intellectual development. Poor external communications helped to train the ancient cities in social self-sufficiency. They managed to be self-centred without being parochial. Their limitations, which appear to us so crippling, proved to them a blessing. Aristotle, reflecting on the greatness of Athens, declared that a large state was as absurd as a ship two furlongs long, that men should know the characters of their fellow-citizens if they were to judge them. 'A nation' was a barbarous conception. 'Who could be the herald of such an unwieldy multitude except a stentor?' To the Greeks there was nothing paradoxical in the association of great men with small communities.

It was an extraordinary phenomenon. In a few small cities on the rocky promontories and islands of the Aegean all our arts and sciences were founded in a few generations. Then followed centuries of imperial and feudal stagnation. Was the explanation racial? No, for the Greeks were mongrels. It concerns the nature of man. If Aristotle was wrong, what better interpretation of this marvel can sociology offer?

At the moment even if it was admitted that the small community was the best nursery for genius and freedom, everything is against it. Ancient Greek liberty was as precarious as it was lovely and it is doubtful if any modern Greek would accept it. How many blessings descend on those who are content with less! The Italians, even the tyrant de Vecchi, were extremely indulgent to Rhodes, so that liberty would not now be half so dear to the Rhodians if it were not sweetened with many fiscal concessions. For example, they get their sugar for 5 drachmas the kilo, while the Cretans, with whose affections no wealthy foreigner has tampered, have to pay 10 drachmas at least.

And apart from the question of groceries, there is that of security, so that in fact few sensible men believe that it is wise for small peoples to wish for independence. It has long been so. Mahaffy, the Provost of TCD, loved freedom and was an ardent phil-Hellene. Describing very readably his travels in Greece with Oscar Wilde, he faced squarely certain ambiguities in his concern for liberty, which as an Irish imperialist he could not dodge. He thought that, when England occupied Malta and the Ionian Islands, she should have taken Sicily and Southern Greece as well.

> What precious results [he wrote] might have been gained for these countries themselves and for Europe at large! While our invalids and sybarites would have spread wealth and refinement through the beautiful uplands of Sicily, our route to India would have lain through Greece. . . Greek art and antiquities would have become the household property of good society, instead of being seen only by a few privileged people to the great disgust of their envious neighbours.

Except that they would have disagreed as to whose invalids should refine the Sicilians, the tyrant de Vecchi would have fully understood this point of view which still survives in many respectable bosoms. I felt it stir in my own, when at Corinth our guide told how she had taken round a party of English journalists concerned about Cyprus. She spoke of the monuments they had seen, the banquets they had eaten, the contacts, the camaraderie and 'the greater mutual understanding' that had ensued.

'Softening-up process!' interjected one of my fellow-travellers.

'Brain-washing!' said a second.

A third was more explicit: 'I think you were cheating. You were using your beautiful country to influence a political decision.'

I felt neutral, for it is the Greek intention to bring Cyprus directly under the Athens Government, as Crete is. No doubt that is what the Cypriots want, but I cannot suppress my conviction that Hellenic liberty was the discovery of small pig-headed communities, which resisted assimilation to larger ones at the price of security. It was almost a definition of liberty that it should be insecure. Groceries or no groceries, it might be easier for Cyprus to extricate herself from the bored clutches of an alien than from the tender and suffocating embraces of Mother Greece.

Certainly Mother Greece loves Crete in a very possessive way. Though we never heard sedition preached there, there is a constant grumbling about taxes and jobs. As regards jobs, it was odd that the admirable guide, who showed us Cnossos and Phaestus as well as Rhodes, was an Athenian. Are there no unemployed intellectuals in the land of Kazantzakis, whom I believe to be a major European novelist? And was the tourist policeman who sat beside the guide an Athenian too? It was his job to go ahead of us and refine the Cretans. Once when we stopped in a village for a drink he dashed into the café first and we found him engaged in a fiery battle with the proprietor and his waiters. We begged for our drinks, but Greek had met Greek and they had no time for us. The policeman was telling them that they should have clean shirts on and a black tie for the tourists, and the waiters were roaring back, 'Why didn't you 'phone us from Iraklion and warn us they were coming?' The policeman stamped his foot and said, 'Can't you understand that you have to have clean shirts for the *whole* of the tourist season?' The monstrous absurdity of this left the waiters speechless, and we managed to order our drinks.

As a civilizing influence would Mahaffy have been pleased with us? In his day, when an unrefined people was to be refined by an imperial one, the patient had to be put in some sort of political strait-jacket and culture had to be pumped in by resident expatriates. But now refinement comes by plane and train and bus from every land of the west. Such progress has been made in the canning and sweetening of culture that huge concentrated doses, capable of neutralizing the toughest insularities, the most obstinate regional idiosyncrasies, can be dumped anywhere by anyone, and they will be greedily absorbed. Culture vibrates through the air and croons and quivers on celluloid. When we landed in Crete we heard a voice warbling in our own tongue from the charabanc that had come to meet our plane: 'I guess I'll have to dream the rest!' it managed to say before we extinguished it. At Cnossos and at Mallia the chauffeur remained with his discs in the charabanc and the warbling would start up again, transporting him to distant lands and remote experiences more effectively then we, the raw unsweetened products of those lands, could ever do. In fact he did not like Anglo-Saxons in the flesh and when we passed the American air-base near Mallia he wrinkled up his nose to illustrate how aloof the Americans were. Pointing at the rocket-site, he said: 'They make Crete very important place; we all get blown up in next war. Greek Government want to be important, Cretymen not.' Cretans and Anglo-Saxons meet each other like shadows beyond the Styx. We saw an American airman looking at Minoan pots; a patch on the back of his tunic five times the size of the Phaestos disk was embroidered with a map of Crete, the word IRAKLION and many letters and numbers, as though he had come to Crete in the mail-bag. The travels recorded on his spine had left no imprint on his face, which was amazingly blank.

In Rhodes at the lower end of the Street of the Knights, we met a crowd of German soldiers dashing with tanks under an ancient archway. Under their Nazi helmets black Greek eyes were sparkling. They straggled back twice and dashed through again, then a third time *da capo*. There was a tourist policeman there, but we were too middle-aged to need his reassurance that there was no cause for alarm. In fact David Niven and Gregory Peck and a host of cameramen and supers and secretaries were at work on their film in the huge and sprawling Hotel Miramare on the road to Cameirus. In an annexe was a publicity department daily sending out advance notices to Arizona and Malaya. A couple of million pounds was to be spent on the film, and half of this, we were told, would be spent in Rhodes. In a few months the film will rise like a rocket and encircle the globe, and before the last vibration of this mighty effort of the human imagination has died down enough gold will have been stirred round to rebuild the Colossus of Rhodes ten times over.

But here we have to ask how far we have damaged the intimate relationship between a creative mind and its milieu by distending almost limitlessly the field of vision and hearing, dulling the impact of experience on our senses by exposing them incessantly to titillations from afar? Rhodes is a suitable place in which to ask this question, because it was to Cleobulus, the Rhodian sage, that the Greeks attributed the famous maxim *mēden agan* or Nothing to Excess. In the lounge of the Miramare did I only fancy that the film-folk passing by were practising some kind of intellectual levitation and only made contact with Rhodes through the soles of their alpagatas? They had the constipated look of men who have consumed more irrelevant experience than they can digest. In the corner a man was chalking up the names of horses on a blackboard. As he wrote, the mimosas seemed to wilt and the skies to become grey. We were at Aintree. We had to wait at a table with picture papers on it and for ten minutes we were transported to Paris and New York and some provincial town, I think, Leeds. And this is happening to most of us the whole time. Impressions from far away as soft as snowflakes are choking up the channels of perception, making sharp corners into curves, generalizing what is particular, reducing everything to a boundless colourless uniformity. There is now no escape from *agan*.

The Age of the Parasites, which runs concurrently with the Age of the Satellites beyond the Oder, may last longer than the Age of the City-State did, but it cannot last forever. Whatever their inward affinities, the Parasites and Satellites daily prophesy for each other inevitable dissolution. And indeed it seems that sooner or later these great commensal communities, consolidated by fear and greed, will disintegrate. Giant states are only suitable for dwarfs. Full-sized humans cannot be fed on abstractions and build a society with others, whose existence can only be deduced from statistics, from digests of opinions and mechanical projections of voices and profiles. An idea, which is to travel far by modern means, must like an air-passenger's luggage be meagre. That is why small thoughts and personalities, which would have met with a rejoinder of their own size in the agora at Cameirus in 300 BC, ripple round the world unchallenged.

And in fact all these engines of refinement, which are supposed to spray the wilderness with culture, always slip into reverse and operate as suction pumps. Those men who are susceptible to external influence are drawn away to the cities leaving the torpid and incurious behind. For various reasons no one minds this much. Our chauffeur in Crete was proud that they had had no civil war there comparable to that on the mainland and very little

Communism. 'You see,' he said, 'we have our family wars. That is enough.' And he explained that his stay-at-home relations with a full-time vendetta on their hands, ramifying through distant cousins and unrelated namesakes, had no time for international politics. In Rhodes sophistication has settled in one corner like currants in a badly cooked cake, leaving the interior ignorant and primitive. I walked round a grave-yard in the village of Archangel and it seemed to me that the peasants, their school-teachers and their priests must be as poor and illiterate as in the days of Cleobulus. The names of the dead are roughly scratched with a nail in cement slabs fringed with bathroom tiles. In the phrase *Enthade Keitai* (Here Lies), I read on various tombs, 'keite, kite, keetai, kitai'. One would not find so much misspelling on the memorial slabs which the Italians unearthed in the ancient Rhodian cities.

These peasants are the sediment which half a dozen infusions of foreign culture have failed to dilute. Sophisticated foreigners in revolt from their age find a certain sweetness in their mummified traditions. There is an epicene pleasure in watching others believe things which we no longer believe ourselves. Lawrence Durrell, whose book on Rhodes is so subtle and observant, sternly censures the village poet because he only half believed in the efficacy of the sacred pool at Soroni, in which two old nuns, wading about in nightdresses, were immersing the village idiot. For the poet's scepticism he blames 'the village schoolmaster and lawyer, those heirs to the vague radicalism and agnosticism, which is poisoning the whole source of our culture'.

Mary Renault, in her charming novel about Theseus, also recoils in this odd direction from what she calls 'the levelling fashions of the day' and 'the standards of Admass', and tries to make credible those stories about Crete and Minos, of which the Greeks themselves were sceptical.

Nostalgia for lost innocence is an affliction of the over-civilized from which country intellectuals are immune. All the best verse about bean rows and simple sacrifices to rustic gods was inspired by the roar of Oxford Street or the Roman Forum. Such sentiments were alien to the Hellenes, a half-rustic people, vaguely radical, vaguely agnostic, who rose to glory and laid the foundations of our culture by extricating themselves from primitive superstition and outworn political forms.

We have locked the Hellenes in a museum because the small

communities in which they thrive seem to belong irrevocably to the past. Though our eyes have rested on the lavatory seat of the Queen of Cnossus, and our local branch of the Town and Counties Bank is a close replica of the Temple of Zeus at Aegina, the Greeks themselves are more irrelevant to us than they used to be. Only a very young undergraduate would dare to take Aristotle seriously and to ask whether in ancient Rhodes a citizen could realize his faculties more fully than we can, whether fewer talents were wasted, fewer brains distorted. Few would speculate whether there was less *Angst* and ulcers among its painters and writers than among the gifted artists at the Hotel Miramare. Yet these questions are as pertinent to human society as those which sociologists normally ask.

I think we can acknowledge squalor and slavery and spasms of barbarism, and yet say that, when Lindos and Cameiros were thriving cities, the Rhodians had some precious gift of reconciling disparate things which we have lost. Society was closely knit without curtailment of variety. Ideas were freshly minted from experience, curiosity moved freely and truth was not yet imprisoned in quotation marks. The temples often combined the functions of city-churches and municipal galleries and archives. Religion adapted itself to the vaguely agnostic trends of the time. Pindar, whose ode to the Rhodian boxer, Diagoras, was preserved in letters of gold in the Temple of Athene at Lindos, was very devout but he had, like many others, manufactured his own beliefs, discarding discreditable stories of the gods, even when, as often, these were the most ancient and traditional. In the temples the integrity and independence of the artist were fanatically respected, if one is to believe the old story of Protogenes and his picture of the Satyr – and why should one not believe it? He had painted a partridge on a pillar beside his satyr, so lifelike that all the partridge-breeders of Rhodes (they still breed them there) had brought in their pet partridges to cluck at it. Protogenes considered that this showed such disrespect to the Satyr, his masterpiece, and so vulgar a misunderstanding of art, that he had asked permission of the temple authorities to paint out his partridge. Permission was granted.

Later, of course, Rhodes against her will became involved in the gigantic imperial designs of the successors of Alexander and, in the homeland of Cleobulus, the Colossus, that great ebullition of excess, was erected. It lasted only fifty years, crashing in the earthquake of 227 BC. The Rhodians lived among the fragments for nine centuries, then a Jew from Syria bought them for boiling down. There were, we are told, nine hundred camel-loads to be carried away.

If in some man-made earthquake our colossal enterprises were to collapse today, it would be as hard to tidy up after them, nor does disaster seem to curb the appetite for excess. On the other hand, these enterprises, as their social sterility becomes apparent, may slowly cease to dominate our imaginations. They may yield priority to the study of human relations, at which both in their theory and in its practical application, the Greeks so enormously surpassed us.

[1961]

22

LAMENT FOR ARCHAEOLOGY

I. THE LAY PRETENDERS

We live in the age of the institution and the expert and mostly consult them with respect and gratitude, but archaeology is the latest of the sciences to be institutionalized and the authority of the expert is still frequently challenged.

A few years ago the site of a Danish settlement in Dublin, Wood Quay on the Liffey, was threatened by the Corporation building surveyors and it was planned to erect municipal offices on the half-excavated site. There was an unprecedented outcry not only from Dubliners but from interested people all over Ireland. They were outraged that ancient traces of Danish Dublin should be revealed only to be covered over again. There were big demonstrations, headed by the vigorous and devoted Father F. X. Martin, and busloads of people from the provinces came up to take part in them.

I believe in demonstrations. In the past two or three years two of our principal Norman mottes in Kilkenny, at Tibraghney and Knocktopher, both associated with English kings, John and Richard II, have been bulldozed away for agricultural purposes, and three or four eighteenth-century bridges have been partially destroyed. Only in the case of the beautiful Thomastown bridge did we have a demonstration and if we had acted earlier, I believe, we might have saved it. The Corporation received our belated deputation kindly, and, like everybody else, we used a bit shamefacedly the tourist gimmick and told of the increasing number of foreign canoeists who are using our lovely rivers, the Nore, the Barrow, the Suir. From the river there is a secret charm in sliding under the dark arches of the high-parapetted bridges and finding our little towns concealed behind them. Now, with the bridges broadened for lorry traffic, we just see a moving panorama of legs and wheels.

So at Wood quay I was shocked that there was no unqualified support for the demonstrators from the 'authorities' in the National Museum and the universities. It was said that all the available evidence had been collected from the site and that there were other sites from which corroboration could more easily be secured.

Yet the demonstrations went on and the Corporation scheme was delayed for months. Had the defenders of Wood Quay had the support of the experts, the Danish site would have been saved. Their final failure was tragically significant. The disagreement between the supporters of office blocks and of archaeological sites does not need investigation. It is the conflict between the demonstrators and the experts that is of permanent interest.

Of this conflict we had revealing evidence at the time. An expert from one of the universities, in an article in *The Irish Times*, attacked the demonstrators, describing them as 'lay pretenders'. He suggested that they were survivals from the romantic antiquarianism of the nineteenth century, which held Irish archaeology in its grip till rescued by a tiny band of devoted men, who sometime in the thirties 'secured a respectably high position for Irish archaeology among related sciences throughout the world'. Judging by reports of what is happening in the National Museum and the fate of various small collections stored there in the basement and at Kilmainham, we are now at the nadir of Irish archaeology. The peak was sometime in the 1850s. I am convinced that when the experts talk of 'romantic antiquarianism', they are thinking of Vallancey and Betham, Beauford and Beaufort, who pioneered Irish archaeology at the end of the eighteenth century. Yet it is manifest that their intellectual influence had totally faded by 1833, when Petrie scourged them in his book on round towers (rather uncharitably, considering how fanciful and dogmatic he could often be himself). In Irish scholarship few disputed the supremacy of O'Donovan and to a lesser extent O'Curry, both of them Petrie's colleagues in the Ordnance Survey. In the Kilkenny Archaeological Society, which after 1848 became one of the leading provincial archaeological societies in the British Isles, I can find only one reference to Vallancey which is not disparaging, a comment at a General Meeting: 'Despite Vallancey's questionable theories, he had done much good in arousing attention to Irish archaeology at a time when it excited little interest.'

After Petrie, as is well-known, came Graves and Prim, Wakeman, Brash, Lawlor, Westropp, Todd, Reeves, Standish Hayes O'Grady, Richard Butler, Wilde, Windele, Prendergast and many others. Most of them were good classical scholars who saw Irish history in its European setting. Those of them who were Irish scholars seldom pretended to subtleties of understanding they did not possess. The antithesis of professional and amateur had scarcely been invented, yet which of these men was 'a lay pretender'?

In the 1850s many provincial societies flourished and carried out functions that now have to be shared between several government-subsidized departments. They considered themselves the guardians and recorders as well as the interpreters of their own antiquities. Not only did the KAS watch over and publish the vast collections in Kilkenny Castle muniment room and much regional material that was later removed for greater safety to the Four Courts and burnt there; they arrested also the decay of Jerpoint and Clonmacnoise, and prosecuted vandals. Graves himself, in a famous and fiery correspondence, tackled Lord Templemore's agent, who claimed that by taking down a portion of Dunbrody Abbey he was 'only improving it'.

Had the Society after the death of Graves and Prim confined its activities to its corner of Ireland, it might have survived there. But the temptation to become a nation-wide society was irresistible. When that happened it was not long before museum and library headquarters were transferred to Dublin, and the influence of the Society slowly retreated from Kilkenny, where it had been born.

A century ago it would have been less easy for the Tibraghny and Knocktopher disasters to have happened. When in 1850 Sir Richard Langrishe of Knocktopher heard that a tenant of his was about to destroy the huge Ballyboodan ogham stone, he promptly stopped him. The KAS had to contend with the same barbarism and it is due to their patient efforts that, till about ten years ago, farmers still had a respect for the antiquities of their neighbourhood. When in 1848 Graves and Prim heard that the local landowner at Dunbell was digging up one of the numerous raths that lie between Bennettsbridge and Maddockstown, they discovered that his workpeople had smashed up the two famous Dunbell ogham stones into small pieces. Graves detected, however, that the ogham stones were made of red sandstone while the prevailing local stone is blue limestone. After hours of careful labour he and Prim managed to sort out the fragments from the dump and tentatively piece them together. When they returned the next day, the workmen, realizing the fragments were valued, had concealed them and would not give them up unless they were paid £30, a huge sum for the young Society to pay and an appalling precedent for future discoveries. By tact and firmness the ogham stones were after three weeks recovered and lodged with many other Dunbell finds in the museum.

They stayed there till, after the deaths of Graves and Prim, the rot had set in. They were then transferred with everything else to the National Museum.

As they were on loan I hoped they would soon be returned to Kilkenny when we tried to revive the Society as it had once been and started a small collection which was ultimately transferred to Rothe House. Far from it. Even when some years ago the whole area, which Graves considered to be rich in archaeological promise, was taken over by Quigley Magnesite and subjected to open-cast mining for dolomite, I could not persuade the National Museum to send down the objects which had been found at Dunbell, for local display. Therefore, I made xerox copies of Graves' drawings in the *Kilkenny Archaeological Journal* for 1852 of sample finds in wood and stone and jet, bone and flint, and gave them to the manager. He was entirely co-operative, but space-age machinery precludes detailed investigation and nothing has turned up.

Apart from their great intellectual achievement, these provincial societies were a source of harmony and reconciliation. The KAS, by its Rule 7, excluded 'all matters concerning our political and religious differences' from its papers and discussions. Through the stormy days of Church Disestablishment and the Land League, when its members, outside the Society, freely expressed loud and contrary opinions, complete harmony prevailed within. Yet Graves was a Protestant clergyman, Prim the editor of a Protestant newspaper, the organ of the landed gentry. Explosive material lay about but no explosion occurred inside the Society.

It occurs to me that the post-Treaty scholars would like to believe that their illustrious predecessors had never existed. Not long ago on the radio an Irish scholar maintained that societies like KAS depended on 'large expensive private libraries, which when social change redistributed wealth, could no longer exist'. This is nonsense. The KAS library was founded by John Prim, a country newspaper proprietor, and James Graves, the rector of a small country parish. Graves, because of his devotion to archaeology, lost promotion in his Church, earning nothing till he was old and got a civil list pension of £100 a year from the British Government. The Society was not exclusive as anyone who could pay his subscription was welcome. There were, of course, great house libraries but scholars were given ready access to them. In this county they were mostly burnt in the twenties as in Woodstock, Desart Court and Bessborough, or sold as in Kilfane and Kilkenny Castle.

As for 'the respectably high position that Irish archaeology has now reached among related sciences throughout the world' it is true that just before the war we had an eminent Nazi prehistorian, Adolf Mahr, as Director of our National Museum (suspected by Military Intelligence of being a spy), and another eminent prehistorian, Dr Sprockhoff, a protégé of Himmler, was invited to join in the centenary celebrations in 1949 (God Help Us!) of Graves' and Prim's great achievements. Yet surely we were more in touch with international learning, indeed ahead of it, when in 1852 the KAS made Boucher de Perthes, 'the Father of Prehistory', our 'Honorary Corresponding Member'. This was five years before his 'discovery' of prehistoric man had been internationally acknowledged. Boucher sent several volumes of his writings to the KAS simply because he recognized the Society as of the same calibre as his own Société d'Emulation at Abbeville, in which one of the great discoveries of the nineteenth century was made.

When transferred to Dublin, Boucher de Perthes' gifts to the Society were lost; similarly, the contents of the Kilkenny Museum were mixed up with everything else in the National Museum and are now irretrievable.

Boucher de Perthes was a customs officer at Abbeville, who grew prize pears, organized a public swimming bath, and wrote poor plays and lively travel books. He was the quintessential 'amateur' or lay pretender and gloried in it. 'I know as much about science,' he wrote, 'as a donkey does about music. . . Ignorance is a field in which nettle and thistle never took root, so they do not have to be grubbed up.'

Boucher and the other two great nineteenth-century pioneers, Schliemann, the indigo merchant, and Arthur Evans, the Balkan war-correspondent and rebel, who revealed the Mycenaean and Minoan civilizations, could also in their day have been called 'romantic antiquarians'. Their great discoveries were hatched in a cocoon of lively guess-work. Ventris, who nearer our time deciphered and revealed the Greek affinities of Linear B, was an architect, who 'did a bit of Greek', he admitted, at Stowe School. Archaeology, in fact, owes an incalculable debt to the lay pretender, and when professional integrity had died, as happened lately for long periods over much of Europe, the lay pretender survived.

When some time in the eighties of the last century the experts removed a vast quantity of our parish registers and other valuable material to the doomed Four Courts for safe-keeping, they were only robbing us of paper. What they are doing now is robbing us of men and women. In the last century those who had a sense of the past used it so that, in Camden's phrase, they should not be 'Strangers in their own land and forrainers in their own cities.' Now it opens the door to a university course in archaeology and 'a job'. And if there is not one in Ireland they look for it in some English or American university.

All those who see that they can make a career out of what used to be called 'a sweet food of the mind' are irresistibly tempted away. If they come home again it is as talent-spotters, and we have in many cases to get 'forrainers' to teach us about our own city. Urban pundit and country puppet nourish each other. There are, of course, brilliant exceptions, men and women who struggle against the tide. There is nothing unique to Ireland about this. It is happening all over the world and meeting varying degrees of resistance.

II. DEATH OF TWO SISTERS

It is a platitude to say that the pursuit of science is no longer of necessity an honourable one. Most sciences have now been institutionalized and though half of man's mind may be on the discovery of truth, the other half is on chairs and grants and exams and whatever great power endows the institutes. One thinks first of physics and the scramble by the British and Americans to snatch Wernher von Braun from Krensburg prison before the Russians got hold of him. It was he who had launched the twenty-seven V2 rockets on London from Peenemunde and it was Himmler who had equipped him with assistants from the concentration camps. They worked, for security reasons, in stinking caves under the Harz mountains. But knowledge, of course, 'belongs to the world' and when von Braun, handed over to the Americans, turned his brains to 'the conquest of space', everyone was delighted with him. There were those who wanted him awarded the Nobel Peace Prize.

It was not long before the dark shadow that had fallen on physics and its related sciences had enveloped them all.

The subject is richly documented. The best book I know about it, Frederick Lilge's *The Abuse of Learning: The Failure of the German Universities,* was published soon after the war and is still highly relevant. The Germans were pioneers in Scientific Method which the rest of the world soon gratefully adopted. The Higher Learning, with its rigorous Teutonic ideal of *Wissenschaft,* spread to America after the Civil War. Knowledge, there, was and still is in danger of disintegrating into multiversities, where degrees are given for pastry-making, and the Higher Learning shone down upon this trackless confusion like a beacon of Integrity and Truth. For many years it was wonderful and great institutes like the Johns Hopkins were founded and prospered.

Then suddenly a terrible disease fell upon the Higher Learning in the country of its birth and spread, in a less virulent form, to America and the rest of Europe.

Lilge's diagnosis is that the tradition of 'scholarly objectivity' and 'the neutrality of science' made the academic the slave of the governments and corporations, which alone had power to pay for abstract studies; these could never, like pastries, pay for themselves. Freed from economic cares, from moral and spiritual responsibilities, the academics shared out the Quest for Truth among themselves as if it was a pork-pie.

> They had [writes Lilge] the happiness of permanent employment and of concealing from themselves the futility of their efforts and their lives.
>
> Departmentalism unleashed all that competitiveness, that currying for favour, that attention to public relations, that scrambling for students, that pettiness and jealousy, which made the university indistinguishable from other organizations.

Obviously it is in Germany where it began that the rise and

fall of the Higher Learning can best be studied and of all the sciences the degradation of the sister sciences, Anthropology and Archaeology, are the most revealing for they are the most related to Man and to Human Life. The most damning evidence comes from before the war, when intellectual resistance was still possible, and I know no better account of what happened than that by Eva Lips, the wife of the curator of the Anthropological Museum in Cologne and an anthropologist herself. She wrote in 1938:

> The anthropologists of Germany, at the outbreak of the Third Reich, hastened to destroy what they had previously revered; truth in research and freedom in teaching. The sphere of activity of these men of science was the world. No science was so well fitted as anthropology to protest against the madness of classifying races according to a scale of values. But they knew also the sacrifices and dangers that a public stand for truth would entail. Not a single man rose up to lift his voice for truth and freedom in science, content to face the certainty of want and persecution if he could but retain his honour.

This, of course, is a world tragedy, not a German one. In the days of Voltaire and the Encyclopaedists it was possible to talk of Science having no frontiers, but this became the emptiest of slogans as soon as learning was officially subsidized. Anything that is paid for by the state is the concern of the state, and in a time of crisis it is easy to justify any form of capitulation or connivance. 'If I go to prison, what happens to my library, my laboratory, my half-classified collection?'

Listen to the advice that Herr van Rautenstrauch, the founder of the Cologne Anthropological Museum and a stalwart enemy of the Nazis, gave to Professor Lips:

> Your attitude strikes me as neither practical nor wise. I would avoid everything that would irritate those now in power and place obstacles in the way of mutual understanding, whereas if you will now wholeheartedly agree to all reasonable requests, I am confident that you can continue your scientific activities indefinitely at the museum.

I believe that is the way in which all directors of all institutes would react in times of stress. Frau Lips calls them 'co-ordinated jellyfish' but it must be admitted that for the purely physical survival of a cultural organism, the jellyfish tactics are best. Professor Lips, as an alternative, tried a silly-clever experiment but failed. He installed as his successor a jellyfish so loathsome in his ignorance and venality that he was sure the authorities would come to their senses. But, of course, he was wrong. Institutes that depend not on men but on administrative machinery will go on churning out degrees and chairs, Festschrifts and journals, though the air is thick with the smell of corpses.

The museum survived but its complicated mechanism was put neatly into reverse. Anthropology, whose object had been to stress the unity of mankind, had become a neat dove-tailing of disparate technologies and it was possible for it to be turned upside down without falling apart. The museum was henceforward used to demonstrate that mankind is in fact so varied that some races can be reckoned as subhuman and treated like animals.

In a very short time, to reinforce the new message, Himmler, who was the most generous patron of Anthropology and Archaeology Germany had ever known, had established at Strasburg an SS Institute for Anthropological Research, under the supervision of Professor Hirt, Director of the University's Anatomical Institute. Hirt had a magnificent collection of skulls of all the races of the earth, but it was defective in Jewish and Russian specimens till the war in the east offered an abundance of excellent quality. Edward Crankshaw has printed Dr Hirt's fascinating instructions to the Wehrmacht for the collection and dispatch of the heads of Jewish Bolshevik commissars. The commissars were to be treated with great care, photographed, measured and all relevant facts recorded, before the heads were expertly severed by a Wehrmacht physician and sent in cans of preserving spirits to Strasburg.

Professor Hirt was later hanged, but in fact he was little worse than a thousand other scholars who at the price of silence bought governmental support for the advancement of learning. The commissars would have been killed in any case. Had not Himmler in his speech at Weselburg dwelt on the necessity of exterminating 30,000,000 Russians? The professor's concern for their skulls may have saved them preliminary discomfort.

By 1933, eleven per cent of all the university faculty members of Germany had become nazified and the others argued no doubt that Science and Culture were beyond politics and that Art had no frontiers. They were surely victims not of German history or temperament but of an occupational disease, which is now afflicting all universities everywhere.

Their own scholars had predicted it generations before. Von

Humboldt, for example, who became Prussian Secretary of Education in 1809, believed that 'the aim of all scientific work is not knowledge but the enlargement of man's character'. What you learn must be integrated with all that you know. 'As soon as a man deludes himself that knowledge does not depend on creative imagination but can be put together mechanically, all is irrevocably lost.'

By 1933 all was lost.

Unfortunately there is no Frau Professor Lips to tell us how archaeology died and when. Was it when Himmler made twenty-five new chairs of archaeology and found twenty-five learned men to fill them? Was it when he sent Sprockhoff to dig for Aryans under Vidkun Quisling? Was it when he sent an expedition to search for the traces of Aryanism (Tokharian?) in Tibet?

I think myself that archaeology did not really die till all international scholars decided that it would be wise and generous to let bygones be bygones. After that all the eminent scholars of Europe, America and Russia, and even a Jew or two, signed a Festschrift in honour of Professor Sprockhoff's sixtieth birthday and he was an honoured guest at conferences such as ours in Kilkenny.

The point that Humboldt, Ortega y Gasset, Lilge and others have made is that the departmentalization of learning had destroyed it. It had ceased to be an integral part of an educated man, transfusing everything. It was detachable, and profound studies about skulls could be pigeon-holed in the mind separately from the question of severing and pickling them. In this way archaeology, which had been born beside ruined abbeys and whose purpose had not been knowledge but to keep alive in a small community the sense of the past and the continuity of history, became one of the whore sciences whose poxy favours can be bought by any government prepared to pay for them.

In fairness one must admit that knowledge basely acquired has once or twice been destroyed. When the allies reached Dachau they burnt all the valuable evidence that Dr Rascher had acquired about high altitude flying – he kept prisoners in ice-cold water tanks or special vans from which air could be extracted till they died of haemorrhage. But probably that was because no 'expert' was present.

Listen for instance to Dr Grahame Clark on this subject:

> Though the motives of the Nazi leaders were nefarious yet they showed a clear recognition of the value of archaeology for enhancing solidarity. . . nor need we find it difficult to admit that some of the research they made possible was of a high technical standard and yielded solid results.

Should we not, therefore, respect 'solid results', however acquired?

Unlike archaeologists, anthropologists have shown themselves ready to admit that their science is dead. Kathleen Gough, a Canadian university lecturer, writes that anthropologists, through claiming that their science is 'ethically neutral', have lost sight of the human goals to which it was once directed. They have ceased to be its masters and become its slaves.

For example, in November 1966 the Association of American Anthropologists passed a resolution which was tantamount to a condemnation of the war in Vietnam. Yet some score of anthropologists were sent out east because their knowledge of primitive customs could be useful in the American counter-insurgency programme, Project Agile. By offering to the military their knowledge of primitive people, they bought themselves out of the job of killing them.

As a human science I do not think archaeology is half as dead as anthropology, simply because we have the example of a century ago to guide us. At the present time, to recover what we have lost is an almost insuperable task. In Ireland the old county societies were linked with a variety of social circumstances which no one would wish to restore even if that had been possible. Yet revivals of earlier ways of thinking have often been adapted to changed circumstances and we need not despair.

[1984]

PART THREE
EASTERN EXCURSIONS

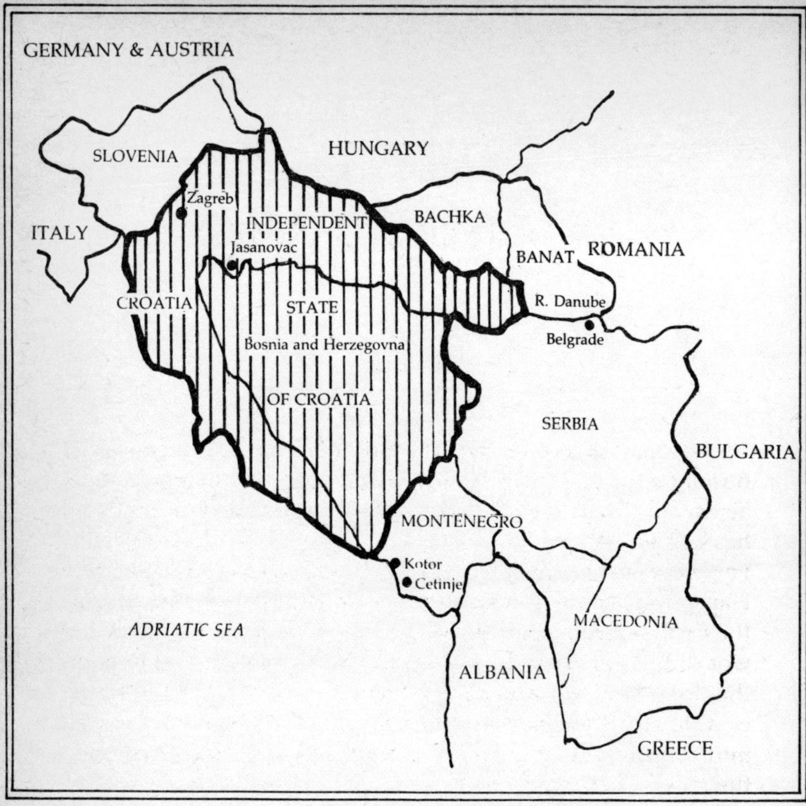

INDEPENDENT STATE OF CROATIA AND
DISMEMBERMENT OF YUGOSLAVIA 1941–45

Frontiers of pre-1941 Yugoslavia marked in bold

Independent State of Croatia	*This included Bosnia and Herzegovina*
Serbia	*Nominally independent under puppet general Nedich*
To Italy	*Montenegro, much of Dalmatia, western Slovenia*
To Hungary	*Bachka and other small frontier regions*
To Bulgaria	*Eastern Macedonia*
To Albania	*Western Macedonia*
Under German control	*Banat and eastern Slovenia*

23

MR PFEFFER OF SARAJEVO

It must have been in the late twenties that the first wave of nostalgia for imperial Austria, its glamour and its grace, swept across the theatre and the screen. Later, it invaded the study and has long given a giddy twist to many serious historical researches. For very many people, whose parents fought against the Hapsburgs, the assassinations at Sarajevo have come to mean the first great irruption of violence into a prosperous and orderly world, the signal for the decay of romance, colour and freedom, the prelude to the crude despotism of the bully and the statistician. In fact, there was never a time when it was harder to enter into the minds of those who saw the Sarajevo assassinations as the dawn of liberty.

But the record of the monuments on the Latinska bridge in Sarajevo shows that there was no simple struggle between poetry and prose, between tradition and anarchy. There was a duel to the death between two rival ideals, one died and the other was stricken with a mortal illness.

The large Austro-Hungarian monument to the Archduke and his wife, with its crowns, columns and marble mourners, stood on the bridge for only two years. It was smashed by the Serbs in 1918 and in the presence of an archbishop a tablet was set in its place to the memory of their assassin, Gavrilo Princip, and to the dawn of Yugoslav freedom. At the same time the bones of Princip and his fellow conspirators were collected from the prison cemeteries of Czechoslovakia and lower Austria and given a splendid interment. The tablet stayed there for twenty-four years and then it was torn down and sent to Hitler at Berchtesgaden by one of his loyal generals. After the Germans, Italians, Croat separatists and finally Communists held the bridge. Today

Princip's romantic dreams seem scarcely more compatible with the public aspirations of his countrymen than do the ingenious political constructions of imperial Vienna. They are revered, of course, like a historic blunderbuss in a show-case, but they are not for handling.

The real tragedy of Sarajevo was never commemorated on the bridge and yet it was more momentous than the collapse of imperialism or the rapid degradation of the nationalism which superseded it. All through the empire and through Europe there were men of liberal outlook who foresaw the fatal collision and tried in vain to prevent it. Their failure meant the disgrace and finally the extinction of liberalism. If another commemorative monument were ever to be erected on the bridge at Sarajevo it ought to be to Mr Leo Pfeffer, the examining magistrate at the trial of the assassins; a liberal, he defended his creed as stoutly as Princip and Franz Ferdinand defended theirs and his defeat, too, was symbolic.

It was not till 1934 that Mr Pfeffer, a Croat and a Catholic, brought his manuscript account of the preliminary examination and his comments on it to my friend, Dr Churchin of Zagreb. Churchin was at that time editor of *Nova Evropa*, the only liberal monthly of consequence to be published in the Balkans. He printed the manuscript in instalments and asked my help in preparing an English translation. But it was a bad time. The rise of Hitler made it hard to focus the attention on Mr Pfeffer's scrupulous analysis of these complex distant events or to make them interesting to others. His book is still unpublished.

Mr Pfeffer, an expert in the law of the Austro-Hungarian Empire, tried to administer it with justice and charity. He treated the assassins as what they were, men of honour and principle, who had acted deliberately and did not wish to shift the responsibility for their acts onto the shoulders of others. They resisted the bullying of the police but they were ready to co-operate with Mr Pfeffer, with the result that we have an all but complete picture of the passage of six bombs and four revolvers from Belgrade through the Bosnian highlands to Sarajevo, of the endless variety of men and women who handled them and hid them in cow byres and in reading rooms and under pillows and in loaves of oaten bread, till finally the Heir Apparent lay dead on an iron bed in the governor of Bosnia's palace.

When Mr Pfeffer had ordered the arrest of a student Grabezh, whom he had correctly associated with the assassination, the young man, the son of an Orthodox priest near Sarajevo, was led to him, filthy and soaking and defiant. The police had tried to force him to tell them where he had hidden the bombs he had failed to throw; they had ducked him in the river and in the town drain. Mr Pfeffer spoke to him in his usual way.

I am the examining magistrate and I am going to call you 'thou', not from any lack of respect but so that we may understand each other better. I do not consider you a common criminal, you acted from political conviction and history will decide whether you were right. But the court must prosecute you for your act. It was not with my knowledge or approval that the police tortured you. If you do not tell me where the bomb was hidden it will explode and injure some innocent person.

Grabezh promptly answered: 'You are the first person who has spoken to me like a human being, so I will tell you.' And half-an-hour later the bomb was found in the earth closet of a hotel belonging to Grabezh's cousin. Another chapter was added to the story of the crime and the chief of police liked Mr Pfeffer even less than before.

If it was due to Mr Pfeffer in the first place that the conspirators were detected, it is also because of him that they remain more than mere names carved in marble or woven into patriotic ballads. We know their hesitations as well as their final resolve and in them we see the reflection of an entire nation in revolt.

After the tension and the triumph of the Balkan Wars the Serbs were more proud and prickly than ever and Mr Pfeffer, a Croat, gives a good picture of the small mortifications that the non-German subjects of Franz Josef had to endure. Bosnia, which borders upon Serbia and has a mainly Serbian population had been recently annexed. It was being given railways and hospitals, but every spoonful of jam had its pill and the local Austrian officials often scraped off the jam for themselves. For example, every town had its Beamtenverein, a small club for government clerks, but though the majority of the members were Slav, there was an unwritten law that all the committee should be German. Mr Pfeffer tells how he and some friends managed once to canvass the voters so that the committee of the club was controlled by Slavs and its name altered. This triumph lasted for one month and then all the Slav committee members were transferred to posts in other towns. But the members elected more Slavs to the committee. Then the Germans all withdrew and formed a *Herrenklub* of their own.

If these lofty ways could exasperate a civil servant like Mr Pfeffer, a more violent reaction can be imagined among the Serbian patriots. When the old Emperor Franz Josef came to Sarajevo in 1910, a student called Jeracic decided to kill him. But, touched by his age and frailty, he flung his bomb at the governor of Bosnia instead, missed, and then killed himself. Jeracic became a great hero, poems were written about him, declamations were made and dozens of students, including Princip himself, swore upon his grave that he would be avenged. The excitement spread to Croatia and four attempts were made upon the life of the governor in Zagreb.

Franz Ferdinand, the Heir-Apparent, was supposed to be mildly Slavophile, and to favour the creation of a trialist monarchy in which Austrians, Hungarians, and Slavs had equal rights. His views made him enemies in Vienna and Budapest but no friends in Bosnia. He was a Hapsburg and that was enough.

The circumstances of his visit to Sarajevo are so strange that Mr Pfeffer raised a doubt that has had frequent echoes and has never been satisfactorily laid to rest. Was the visit a provocation? Did the Vienna Government want some incident to occur that would give an excuse for the subjugation of Serbia? Mr Pfeffer can explain in no other way the absence of police and military from the streets (very strange when you recall that there were manoeuvres on and troops in abundance outside the town). And how was it possible for a second assassin to have another try half-an-hour after the first had failed? The photographs have survived and you can see the archducal car proceeding down an almost empty street. A small boy waves his hat from the quayside, while on the opposite pavement, Mr Pfeffer tells us, six assassins were stationed at intervals (the photographer had marked one of them with a cross), but not a single policeman. Then why ever did the royal visit take place on Vidovdan, a great day of mourning for the defeat of the Serbs by the Turks in the fourteenth century, a defeat which the Serbs had just so triumphantly reversed?

But one must not oversimplify. Of course there may have been some high official who said, 'The Archduke thinks he's so popular with the Serbs, let him find out for himself!' and then cynically relaxed security measures. Baron Bolfras, for example, who accompanied the Archduke, expressed that opinion in his reminiscences. But I doubt whether respectable bureaucrats often consciously plan for assassination. I think, when they want a major blunder made, they delegate authority to some naïve and irreproachable subordinate. One can imagine some minor diplomatic personage getting fuddled by the mystique of royalty and Austria's cultural mission to the Balkans. He would specially choose Vidovdan for the visit. 'We must teach Serbs and Turks to forget about these ancient quarrels,' he would argue, 'and to bury the hatchet. We must show them how our royalty moves freely and fearlessly among its subjects. We put our trust in Providence.' Then the assassination would be deemed the violation of the most sacred trust, and the ultimatum to Belgrade would seem to have been countersigned in Heaven. They could settle down to the absorption of Serbia with the easiest of consciences.

As the days passed, the mourning for the royal couple assumed a majesty that must have made it very hard for Mr Pfeffer to keep his head. The royal corpses passed out of the hands of the doctors and the police and lay in state with a hundred tapers blazing. They travelled overland and by sea to Trieste with solemn ceremonies at every halt. Finally, at midnight, they reached Vienna; with torches and muffled drums and a cavalry escort, they were brought to the church of the Hofburg. The next day the old emperor drove up from Schonbrunn to the service while his ministers got ready for the annihilation of Serbia.

Meanwhile in Sarajevo, Mr Pfeffer looking out of his window saw a procession of boys and girls issuing from the police station with a large portrait of the Archduke draped in crape. A wave of mourning was followed by a wave of indignation against the Serbs. Their shops, hotels, reading-rooms were wrecked. The police knew that provided you organize the mourning, there will always be volunteers to carry through the retribution.

Mr Pfeffer slowly pieced together the whole of the story of the assassinations. Very many Serbs in Bosnia and outside it, as well as some Croats and Moslems, were linked in the conspiracy. The individual had set himself in a big way against the state but nothing appeared to prove the complicity of the Serbian Government which the Austrian ultimatum assumed.

There was, of course, a link between the political intrigues of Belgrade and the young Bosnian rebels, but Pfeffer, after a detailed examination of all the evidence, decided that encouragement from Serbia had been unofficial and half-hearted. Captain Tankoshitch, a hero of the Balkan Wars, had indeed got the bombs for the Bosnian students, when they had come to him in Belgrade, begging his assistance. He was a member of the Black Hand,* a Serbian organization for the liberation of the Southern Slavs of the Austro-Hungarian Empire. It had seemed to him and others that the Archduke's visit and military manoeuvres in Bosnia, which, as Supreme Commander he came to supervise, were sly preliminaries to an attack on Serbia. Possibly, they thought, a bomb or two might warn the Austrians of the resistance they would meet, though the conspirators did not seek the approval of the Serbian Government, which knew nothing of their schemes. Soon after the bombs had been provided, the leaders of the Black Hand had misgivings. Not in their wildest dreams had they thought that the Archduke would be so carelessly guarded that the assassination might succeed, but the young men seemed too ingenuous to be trusted. Sharats, a theological seminarist, was sent post haste to Sarajevo to stop the enterprise, but the bombs were already on the way, the students had made up their minds. They would not listen to him.

Mr Pfeffer secured abundant photographs. Alone of all the conspirators, the guerrilla Tankoshitch faces the camera with dandified composure, spruce moustachios and a chest criss-crossed with bandoliers. We know the others only from prison photographs. There are about a dozen university students, a village schoolmaster, a prosperous citizen of Tuzla who had opened the first cinema, a patron of gymnastic clubs and reading-rooms. There is a peasant farmer, a very handsome old man in the white tunic and gay woven girdle of the Bosnian highlands. His son, a pastoral figure from the Old Testament, appears with his hands lightly clasped. He is grave, bewildered and yet relaxed, strangely different from the tense figures of the townspeople. You can see in their eyes that their resolution was shaped by text books, newspapers, committees, while for the peasants the tragedy of Vidovdan was the fulfilment of old legends, ancient curses. For them the Archduke must have been a shadowy figure not easily to be distinguished from the Turkish

* There are some who now dispute Pfeffer's conclusion, e.g. Joachim Remak, an American professor, who thinks that the whole assassination was organized by Apis (of the Black Hand) in Belgrade, but I don't believe he proves his case at all.

overlords of the past. The bombs which the students brought them slipped into their broad girdles all too naturally.

These bombs must have changed hands twenty times on their way to Sarajevo. Let me describe a single episode, one of many similar ones. One June day a fortnight before the assassination, Chubrilovitch, the young teacher of a church school near the Serbian frontier, was riding beside the village priest to buy lambs. He had offered to help the priest ford a river swollen by the floods, but before they reached it a ploughman came out of the woods to say that two students wanted to see the schoolmaster. As soon as the priest had gone, the students, whom the ploughman had helped across the frontier, crept into the open. They explained that in their rucksacks were bombs for the murder of the Archduke. These would somehow have to be brought to Tuzla, the market town, and left with the cinema proprietor for the next stage of their journey to Sarajevo. The schoolmaster put the bombs into the panniers of his horse and took the students to the large farmhouse of his godfather, Kerovitch. The whole family came in to discuss how to get the bombs to Tuzla. One of the sons of the house had cut his hand scything; he had to go to town to see the doctor; then he remembered that their neighbour had to take out his horse and cart to fetch a trunk belonging to a brother who was leaving his school at Tuzla. When night fell they set off, skirting the village where there were military barracks, sitting at different tables whenever they stopped at taverns, till after many adventures they reached the reading-room over which the cinema proprietor had his flat.

Even so crude a summary may illustrate how the Austrian annexation of Bosnia had brought two worlds into violent collision; it shows that the assassination was not hatched in an anarchist cellar. In the wild barren mountains, which the Turk never completely subdued, the fierce spirit of independence, though it might exchange ballads for reading-rooms, daggers for bombs, was scantily concealed.

Princip and Chabrinovitch, the two students who actually used the weapons on Vidovdan, were reading-room rather than mountain trained. Mr Pfeffer speaks well of their courage and sincerity. When the trial was over the judge called on those prisoners who repented of their crime to stand up. They all stood up except for Princip. When interrogated, he replied that he was sorry that he had robbed some children of their parents and that he had killed the Archduchess, particularly as she was a Czech, but he was not sorry he had killed the Archduke. He had intended to do so. Then Chabrinovitch, confused and ashamed, sat down again. He had changed his mind, he said; he wasn't sorry either for what he had done.

Chabrinovitch was a nineteen-year-old printer. His evidence was heard with difficulty because the cyanide, which he had tried to swallow at the moment of arrest, had burnt his lips. He was a more theatrical type than the others. He longed to be conspicuous and was so unwisely talkative that the other two students, Princip and Grabezh, had separated from him on their journey across the mountains. There had been ructions in the Chabrinovitch household the day before Vidovdan, when he had hidden the imperial standard which his father intended to hang out of the window. He had made his preparations for immortality rather elaborately, getting photographs of himself to present to his friends, consigning his watch and his savings to his sister. After his bomb had missed he had leapt into the river with the cyanide between his teeth. But everything went wrong; the river washed off the cyanide and his terrified friends destroyed his photographs. He died in prison at the moment when Serbia had suffered her greatest defeat.

Their nationalism was of the traditional kind. Princip declared that Serbs and Croats were one people and that Yugoslavia must be united as Italy and Germany had been. They must throw out the Austrians as the Italians had done. They were quite unlike the subsidized revolutionaries of later days; indeed they were always penniless. A week or two before the assassination the director of the academy library had noticed that Princip always read on through the lunch hour; finding that he had no money for food, he offered him some. Princip refused but agreed to earn a few shillings by copying out the minutes of a committee meeting. A couple of months later, when it was discovered who had copied them, the offensive pages were solemnly erased.

Mr Pfeffer wrote his book at a time when the Croats were suffering as much from Serbian despotism as under Austria-Hungary. King Alexander's police surpassed the Austrians in brutality and a Croat might well have been tempted to regret the world of culture and learning destroyed on Vidovdan.

But in Mr Pfeffer's pages we see the empire fading naturally and inevitably as a flower. It could not be saved, but the ground might be got ready for its seeds. Mr Pfeffer and others were doing this, but most of the Austrian officials could not face the truth. Their diplomacy had become a network of lies and tricks in which they strangled as many friends as enemies. We see this happening even in Sarajevo. The Austrians were trying to conciliate the Moslems in Bosnia in order to counterbalance the Croats and Serbs, who formed the majority. Perhaps they had some prevision of their war-time alliance with Turkey. Their Bosnian regiments wore the fez and a hideous Turko-Viennese town hall was erected at Sarajevo. The authorities were therefore displeased when Mr Pfeffer discovered that one of the young men who waited on the quayside with a bomb for the Archduke was a Moslem. He was twice imprisoned and twice escaped with the connivance, Mr Pfeffer was convinced, of the police. He was never brought to trial or charged.

And there were fatuous, place-hunting lies as well as mean, political ones. Contrary to custom, Mr Pfeffer was not asked to be present at the examination of the bodies of the royal pair, but he was expected later to sign the official report testifying to facts he had not seen. He indignantly refused. Later he learnt that he had not been asked in because of his grey suit. In the presence of royalty, even dead royalty, a frock coat is obligatory. Also decorations were to be awarded to all those present on that solemn occasion and his rank did not qualify him for one.

The convicted students were under twenty and therefore exempted by Austrian law from hanging. But they and most of the others died after a year's imprisonment; Mr Pfeffer does not attribute this very strange fact to Austrian cruelty. TB can, perhaps, account for two out of a dozen. One of them went mad. Is it possible that these unsophisticated people simply sank under the gigantic consequences of what they had done? At times they may have had some intimation of the honour in which they would later be held, but more often they must have thought of the German and Austrian armies advancing everywhere and the Serbians hopelessly crushed. Night and day five soldiers watched over Princip in his cell at Theresienstadt, one in his room, two in the passage, two outside the window. He can never have learnt that the empire he had challenged was collapsing.

The Austrian authorities strongly disapproved of Mr Pfeffer, but he had done his work well and could not be dismissed. With ingenious malice the minister succeeded in transferring him to

Tuzla, the home ground of so many of the conspirators whom he had brought to trial. When the war ended, the Tuzla town council pressed for his trial, but the brother of the schoolmaster, Chubrilovitch, who had been hanged, came to his defence and he was allowed to retire into private life.

He was universally detested and yet it was clear that he had acted in the only possible way that an Austrian official could honourably act. He had fixed the guilt clearly and categorically upon individuals who were ready to shoulder it. He had tried to dispel the clouds of dark suspicion and vague accusation from which wars arise. He had localized and isolated a crime at a time when the Austro-Hungarian Government, with the German Empire behind it, was trying to put a whole nation in the dock.

He failed; but in honouring what was generous and self-sacrificing in a young nation which claimed its rights, he upheld better than its own ministers the honour of the doomed old empire which he served.

EPILOGUE

The Sarajevo conspirators were Croats, Serbs and Moslems, and they aimed at a nation in which the diverse peoples of Yugoslavia should live in free and equal union. They were mostly republicans and the movement to which they belonged was not tainted with racialism till the new state was set up under the Serbian king. It was racialism, not nationalism, that undermined Yugoslav unity, but this vital distinction is seldom observed and when 'petty nationalism' is attacked as the source of our troubles, the 'petty nations' seldom defend themselves. Unlike monarchies, empires and Communist states, they have no trade union nor have they developed a common philosophy. They have few arguments to oppose to the universalists and imperialists, who believe that incompatibilities of language and culture are best ironed out by the kindly pressure of a dominant race. In fact, the small peoples often subscribe to this belief themselves. Frequently you will hear an Irish nationalist lamenting the collapse of Austria-Hungary and explaining that Yugoslavia and the other succession states were mere puppet contrivances of the League of Nations, rag-bags of racial oddments, doomed to disintegrate. He ignores that these states all have living languages and often a more distinctive culture, a longer history of independence than our own. And since the Succession States owed their existence to England and France, their citizens often scoffed at Ireland's independence. The Croats used to call themselves 'the Ulster of Yugoslavia' because they considered the Six Counties as progressive as themselves and in equal danger of being absorbed into the peasant economy of a more primitive people.

What then is nationalism and how can it be distinguished from racialism? Thomas Davis, being only half-Irish, is probably a sounder nationalist, more immune from racialism, than Mazzini and the other Victorian apostles of the resurgent peoples. He would have said that a country belongs to the people who were born in it and intend to die there and who make its welfare their chief concern. There is no mention of 'minority rights', because these were assumed. Even in Ireland not many think like that now. Read the speeches reported in the press. Where one man talks of national unity, a hundred will talk of some unity that is racial, confessional or political.

It was because nationalism lacked a philosophy that in the early twenties it began to decay and racialism took its place. The first sign of this degeneration came in 1923, when by the Treaty of Lausanne in exchange for Turks from Europe over a million Greeks were moved from the coast of Asia Minor, where they had lived for three thousand years. This ghastly crime was committed so efficiently under the auspices of the League of Nations that it won universal applause. What Churchill was later to call 'the disentanglement of populations' began to seem a sensible and modern way of solving finally an ancient problem.

The old view that men should enjoy equal rights in the land of their birth began to seem hopelessly out of date, and soon Hitler and Mussolini and Stalin were eliminating causes of friction by large and admirably organized population exchanges in the Tyrol and the Baltic States. The war had hardly started, when it became obvious to all sensible Germans that, if there was ever to be world peace, all conquered peoples should be either Germanized or deported. That much-respected man, Dr Oberlander, who later became Adenauer's Minister for Refugees, said with reference to the Poles: 'It is better to be harsh now than have petty warfare waged for generations.' Soon the contagion of this generous realism reached the Allies, and in 1940 we find Benes writing in *The Nineteenth Century* that three million Sudeten Germans should be 'amicably and under decent human conditions' expelled. When the time came they were expelled. Again, Churchill in 1944 expressed the opinion that expulsion was 'the most lasting and satisfactory method' of dealing with the 7,500,000 Germans of the East. They, too, were satisfactorily expelled.

When we recall such gigantic endeavours, scientifically conducted, to sort out the old rag-bag nations of 1918 into homogeneous states, how petty and parochial seem the dreams of the Sarajevo conspirators, and the poor old League of Nations with its condominiums and Free Cities and minority rights! And how more than dead are Davis and Herder and their romantic insistance on Homeland and Nationhood! One has to listen hard to catch the least echo of that extinct ideology. Yet here is one from the most improbable source of all, from Germany, which once led the world in the social science of Disentanglement. It comes from The Exiles' Charter, an appeal for Heimatrecht published on behalf of those 7,500,000 German refugees from the East.

> God placed men in their homes. To drive men out of their homes spells spiritual death. We have experienced this fate. Hence we feel called upon to demand that the right to one's home be recognized as one of the basic rights given by God to man.

[1956]

24

THE LAST IZMIRENJE

For three days the rain had fallen steadily. When we arrived in Kotor, the top of Lovcen was invisible, and festoons of moist cloud swam across the mountains behind us. Nonetheless, there was a band to meet the boat and a great crowd, and on an iron mooring post a youth was arranging salvoes of welcome. Every now and then there was an enormous bang, and he disappeared in thick white smoke, for explosions are the Dalmatians' favourite way of celebrating great occasions, and today was a feast day in both the Catholic and Greek Churches. It was Easter Day for the Orthodox, while for the Catholics it was the feast of St Hosanna, a nun whose mummified body lies below an altar in one of the Kotor churches.

I pushed my way through the crowd, and asked the first likely person I met where the monastery of Grbalj was, and what time the 'izmerenje' was to be. Nobody knew, though I had heard in Belgrade about it three hundred miles away, while here it was only half-an-hour's drive by car. It was not till I had searched the town for information that I found, at last, that I was a day too early. I was rather relieved; perhaps the next day the rain-clouds would have lifted.

In the afternoon, with two others, I made a half-hearted attempt to drive to Cetinje, but soon after we had passed the old Austrian customs house, at the frontier of Dalmatia and Montenegro, we were in dense fog and the whole panorama of Kotor Bay, which must be one of the loveliest in the world, had disappeared, and we were shivering with cold and damp. We went back; and that evening, when I was having tea in one of the old houses at Dobrota, I was told the story of the Montenegrin blood feud by a lady who had studied law and had attended the trial of Stevo Orlovich in an official capacity.

The Orlovichs and the Bauks were two families living some fifteen miles from Kotor, not in Montenegro itself, but observing the old Montenegrin customs. Two years ago the Orlovichs had made enquiries and learnt that Stjepo Bauk, whose father was dead, would let his sister accept a proposal from Stevo Orlovich. Stevo, thereupon, set out with a group of his relations to make a formal offer, carrying firearms, as was the custom, so as to celebrate the betrothal with the usual explosions. When they reached the Bauks' house, they were told that the offer was refused.

It appeared that an old uncle of the Bauks had been greatly insulted that his permission had not been asked. He had made a row, and Stjepo had given in to him. Stevo Orlovich was outraged and indignant, and whipping out his gun he fired at Stjepo Bauk and hit him in the leg. Bauk fired back and injured Orlovich – there was a scuffle and the Orlovichs took to their heels. A few days later, Stjepo Bauk's leg had to be amputated, and he died. The case was tried in the courts, and Stevo Orlovich was sentenced to three years' imprisonment.

But the Bauks were not in the least pacified by this; they held to the old Montenegrin tradition that blood should be avenged by blood, and the Orlovichs continued to feel uneasy. Near Podgorica, in Montenegro, just such a murder had taken place in 1930, and since then thirty murders have followed it in alternate families, the last one six months ago. It has been impossible for the courts to collect satisfactory evidence; though the relations of the victim in most cases knew the murderer, they would scorn to hand him over to justice. Revenge is a private, not a public, responsibility. But there was a way out, and this the Orlovichs took.

Some ten months ago, when Stevo Orlovich had had the rest of his sentence remitted for good behaviour, twenty-four 'good men' of the Orlovichs called on the Bauks, and asked them to agree to the izmerenje ceremony. The Bauks refused. Five months later, the Orlovichs appealed again, and this time they were granted a day's armistice for every member of the deputation, that is to say, twenty-four. After that they came a third time, and at last the Bauks granted their request. It would be the first izmirenje celebrated in the neighbourhood for more than a generation, and it was this ceremony that I had come to Kotor to see.

'Of course,' my friend said, 'it won't be nearly as elaborate an affair as it used to be. In the old days the murderer had to crawl on his hands and knees and beg forgiveness; and then he must give a gun to the head of the other family as a token. And then there were the babies at the breast. Seven women of the murderer's family had to come with their seven babies in cradles, and ask the head of the family of the murdered man to be the "kum" or godfather, and he was obliged to accept.

'That shows what size the families were,' she added. 'Today, in all Dobrota, you couldn't find seven babies at the breast, far less in one family.'

The birds were singing next morning at six o'clock, and the fog seemed to have lifted completely from Lovcen. It looked as if the day was to be fine. I was told to be ready on the quay at 7 a.m., and was to share a car with the two judges who had sentenced Orlovich, two local correspondents of a Belgrade paper, and one of the hundred guests invited by Orlovich. This guest was so confident that the ceremony would wait for him that we were an hour late in starting. To get to the monastery of Grbalj you must climb up the slope of Lovcen out of the Boka, and then down again towards Budva on the open sea. Most of the district is a 'polje' or flat space between the mountains, and relatively fertile; the peasant houses are placed for the most part on the rocky, barren slopes, where nothing grows except scrub or wild pomegranates and stunted oak; their farms lie below them in the polje, full of vines, fig-trees, beans and potatoes, market crops that they can sell in Kotor.

The people of Grbalj were always an enterprising community from the time of the great medieval Tsar of Serbia, Dushan; they had their own laws, and the Venetians, when they occupied the Boka and its surroundings, respected the Grbalj Statute, which was only abolished when Dalmatia was seized by Austria after the Napoleonic wars.

We soon saw the monastery perched on a hill on the left – an unexpectedly small, insignificant building, its courtyard black with moving people. The larger half was completely new.

'The old building was raided and burnt by the Montenegrins themselves during the war,' the judge told me. 'They say the Austrians were using it as a store for ammunition. It was rebuilt, and they opened it again last year. There are some twelfth-century frescoes in the end of the chapel, but they're badly damaged by damp, as it was roofless for so long.'

Behind us, a mile or two away, but plainly visible as it lay open on the rocky face of the mountain over against the monastery, was the cluster of houses where the Bauks and the Orlovichs lived. They were large red-tiled farmhouses two or three storeys high, with big windows and several annexes. The Bauks' house was the bigger of the two.

'The Bauks have a dozen families scattered over the place,' said the judge, 'but the Orlovichs only have two, so I don't know how they'll pay for the dinner; you see, they must bring a hundred of their supporters and the Bauks must bring a hundred of theirs: the Bauks will be the hosts, but the Orlovichs must pay for it all. It may run them into a couple of thousand dinars [about £8]. If either side brings more or less than a hundred, it's a gross insult, and they'll have to start the whole business over again.'

The hundred Orlovich guests were already there when we arrived; outside the wall of the churchyard a group of women and neighbours, whom neither side had invited, were leaning watching. The women, in Montenegrin fashion, had their thick black hair wound across their foreheads in heavy plaits, a black lace veil fell from behind to their shoulders.

There were two long tables stretched out in the courtyard covered with brown paper, but the Orlovichs were most of them sitting upon the wall. The six 'good men' who headed the Orlovich deputation were in the vestry when we arrived, drinking Turkish coffee. One was a fat, pleasant-looking priest in a grey soutane from a neighbouring parish. Two seemed prosperous town relations in smart overcoats, clean-shaven, with gold teeth and Homburg hats; two were well-to-do farmers in full Montenegrin dress, round caps with red crowns embroidered in gold and the black bands that all Montenegrins wear in mourning for the battle of Kossovo, when the Serbians were defeated by the Turks in 1399. They had red waistcoats with heavy gold embroidery, orange sashes and blue breeches with thick white woollen stockings and string shoes. The other ninety-four Orlovichs had compromised about their clothes; they nearly all had the caps and some had either the breeches or the waistcoat, but they mostly had an ordinary Sunday coat on top of it. They all had black moustaches, and held either a heavy stick or an umbrella in their hands. I saw one or two men who had both.

One of the journalists from Kotor beckoned me into the church, and introduced me to the priest and a small dark man with terrified eyes who stood beside him.

'That's the murderer,' he told me. 'You are the murderer, Stevo Orlovich, aren't you?' he asked to make certain.

'Yes' – and we shook hands.

We shook hands with his brother, too, an older, solid-looking man. He, too, had received a bullet wound in the leg as he was running away from the Bauks' house. Stevo Orlovich shrank away behind the chapel walls as soon as he could; he was very slightly built, and had black bristly hair and a small Charlie Chaplin moustache; he wore a neat but worn black suit, with a fountain pen clipped in the breast pocket. He was evidently in an agony of shame and embarrassment about the ceremony he was going to have to go through. But he was sufficiently collected to make it clear that he wasn't pleased to see us.

All at once a boy began to toll the three small bells of the chapel, and five or six people went in to hear the priest celebrate the short Easter Mass according to the Greek rite. I saw the correspondent of the Belgrade *Politika* standing beside them leading the responses in a booming voice.

'Christ is risen!'

'Lord, have mercy on us!'

The priest was swinging a censer vigorously, and the whole courtyard was filled with sound and the smell of incense.

It lasted a quarter of an hour. When I came out of the church one of the Orlovichs who was sitting on the seat, cried out, 'Hello, boy!' and I went and sat down beside him. He had been at the copper mines at Butte, Montana, and said that at least ten others present had been there, too. I complimented him on his gorgeous embroidered waistcoat, but he said it was nothing to what they used to have. Times were bad. . .

'Montenegrin mans should do like Irishmans,' he said, 'raise hell, holler!'

Evidently, a good deal of information about Ireland had filtered via Butte, Montana, to Grbalj, because he had a muttered conversation with his neighbour about de Valera and the Lord Mayor who had died after a seventy day hunger-strike.

'I was telling him about the Liberty Irish State,' he said.

The six good men walked out of the church yard and he said:

'You see that bunch? They go fetch the otha bunch!'

But the six Orlovichs returned alone and another hour passed before down the mountain slope the procession of the Bauks, a long black line like a school crocodile, issued slowly from behind a little wood. They were a long way off still. From the terrace of the priest's house I watched them going down a small lane through an olive grove into the main road, crossing the wooden bridge over a very swift stream then climbing up the hill towards the monastery.

A man came out of the monastery with a big basket of bread and he was followed surprisingly by a sailor with some paper table napkins. Carafes of rakkia were planted at intervals along the table. . . The Orlovichs got up and walked leisurely towards one side of the churchyard, they formed themselves in a long row, fifty abreast, two deep. In the back row towards the end I saw the murderer flatten himself against the wall. He was fingering his fountain pen nervously. His brother was beside him.

The little priest in the grey soutane came bustling out of the church.

'Take off your hats,' he said, and we all did so.

Then the Bauks came in, headed by two handsome elderly priests with black beards, then four other good men.

They lined themselves opposite the Orlovichs, exactly a hundred, with their hats still firmly on, facing a hundred with bare heads. It was like Sir Roger de Coverley.

There was a long silence and then one of the Bauk 'good men', a professor from Kotor, came out into the middle and in a loud voice read the sentence. This is a slightly abbreviated version of what he read:

In the name of Christ the Saviour Who is eternal peace between men.

Today, when the Ascension is near at hand, in the year of Our Lord 1937 in the monastery of the Blessed Virgin of Grbalj good men have met together and pleaded with the families of Bauk and Orlovich to lay aside their blood feud which arose in the month of February 1935.

In the name of God from Whom all true justice proceeds and after long cognition, they pronounced this sentence which shall be executed on the third day of Easter, 1937, in the monastery of the Blessed Virgin of Grbalj.

Seeing that God's justice fell upon the wounds of Stjepo Bauk, the son of Vuk and Stevo Orlovich, the son of Lazo, who remained alive after wounds received, and seeing that Mirko Bauk valiantly forgave the murder of his brother Stjepo and reconciled himself through God and

St John with the Orlovichs, we declare this sentence:
1. That the brothers Orlovich wait with a hundred of their people on the Bauks with a hundred of theirs.
2. That the Orlovichs humbly, according to custom (but not carrying firearms), shall approach the Bauks who shall embrace them in this order.

Mirko Bauk, the son of Vuk, shall kiss Stevo Orlovich, the son of Lazo.

Vaso Bauk, the son of Rado, shall kiss Ilya Orlovich, the son of Lazo.

3. That at the first baptism of a child of theirs the Orlovichs shall ask Bauk to be godfather and he shall accept.
4. That from this reconciliation everlasting friendship and mutual respect for their mutual honour in word and deed shall proceed and that this blood feud shall be ended for all time.

Each family must receive a copy of this sentence and one must be preserved in the archives of the monastery where this reconciliation was made.

Drawn up by the undersigned: [Here follow the signatures of the six good men of the Bauks and the six good men of the Orlovichs.]

The professor stepped back into the Bauk ranks and put the sentence back into his leather portfolio.

Then one of the Orlovich good men cried out in a voice breaking with emotion:

'Stevo Orlovich!'

The murderer folded his arms across his breast and bending down from the waist he darted forward from the wall. He was like someone in a trance. He did not see where he was going and butted his bowed head into a man in front. It was a second before he had disentangled himself from the overcoat and was heading once more for the Bauks. Mirko Bauk, a fat young man with fair hair and moustache, all in black except for the red crown of his Montenegrin cap, stepped out and raised him up.

'Forgive me!' said Orlovich.

'I forgive you my brother's blood,' Bauk answered and they kissed each other on both cheeks. I heard people sobbing behind me. Then Vaso Bauk, who was small and puny, embraced Ilya Orlovich and finally all the hundred Bauks stepped forward and shook hands and greeted the hundred Orlovichs. Then they all took their seats at the table, the Orlovichs sitting at one table, the Bauks at another. Stevo Orlovich did not appear but stayed in the monastery with his brother.

I and the four men from Kotor were preparing to go home but the Bauk professor pressed us to stay.

'The Orlovichs would like to ask you,' he said, 'but they have to be so humble today – it isn't the custom – so we invite you.'

A table was brought out from the vestry and a red table cloth and we sat by ourselves in the other side of the courtyard.

Before we started to feed, the Bauk priest got up and began an Easter hymn. . . and once more the journalist's big voice filled the courtyard.

A lot of forks arrived and a platter heaped with boiled beef. Someone else explained to me that when the monastery had been rededicated last year, there had been six hundred guests and each had a knife for himself and also a tumbler; but today it was different – it was custom. So there were no tumblers and we pushed round from mouth to mouth, first a big bottle of rakkia, then a big flask of an excellent red wine.

'Please you thank you, Mister!' the journalist with the big voice said every time he gave the flask a shove in my direction.

He then muttered very rapidly into my ear a couple of verses of a poem beginning:

My 'ome iz zy ocean
My 'arth iz ze ship!'

The meal was quite good and the platters were constantly replenished by the sailor and two men running backward and forward with white napkins held in their teeth. After the beef came boiled ham. Except at our table nobody talked very much. There seemed to be no fraternization between the Bauks and the Orlovichs. First came forgiveness, a little later, perhaps, friendship would follow.

They must have had an extraordinary capacity for keeping the practical and the emotional side of their lives distant for on the slope of the hill their two houses seemed only a few hundred yards apart. Their sheep must graze the same mountains, they must use the same tracks. How had they managed to pass two years so close without lending things and without borrowing things?

There could be no doubt, anyway, that the quarrel had at last been settled. The sentences of the law courts usually leave bitterness and dissatisfaction behind but the ceremony at Grbalj, so impressive and deeply moving, aimed at something far higher. Did it achieve it? I thought so, but couldn't be sure. Did Mirko perhaps look a bit too self-righteous? Does one ever feel very friendly towards people who force on one too abject an apology or towards one's relations who watch it? I think Stevo may go to Butte, Montana.

Most European law is based on compensation and punishment, justice is important, but it is also impersonal. Montenegrin custom on the other hand takes into account forgiveness which English justice ignores, and because of that, when 'izmirenje' passes away, as pass it must, an important element of justice will have gone with it.

The journalist borrowed the copy of the sentence from the monastery achives.

'Meet me in the Café at Kotor,' he said to me, 'and I'll let you have a read of it.'

And we crammed in eleven of us, for some of the Orlovich friends came too, into the car. . . There was some angry tooting behind us and a lemon-coloured sports car thrust past, containing the professor and two of the Bauk 'good men'.

A moment later we were on the main highway to Cetinje, negotiating the hair-pin bends of that incredible road. Every now and then we passed policemen with fixed bayonets and we dodged a charabanc full of German tourists. Below us at Kotor a yacht lay at anchor by the quays, a procession of soldiers was marching through the streets which were green with acacia trees. The grimness of the mountains lay behind us and we were in the twentieth century again.

'It's beautiful,' I said to one of the judges.

'Yes,' he replied, 'but you should have seen it when the King and Mrs Simpson were here. The evening they arrived all the bay from Tivat to Kotor was illuminated – bonfires and petrol. It was wonderful. One of the bonfires set alight to some dry grass where there were some young trees. Not much damage done, but it made a wonderful blaze!'

By the time our car had drawn up at the Town Katana, the izmirenje at Grbalj was like something that happened in a dream. Will there ever be another one in Montenegro? I can hardly believe it. The 'good men' in the Homburg hats were getting self-conscious about it and I am convinced I heard the murderer and his brother grumbling about the journalists behind the chapel wall. I was glad he didn't know that someone had suggested bringing a film apparatus. Nowadays, too, one can always interrupt blood feuds by going to Butte, Montana.

[1947]

25

THE SUB-PREFECT SHOULD HAVE HELD HIS TONGUE

In countries where the old beliefs are dying it is the custom for educated people to handle them with nostalgic reverence. It is thought crude and undignified for a sophisticated man to take sides in a religious squabble, and it often happens that, the less he believes in himself, the more indulgent he is to the time-honoured beliefs of others. I have been reproached several times by sincere and civilized unbelievers for my efforts to find out the details of the vast campaign in Croatia in 1941 to convert two and a half million Orthodox to Catholicism. 'Why not let bygones be bygones?' they say. 'If we rake these things up we'll merely start trouble at home and play into the hands of the Communists. And anyway, they are always killing each other in the Balkans.' I once heard an ambassador in Belgrade argue like that, and indeed I have never heard a British or American official abroad argue in any other way. When in 1946 I went to Zagreb and looked up the files of the war-time newspapers of Croatia in which the whole story was to be read, it was obvious that no foreign inquirer had handled them before, and the library clerks regarded me with wonder and suspicion.

Yet it seemed to me that for a man as for a community too high a price can be paid for tranquillity. If you suppress a fact because it is awkward, you will next be asked to contradict it. And so it happened to me when I got back to Ireland, and gave a talk about Yugoslavia, the country and its people, on Radio Éireann. I did not mention the Communist war on the Church, or Archbishop Stepinac, who had just been sentenced to imprisonment for collaboration with Pavelitch, the Quisling ruler of Croatia, and for conniving at the forced conversion campaign. I could not refer to the Communist persecution of religion without mentioning the more terrible Catholic persecution which had preceded it, so I thought silence was best. But silence did not help me. In the following week our leading Roman Catholic weekly, *The Standard*, published a long editorial diatribe against myself and against Radio Éireann. I had not, it declared, said a word about the sufferings of the Church and its ministers under Tito and, by sponsoring me, Radio Éireann had connived at a vile piece of subversive propaganda. The officials of Radio Éireann, knowing I was no Communist, supported me, and finally *The Standard*, under pressure from my solicitor, agreed to print a long reply from me. I received the proof-sheets, corrected and returned them, but the reply never appeared. Months later, a muddled, amiable explanation reached me, and my friends said 'let bygones be bygones'. I did. That is the way things happen in Ireland.

But it became increasingly difficult to be silent. The foreign editor of *The Standard*, Count O'Brien of Thomond, published a little book called *Archbishop Stepinac, The Man and his Case*. It had an introduction by the Archbishop of Dublin, and commendation on the dust-cover from a couple of cardinals, Canadian and English, and half a dozen bishops and archbishops. Cardinal Spellman laid a copy of the book on the foundation stone of the new Stepinac Institute in New York, USA, and told 1700 schoolgirls, drawn up on a polo-ground in the form of a rosary, what they were to think about Croatian ecclesiastical history. Yet it seemed to me that there was a major error of fact or of interpreation, or a significant omission, on almost every page of this book. Meanwhile all the county councils and corporations in Ireland met and passed resolutions. Extracts from Count O'Brien's book were hurled about, and fiery telegrams despatched to parliaments and ambassadors.* But the climax of my discomfort was reached when our Minister for Agriculture, Mr Dillon, addressing some law students, advised them to model themselves on Mindzenty, Stepinac and Pavelitch, who had 'so gallantly defended freedom of thought and freedom of conscience'. Those who knew Yugoslavia were aghast, for Pavelitch, one of the major war criminals, was the Yugoslav counterpart of Himmler, and it

* In my own county town, Kilkenny, a muddled but enthusiastic alderman insisted that Tito was in Dublin in the capacity of Yugoslav ambassador, and proposed at the Corporation meeting that he should be told 'Get out, Tito!'

was under his rule that the gas chamber and the concentration camp were introduced into Yugoslavia and the forced conversion campaign initiated. Clearly Mr Dillon was speaking in ignorance, not in bigotry, but ignorance rampaging with such assurance and harnessed to religious enthusiasm is like a runaway horse and cart. It must be stopped before serious mischief results.

I felt that the honour of the small Protestant community in Southern Ireland would be compromised if those of us who had investigated the facts remained silent about what we had discovered. In many Roman Catholic pulpits the sufferings of the Catholics under Tito were being compared to the long martyrdom of Catholic Ireland under Protestant rule. 'Yesterday and today Herod abides.' If we agree that history should be falsified in Croatia in the interests of Catholic piety, how could we protest when our own history was similarly distorted?

In letters to the newspapers I replied to Mr Dillon and many others who had expressed similar opinions. A well known Irish Jesuit, Father Devane, assuming a Slav name, Mihajlo Dvornik, to lend force to his accuracy, solemnly declared that there had been no forced religious conversions in Croatia, but I could find no one ready to argue the details. Mostly they quoted at me passages from Count O'Brien, or, on *a priori* grounds, accused me of vile slander. 'The Catholic Church had always insisted that conversion must be from the heart. *Ad amplexandam fidem Catholicam nemo invitus cogatur.*' I was alleging the impossible.

Soon afterwards it was announced that Tito was to visit London, and in Ireland, as in England, various anti-Yugoslav demonstrations were arranged. My friend, Owen Sheehy-Skeffington, a lecturer in Trinity College and now a member of the Irish Senate, invited me to a meeting of the Foreign Affairs Association, at which the editor of *The Standard* was to read a paper on 'Yugoslavia – the Pattern of Persecution'. The Association had been modelled on Chatham House as an international fact-finding society and Arnold Toynbee himself had come over to give his blessing to the first meeting. In the *Survey of International Affairs* of 1955 he was later to express himself as strongly as I had about the persecution of the Orthodox. This is an undenominational society with a tradition of free speech. The lecturer had never been to Yugoslavia, and I believe that all the others on the platform were in the same position, though one of them said that on a cruise down the Dalmatian coast he had met members of a

Yugoslav football team. I decided that at the end of his paper I would try to make those points which he had failed, despite his promise, to publish for me. I would try to show how variegated was the pattern of persecution in Yugoslavia, and how misleading our crude simplifications would be. What followed has been told by Paul Blanshard, whom I met for the first time that evening, in his book *The Irish and Catholic Power.* It is enough to say here that the Chairman's attempt to close the meeting at the end of the paper was ruled out, on a vote, as unconstitutional. I got up, holding in my hand *The Martyrdom of the Serbs,* a book published by the exiled Serbian Orthodox Church in Chicago, in case anything I said required authoritative corroboration. It had been given me by archpriest Nicolitch, the head of the Serbian Orthodox Church in England. But I had spoken only a few sentences when a stately figure rose from among the audience and walked out. It was the Papal Nuncio, of whose presence I had been unaware. The Chairman instantly closed the meeting, and there was an appalled silence, followed by a rush of reporters in my direction. They had understood nothing in the confusion. There was, consequently, some lively reporting, and two leading dailies quoted me as saying that the Orthodox Church, not the Communists, had initiated the persecution of the Catholics in Yugoslavia. In gigantic letters in the *Sunday Express* (Irish edition) I read: 'Pope's Envoy Walks Out. Government to Discuss Insult to Nuncio.'

Blanshard has described the measures taken against Skeffington in Dublin and myself in Kilkenny. The persecution was of a familiar pattern, and I try to see in it not a personal hard-luck story, but material for a study in the modern indifference to evidence, but I think both of us knew that had we been less fortunate in our backgrounds we would have been ruined. Skeffington, the son of a father executed by the British in 1916 – or, to be more accurate, murdered at the orders of a hysterical British officer – is at his happiest when he is fighting, and shortly afterwards he had fought his way into the Irish Senate. For myself, I am grateful for the few inherited acres which have helped me to survive the disapproval of my neighbours. All the local government bodies of the city and county held special meetings to condemn 'the Insult'. There were speeches from mayors, ex-mayors, aldermen, creamery managers. The County Council expelled me from one of its sub-committees, and I was obliged to resign from another committee. Although my friends put up a fight, I was forced to give up the honorary secretaryship of an archaeological society which I had myself founded and guided through seven difficult years (see Appendix). My opponents hoped that my liquidation would be decorous and quickly forgotten, but my friends and myself were little inclined to oblige them, and for a time our small society enjoyed in the metropolitan press a blaze of publicity which its archaeological activities had never won for it.

I decided that before I resigned I would tell our two or three hundred members something about the forced conversion campaign in Yugoslavia. Much of the evidence, including the utterances of the Orthodox Church and its bishops, and Archbishop Sharitch's 'Ode to Pavelitch', with its sonorous denunciations of Serbs and Jews, I put aside, because I was certain that it would not be believed. Finally, I decided to publish the long letter written by Stepinac to Pavelitch on the subject of the forced conversions. I had translated it from a typescript in Zagreb in 1946, and it seems to me a document of vast importance which deserves a prominent place in the annals of religious history. Its reception was disappointing. Many were confused by the outlandish names and inextricably complicated series of events, and I was taken aback when one friendly disposed reader congratulated me on 'my interesting article on Czechoslavia'.

There is in Ireland a historic loathing of proselytism. The well-meaning Protestants who plied the starving peasants of the west with soup and Bibles after the famine of 1846 have never been forgiven. Religious apprehensions as strong as these survive in Yugoslavia, and I had hoped that some of my neighbours would be capable of the necessary mental adjustment and would see the parallel. Surely it would be obvious to them from the Stepinac letter that the Croatian bishops, while denouncing the use of force, were delighted with the opportunities for mass conversion which the chaos and defeat of Yugoslavia afforded them. There was, for example, Dr Mishitch, the Bishop of Mostar and the kindliest of mortals, whom even the Communists have praised for his clemency. He too had made quite plain the hopes which he had entertained at the beginning of Pavelitch's régime:

> By the mercy of God [he wrote] there was never such a good occasion as now for us to help Croatia to save the countless souls, people of good will, well-disposed peasants, who live side by side with Catholics. . .

Conversion would be appropriate and easy. Unfortunately the authorities in their narrow views are involuntarily hindering the Croatian and Catholic cause. In many parishes of (my) diocese. . . very honest peasants of the Orthodox faith have registered in the Catholic Church. . . But then outsiders take things in hand. While the newly-converted are at Mass they seize them, old and young, men and women, and hunt them like slaves. From Mostar and Chapljina the railway carried six waggons full of mothers, girls, and children under eight to the station of Surmanci, where they were taken out of the waggons, brought into the hills and thrown alive, mothers and children, into deep ravines. In the parish of Klepca seven hundred schismatics from the neighbouring villages were slaughtered. The Sub-Prefect of Mostar, Mr Bajitch, a Moslem, publicly declared (as a state employé he should have held his tongue) that in Ljubina alone 700 schismatics have been thrown into one pit.

Elsewhere in his letter the Bishop wrote:

At one time there was a likelihood that a great number of schismatics would be united to the Catholic Church. If God had given to those in authority the understanding and the good sense to deal effectively with conversion, so that it could have been carried through more ably, more smoothly and by degrees, the number of Catholics might have been increased by at least five or six hundred thousand. Such a number is required in Bosnia and Herzegovina, if there is to be an increase from 700,000 to 1,300,000.

The other three bishops, whose letters Stepinac quoted, all took the normal human view that it is inadvisable in the name of religion to throw waggon-loads of schismatics over cliffs; they were critical of the conversion campaign, but they did not find the occasion for it unseasonable. Had there been no cruelty, and if possible a little soup, they would have welcomed it. But compared with Mgr Mishitch's letters theirs are cold, calculating and self-righteous. Archbishop Sharitch opined that the town council of Sarajevo was imposing too high a tax on the Bosnian Orthodox for their change of religion. The Bishop of Kotor, Dr Butorac, declared that the missionaries to the Serbs must be wisely selected. 'We must not entrust the problem,' he wrote, 'to monks or priests who have no tact at all and who would be much better suited to carry a revolver in their hands than a cross.' And he expressed the fear that if the Serbs were driven too hard they might, out of defiance, pass over in a body to Islam.

I must confess that I find Mgr Stepinac's comments on these

letters and the situation that provoked them curiously narrow and thin-lipped. He scolds the miserable, hunted Orthodox for their terrible errors, deriving, he declares, from 'hatred and schism', and he blames them for the Russian Revolution, just as he blames the crimes of Pavelitch and his gang on the Chetniks – that is, the followers of Mihailovitch – the Communists, and the Royal Yugoslav Government. He considers that the best way to convert the Orthodox might often be found through the medium of the Greek Catholic Church, which recognizes the authority of the Pope while preserving its Orthodox ritual. He ends his letter, as he began it, by exonerating Pavelitch from all blame in the crimes that had been committed.

Yet Count O'Brien tells us in his little book that at this time, in defence of the Orthodox, the Archbishop had swept into Pavelitch's office. '"It is God's command!" he said, "Thou shalt not kill!" and without another word he left the Quisling's palace.'

Stepinac's long and respectful letter to Pavelitch at this date proves the anecdote to be a hagiographical fabrication. Yet it was quoted at me several times in the press of Kilkenny and Dublin. The letter was obviously the longest and most important that Stepinac had ever written, and it struck me as odd that though I had published it twice in Ireland – for my critics in Kilkenny and also in *The Church of Ireland Gazette* – nobody in the British Isles, at a time when so much was written and said about the imprisoned Archbishop, ever commented on it, quoted from it, or wrote to me to enquire how I had secured it. Three years later, however, Richard Pattee published in America a lengthy book in defence of Stepinac, and among his documents the letter belatedly appeared. Yet I believe that my translation is the more accurate of the two. Mr Pattee has thought it best to omit a sentence or two here and there. He leaves out, for instance, Mgr Mishitch's calculations of the number of conversions required in Bosnia and Herzegovina. Again, wherever the word 'conversion' appears in the text Mr Pattee reads it as 'legitimate conversion', thus adding an epithet which I could not trace in the original. Stepinac's admiring description of the Bishop of Banja Luka as 'that old Croatian warrior' likewise disappears, presumably because Mr Pattee does not wish his readers to infer that the bishops were Croatian separatists trying to ingratiate themselves with Pavelitch.

About the same time Mr Michael Derrick published in *The Tablet* a paragraph or two from Mishitch's letter, but he attributed it to Stepinac, and he omitted the extraordinary parenthesis about the Sub-Prefect who told of the barbarities inflicted upon the Orthodox, and the bishop's comment that 'as a state employé he should have held his tongue'. In the succeeding issue of *The Sword*, Mr Derrick published my translation of Stepinac's *The Regulations for Conversion* without acknowledgment! Anybody who read these regulations with an open mind, and particularly an Irish Catholic with his inherited horror of 'souperism', would have to admit that they bore every trace, except soup, of *illegitimate* conversion. For instance, Clause XI, an appeal that the Orthodox be granted full civic rights, has been much applauded, but it begins, 'A psychological basis for conversion must be created among the Greek Orthodox inhabitants.' If still in doubt as to the bearing of these regulations one would have only to read the manifesto of Dr Shimrak, editor of the leading Catholic daily, and chosen by Stepinac as one of his two colleagues in the supervision of conversion:

Every priest must have before his eyes that historic days have come for our mission. Now we must put into practice that which we have spoken of in theory throughout the centuries. In the matter of conversion we have done very little up to this, simply because we were irresolute and dreaded the small reproaches and censure of men. Every great task has its opponents, but we must not be downcast on that account, because it is a question of a holy union, the salvation of souls and the eternal glory of the Lord Christ. Our work is legal in the light of the ruling of the Holy See. . . also in the light of the ruling of the Holy Congregation of Cardinals for the Eastern Church. . . and finally in the light of the circular sent by the Government of Independent Croatia, July 30, 1941, whose intention it is that the Orthodox should be converted to the Catholic faith (*Diocesan Magazine of Krizhevtsi*, No. 2 [1942], pp. 10-11).

Count O'Brien, an Austrian of Irish descent, had been until he came to Ireland after the war the editor of an important Viennese paper, and he claims in his book to have known Shimrak intimately for twenty years. He also writes that all the Croat bishops had opposed Pavelitch's 'evil plan' for the forced conversion of the Orthodox. This seemed in such strong conflict with Shimrak's declaration that long before the 'Insult' I had visited Count O'Brien to ask for an explanation. An explanation was forthcoming. The Count replied at once that Shimrak had not been a bishop at the time, but only an administrator. It appeared from his reply that it was actually after he had proved himself in sympathy with Pavelitch's plan that Shimrak was appointed to the bishopric and to Stepinac's committee for regulating conversion. I then asked how it came about that, if all the bishops were hostile to Pavelitch and his plans, Archbishop Sharitch of Bosnia, one of the greatest of them, had been able to print his *Ode to Pavelitch* in the ecclesiastical papers of his own archdiocese and that of Zagreb. I had made a translation of his ode in twenty-six verses, describing his meeting with Pavelitch at St Peter's in Rome, and I now ventured to remind Count O'Brien of a few lines:

> Embracing thee was precious to the poet
> as embracing our beloved Homeland.
> For God himself was at thy side, thou good and strong one,
> so that thou mightest perform thy deeds for the Homeland. . .
> And against the Jews, who had all the money,
> who wanted to sell our souls,
> who built a prison round our name,
> the miserable traitors. . .
> Dr Ante Pavelić! the dear name!
> Croatia has therein a treasure from Heaven.
> May the King of Heaven accompany thee, our Golden Leader!

Count O'Brien had an explanation for that, too. He said: 'The Archbishop was an abnormal man, very emotional. He was always embracing people. Whenever we met, he used to kiss me on both cheeks. He can't be taken seriously.'

These replies made me feel very helpless, since they could not have been made if venal indifference had not reigned around us. When I went home I was feeling as emotional as the Archbishop, and I remember that I wrote a poem myself on the Massacre of the Orthodox, though I must admit that it was the massacre of the truth that really outraged me.

> Milton, if you were living at this hour,
> they'd make you trim your sonnet to appease
> the triple tyrant and the Piedmontese.
> 'Why for some peasants vex a friendly power?
> We'd like to print it, but Sir Tottenham Bauer
> and half the Board would blame us. Colleen Cheese
> would stop its full-page ad. They're strong RCs.
> It's old stuff now, and truth, deferred, goes sour.
> So cut those lines about "the stocks and stones"
> and "slaughtered saints", or keep for private ears

that fell crusade, for even in undertones,
it breeds disunion and the Kremlin hears.
Say nothing rash or rude, for it is right
that all the godly (west of Kiel), unite!'

I thought my poem almost as good as the Archbishop's, but I had some difficulty in getting it published. In the end it appeared in a pacifist weekly, but very inconspicuously and in very small print. The Archbishop had been luckier. His had appeared in *Katolicki Tjednik (The Catholic Weekly)* on Christmas Day, with a signed portrait of Pavelitch and a decorative border of Christmas tree candles and little silver bells.

I suppose that the small community in which I live has about the same significance for the world as the community of Mr Bjitch, who as a state employé 'should have held his tongue' about the massacres, so I need not apologize for returning to it. My friends and neighbours were memorably kind and supporting; for they knew that I had not intended to insult anybody. But others were puzzled. I was not, like Mr Bjitch, a state employé , and some found it difficult to make their disapproval materially felt. This problem would not have baffled them for long had it not been for the courtesy and good sense of the local Catholic clergy. I was most vulnerable through the Kilkenny Archaeological Society. This had been a famous Victorian institution, with the Prince Consort as patron and the Marquess of Ormond as President, but it had shifted to Dublin as an All-Ireland Society, and when I revived it in Kilkenny in 1944 it had been dead there for half a century. In a couple of years the new Society became a real bridge between Protestant and Catholic, Anglo-Irishman and Celt. The friendliness which it created was perhaps our main achievement, but we did other things, too. Mr O. G. S. Crawford made for us a photographic survey of old Kilkenny such as no other Irish provincial town possesses; Dr Bersu, the Director of the Institute of Frankfurt, made his principal Irish excavation on a hill fort outside Kilkenny and reported it in our journal; we had a centenary celebration of the old society in Kilkenny Castle; and the National Museum co-operated in a very successful Kilkenny Exhibition. But I think I was proudest of having organized a week's visit from the principal archaeological society in Northern Ireland; for cultural fraternizations between North and South are as rare as they are valuable. I feared that all this work would be wasted, so I decided to appeal to a certain Stephen Brown, a Jesuit, who had attended meetings of our Society. He had escorted the Nuncio to the fateful meeting, and afterwards in the *Irish Independent* had defended the Croatian hierarchy against the charges of illegitimate proselytism, with copious quotations from Count O'Brien but, as it seemed to me, with a total ignorance of Yugoslav conditions. Father Brown received me warmly. He said he was satisfied that I had not intended to insult the Nuncio, that he strongly disapproved the introduction of the incident into the affairs of an archaeological society, and that in any case the Nuncio had visited the meeting by mistake under the impression that he was bound for a meeting of a Catholic society with a similar name. Father Brown said that he would send me a letter making these three points, and that I might publish it in any paper I chose. The letter never arrived. It seemed, however, that a compromise had been reached in the matter, for a few days later a paragraph appeared in *The Standard* under the heading 'Mr Butler rebuked'. After commending all the denunciations by public bodies, the passage ended:

> It is well that such repudiation should be known. But we doubt if any good purpose would have been served by the proposed step by which Mr Butler would have been deprived of office in, say, the Kilkenny Archaeological Society, of which he is presumably an efficient functionary, and into which he can scarcely introduce sectarian issues. If he has any regard for public opinion he must know by now that his action met with not alone local but national disapproval. That is sufficient.

It was difficult for me to return as a presumably efficient functionary to a Society which I had myself founded, so I never after attended a meeting, but my friends, both Catholic and Protestant, still support the Society and I am glad today that it continues.

I hope I have not appeared to diagnose in my Catholic countrymen a unique susceptibility to a disease with which we are all of us more or less infected. Speed of communications has increased, and we are expected to have strong feelings about an infinite series of remote events. But our powers of understanding and sympathy have not correspondingly increased. In an atmosphere of artificially heated emotionalism truth simply dissolves into expediency. This shifting current of expediency may be illustrated by a chronicle of the changing attitudes to Pavelitch in the past ten years. In Croatia, upheld by the victorious Germans, he had for four years been regarded as a great Christian gentleman and patriot. All the Catholic bishops and the Evangelical bishops were among his panegyrists and had received decorations from him. Then the Nazis collapsed, and Pavelitch was regarded by the outer world as one of the basest of war criminals, while in Croatia all the dignitaries hastened to disavow the compliments they had paid him. A former Italian Fascist, Malaparte, in his book, *Kaputt*, has described how, as correspondent of *Corriere Della Sera*, he visited Pavelitch in his office in 1942 and saw behind him what appeared to be a basket of shelled oysters. 'Are these Dalmatian oysters?' Malaparte asked. 'No,' Pavelitch replied, 'that's forty pounds of human eyes, a present from my loyal Ustashe in Bosnia' – eyes, that is to say, of the Serbian Orthodox. I am ready to believe that this story is an invention, like Stepinac's visit to 'the Quisling's Palace', and that stories like this were repeated by the ex-Fascists, who thought that if they made the whole world black their own shade of dirty grey would be less conspicuous. But in 1948 no one told Malaparte that he was a liar. Indeed, writing about *Kaputt* in *The Irish Times*, Mr Kees van Hoek, the biographer of the Pope, said that Malaparte was 'the most accurate observer and reliable witness'.

That was the universal western view of Pavelitch seven or eight years ago – a monster of iniquity, an ogre out of a fairy-tale. But since then Pavelitch has become more respectable, and if he was wanted again in a campaign against Communism in the Balkans it is possible that he and his friends would be used. He now lives in South America and two or three papers and journals are published in his interest. Five years ago he issued postage stamps commemorating the tenth anniversary of Independent Croatia, and he has cashed in very effectively on the Stepinac legend, since one of his Ustasha clubs in the Argentine is called after the famous Cardinal. Archbishop Sharitch, the devoted admirer of both Pavelitch and Stepinac, lives in Madrid, but still publishes his odes (rather modified), as well as ecstatic reminiscences of Stepinac, in *Hrvatska Revija*, a Croatian separatist quarterly of Buenos Aires. I once visited Mgr Stepinac in prison and found him a gentle and serious man, who obviously acted as he thought was right. Surely it must be one of the hardest blows that fate has dealt him that both Pavelitch and Sharitch speak well of him?

In one way or another the memory of a terrible crime against humanity is being confused and effaced, so that many people believe that it never happened at all or that it has been monstrously exaggerated. I have seen Pavelitch compared in Irish papers with Roger Casement and Patrick Pearse as a simple-hearted patriot who merely did his best for his country in difficult circumstances. In October 1952 he was interviewed for an Italian picture paper, *Epoca* of Milan. He was photographed basking in the South American sun with his wife and family, stroking a pet dog. He told how he had escaped from Croatia through the Allied lines, how he had paused for weeks at a time in Naples, the Vatican City, and Castel Gandolfo. He was to be considered a romantic fellow, the carefree immunity which he enjoyed no more than his due.

How has all this happened? Three centuries ago Milton give undying notoriety to the massacre and forced conversion of the Waldenses, and Cromwell sent out emissaries to collect information about the sufferings of this tiny Alpine community. We are mostly now immune from the religious fanaticism which once intensified racial antipathies and to which Cromwell himself was no stranger; why has it become unwise to censure or even to take notice of an explosion of those ancient passions fifty times more devastating than that which Milton observed? There were scarcely ten thousand Waldenses to be persecuted in Piedmont, while the decrees of Pavelitch were launched against more than two million Orthodox, and 240,000 were forcibly converted.

Looking for a reason, I can only conclude that science has enormously extended the sphere of our responsibilities, while our consciences have remained the same size. Parochially minded people neglect their parishes to pronounce ignorantly about the universe, while the universalists are so conscious of the world-wide struggles of opposing philosophies that the rights and wrongs of any regional conflict dwindle to insignificance against a cosmic panorama. They feel that truth is in some way relative to orientation, and falsehood no more than a wrong adjustment, so that they can never say unequivocally 'that is a lie!' Like the needle of a compass at the North Pole, their moral judgment spins round and round, overwhelming them with information, and telling them nothing at all.

[1956]

26

THE ARTUKOVITCH FILE

I. REFLECTIONS ON A CROATIAN CRUSADE

Some years after I had written 'The Sub-Prefect Should Have Held His Tongue', I was in New York and read how the Yugoslav Government was urging that Artukovitch, Pavelitch's Minister of the Interior, who was living in California, should be extradited. I went to the Yugoslav Consulate to enquire about this and was handed a fat yellow booklet called *Artukovitch, the Himmler of Yugoslavia* by three New Yorkers called Gaffney, Starchevitch and McHugh.

Artukovitch first won notoriety in October 1934. He had gone to England at the time of King Alexander's murder at Marseilles. After his visit to Paris, the king had intended to see his son, Crown Prince Peter, at Sandroyd School, so, in case the Marseilles attempt failed, Artukovitch had been deputed to arrange for the king's assassination in England. It did not fail so Artukovitch waited in Czechoslovakia and Hungary till the Nazi invasion of Yugoslavia. He then returned with them and held various ministerial posts under Pavelitch from 1944 to 1945 in the Independent State of Croatia. Very few people have heard of him, yet if his story were told with remorseless candour, we would have a picture not only of Croatia forty years ago, but of all Christendom in our century. Everything that the New Yorkers relate was already known to me, except for one startling paragraph, an extract from a memoir by Artukovitch himself. After describing how he escaped to Austria and Switzerland in 1945, he goes on:

> I stayed in Switzerland until July 1947. Then with the knowledge of the Swiss Ministry of Justice I obtained personal documents for myself and my family, which enabled us to travel to Ireland. Using the name of Anitch, we stayed there until 15th July, 1948. When our Swiss documents expired, the Irish issued new papers and under Irish papers we obtained a visa for entry into the USA.

So evidently we in Ireland had sheltered this notable man for a whole year. He was not, like Eichmann, a humble executive, but himself a maker of history, dedicated to the extermination not of Jews alone, but also of his fellow-Christians, the Serbian Orthodox. He was a member of the govenment which in the spring of 1941 introduced laws which expelled them from Zagreb, confiscated their property and imposed the death penalty on those who sheltered them. Some twenty concentration camps were established in which they were exterminated. Why do we know so little about his sojourn among us? Did he stay in a villa at Foxrock or in lodgings at Bundoran or in some secluded midland cloister? And who looked after him? The Red Cross? And did we cherish him because he presented himself to us as a Christian refugee from godless Communism? That seems to me rather likely.

Nowadays we usually estimate cruelty by statistics and Gaffney and Co. use the figures normally recorded for Croatia by Jewish and Orthodox writers, that is to say, 30,000 Jews and 750,000 Orthodox massacred, 240,000 Orthodox forcibly converted to Catholicism. Even if these figures are exaggerated, it was the most bloodthirsty religio-racial crusade in history, far surpassing anything achieved by Cromwell and the Spanish Inquisitors. I am sorry that Gaffney and Co. give so many photographs of headless babies, of disembowelled shopkeepers, of burning beards soaked in kerosene, for Artukovitch was, like Himmler, a 'desk-murderer', who deplored the disorderly and sadistic way in which his instructions were carried out. He was respectable, and it is the correlation of respectability and crime that nowadays has to be so carefully investigated.

The three writers tell Artukovitch's story with much emotion, because, as is plain, they want him to be extradited and hanged. But in itself the story is of the highest importance, for no earlier crusade has been so richly documented. If the abundant material were coolly and carefully studied, how much could we learn about human weakness and hypocrisy! We could observe how adroitly religion can be used in the service of crime. When Pavelitch and Artukovitch and their armies retreated, they were sure that, on the defeat of Germany, England and America would turn upon Russia and they could return to Zagreb. Therefore nothing was destroyed, the state documents were stored in the Archiepiscopal Palace, the gold (dentures, wrist-watches and all) was hidden below the deaf and dumb confessional in the Franciscan monastery and cemented over by the friars themselves. The newspapers of the time, secular and ecclesiastical, are still to be seen in the Municipal Library, but this huge pile of documents, the Rosetta Stone of Christian corruption, has not yet been effectively deciphered.

These terrible Church papers, 1941 to 1945, should destroy forever our faith in those diplomatic prelates, often good and kindly men, who believe that at all costs the ecclesiastical fabric, its schools and rules, its ancient privileges and powers, should be preserved. The clerical editors published the Aryan laws, the accounts of the forced conversions, without protest, the endless photographs of Pavelitch's visits to seminaries and convents and the ecstatic speeches of welcome with which he was greeted. Turn, for example, to *Katolicki Tjednik (The Catholic Weekly)*, Christmas 1941, and read the twenty-six-verse 'Ode to Pavelitch', in which Archbishop Sharitch praises him for his measures against Serbs and Jews. Examine the Protestant papers and you will find the same story. Is it not clear that in times like those the Church doors should be shut, the Church newspapers closed down, and Christians, who believe that we should love our neighbours as ourselves, should go underground and try to build up a new faith in the catacombs?

Why did our professional historians not deal with all this long ago? They seem to wait till history is dead before they dare to touch it. But does a good surgeon only operate on corpses? They have wholly misinterpreted their functions, for it is their duty to expose the liar before his contagion has spread. While Artukovitch was on his way to Ireland, a Dublin publication told us authoritatively that the massacre of the Serbian Orthodox had never happened. In Count O'Brien's book* on Mgr Stepinac, to which I have already referred, we read:

> They [the Orthodox] were offered by Pavelitch the choice between conversion to the Catholic faith or death. . . But the Catholic Church as a whole, all her bishops and the overwhelming majority of her priests, led by the Archbishop of Zagreb, made this evil plan impossible.

Some of the correspondence between Artukovitch and Stepinac has been published in English by Richard Pattee† and,

* A. H. O'Brien, *Archbishop Stepinac, The Man and His Case* (London 1947).

† Richard Pattee, *The Case of Cardinal Aloysius Stepinac* (London/Milwaukee 1953).

collating with Gaffney, we see how Stepinac, a brave and merciful though very simple man, was hopelessly compromised by his official connection with the state. It was only his own flock whom he could help, and even them very little. For example, he appealed to Artukovitch on behalf of one of his priests, Father Rihar, who had defied Pavelitch. His failure was absolute, for this is how Artukovitch replied:

> Zagreb. 17th November, 1942. In connection with your esteemed request of 2nd November, 1942. . . notice is hereby given that Francis Rihar by the decree of this office of 20th April, 1942, No. 26417/1942, was sentenced to forced detention in the concentration camp at Jasenovac for a period of three years. . . because as pastor at Gornja Stubica he did not celebrate a solemn high mass on the anniversary of the founding of the Independent State of Croatia. . . nor did he consent to sing the psalm *Te Deum Laudamus*, saying that it was nowhere prescribed in ecclesiastical usage. . .

Stepinac appealed again, but Rihar had been already three months at Jasenovac and, therefore, according to the rules of this camp, he was killed.

How, anyway, could Stepinac defend Father Rihar with any authority, since he himself had done what Rihar refused to do? Gaffney and Co., on page 42, reproduced seven photographs of the celebration of Pavelitch's birthday on 15 June 1942, and a letter from the Archbishop exhorting his clergy to hold a *Te Deum* after High Mass the following Sunday, 17 June, because of 'Our Glorious Leader'.

Since Pattee omitted this very relevant letter, it is strange that he printed Stepinac's correspondence with Artukovitch about the Jews, for this makes it clear that in acknowledging the authority of Pavelitch, the Archbishop, for diplomatic reasons, felt obliged to accept the terminology of the anti-semites and their human classifications. For example, on 30 May 1941 he urged Artukovitch 'to separate the Catholic non-Aryans from non-Christian non-Aryans in relation to their social position and in the manner of treating them'.

Much has been written about Communist distortions of history, but only recently has our own inability, as Christians, to report facts honestly been closely investigated. Now, after twenty years, the dam has burst and the truth, a turbid stream, is inundating our self-complacency and irrigating our self-knowledge. Catholic scholars are leading the way. For example, Professor Gordon Zahn has shown how selective is the documentation on which the biographies of Christian heroes of the resistance are based. Their sermons and speeches were pruned of all the compliments they paid to Hitler and his New Order and no row of dots in the text marks the excision of these now-embarrassing ecstasies.

In the long run, remorseless truth-telling is the best basis for ecumenical harmony. Hitler once explained to Hermann Rauschning how he intended to use the Churches as his propagandists. 'Why should we quarrel? They will swallow anything provided they can keep their material advantages.' Yet Hitler never succeeded in corrupting the Churches as effectively as did Pavelitch and Artukovitch, who professed to be Christians. We shall not be able to estimate the extent of their success and how it might have been resisted, while a single fact is diplomatically 'forgotten'. It is well known that those who suppress history have to re-live it.

* * *

How did Artukovitch (alias Anitch) get to Ireland? I wrote to Yugoslavia, to America, France, Germany and questioned Yugo slavs in Dublin and London. The Yugoslavs, both Communist and anti-Communist, had no information. A friend in London, who had been to Trinity College, Dublin, remembered someone saying: 'I'd like you to meet a very interesting chap called Anitch', but the meeting had never happened. In the end Branko Miljus, a former minister of the pre-war government in Belgrade, who now lives in Paris, got some news for me from a friend in Switzerland. If I seem to give too many names and details, it is so that his story can be checked and completed.

The first stage of the journey is fairly well known. Pavelitch and Artukovitch had escaped to Austria when the Croatian state collapsed. They seem to have been arrested by the British in Salzburg and, after 'a mysterious intervention', released and there was an interval of hiding in monasteries at Sankt Gilgen and Bad Ischl. The Yugoslavs were in hot pursuit, so Pavelitch fled to Rome, disguised as a Spanish priest called Gomez. Artukovitch stayed on till November 1946, when he met the learned Dr Draganovitch, Professor of Theology at Zagreb, who was touring the internment camps with a Vatican passport. He had secured the release of many hundreds of Croat priests who had fled with Pavelitch. Now he obtained for Artukovitch papers under the name Alowz Anitch and put some money for him in a Swiss bank. Two other priests, Fathers Manditch and Juretitch, also came to his aid. The former, the treasurer to the Franciscan order, controlled a printing press at the Italian camp of Fermo and assisted the Ustashe (Croatian nationalist) refugees with funds and propaganda. Juretitch had been sent on a mission to Fribourg by Archbishop Stepinac, so he and Manditch, both former students of Fribourg University, were able to secure a welcome there for Artukovitch. Archbishop Sharitch, Pavelitch's poet-champion, had got there ahead of him. Both Draganovitch and Juretitch had been appointed by Mgr Stepinac to the Commission of Five for the Conversion of the Orthodox in November 1941. These three were important people to have as sponsors. The ecclesiastics of Fribourg must have been impressed. They recommended Artukovitch to the police who got him a *permis de séjour*. There were other difficulties, which, according to report, Artukovitch smoothed out by the gift of a Persian carpet to an influential official.

But meanwhile the Federal Police had learnt that Anitch was the war criminal Artukovitch. They told him he had two weeks in which to leave Switzerland. Once more the Franciscans came to his aid. The prior of the Maison Marianum at Fribourg recommended him to the Irish Consulate at Berne. And so it happened that in July 1947 Artukovitch landed with his family on the Isle of Saints, sponsored by the disciples of that saint, who had prayed:

> Lord, make me an instrument of Thy peace!
> Where there is hatred let me sow love,
> Where there is sadness, joy!

I do not know where Artukovitch spent his Irish year, but one day, as a matter of history, and perhaps of religion, we shall have to know. If Artukovitch had to be carried half-way round the earth on the wings of Christian charity, simply because he favoured the Church, then Christianity is dying. And if now, for ecumenical or other reasons, we are supposed to ask no questions about him, then it is already dead.

On 15 July 1948 Artukovitch with an Irish identity card left Ireland for the USA where he settled as a book-keeper, near his wealthy brother in California, still under the name of Anitch. It was over two years before his true identity was discovered. The Serbian Orthodox were slow to move. Oppressed by the Communists at home, dispersed as refugees abroad, they still managed to publish the facts in books and papers in London, Chicago, Paris. In 1950 Branko Miljus, and two other prominent monarchist politicians in exile, sent a memorandum to the Fifth Assembly of the United Nations urging it to implement its resolution of December 1946, which had branded genocide as a crime against international law. They asked that its member states should take into custody, till a Commission be appointed to try them, some 120 Croat nationals, who had taken refuge among them. On the long list appended, the names of Artukovitch, Archbishop Sharitch, Fathers Draganovitch and Juretitch and many Franciscans were mentioned, and some of the scarcely credible Franciscan story was related. It is stated that a Franciscan had been commandant of Jasenovac, the worst and biggest of the concentration camps for Serbs and Jews (he had personally taken part in murdering the prisoners and Draganovitch, with the rank of Lieut.-Colonel, had been the chaplain). The memorandum relates how the focal centre for the forced conversions and the massacres had been the Franciscan Monastery of Shiroki Brijeg in Herzegovina (Artukovitch had been educated there) and how in 1942 a young man who was a law student at the college and a member of the Catholic organization, The Crusaders, had won a prize in a competition for the slaughter of the Orthodox by cutting the throats of 1360 Serbs with a special knife. The prize had been a gold watch, a silver service, a roast sucking pig and some wine.

How can this be true? One recalls that great hero of Auschwitz, the Polish Franciscan Father Kolbe. But it *was* true and rumours of it had reached Rome. Rushinovitch, Pavelitch's representative at the Vatican, had reported to his Foreign Minister in Zagreb the remarks of Cardinal Tisserant, with whom he had an audience on 5 March 1942:

> I know for sure that even the Franciscans of Bosnia-Herzegovina behaved atrociously. Father Shimitch, with a revolver in his hand, led an armed gang and destroyed Orthodox Churches. No civilized and cultured man, let alone a priest, can behave like that.

Tisserant had probably got some of his information from the Italian general of the Sassari division at Knin, who had reported that Shimitch had come to him as local representative of the Croatian Government and had told him that he had orders to kill all the Serbs. The general had had instructions not to interfere in local politics, so he could only protest. The killing, under Franciscan leadership, had begun. The following year the Superior of the Franciscan Monastery in Knin was decorated by Pavelitch for his military activities with the order of King Zvonimir III.

The Croat bishops themselves were aware of what was happening. The Bishop of Kotor, Dr Butorac, while agreeing that the moment was propitious for mass conversion, wrote to Mgr Stepinac (4 November 1941) that the wrong type of missionaries were being sent – 'priests in whose hands revolvers might better be placed than a crucifix'.

In parenthesis, I should say, how fascinating are Rushinovitch's accounts of his audiences in Rome with Pius XII, with Cardinals Tardini, Maglione, Sigismondi and Spellman. Only Tisserant, and to a lesser extent Mgr Montini, the present Pope, appear to have fully grasped what was happening in Croatia. In Cardinal Ruffini the Ustashe had a firm supporter.

The memorandum made little impression on the United Nations, since it had no member state behind it. It had accused Tito's Government, which *was* a member state, of sheltering many Croat criminals and using them to break down the anti-Communist resistance of the Serbs. However, in 1952 Tito appealed to the USA for the extradition of Artukovitch. The California Courts to whom the case was referred argued that the extradition treaty of 1901 between USA and Serbia had never been renewed and that therefore Artukovitch could not be handed over to Yugoslavia. Six years later the Supreme Court rejected this view (by 7 to 1) and decreed that the case must be tried again in California. In the meantime Artukovitch had become a member of the Knights of Columbus and a much-respected figure who gave lectures to institutes and interviews on TV. When he was arrested again 50,000 Knights sent petitions on his behalf to Congress, and the West Pennsylvania Lodges of the Croatian Catholic Union forwarded a resolution that 'his only crime is his ceaseless fight against Communism' and that he was a champion of the rights and freedoms of all the peoples of the world.

That was the way his counsel, O'Connors and Reynolds, presented him, too, and Father Manditch, who had helped him in Switzerland, was once more by his side, in charge of another printing press and now Superior of the Franciscan Monastery in Drexel Boulevard, Chicago. His papers *Nasha Nada* and *Danica* (*Our Hope* and *Morning Star*) not only supported him but in their issues of 7 May 1958 urged their readers to send subscriptions for the Ustashe refugee fund to Artukovitch at his address in Surfside, California.

Another very useful ally was Cardinal Stepinac's secretary, Father Lackovitch, who had sought asylum at Youngstown, Ohio. In Europe Stepinac had been almost beatified for his implacable hostility to Pavelitch and Artukovitch, but now *The Mirror News* of Los Angeles (24 January 1958) reported Lackovitch as saying that he had seen Artukovitch almost daily and that he had been 'the leading Catholic layman of Croatia and the lay spokesman of Cardinal Stepinac and had consulted him on the moral aspect of every action he took'. The murderers of the Old World had become the martyrs of the New.

The American public was so ill-informed that it was possible to get away with almost anything. Pattee prints a statement that 200,000 of the converts from Orthodoxy were returning 'with a right intention' to a Church, which 'for political reasons' they had been forced to abandon. In fact, of course, the Serbian Orthodox had been in schism for some three centuries before the Protestant Reformation. Cardinal Tisserant, who had a rare tolerance of disagreeable truths, denounced Rushinovitch vigorously when he tried out this argument on him:

> I am well acquainted with the history of Christianity and to my knowledge Catholics of Roman rite never became Orthodox. . . The Germans helped you kill all the priests and you got rid of 350,000 Serbs, before you set up the Croatian Orthodox Church. What right have you to accuse others and keep on telling us that you are guardians of culture and the faith? In the war with the Turks the Serbs did just as much for Catholicism as you did and perhaps more. But it was the Croats, all the same, who got the title of *Antemurale Christianitatis*.

When I was in California, I went to see Father Mrvicin of the Serbian Orthodox Cathedral at West Garvey, near Los Angeles, and asked him why the Orthodox and the Jews of California had tolerated so many lies. He told me that at the time of the extradition trial he had circularized close on a thousand Serbs, who must have known well about Artukovitch, urging them to give evidence, but very few had replied. Life in USA was hard for them as refugees, they did not want to affront a powerful community, McCarthyism was not yet dead and they were shy of associating themselves with an appeal that came from a Communist country. A naturalized American, who took the matter up, died violently and mysteriously.

As for the Jews, though 30,000 with their 47 rabbis had been murdered in Croatia, Croatia was far away, and many who had escaped to USA had owed their safety to holding their tongues. Even so, the Jewish War Veterans of California, *The Valley Jewish News* and some Gentile papers like *The Daily Signal* of California came out against Artukovitch. But most Americans felt for the unknown refugee and his five children the easy charity of indifference. Finally the Yugoslav Government did some profitable deals with the USA and became indifferent, too. It is now interested only in proving that Artukovitch was a helpless stooge of the Nazis and that therefore the Bonn Government should pay compensation to Yugoslavia for the damage that he and the Ustashe had done.

The other day I came across a *History of Croatia*, published by the New York Philosophical Library. The author, Mr Preveden, acknowledges various 'inspiring messages of commendation and encouragement'. One of them comes from 'Dr Andrija Artukovitch of Los Angeles'. He is quite a public figure. He may have changed his address but his telephone number used to be Plymouth 5-1147.

Now many people want him hanged but there would not be much point in it. He was an insignificant man, who got his chance because there had been a great breakdown in the machinery of Christianity and he was able to pose as its protector. Why did this breakdown occur? Can it be repaired and, if so, how? So long as we are obliged to pretend that the breakdown did not happen, we shall never find out.

[1970]

Postscript 1971. There has since been an easing of tension between Communism and Christianity, most notably in Yugoslavia, where diplomatic relations with the Vatican have been resumed and there has been friendship between Catholic and Orthodox.

For example, in a Christmas message, Bishop Pichler begged forgiveness of the Orthodox Church and their Serbian brothers for all the wrongs done to them and funds have been raised by Catholics to restore the destroyed Orthodox churches.

Some of the leading Orthodox are not wholly happy about all this. Is it spontaneous or Government inspired? Is it possible that Tito fears the deep-rooted and passionate nationalism of the Orthodox more than Catholic universalism, which can be manipulated by external arrangements? Under the amnesty to political offenders, many Ustashe have returned home, notably Father Draganovitch, one of the five 'regulators' of the Forced Conversions, who escorted Pavelitch and Artukovitch to safety. He is in a monastery near Sarajevo editing the Schematismus, a sort of ecclesiastical year-book, whose publication has been suspended since 1939. Some of his returned colleagues are more active politically.

There is, of course, everything to be said for peace and conciliation, but the brotherly love that is brought about by diplomatic manoeuvres is often a little suspect.

II. IN SEARCH OF A PROFESSOR OF HISTORY

I could not get it out of my head that eighteen years before, Artukovitch had stayed for a year in Ireland. How had he come here? Who had sheltered him and where? In the spring of 1966 I was in Dublin for a week and I decided to find out. I was convinced that only some highly organized international body could have brought a wanted man so secretly and efficiently across Europe and, since the Franciscans had been so closely associated with the Ustashe in Croatia and had many international links I was confident that it was they who had brought him. I have never heard anything but good of Irish Franciscans but they were an institutionalized body and as such able and anxious to protect their members who get into trouble abroad.

There were a dozen Franciscan Houses in Ireland and I wrote to the Provincial in Merchant's Quay, Dublin, and also to four or five other houses, which, because of their remoteness, I thought were likely. Most of them answered with polite negative replies. The Provincial told me there had been a Croat Franciscan at their Galway house for some time but his name, Brother Ivanditch, was on the list of their Order and they had no doubt of his identity.

It was not till Branko Miljus sent me his copy of *The Mirror News* of Los Angeles that I made any progress. Artukovitch had been interviewed by the reporter, Henry Frank, who for the photograph had arranged him at a piano, grouping his wife and five handsome children round him. The Rev. Robert Ross of the Blessed Sacrament Church was there too as a friend and advocate. He told Frank how, as Minister of the Interior, Artukovitch had helped the Jews and been a formidable foe to the Communists.

'Artukovitch listened gravely and said with quiet dignity, "'I put my faith in God".'

Frank spoke of Artukovitch's 'strong, seamed face' and his 'modest well lived-in living-room'. He told how his daughter, Zorica, had won an essay competition in Orange County High School and his nine-year-old son, Radoslav, had been born in Ireland.

Here was a clue. The children had been exploited sentimentally to mask the truth, so they could be used to rediscover it. I went to the Customs House and after prolonged search I found Radoslav Anitch's birth certificate (A.164, No. 75). He was born on 1 June 1948 at the Prague House Nursing Home, 28 Terenure Road East; he was the son of Alois Anitch, Professor of History, of 6 Zion Road, Rathgar.

On the strength of this discovery. I sent a letter to all the Dublin dailies, explaining that I was writing an account of the Independent State of Croatia (1941-45) and that I wished information about the former Minister of the Interior, Andrija Artukovitch, (alias Alois Anitch) who had lived at 6 Zion Road, Rathgar, in 1947. Only *The Irish Times* printed my letter, turning him into a lady called Audrey.

In the meantime I visited the two houses, which were close to each other. No. 6 Zion Road is a two-storied house of red brick with an ivy-tangled sycamore and an overgrown privet hedge, but it had changed hands so often that it told me nothing about Artukovitch's Irish sponsors.

No. 28 Terenure Road, a tall building of red and white brick with much ornamental ironwork, has ceased for some years to be a nursing home. Nobody knew where the former owner had gone and it was not till I had paid two visits to the Guards Barracks at Terenure that one of them recalled where she now lived. It was not far off at 7 Greenmount Road and I went there immediately. The matron was a charming and intelligent woman and after eighteen years she remembered the Anitches perfectly. She had found them a pleasant and pathetic couple. He had spoken little English, Mrs Anitch had spoken fluently and, because of that, she had asked that he should have lunch with her in the Nursing Home. 'He is my baby,' Mrs Anitch had said, 'he wouldn't know how to get lunch without me.' They had two little girls who were at the Sacred Heart Convent, in Drumcondra Road, and now they wanted a boy. 'If it's a girl,' said Mrs Anitch, 'don't call him till the evening.' But when on the morning of 1 June Radoslav had been born, she was so delighted that she said her husband must be called at once. Anitch came and in his joy he had embraced the matron, much to her embarrassment. The Anitches had behaved nicely paying all their debts with money from America. After they had gone some months Mrs Anitch had written a grateful letter, which the matron showed me.

Only one person besides her husband had visited Mrs Anitch in the Nursing Home. He was a Franciscan who had been in Croatia, but the matron was not clear whether or not he was a foreigner. The Anitches had told her that the Communists had been particularly vindictive against the Franciscans.

My anticipations that the Franciscans had helped Artukovitch in Ireland had now been confirmed so I went to see the Provincial at Merchants' Quay. This time he agreed with me that the friar at the Nursing Home must have been the Croat at the Galway House. His name, he said, was Ivanditch. He was a supporter of Pavelitch and had often gone from Galway to Dublin.

Yet a Croat friar could not have made all these arrangements without powerful Irish assistance. Where had it come from?

The process by which a great persecutor is turned into a martyr is surely an interesting one that needs the closest investigation. I had only four days left in Dublin, so I could not follow up all the clues, but I made some progress.

First I went to the Sacred Heart Convent, 40 Drumcondra Road, a big red building on the left hand side of the street. I was shown into a little waiting-room and was received by a charming and friendly nun. I told her I was trying to trace the family of two little girls called Zorica and Vishnya Anitch, who had been at the convent in 1947 when they were four and five years old. She went away to look them up in her register and I sat for a very long time contemplating the plate of wax fruit and the little figurine of St Anthony. Then the nun returned and told me that the two little girls (but they were called Katherina and Aurea Anitch) had been admitted on 9 August 1947. Their parents had lived at 7 Tower Avenue, Rathgar and had taken the children to USA on 15 July 1948. She did not recall them herself but suggested that I ring up an older nun, Sister Agnes, who would certainly remember them. She was at St Vincent's Convent, North William Street. I rang Sister Agnes, who remembered them all vividly. The little girls were sweet and she had found the two parents 'a lovely pair' and Dr Anitch was 'a marvellous musician'. She did not remember that anybody came to visit the children except their parents, but a Franciscan monk, a nephew of Dr Anitch's, who had escaped with them from Croatia, was with them and had helped them to find lodgings.

Next I visited 7 Tower Avenue and was directed to a previous tenant, who worked in an ironmongery in D'Olier Street. He said he did remember having a lodger with a name like Anitch. He added, 'He was black, you know.' I tried other houses in Tower Avenue. Everybody was helpful and interested but I got no further clues.

After this I returned to Mrs O'Donoghue in Greenmount Road and found she had been keenly interested in what I had told her and herself had been trying to find out who had been the landlord in 6 Zion Road when the Anitches had lived there. She said I should get in touch with Patrick Lawlor, 32 Hazelbrook Road, who had sold the house to some woman in 1947.

I wrote to him and the next day he rang me up. He said it was so long ago that he could not remember the woman's name, but the auctioneer might know. After that I made some dozen visits and twenty telephone calls. They would be boring to relate but I found them exhilarating, as each clue led to another clue. I telephoned the doctor who had delivered Radoslav and examined the parish registers in Terenure and Rathgar for christenings. I went to the Valuation Office and telephoned the Voters Register, the Irish Red Cross, the Aliens Office and the International Office of Refugees. I enquired at the City Hall about Corporation Rates. In the end I got onto the solicitor who had acted both for Mr

Lawlor and for the woman to whom he had sold 6 Zion Road. His clerk made an unsuccessful search for her name and then suggested, 'Why not call on Thom's Directory?'

I went there the next day and the secretary took down from a shelf the directories for 1947 and 1948 and found Patrick Lawlor's name in both. 'But that's impossible,' I protested. 'He sold the house to a woman in 1947.' 'Yes, but there might have been a delay in publishing after we collected the information.' She took down the directory for 1949. 'The woman's name was Kathleen Murphy,' she said. I was off like a shot to a telephone-box.

There were three Miss K. Murphys in the directory and five Mrs Kathleen Murphys and several K. Murphys, who might be either male or female. It was a lengthy business for some were out and I was asked to ring later and some were testy at being catechised by a stranger. The fifth answered very suspiciously. 'Who are you? Why do you want to know? Yes, I was at 6 Zion Road, but if you want to know more you must come down. I remember the Anitches and, if you're friends of theirs I'd be glad to see you. Do you know them?' I said I did not but that a friend of mine in Paris, M. Miljus, would like to get in touch with them.

So we drove down to 6 Barnhill Road, Dalkey, a fine broad street with handsome villas. My wife waited outside in the car writing letters, while Mrs Murphy, a friendly middle-aged woman talked to me in her drawing-room. A friend of hers was just leaving when I came in, an Ulsterwoman with a nice downright manner, whose husband had been a bank manager in Kilkenny. She remembered us straight off when I said my name. 'Yes, I know who you are. I read your letters and articles in *The Irish Times*. I remember you got into a row with the Nuncio, Dr O'Hara, and it was on the head of you he got the boot!' She and Peggy talked together while I was with Mrs Murphy, who I could see had a powerful affection for this foreign family who had lodged with her. In particular she admired 'Dr Anish', whom she connected with 'Czechoslavia'. This confusion is not very surprising. Artukovitch would not have mentioned Yugoslavia, which did not exist for him, and not much was known in Ireland of Croatia, though one of those who were kind to him in Dublin said he came from Craishe. In general he was befriended as a foreign refugee from Communism and hitherto I have found no trace of sinister international intrigue among those who gave him hospitality.

Mrs Murphy reproached herself repeatedly for not having kept in touch with the 'Anishes' in California. Several times they had written charming letters. What a delightful family they were! 'They made a wonderful impression all round,' she said. 'I'd like to show you some snaps I have of them.' Mrs Murphy took down a photograph album with a large bundle of snaps in the middle. She rummaged through them all the time we were talking but never found what she was looking for. I explained to her that some time after Dr Anitch had got to California he had been the subject of bitter controversy and I showed her the picture of the family in *The Mirror News*. 'Ah, how old he has got to look, poor man! And that big girl must be Katerina and that one Aurea. And goodness me that young chap must be Radoslav! How time flies!' When I told her what his enemies were saying she shook her head indignantly. 'People will say anything! I don't think he thought of politics at all. All he cared about was his family. He was a wonderful father and husband! He was a very good man you know. He was rather like President Kennedy. He wanted justice for everybody. And he loved the Church. They were daily communicants.' Then I asked her how she had met him in the first place and she said she thought it had been at some party. Maybe some priest had introduced them. She became a little vague on the whole in this pregnant conversation. I was being the sly one, she the candid one. I asked did she meet a Franciscan with him and she said, 'Oh, yes, there was one came to lunch a couple of times. But the Anishes lived very quietly. They hardly saw anyone. You see he was a very retiring scholarly man. He once or twice gave a lecture at UCD, but otherwise they just thought of the children.' I subsequently made enquiries about those lectures at UCD but with no success.

Then I told her what remorseless enemies he had and explained something of the collapse of Yugoslavia. I showed her *Artukovitch, the Himmler of Yugoslavia*, turning the pages rapidly so as to reach some not too emotive pictures of him in the days of his glory. There he was giving the Nazi salute to a German general and there again greeting Hitler's envoy at the head of his Security Police, and there with his wife at a cocktail party in the Hungarian Embassy. I skipped some horror pages, headed with heavy irony ANDRIJA ARTUKOVITCH'S HEROIC DEEDS and including a picture of a soldier scissoring off the head of a seated peasant with some shears. Except for their attribution, such photographs are probably genuine. As I have said, Artukovitch was probably a desk murderer only. Mrs Murphy must have caught a glimpse of the scissored head for she stiffened and started to fumble again in her album for her friendly snapshots.

'Everybody in Dublin seems to have liked him,' I said, 'but why did he come here with a false name?'

'Probably he was forced to. Lots of people are. He couldn't have been a Nazi, though he may have been forced to take that side. I'm a good judge of character. I've travelled in sixteen countries and know a good man when I see one.'

'But he signed all those laws against the Jews' (I thought it would be too complicated to talk about the Orthodox she might not know who they were).

'Well, look what the Jews are doing to other people!' (I suppose she was thinking of the Arabs.)

Then we said good bye. As I left she repeated; 'They just lived for their children. They thought the world of them.'

The next place I had to visit was the Franciscan House in Galway from which Dr Anitch's nephew, Brother Ivanditch, paid visits to Dublin to see him.

When we reached Galway I went round to the Franciscan House, which is a few streets away from Eyre Square. Beside the big church I saw a small private door through which some travelling clerics with suit-cases were being hospitably ushered. I waited till they had all been welcomed before I went in and, after a few moments, the Father Superior appeared. Though he was preoccupied with his visitors he received me kindly. Seeing my attaché case he thought I was a commercial traveller, but when I explained I had come as a historian interested to find out about a Croat friar called Ivanditch, who was in Galway in 1947, he said, 'I'm afraid I don't know the good man. I'm only here three years, but, if you come tomorrow, when we've a bit more time, I'll get Brother Bede onto you. He was here in 1947.'

The following day I went round to the Franciscan House at 11.30 and Brother Bede received me. Yes. He remembered Brother Ivanditch well and had looked him up in the 'Schematismus' of the Order. He was from the province of Bosnia, near Sarajevo. He was a very striking looking chap and must have been over six foot. He was born in 1913. 'He wasn't here but at our hostel, St Anthony's College along the Moycullen Road, so

I didn't see much of him. But they say he spent all his time at the wireless listening to the news in German, French, Italian, Spanish; he was a very intelligent fellow, learnt English quickly. But he was broody, reserved and melancholy. All soul, you might say.'

Brother Bede had spent the war years in Rome. In the Franciscan headquarters the Croats had been more prominent than any other Slav group. Apart from Father Manditch, the treasurer of the Order, there was Father Jelachitch, a great canon-lawyer, and Brother Balitch, an eminent palaeographer who had written about Duns Scotus. 'You've no idea what confusion there was in Rome at that time. As for us, we put all the Slavs in one basket, a terribly passionate lot. We couldn't unscramble them.'

'Who sent him here? Oh, I suppose it was the General of our Order in Rome. I think it was Schaaf at that time, but I could look that one up. It was a question of obedience, you know.'

I told him that the Ustashe ambassador to Rome, Rushinovitch, had been given audiences by many cardinals and had sent his impressions of them back to Zagreb. It was obvious that not only the Irish but all the clerics at Rome had been highly confused by what was happening in Croatia. Only Cardinal Tisserant, I said, had a clear idea. On the other hand Cardinal Ruffini was a vigorous supporter and protector of the Ustashe!

'Ruffini!' Brother Bede laughed. 'Yes, indeed. He was a Sicilian, a great nationalist! They are as excitable as the Slavs. We took everything they said with a pinch of salt.'

As for Ivanditch, he had stayed for about a year in Galway and then gone to Canada. But there was a rumour that he was in Valencia, Spain, now. He was still alive or he wouldn't be in the Schematismus.

Brother Bede did not think I would get much more information from St Anthony's College as they were always changing their staff there, but there was a Brother David who might remember him. 'Worth trying anyway. Cross the salmon-weir bridge and along the Moycullen Road till you come to a long grey building on the left.'

They were widening the road and the surface was terrible so it must have been very close to the Brothers' dinner-time when I got to St Anthony's. The most pleasant thing about the building was the fine stone wall, a new one, that surrounded it. Most of the Galway walls are still excellently built and of stone, as unlike as possible to the new walls of the midlands, which, maybe because of the rich stoneless soil, are built of concrete, which submits itself readily to many vulgar and modish fancies.

I waited in a very clean and polished parlour under a picture of Jesus meditating on the Mount of Olives, till Brother David came along. He and his colleague, Brother Edmond, remembered Ivanditch well, and Brother David showed me a photograph of himself and Brother Ivanditch and a Galway lady, Mrs O'Halloran. They were a handsome group. Ivanditch, whose religious name was Brother Louis (Croatian Luji), was dark, clean-shaven, spectacled. A pleasant serious person he looked in his long brown habit with its white cord.

'But he was very hysterical,' Brother David said. 'He'd been sentenced to death by the Communists and he spent all his time listening to the ups and downs of Communism on the wireless. He was with us about a year, sent here by the General at Rome, waiting for instructions where to go. He was a professor of Dogmatic Theology. According to what he said, he was second-in-command to the Provincial at Zagreb. He had been given the seal of the Province of Croatia – he had it with him here – when the Provincial was imprisoned.'

I asked him if Artukovich (Anitch) had ever been to visit him. 'No, he had no visitors at all though once or twice he went to Dublin.'

'He brooded the whole time. He said the only hope for us was to have a third world war immediately. He thought us a very weak lot. There was a milk strike in Galway at the time and he could not understand why we did not settle it straight away by shooting the milkmen. And we should invade the six counties and settle that matter too *immediately*.'

'What amazed us about him,' Brother Edmond said, 'was the way he ate jam for breakfast. . . sometimes nearly a whole pot, and without any bread, just with a spoon. And though he got to know English very well, he used some very funny expressions. When we used to ask him if he would like another helping of anything, he would say, 'Thank you, no, I am fed up!' But he made a great friend in the town who could tell you more about him than I can, Joe O'Halloran of the Corrib Printing Works. He was working in O'Gorman's book shop in those days and he and Brother Louis used to see a lot of each other. Joe is the son of Mrs O'Halloran you saw in the snap shot.'

It was difficult to believe that the Galway Brothers belonged to the same order as the Ustashe Franciscans. What was nearest to Brother Edmond's heart was a scheme for building houses for the homeless by voluntary groups. He had been considering this idea, while he was with the Order in Louvain.

Joe O'Halloran was in a white coat working at the Corrib Printers when I called. He asked for a few moments to change and then he joined me at the Imperial Hotel and we had vodka and orange together. He had only been eighteen when Brother Ivanditch was in Galway, and he had been hugely impressed by this glamorous and passionate foreigner who had fled from his country under sentence of death, who had seen his Provincial sentenced to five years' penal servitude and his Primate, a world famous cardinal, condemned to sixteen years imprisonment by a Communist government. They had spent every Sunday together and Joe's parents had been equally captivated by this engaging person, who bore with him the seals of the Franciscan Order in Croatia and the responsibility to make its sorrows known to the world. It was his dream to establish a Croatian Seminary in Dublin. Ireland must know what Croatia had suffered and was still suffering in the name of Christ. She must know that the fate that had befallen Croatia awaited all Europe. They must be prepared.

Brother Luji counted on Joe O'Halloran's support in this sacred cause. But after a year the orders came from Rome for him to cross the Atlantic. He sailed from Liverpool to Montreal and Joe O'Halloran saw him off in Dublin. But though he had left Joe in charge of a sort of crusade, he had not replied at all regularly to his letters and slowly they had lost touch with each other. Joe learnt, though, that Brother Luji had been appointed chaplain to the Croat workers at Windsor, which is on the Canadian side of the Detroit river. They worked in the Ford factory at Dearborn and Brother Luji built for them the Chapel of St Joseph. Later on he had heard that he had been secularized and had left the Franciscan Order and it now occurred to Joe O'Halloran that this might have been because the French-Canadian Franciscans did not like Ivanditch's Croatian politics, which a few years later resulted in the murder of the Yugoslav consul in Stockholm and a curious entente with the Communists.

I asked about Artukovitch-Anitch and also about Count O'Brien, but Joe knew nothing of them. The only layman in Galway that Ivanditch saw was Mr O'Flynn, the County Manager, who invited him to tea, because his niece had once taught in Zagreb. Ivanditch had however told Joe that he had an uncle in Dublin who had been a Minister in the government of Croatia. Joe O'Halloran stressed that Ivanditch had totally failed to inflame the Franciscans in Galway and was very much disappointed in the Irish. He had been in Galway when the Republic was proclaimed in Eyre Square, and he was amazed that the Government had tolerated an opposition for so long. Why had not they just shot them?

In the past eighteen years Joe had changed. Ivanditch, were he to return, would no longer have the intoxicating effect which he had had on him as a very young man. In those days he had been puzzled that his elders should be so apathetic. For example, Father Felim O'Brien, a well-known Franciscan, had been lecturing in Galway and had treated very coolly Ivanditch's passionate appeals for a crusade. O'Brien was known all over Ireland for his dislike of 'liberalism'. Two or three years later, in 1950, he engaged Owen Sheehy-Skeffington in a long controversy in *The Irish Times* later published as a pamphlet, on *The Liberal Ethic.* I had contributed to this controversy so I have kept some records of it. O'Brien had maintained that in Ireland we owe our freedom of expression more to the clerics than to the liberal doctrine of tolerance, and that in Europe the Catholic clergy are the chief champions of liberty.

We got back late from Galway and it was a day before I was able to look up Ivanditch in my books. I found only one reference to him. He was referred to on page 20 in the report of the Stepinac Trial, *Sudenje Lisaku, Stepincu, Salicu I Druzini,* in connection with the trial of the Provincial of the Franciscan Order, Father Modesto Martinchitch. The Provincial is said to have given Brother Luji (Ivanditch), an Ustashe, a large sum of money to enable him to escape abroad. Brother Luji was not one of the five friars who helped the Provincial bury the thirty-four trunks of Ustasha treasure under the confessional in the Franciscan Church in May 1945, and I find no record of any activities that in Communist eyes were criminal. I think that when he claimed to have been sentenced to death by the Communists, Ivanditch was trying to make himself more glamorous. He seems to have escaped early on with an ample travel allowance and the seals of the province.

Whether or not Artukovitch was really his uncle, it may have been his task to escort him abroad in safety.

Since Brother Bede had mentioned Dr Balitch, the eminent palaeographer, at the Vatican, I looked him up in the vast book *Magnum Crimen* by Professor Victor Novak of Belgrade, not expecting to find anyone so scholarly and remote in this record of horror. But there he was on page 900. 'Brother Doctor Karlo Balitch, Professor at the Franciscan University at Rome.' His offence seems to have been slight but significant. When Marshal Kvaternik, the Commander of the Ustashe Forces, had arrived in Rome and visited the Institute of St Jerome in February 1942, Professor Balitch had been there to receive him, together with several other distinguished Croatian clerics and the whole staff of the Institute. Dr Balitch seems to have listened appreciatively while Dr Madjerec, the Rector, praised Kvaternik and the leader Pavelitch for their illustrious deeds in the cause of Christ.

The St Jerome Society was a very old and established Croat Institution with headquarters at Rome. Every year, even when Novak published his book in 1948, there were celebrations there in honour of Pavelitch's birthday, attended by Croat Jesuits, Dominicans, Capuchins, Benedictines. When Marshal Kvaternik addressed the Institute praising its work for the Ustashe there was loud and prolonged applause. This was in Rome, yet we have been told repeatedly that it was only under the strongest pressure that in Croatia itself the hierarchy lent their support to Pavelitch.

After the St Jerome Society had been suppressed in Croatia by Tito, Mgr Stepinac declared in his speech of defence: 'The St Jerome Society has ceased to exist. Its suppression is a grave offence against the whole people.' But surely it was rightly suppressed.

In an authoritarian community, when there is hypocrisy and connivance at the centre, the ripples from them spread outwards to the remote circumference: 'In vain do they worship me, teaching as their doctrines the precepts of men.'

In 1985 there is news of Dr Draganovitch, who helped Artukovitch to escape. I have been reading Tom Bower's story of Barbie, 'the Butcher of Lyons' who eluded French justice after the war in 1951 by the 'Rat Line', an escape-route which the Americans set up for people who were valuable to the CIA. They were equipped with fake passports and identity cards, but a contact was needed in Genoa, the port of embarkation, to supply the Rats with immigration papers for South America. Draganovitch, who had helped so many Ustashe escape to the Argentine, was obviously the man for the job. His fees for the Rat Line, according to Tom Bower, were $1000 for adults, half-price for children and $1400 for VIP treatment.

Surprisingly, though his services to the escaping Ustashe were well-known and though he had been on the infamous Committee of Five for the conversion of the Orthodox, he was permitted legally to return to Yugoslavia.

Is it possible that just as Barbie had useful information to give the Americans about the Communists, so Draganovitch had useful information to give the Communists about the Americans?

Artukovitch himself is still in California and, as I have related, sometime in the sixties the Yugoslav Government tired of asking for his extradition. Among other reasons, maybe, they thought that a sensational state trial in Zagreb might revive animosities between Serb and Croat.

However, in July 1981, the Board of Immigration Appeals in the USA, in view of a 1979 ruling of Congress, ordered that Artukovitch be deported. This was followed by further legal proceedings, appeals, counter-appeals, hearings and re-hearings.

The US Justice Department acted on a legal reform excluding 'Nazi collaborators' from seeking refuge and on 14 November 1984 'three carloads of federal marshals, guns drawn,' burst into Artukovitch's house at Seal Beach and took him into custody (*The Sunday Times*, 12 January 1985). He is now eighty-five and, according to his Dublin-born son Radoslav, he has Parkinson's Disease, a congestive heart condition, and is also blind and suffering from delusional paranoia. It is uncertain whether he will be competent to take part in an extradition hearing and its sequel, deportation to Yugoslavia and a show-trial at Zagreb. [1985]

Postscript 24 September 1986 He was finally extradited to Yugoslavia on 12 February 1986. On 15 May, after a four-weeks' trial, death sentence was pronounced. Twenty-six witnesses were called, evidence of much brutality given. Yet Artukovitch maintained that he was innocent and his duties chiefly administrative: 'I have always acted according to my conscience and the teachings of the Catholic Church.' Security for the trial was tight; policemen patrolled neighbouring streets with machine-guns and muzzled dogs. There has been no word of Artukovitch's execution. I believe he is still alive.

27

PETER'S WINDOW

No. 59 Chernishev Pereulok was a large plum-coloured block of bourgeois flats near the Yekaterinsky Sad (the Catharine Gardens), and the Archangelskys' flat was on the fifth floor. The lift had not worked since 1917 and sat in the well of the staircase, full of tram tickets and old newspapers. There was still a large gilt mirror on their landing, though all the others had been removed by the Jacht or House Committee. Darya Andreyevna, the former owner of the flat and its 'responsible tenant', set great store by all these traces of former grandeur and the Jacht had yielded before her fury when the mirror was threatened.

When my wife, Peggy, and I and our friend Archie Lyall, first came to Leningrad in 1932 on the *Alexei Rykov*, a tourist ship, the Archangelskys had made a special effort to welcome us. We brought news of Nikolai Mihalitch's old friends in England with whom he had had no contact since his wife, Connie, and baby son had left. They had gone home three years ago when the NEP period had given place to the rigours of the Five Year Plan and milk and baby-foods became scarce. We got the introduction to Nikolai Mihalitch through my cousin, Willy de Burgh, Professor of Philosophy at Reading University. Nikolai's father had been a priest in Tiflis and they had fled from the Bolsheviks to the Crimea (for a short time in White Russian hands). There, his sister had married an Englishman, an officer in the British interventionist forces, whose home was in Reading. When the Bolsheviks seized the Crimea, Nikolai was sent to England and became one of the most brilliant of de Burgh's pupils. It was there that, later, he married Connie, a fellow student, and influenced by the left-wing intellectualism of the time, they became Communists and decided to join his widowed mother in Leningrad.

When we first called there were biscuits and tea with hot milk, and strawberry jam in saucers, and his mother was in a state of collapse compounded of hospitality and suspicion. Nikolai had asked a friend of his, Major Tihomirov, a teacher in the Military Academy, to meet us and a colleague of his own, Baroness Garatinsky, was anxiously awaited. Nikolai Mihalitch had told me her story. She had been an old revolutionary and in 1917 her peasants, who had taken over her estates in Central Russia, had made her their manager. Five years later her position had became impossible and she was now teaching languages in Leningrad. Through the open window we saw her limping slowly up the street, pausing and glancing up and down to see that it was empty before she turned in. 'It isn't very safe for us to visit each other,' he said; 'in any case she doesn't like the stairs with her lame leg, but this is a special occasion.' He told me that because of her origins, she was suspect politically. She had a daughter in exile in Siberia and a son in Solovietski Island. In Goskurs, the Polytechnic where she taught, she was the victim of petty persecution. 'Women are the worst,' he said, and he was explaining how in Leningrad an arts education was more accessible to the female than to the male bourgeois, when the baroness walked in. She paused in the doorway, leaning on her stick, and diverted with a smile his mother's effort to introduce us and give her a chair. 'Later, later, Nina Gavrilovna.' To us she said, 'Women are allowed a bit more licence, because even here they aren't taken seriously. Masculine unreliability matters more.'

She had a sharp rather cantankerous manner but spoke English well in a beautifully clear voice. She always talked rapidly and provocatively when she was manoeuvring into chairs or difficult positions, as if to distract attention. She looked coldly into people's eyes when she talked to them. She herself had a lack of personal inquisitiveness that was almost unfriendly. It was as if she could only argue or disagree and did not waste time in liking or disliking.

Nina Gavrilovna was a crushed, dark little woman. She followed our English talk anxiously with her bright black eyes, interrupting her son with nudges and murmurs, when she could: 'Kolya, ask the lady after the Professor's wife's health!' 'Kolya, you are talking so much you have not noticed the lady has nothing on her plate!' (Only Nikolai's mother called him Kolya, as I will for brevity, but actually everybody in the flat was very formal and used patronymics. Even his closest friends called him Nikolai Mihalitch.)

She guessed correctly that her son was being indiscreet but could never learn that it made him worse to interrupt. The baroness, seeing her agitation, said to me, 'You mustn't think that because we have much to complain of, we are enemies of the Revolution. The Revolution had to happen, it was the result of generations of suffering and plotting. All the great Russians of the past have played a part in it. It is a historical fact, a great convulsion of human nature. If we are to go on living we must accept it, and I have always done so gladly.'

Before we could reply Tihomirov succeeded in changing the conversation. He spoke English in the genteel, mincing way of some educated Russians. He had gold teeth and a moist, glinting smile.

As we left, Kolya said to me, 'When you come back from Rostov, you must stay with me. I will get you a job teaching.' He translated this to his mother, who gave a glance of agony. 'But there is no bed. What will Darya Andreyevna say?' He ignored her. 'I will arrange. I will get you a bed. You must stay a term.'

We went down the Volga and visited Moscow and Rostov. Archie Lyall wrote a book on our experiences, *Russian Roundabout*, which became a classic for all earlier travellers by Intourist. I came back fearing that Kolya's mother would have dissuaded him from inviting me to stay on. I was wrong. We spent a few days in Leningrad before the *Rykov* sailed back and it was plain Kolya counted on my staying. Smiling and bowing, Alexander Ivanitch Tihomirov came to our hotel and together we went to the military stores, where, under his guidance, I bought myself a camp-bed for forty roubles. The next day the *Rykov* sailed. Kolya, Tihomirov and I went to the docks to see off Peggy and Archie. It was a strange departure, for there was a young woman among the passengers who had had a nervous breakdown. She had been recommended a 'complete change' and she and her parents could think of nothing better than a trip to Russia. While there she had gone mad and had to be dragged aboard kicking and struggling and finally lifted up the gangway, screaming.

That afternoon I installed myself in Chernishev Pereulok. It was the name-day of all the Sonias and Nadjezhdas, and their friends were hurrying up and down the streets carrying bunches of over-blown dahlias. A few foreigners were still bathing on the broad strand by the Peter and Paul fortress but the melon pips, which had started to sprout by the water's rim, had been nipped by an early frost. Workmen were wrapping up the heads of delicate shrubs in the Summer Garden in balloons of paper and taking in the cactuses and coleuses, which ornamented the lawns with hammers and sickles.

In the Archangelskys' flat the Jacht had sent a chimney sweep to clean the flue. Everything I saw was coloured and penetrated for me by the thought of the Revolution. Even commonplace or inevitable things had a bloom of special significance because they had matured at such a time and in such a place.

I pitched my camp-bed between the stove and the window in the room, where we had our tea-party in the summer. Kolya had a divan covered with drab fusty material in the opposite corner. Everthing in the room was shabby and dark. There were large patches on the wall where his son, Misha, a couple of years before had peeled off the wallpaper and scribbled on the plaster. Over the whole flat there was that sweetish, musty smell of black bread and benzine and scent and galoshes that Russians seem to carry with them, even into exile. I felt lonely and ill-at-ease. Nina Gavrilovna plainly did not want me there. She refused to believe that being foreign I could understand anything, unless she shouted at me with plentiful gesticulations. Her bed was in a widening of the passage, which was screened off by a dark curtain. Beyond that were two rooms, where invisible factory-workers lived. To the left was the room of Darya Andreyevna and her husband. In the dark passage outside our room near the front door, Lyubotchka, the Archangelskys' maid, used to sleep on her trunk. Till I had practice I stumbled over her every time I came to bed late. At the far end of the passage was the kitchen, where each tenant had his private Primus, and off that there were two windowless cupboards, the bathroom and the W.C. Darya had asserted her authority in these two rooms by pinning up the pictures that decorated the flat when it had been hers, 'Stags at Bay', 'The Imperial Palace at Gatchina', family groups. They bulged out from their drawing-pins with all the fluff and dust that had accumulated behind them. No one dared to remove them, but during the paper shortage hard-pressed tenants had torn jagged strips from them and from their cardboard mounts.

Kolya had exchanged his Russian white summer suit for a Norfolk jacket and grey flannel trousers. Before he was like an Italian but now he was like a Bloomsbury Asiatic. He had a dark thin fanatical face and abrupt, vehement movements. He did not like to explain or to have his explanations questioned.

My first day I spent alone in the flat writing letters and examining Kolya's books. They were neatly shelved on a pair of skis that he was storing for his elder brother, an engineer. I saw F. H. Bradley, Hegel, Bertrand Russell, Aldous Huxley, D. H. Lawrence. Of Russian writers he had only Lenin and his commentators.

I was interrupted constantly by the telephone. His mother would slip in and answer it, looking at me through the corners of her eyes. 'Ne doma,' she would say bitterly, 'Ne znaioo!' 'He's not at home.' 'I don't know!' This happened two or three times. Then she took out her basket and went marketing, and I was left to answer the next call myself three-quarters of an hour later. It was a lady. 'Where is Nikolai Mihalitch?' From my way of answering she guessed I was English and she went on in English. 'Where can he be? He was due to give his lesson here half an hour ago and I rang up Techmass, but he hadn't given his class there, and at Goskurs it was the same.' I couldn't enlighten her.

At six o'clock his mother let him in and there was a voluble conversation in the passage. He came into the room without greeting me. He looked completely exhausted. 'It is arranged,' he said, but hearing his mother at the door leapt up and seized a plate of over-cooked vegetable marrow from her. 'Isn't your mother going to eat here?' I asked. 'No, it would be better not. She does not understand the English.' Even when it was irrelevant, I made a point of saying I was Irish not English. I made things worse by saying once that the de Burghs were Irish too. It was as a visitor from England, where he had been so happy, that Kolya was welcoming me. For years he had been waiting for an opportunity to return the kindness which had been shown him. Even for his mother the syllables Dee Buggs had some mystic significance. He did not want to be put off by details.

'What is arranged?' I asked, when he seemed ready for a question. 'Your classes are arranged,' he said. 'You will have four classes every evening from eight till midnight. I've made out the list. You will be a member of our brigade. Then there is Olga

Kulgachev two hours and Engineer Stavrogin three hours in a decade, and you've already fixed up with Alexander Ivanitch. They will start next week.' A decade, which sounded to me an eternity, meant ten days. Brigades were groups of friends, who shared out pupils or jobs between each other. There were other brigades for house decoration, theatre craft, translating and all the more specialized arts and crafts. 'But did you spend all this time looking for work for me? You must have missed all your classes.'

'That is of no importance.'

For the next few days he once more gave up all his classes in spite of my protests, and we tramped and trammed from one end of Leningrad to the other, interviewing passport officials, professors, pupils.

One day as we were queuing up outside the offices of the Lensoviet, he tried to explain himself to me: 'I am a Caucasian from Georgia like Stalin, with the same theological background. He was a theological student. He believes like the Manicheans that there is Good and Evil, Black and White, a dichotomy. All this which he thinks Good is Evil.' He waved his hand at the Lensoviet and the long queue.

'Why do you like the English so much then? They are not Manichean. They play down all the major issues of good and evil. They are loyal to small obligations, not big ones. I can't imagine an English teacher neglecting all his classes to help the friend of friends, who were once very good to him.'

He looked hurt, as if I had accused him of being un-English. But I had meant it as a compliment and I could not let the subject drop. I argued that social organization works better in England, simply because the English only made superficial impact on each other. They glide about, cannoning off each other like billiard balls. They can calculate each other's reactions accurately, because they hardly ever impinge. Perhaps the reason why the Russians are difficult to organize is because they make real contact. It's like playing billiards with bull's eyes.

'You forget I am a Caucasian. That's what I hate about the Russians, always prying and enquiring about each other.'

I found his claim to be Caucasian as irritating as he found my claim to be Irish: 'I don't think Russians could ever be detached in the tepid, unemphatic English way. You would merely isolate yourselves.'

After a pause, he said: 'Darya Andreyevna was catechizing my mother about you today. She thinks you are a spy and wants the House Committee to turn you out. She has been to the Upravdom [the President of the House Committee]. Lyubotchka did her best for you. She said she thought you were a harmless idiot because you smile when you talk to her.'

'I only meant to be friendly.'

'Yes, but real Russians only smile at jokes.'

I had no way of paying for my lodgings, so I suggested that Peggy should pay Connie in Eastbourne every week. He refused indignantly. I was his guest. I accepted this but asked Peggy to send suitable things to Connie instead.

But we were to have other complications that evening. Lyubotchka the maid came from Karelia near Finland where not much was known about plumbing. She had broken one of Connie's wedding-present tea cups, and, fearing to admit it, had thrown it down the W.C. and pulled the plug. Darya Andreyevna a little later found the W.C. choked and, groping with her hand, she discovered a piece of Connie's china. With me there without her permission, it was too much for her. Sobbing with rage, she burst through the door and flung the horrible handful on the floor.

In the fury about the tea cup my problem was forgotten. Nobody ever again thought I was a spy. But after that, Darya and Kolya never went to see each other. They communicated, when they had to, by telephone. When our door was open, we could hear Darya Andreyevna's real voice through the passage wall almost as clearly as her telephone voice. Though she lived in the next room for many months, I never saw her again, nor did I ever see her husband though we were incessantly aware of each other.

Darya's husband had been a colonel in the Tsar's army, a very tyrannical one, Kolya told me, and his wife had been an opera singer and quite famous. After the revolution she had sung Soviet songs and had been awarded the rank of 'Naoochnaya Rabotnitsa' or 'Scientific Worker'. Because of this she had first-category food rations and the right to a certain floor space in her old flat. In relation to the Jacht she became 'the responsible tenant'. With her food tickets she could get, among other things, macaroni. Nina Gavrilovna could never forgive her this. A Tsarist colonel's wife got macaroni, while her son, a Marxist professor and Privat

Dozent at the Oriental Institute, had to live on vegetable marrow. Incessantly nagging Kolya about this, she had made it psychologically impossible for him ever to get a first-category food ticket. All that was necessary was for him to fill in a few forms, but nothing would induce him to do so. Whenever macaroni was mentioned, his face went dead and cold and Manichean.

Soon after this my classes began. The last tourists had disappeared from the streets and I felt like a privileged member of the audience who goes home with the actors after the play. Stacks of logs were being piled in the courtyards and back streets and one heard the whine of saws. The streets got emptier and footsteps echoed. Everyone except Kolya sealed up his double windows with gummed paper and closed the phortochka, the little ventilating window by which they were pierced. Everyone bought galoshes, for the pavements were like troughs and held water.

I had no winter clothes and clothing became an obsession, for my arms were too long for everything I could afford. Kolya lent me an old coat, and I wedged a pair of undersize galoshes onto my shoes. I could never get them off again, so I used to take off shoes and all at my classes and hide my feet under the desk. Later on I put my galoshes on my indoor shoes, but I had to walk sedately or the galoshes dragged them off again.

One day, as I was walking to my classes in the twilight, I saw a large leather-coated figure lying on the pavement. He had an open dispatch-case beside him with papers scattered about. He was snoring. A woman came from the far side of the Moika river to help me lift him up. 'What a shame,' she exclaimed, 'to see such a beautiful coat lying in the mud!' We examined it together. 'I bet he's a commissar!' she said. 'One can only get a coat like that with valuta.' We dragged him to the Mariinski Theatre and propped him up, sitting against one of the columns of the portico. I told her I had valuta and needed a coat, so she took a pencil and piece of paper out of his dispatch-case and wrote the name of the place where I could get one like it.

Next day I went there. There was only one possible coat but it was still too short in the sleeves. Nina Gavrilovna did not seem to like my wearing Kolya's coat, so I went back several times but could not make up my mind to spend so much money on a coat that did not fit.

Kolya had brought back from England an obsession about fresh air, and was proud that he was the only man among his acquaintances who kept his phortochka open day and night. Alexander Ivanitch Tihomirov told me that Max Müller had once come to Petersburg to lecturer on Fresh Air but had to postpone his lecture because he had lost his voice. My experience was the same. I always woke up with a sore throat, but it was a point of honour with Kolya not to close the phortochka.

Kolya had two other friends who taught English, besides Tihomirov and Vera Garatinsky. Both of them, Yegunov and Lihachev, came of wealthy families, who had governesses. Yegunov had had a Scottish governess, whose Glasgow accents reproduced themselves in all his pupils. Lihachev was in the navy and only settled in Leningrad during the winter, when he taught at the Marine Academy. His English was the strangest and the most fluent. Onto a precise bookish English he had grafted a cosmopolitan sailor's slang derived from conversations in the *lingua franca* at Baltic ports. He was never at a loss for a word. We only got two roubles an hour for our classes and big deductions were made for holidays. There were also 'voluntary' contributions, which were compulsory; only Kolya did not pay them, as he disapproved on principle.

Alexander Ivanitch, in those days, was a bachelor with close-cropped hair and a smart military appearance. He had been a Tsarist officer. He was courtly and considerate. He described himself to my wife as 'very Victorian'. But when he deplored the new ways, he did not mean Bolshevism, but foxtrots, red fingernails, James Joyce. The Revolution had been such an overwhelming experience that I doubt if he ever criticized it, even to himself. All the same, to save his self-respect, he permitted himself some tiny heresies, about women in public life, for example. In most totalitarian creeds there is an unimportant corner, like a game-reserve, retained for harmless scepticism and good-humoured satire. Alexander Ivanitch knew his way about it perfectly and for some time appeared to me to be a highly emancipated person.

He had learnt English by the 'Williamson Method' and used to compare his face in a looking-glass with a series of enlarged coloured pictures of the mouth and tongue. He was very conscientious and wished to capture the spirit of the language as well as the idiom. In addition to the mouth-pictures he had a collection of English political speeches on gramophone records.

Also he recited to me once a week a leader from *The Manchester Guardian*, which as an officer in the army he was permitted to take in.

He had other military privileges regarding rations of food and clothing, which he shared generously with his friends and the two devoted old ladies who looked after him. He lived in a stuffy room above a tailor's shop. It smelt of pot plants and leather and kvass. He used to put on a record just before my lesson, so as to get his ear into training. One unseasonably warm afternoon I walked with Lihachev towards his house. The loudspeakers on the street corners, which bawled out the feats of shock workers, were silent as if exhausted by the heat, and I was astounded to hear a cultured and fruity English voice echoing unchallenged through the narrow empty street. The voice came from Alexander Ivanitch's open window; it was Mr Asquith addressing a meeting in Edinburgh seventeen years before: 'We shall not sheathe the sword,' he was declaiming, 'till Belgium has recovered in full measure all and more than all that she has lost, till France. . . '

'It is rare and pleasant,' said Lihachev, 'to hear someone praise liberty who has dined well.'

Alexander Ivanitch was revising a pre-revolutionary grammar of English conversation. The questions of the new Russian tourist, instead of being inquisitive and pleasure-seeking, became didactic and uncompromising. He enquired about wages and factories instead of theatres and laundries. The rigours of his catechism were tempered by a strange jauntiness, in which Alexander Ivanitch took a special pride. 'Is a sportlike way of asking the time to say "What do you make the time?"', he enquired, 'and can one use the phrase "oneish twoish" without a preposition?'

I gave him his lessons under seal of secrecy, lest it should get about among rival teachers that he still had anything to learn. Slavs are too logical to value modesty or self-depreciation. 'If you yourself', they argue, 'think poorly of your faculties, they must be poor indeed.'

One day he told me to be very careful what I said to Nikolai Mihalitch. He was unreliable, he explained, and indiscreet. I did not mention that Kolya had given me similar warnings about him. I gathered that Alexander Ivanitch was in touch with the GPU (the Gaypayoo was the current name in 1931 for the Secret Police). In the end I came to the conclusion that almost all those whom I was able to see constantly had obtained the consent of the GPU and were under obligation to report my movements. I was flattered that they liked my company enough to go to this trouble, but I am sure that Alexander Ivanitch alone attempted a conscientious record of my unmemorable sayings and doings.

He was, in fact, the ideal spy. It was a disinterested pleasure to him to gossip, and it was a bonus for him to feel patriotic. He never did us any harm. Indeed, hovering on the edge of our little group, he was a kind of insurance that we should not be molested. He liked his lessons and wished us well. He once publicly refuted a rival teacher's allegation that I had 'a terrible Irish accent'.

Kolya had made out the curriculum for English literature in Techmass and Goskurs. It was very impressive. Every English writer who had written anything vaguely subversive was included. There were Kingsley's *Alton Locke*, Mrs Gaskell's *Mary Barton*, Charlotte Bronte's *Shirley*. Were these about the industrial revolution perhaps? But why Virginia Woolf, Aldous Huxley and E. M. Forster? Copies of the list were typed and I handed them round to my classes and asked them to bring what books they could. About twelve books came: some Byrons, Wildes, Galsworthys, and a book, author unknown, called *A Fairy Sits Upon My Knee*. A little Jewess, who, I had been told, was a political spy, brought in and insisted on reading a book by Mildred Cram about a man who married above himself in London society and did not know that you had to eat asparagus with your fingers. His wife tried to stifle the artistic side of his nature and eventually he flung it all up and returned to his old simple life. No other books could be found. As a result, most classes had to be improvised, and though my pupils were friendly and interested, there was no interval between the four classes, so by midnight I was often nearly speechless from exhaustion.

That winter the fortieth anniversary of Gorki's 'creative work' was being celebrated. Nizhni Novgorod was being rechristened Gorki, and a bombing aeroplane had been dedicated to him. Though we never talked of politics, we sometimes discussed 'ideology'. A woman said that Gorki was 'a gumanist' (our 'h' is 'g' in Russian) and that a bombing aeroplane would not please him much. I asked them to define 'gumanism'. A man said in English, 'It is what you say "namby-pamby".' The woman was not satisfied and began to protest. It appeared that about half the class thought nambi-pambiness a good thing, but the political spy, a kind woman, who did not want trouble, proposed we go on with Mildred Cram.

The classes were orderly and well arranged, the rooms clean and airy. The Principal of Goskurs had once been Director of the Imperial Ballet and all his staff except two or three were bourgeois, who had learnt foreign languages from governesses and tutors. At the doorway sat the political director, an Armenian called Guzelimian. Every time I passed he examined me fiercely, as if he wished to cathecize me; he had a villainous peasant face and I hurried on pretending not to notice him. One day when we were alone in the hall he beckoned me over. 'When you go to England,' he said, 'will you get me a fishing-rod?' Fumbling with his papers, he took out a picture. 'Like that. I wanted to talk to you several times, but you looked so stiff I didn't dare.'

The other teachers didn't talk to me but I felt an atmosphere of friendliness and goodwill. Once, when a long corridor was empty, an elderly man, who had never spoken to me, came up and presented me with a book. 'This is my book,' he said. 'Don't tell anyone.' He bolted before I had time to thank him. Whenever I passed him later, he pretended not to see me.

The small blue volume was an excellent Russian-English dictionary by C. K. Bojanus and V. K. Muller. Later Kolya told me that he was Professor Bojanus himself, that he intended to marry Mrs Williamson of the mouth-pictures and go with her to England, but did not want to prejudice his chances of leaving Russia by any association with foreigners.

Edmund Wilson (*New Yorker*, 20 April 1963) wrote that Bojanus was liquidated and his name taken off the title page of the dictionary, but the verb 'sostavili', 'composed', was left in the plural, though Muller is named as sole author. I had previously heard that he escaped and worked at the School of Slavonic Studies till he died. I reproach myself that I never enquired about this kind, good man, or sent the fishing-rod to Guzelimian.

Nina Gavrilovna was against me from the start and decided that I was to blame for anything that went wrong in the flat. In Moscow I had been given a sixteenth-century ikon of John the Baptist by Leonid Leonov, whose book *The Thief* I had translated, and one day I showed it to Kolya, who promptly hung it on the wall. His mother, seeing it when Kolya was out, was appalled. 'What will his pupils say? It's pearls before swine.' She laid the ikon reverently in the laundry-basket. When Kolya came back and saw the gap on the wall he marched unerringly to the laundry-basket. The ikon came in and out of the basket several times. Then I said to Kolya, 'I'm a nuisance here. I'd better find a room elsewhere.'

He flared up, 'Are you not comfortable here? No one would have you except me; they would be frightened even if they had room. And at the hotel you would have to pay two pounds a day. My mother will be going to Luga soon. At the New Year I will arrange that we take a few days' holiday and go on an excursion with Lihachev and Yegunov to the South. I will arrange to get teachers' tickets.'

All the same I put several advertisements in the papers and got some replies. I went round to the addresses. Nobody wanted to be paid. In fact money meant very little in Leningrad; they lost all interest in me when they heard I was not a foreign engineer, paid in valuta, and entitled to meal tickets at Quisisana, the Insnab restaurant (Insnab meant Inostranni Snabzheniye or Foreign Provision). One woman thought that as a foreign engineer I would be able to get her coat lined at Torgsin. One letter I did not answer. It was from a Pole called Vaishlé, who offered me a bed in his living-room. His aunt used it in the daytime, but she worked in the post office at night. It would be empty then and I could use it free, if I would help him read an English book on geology. One day when I came back from giving Alexander Ivanitch his lesson, I found Kolya entertaining the Pole, a small fat jolly man. He had brought his lunch and his geology book under his arm. 'I thought you might be too shy to come, so I came instead.' I was relieved to find that in the last resort there was someone in Leningrad eager to house me, and I offered to read some geology with him then and there. As he left, he said, 'I'm in this neighbourhood once or twice a week. I'll just call round and we'll read a bit of geology and I'll promise to keep my aunt's bed free for you.'

I agreed to this arrangement as a sort of retaining fee, and every now and then he came round. He always brought his lunch, but sometimes he came without his geology book just for a talk. Being a Pole, he was the first person I met willing to admit that I was an Irishman. He was greatly interested and told me that Daniel O'Connell's great grand daughter was working in a large china factory on the Neva. He seemed to take it for granted at his first glance at my surroundings that for an Irishman to live in a Russian family was a chemical experiment that might or might not succeed. 'How are things going?' he would ask. 'Remember my aunt's bed is always free.' Once, as he left, he clasped my hand and said: 'You know Russians are Asiatics, they don't understand comfort. I advise you to come to us.'

I had some £25 worth of black roubles, given me by an English sociologist who was staying at the British Embassy. He was going home and no longer needed them. So often I would ask Kolya out to lunch at one of the tourist hotels. After the season the fare was always the same. We had only one course. At the Europa there was a rich-looking paté made of game in aspic, at the October a fish called 'sudak' with Sauce Tartare. Except for ourselves and one waiter, the large dining-rooms were usually empty. The restaurant at the October was below street level and beggars would crouch on the road outside and stretch in supplicating hands through the ventilators. Kolya came reluctantly or else refused. He was very proud. When I pressed him into coming, in order to show that he had not refused from fear of being compromised, he would talk loudly in English criticizing the Soviet régime. I think he was flattered when one day an old woman came up to us outside the October and said: 'Messieurs, votre roi est le cousin de notre empereur.' He gave her a few kopecks. The old woman looked at them for a moment in hurt perplexity and then stuffed them quickly in her skirt.

In the end I believe it was the Pole and not hunger that prevailed upon Kolya to apply for a first-category food ticket. Though I was the cause of so much trouble, he wanted me to stay. He said one evening: 'I am becoming a "naoochny rabotnik". I have arranged that tomorrow there will be a proper English breakfast. There will be porridge and scrambled eggs.' And next morning Lyubotchka produced a thin custardy substance and 'grechnevaya kasha', a sort of gruel made of buckwheat. The buckwheat only lasted a week, for, learning that Kolya was a naoochny rabotnik, Nadya, one of the Kolya's predatory relations, made a claim on it. 'There will be just scrambled eggs,' he said, 'but that will be a change, which is always nice.' 'Yes,' I agreed, 'but next time couldn't Nadya have the change and let us have the buckwheat?'

But he was totally indifferent to food. Once he gave up his sugar ration for a whole month so that he could buy the works of Dorothy Wordsworth, of which a consignment had reached Leningrad.

One day the first snow came and the waters in the canals moved turbidly below a film of ice. Lihachev, who had been in Armenia, was back and we talked of going to ski at Pavlovsk. Everybody became cheerful and excited, the streets were gay and sparkling, and tiny children, so tightly buttoned into shubas that they looked like small sheep, pulled each other about in packing cases in the Yekaterinsky Sad. Once or twice a week we had free evenings and there were theatres and ballets and impromptu parties.

I was the only one who could buy at Torgsin, the foreign currency shop, but my black roubles were running out so I seldom went there or to the hotels. But for our parties I got bottles of sweet Caucasian wine. I had a pupil behind the counter who helped me dodge the queues. In the markets there was always plenty of bread, and different delicacies swept over the city in waves; honey or cheese or stiff black cranberry jam crowded the shops for a few weeks and then disappeared in a night as quickly as they had come. Instead came sock suspenders or celluloid tooth-brush cases and, in the window, a red cloth with a bust of Lenin on it. There were no containers for the honey and Kolya in his English mood refused to carry his jug in his hand down the Nevsky. Inevitably, Nina Gavrilovna blamed it on me that everything in his attaché case, books and lecture notes, were covered in honey.

Baroness Garatinsky came back from a visit to her son, who was imprisoned in Solovietsky Island; every day for five minutes she was allowed with all the other visitors into a long corridor, where behind an iron railing their relations were waiting to see them. So as to be heard, each tried to talk louder than his neighbour and, when it was impossible, they had to communicate by gestures. 'I felt we had stopped being human and become monkeys. Perhaps we have always been monkeys.'

Lihachev usually came with Yegunov, who taught English with him at the Marine Academy. He was a Greek scholar and had translated *Aethiopika,* a third-century Alexandrian novel by Heliodorus. As far as I could judge, Yegunov's translation and its ninety-page introduction would have brought him distinction in England. He was now translating Plato's *Timaeus,* also for the Academia Press, but hesitated to publish it. 'Two friends of mine,' he explained, 'were overheard at a party setting Plato above Karl Marx and they were banished from Leningrad.' 'Don't risk it then,' I said. 'Well, it was not so bad for them,' he answered doubtfully, 'they were unemployed stage managers and they were sent to Orel, where, as it happened, they got jobs straightaway in a new theatre. They sneak back to Leningrad, when they can. But I could not bear to leave Leningrad.' For though Leningrad is the least typical of Russian cities, its citizens love it as Parisians love Paris. They are unhappy away from its grave and charming avenues and gardens, its cold northern sunsets.

Yegunov had tuberculosis. Peter the Great built his city on a marsh for wealthy aristocrats with fur coats and servants with warming-pans and stoves, or else for tough mouzhiks, who would warm themselves with labour and vodka. A generation ago the remnants of a well-to-do bourgeoisie lived there without fuel or fur coats to interpose between themselves and the raw and foggy winters. How could they not get tuberculosis?

Lihachev was always cheerful. His father had been a wealthy doctor, who, at the outbreak of the Revolution, had invited all his relations and friends to share his two-storied house so that they need not have strangers forced on them. They had brought all their most cherished furniture with them. Two uncles had been in the consular service in Africa and had crammed the rooms with bamboo and bark and bronze and stamped leather. He told me that when they had all in the old days lived in different parts of Petrograd, they travelled long distances to quarrel with each other. 'Now it's so easy, there's no sport in it.'

One day in October we were eating raw herring and scrambled eggs, and having the last drop of the brandy flask I had brought from Ireland, when the telephone rang. It was a girl, in the flat above. She said she was a pupil of Kolya's at the Oriental Institute and, as they were having a party and short of 'cavaliers', would we come up and join them? Kolya said he had friends with him. 'Well, bring them all,' she said, so we all trooped upstairs.

The girl opened the door herself, but when she let go the doorhandle she slipped backwards and would have fallen if she had not clutched at Kolya. A girlfriend beside her was scarcely steadier on her feet and, when at last we got into the room, we saw the reason. It was an infinitely more luxurious flat than ours, with pre-revolutionary candelabras, family portaits and wall-hangings, and a long table heaped with grapes and pineapples, every variety of wine and liqueur and plates full of appetizing food. There were men in morning coats and ladies in evening dress. It was astonishing to come from our bleak, dark and damp quarters and to discover so much light and luxury a few feet above us, and in a room the same size and shape as ours. Half dazed, I flopped into a chair beside a plump lady with enormous ear-rings, who poured me out some curação and talked to me in faultless English about Ilfracombe. Then someone told me it was a wedding, and the bridegroom came and asked me very pleasantly to bring up my curação and come to dance in the next room. It was very small and corresponded to one of the factory workers' rooms down below. Lihachev was foxtrotting in the tiny floor and I found a partner and joined him. It was hot and uncomfortable and I sensed that something was wrong, but I could not tell what or why. Suddenly I discovered that the tension, which I had detected, was emanating in dense waves from Kolya, who sat scowling on a sofa beside Yegunov. My partner suggested that we should stop and sample some of the delicious food and I gratefully agreed. Then I saw Kolya talking in a very haughty way to a lady, who I assumed to be the hostess, and who looked embarrassed. All at once he got up and swept us along with him in a puzzled, disapproving crocodile, making it difficult for us to say any thank-yous or goodbyes.

It was not until I got downstairs that I understood what had happened. The two girls, the bride and her friend, both of them Kolya's pupils and both drunk, had dared each other to ask their romantic-looking teacher to the wedding party. Brimfull of hospitality and alcohol, the bride had chortled excitedly down the telephone without thinking of consulting her Mama. She must have been appalled when, instead of the glittering cavaliers she expected, four frowsy intellectuals in shabby suits turned up. Lihachev was the best of us because he was still in his naval uniform. But the bride's mother, a dignified lady with grey hair, came up to Kolya and explained that there had been 'a little misunderstanding': 'We're not the sort of people, you know, who just ask anyone to our family functions.' Kolya had snapped back loudly that it was no pleasure for him to come but the bride had been so pressing on the telephone. A stunned silence of embarrassment fell on the wedding party for two minutes and then was skilfully dispelled by a tornado of convivial noises as we trooped away down the stairs.

Once or twice my pupils invited me to birthday parties. They were mostly easy and pleasant and uneventful. Why does one remember the embarrassing occasions best? There was Olga N.

and her mother, bourgeois, still only half-adjusted to the new régime. Kolya and I arrived at her birthday party with a cake I had chosen with care at Torgsin, covered with crystallized cherries, and I was disappointed when Olga, not looking at it, grandly told the maid to put it with a pile of other unopened presents on the piano. She was a prize pupil of mine and prattled away in a low, quiet, self-important voice in very literary English. When we came in, the mother was saying, 'Oh dear, not enough tea-spoons! Where can the wretched girl have put the spoons?' Olga then said to the company in English: 'My Mother had formerly four dozen tea-spoons, but she was forced to sell three dozen. She is very old fashioned and now greatly regrets the deprivation and cannot reconcile herself to the loss. Consequently she resorts to little subterfuges such as you have just heard.' She herself was worried about the buttons on her blouse. The little red ornaments on them were wearing out, but, because they were enamel, couldn't be painted in, so she was getting a friend, a chemical engineer, to help. He was first of all going to scoop out the centres, and then. . .

These are the things we talked about in Leningrad in 1931: spoons, buttons, macaroni, galoshes, macaroni again. I don't believe I ever heard anyone mention Magnetogorsk or the liquidation of the Kulaks or any of the remote and monstrous contemporary happenings to which by a complicated chain of causes our lifestyle and our macaroni were linked.

Communism is said to inspire a dull uniformity, but Lihachev, who was quite unpolitical, was always seeking and finding coloured variations. In his rooms I met Negro communists and Turks, Tartars and Kirghiz, and one day he took me to the Hispano-American Society. It was held in the room of a Mexican communist, a lady, who dreaded the Russian winter. In the autumn she had shut herself and her family into her room and sealed up the large double window and the phortochka, and then fought the domestic and personal smells with powerful scents. It was not yet mid-winter, but it was plain to all the battle had been lost. Lilies and jasmine had been routed by an appalling primeval smell that was neither Slav nor Latin. Lihachev said it was Aztec. The lady introduced me to a celebrated Mexican writer, but talking meant breathing, and I appeared to him to be dumb, and he went over to Lihachev. For Lihachev, as I heard long afterwards, it proved to be a disastrous meeting. The Mexican was charmed with him, and when he went home he sent his book on Communism for Lihachev to review. Unfortunately the book had Trotskyite tendencies and he was compromised by receiving it. He was dismissed from the navy and he became a literary freelance compiling anthologies of foreign poetry, always lively and occupied. In a large new sombrero, he visited all the Leningrad publishing house and got contracts.

That was the last I heard of him, but before I left Leningrad Vera Garatinksy had told me that in a couple of years there would be enough English-speaking proletarians to replace all the bourgeois teachers and guides and translators. 'That will be the end of us,' she said. 'It's that accursed English woman and her method. Don't let them invent any more clever methods over there, please.'

My way to Goskurs lay along the Moika, the little river that ran from the Winter Palace under the Nevsky and the Vosnesensky to the Neva. It had been a very aristocratic district once. On the far side, in a pale green eighteenth-century house, Pushkin had lived and had died painfully after a fatal duel. The quays and surrounding streets were almost deserted in the winter evenings, and very quiet except for my galoshes slapping loosely on the pavements. In the marsh air the northern sunset quivered from time to time as if it was trapped between the beautiful impassive houses. In the daytime the red proletarian trimmings held the eye and the mind, but in the twilight different obsessions replaced them.

Before I went to Russia, I had been reading Dostoievsky's *The Idiot*. It is the story of passionate people pursuing each other through the streets of St Petersburg, with love, with hate, with revolvers or bundles of roubles. Their feelings and their motives are often obscure, and Dostoievsky, standing outside his own creations, suggests different explanations of their behaviour. Through this, his characters have the freshness of reality, for mostly we only guess at other peoples' minds. Prince Muishkin, the Idiot, is the still centre of the hurricane, the personification of Dostoievsky's belief that 'the Russian heart is more adapted to universal brotherly friendship than that of any other nation'. And indeed perhaps the Russians are more perceptive and, when it is in their power, more ready than others to make allowances for the failures they perceive. The first people to give Prince

Muishkin hospitality, when he arrived poor and shabby in St Petersburg, were the Epanchins, who lived in a large house on the broad bustling Sadovaya, where I caught the tram for my classes. Muishkin was at peace with himself and, despite his simplicity, this gave him a strange authority over others. To Dostoievsky he was the symbol of Russia's unconscious, unexercised power.

I do not believe that the creations of genius die without issue or that, because of a change of government, cities start to breed a different type of man. They dress differently and feed differently, and that is all.

Great writers interpret men to each other by example and analogy. The creative imagination ebbs and flows with some degree of constancy. On the one hand all men have common needs, passions, hopes, which society has to satisfy; on the other hand every man is unique and he must so manipulate society that his nature is fulfilled. The great Russian writers, Tolstoy, Dostoievsky, Chekhov, were almost always more conscious of diversity of temperament than of uniformity of needs. Then Karl Marx and the Revolution created the Economic Man, and while this wonderfully lifelike dummy is in the shop window, what hope is there for the genius that is kindled by human diversity? The fact that there are vast editions of the classics published and sold out keeps the flame alive but cannot fan it.

I once tried to talk about these things at Goskurs during the dangerous half-hour of free conversation, when my pupils and I, under cover of grammar, tried to find out what we were like. One of them helped me out with a cliché, 'ghosts of the past', which quenched what I had to say, and instead I said that Petersburg, like Alexandria and Constantinople, had the tremendous toughness of cities that were built round an idea, not a market. Peter's 'window upon Europe' had been made for autocrats and bureaucrats, but once opened it could not be shut. Marx came through as well as Dickens and Byron and Georges Sand and Henry George and all the strange assortment of foreign influences. Tolstoy, no less than Dostoievsky the Slavophile, had hated Petersburg and its Western culture, as the oyster hates the foreign body it turns into a pearl, but they could not ignore it. And what they had accepted and adorned, their successors could still less ignore.

The weather was getting foggy. Most Russians had sealed up their windows, but whenever I shut the phortochka Kolya opened it again. Fresh air was one of his cherished English traditions, about which he was very sensitive. His love of England was a substitute for religion and I knew that his welcome to me derived from it. There was a legend in Techmass about his 'English reserve', but in fact there was nothing English about it. He was normally impetuous and enthusiastic but in his English mood he alternated between a cold animal torpor and a passionate misanthropy. 'English dissent and socialism,' I said, 'are based on an accidental tepidity or, if you like, sobriety of temperament. Your emotional heterodoxy is something quite different.' I would not have risked saying this but my cold was getting worse and I was scared of getting stranded in Leningrad with bronchitis. The next time I shut the phortochka he looked stern but left it shut.

Once, when I was sitting over my sudak in the October, an Oxford acquaintance, John Lane-Tuckey and his wife, a sleek, self-satisfied university couple, came by. They were tired of crèches and clinics and wanted to see 'real Russians'. It seemed obvious to ask them back and Kolya was pleased. But the moment they came into the room I saw it was a mistake. John asked light ironical questions about Soviet economics – he was a sociologist. Barbara, his wife, was silent, clearly horrified by the squalor of the flat. Something in their manner and appearance turned Kolya into a pillar of Marxist orthodoxy. His open friendliness dropped and he talked to them as if he was giving copy to journalists. I took them back to their hotel. 'But you can't go on living there,' Barbara Lane-Tuckey said, 'the smell, the dark!' She was kind and worried and pressed on me what they'd brought from England and no longer needed, a packet of lump sugar, three lemons and a bottle of hydrogen peroxide to gargle. I felt unsettled, like a child at school who has had a visit from home. I tried to come back into the flat as if it was for the first time, so as to experience what they had seen and smelt. Yes, it was unbelievable. I shut up the provisions in my trunk. Neither of us referred to the Lane-Tuckeys again.

Kolya had appalling moments of self-criticism. Soon after this he stayed up a whole night reading *A Passage to India*. Closing the book at breakfast-time, he said, 'I'm like Aziz. I'm an Asiatic.' He was sombre the entire day, but he felt he had given himself away too much, for a little later he started to refer to Lyubotchka as 'the maid' and to give her lessons in waiting at table. She was always terrified of him when he was being English. He instructed her in a cool, bitter, military voice: 'All over again till you get it right, please.' Lyubotchka reacted as if to electric shocks. She started to jerk and dart about like a rabbit, her eyes glazed with fear. Eating, which she had done all her life, suddenly became black magic.

When I found someone had been rummaging in my suitcase, I kept count of the lumps of sugar and chocolate, and found two or three pieces disappeared every day. They were precious as gold to me in case I got ill and couldn't go out to buy food. Nina Gavrilovna used to do all their shopping in the market, and if I asked her to go to Torgsin, the foreign currency shop, people might think she had been receiving valuta from abroad or hoarding jewellery.

One day a golden-haired cousin of Kolya's called, all charm and friendliness, but Kolya was nervous and abrupt. He obviously wanted her to go, but she stayed on. At last she turned to me and said, 'I wonder if. . . ?' Kolya shot up into the air and came between us, clenching his fists: 'No, that I forbid you to ask him! That you shall not ask! No!' She shrugged her shoulders and left, followed by Kolya raging. The hall door slammed. After a bit the girl came back with a bottle in her hand. 'I wanted to ask you if I could have a drop of peroxide for my hair?'

When Kolya came back I told him that she was welcome to my peroxide but I thought Lyubotchka was stealing things out of my trunk. He became very solemn: 'The matter must be brought before the House Committee.' That evening the curtain flapped ceaselessly over his mother's recess. The murmur of conversation never ceased. When Kolya went out, she emerged and asked me if I wasn't ashamed, a greedy foreigner, who cheated on the currency and had fine meals in the Europa, to count lumps of sugar and persecute a poor servant-girl? And I had lemons in my trunk too, and chocolate.

'How did you know I had lemons in my trunk?' I couldn't stop myself asking. Oh, she crowed, she'd been digging in my trunk had she? What would Kolya say when he heard I accused his mother of being a thief? This I could not answer. My Russian was not good enough for me to pick my way through the tangle of misunderstandings. 'And Kolya has given up his translating in order to show you the way round Leningrad. You don't even pay for your lodgings.'

I tried to explain the arrangement Kolya and I had come to, adding, 'Perhaps he didn't fully understand?'

'So he didn't understand? He can't understand English can he? He speaks it as well as you do, if not better. That'll be news to him he can't speak English.' And then she produced her trump card. 'If the GPU knew you have black roubles. . . Russians have been shot for less!'

At this moment the Pole came to the door. He was very apologetic for interrupting and sincerely anxious that we go on with our quarrel and not mind him. Nina Gavrilovna went out and he produced a slip of paper and explained to me how many weeks I had earned by my translations to use his aunt's bed. But chiefly he had come to ask me to a party. He gave a ceremonious bow. It was for the Fifteenth Anniversary of the Revolution; it was going to be a very special party. I accepted and he told me I would get a formal invitation in a day or two. I had an almost permanent cold now and I kept on wondering what would happen if either the aunt or I got ill. I wished I had paid more attention to the conducted tours round infirmaries and hospitals.

When Kolya came home that night, his mother drew him behind her curtain. Then I heard him leave. He did not come back that night or the following morning. Then the telephone started to ring as it had the first day I spent in Chernyshev Pereulok, and I answered the pupils as his mother had done, 'Ne doma. Ne znaioo.'

He came back in the evening. 'I can't stay in the house with you any longer,' he said. 'I'm going to Lihachev's.' He began to pack a suitcase.

'If you think I'm to blame, I'll go.'

'You've nowhere to go.'

'I'll find somewhere!' I jumped up and put on my coat and hat and, seizing my suitcase, walked out of the room.

Kolya was out of his mind. 'That's my coat,' he said. 'I can't trust you to bring it back. You must leave your suitcase behind instead.'

I threw the suitcase down and flung the coat at him too, in a rage. When I was half-way down the stairs, the door of the flat opened and his mother came running after me. 'Come back,' she said, 'he just lost his temper. He hasn't had anything to eat all day.'

'No, I won't come back.'

'Please come back. If the GPU hears that Kolya turned you out, he'll get into trouble.'

'They won't hear.'

It was not until I was in the street that I realized I had left my passport in Kolya's coat, but nothing would have induced me to return.

Leningrad was very badly lit in the evenings and the directions hard to follow, as the new street names were usually too long to use. The Nevsky, for example, was never called its proper name, October Twenty-Fifth Street. At so late an hour I hesitated to go to Yegunov, who lived nearby. He had a single room in a vast tenement house, honeycombed with arches and passages, the entries blocked with stacks of firewood and stinking rubbish-heaps, and every arch and entry looked alike. The Pole's house was in the outskirts of the city in the Narva district, and I knew I would never find it.

There was a thin coat of snow in the Nevsky that flung back the light of the lamps. All the passers-by had on shubas, or leather coats, except for a few beggars in the archways and the old general standing as always with his tray of transfers and celluloid tooth-brush cases outside the Moscow Station. Yet in spite of the snow I was so angry and excited I did not feel cold. I walked up and down the Nevsky enquiring at all the hotels, big and small. They would none of them take me. They were full up with delegates from the provinces for the Fifteenth Annivarsary. In any case, as I was registered in a private house, I would have first to get my registration cancelled at the police station, and that had closed three hours earlier. At the Gostiny Dvor, the big shopping-centre between the Nevsky and the Sadovya, I ate some pirozhkies, hot cabbage pies, at a stall. There were lights in the Kazan Cathedral, where the finishing touches were being put to an historical exhibition, and outside workmen on scaffolding were nailing up strips of red cloth for the celebrations. Some others were sitting round a brazier eating food out of parcels.

Opposite the Kazan Cathedral was the British Consulate. Mr Bullard, whom I knew, got his food from a London shop. He had deep armchairs and a roaring fire. Several times I had dropped in for a chat and a cup of tea and Huntley and Palmer chocolate biscuits. He was friendly but did not approve, any more than the Russians did, of fraternization. Kolya told me that he had tried to take Connie Archangelsky's passport from her because she was married to a Russian. Rumour said that there was always someone lurking by the cathedral steps making a note of his visitors. He had good manners and would be able to dissemble his satisfaction at seeing somebody paid out for staying in a Russian family. He himself only met official Russians and had to go to Finland to get Russian lessons.

I could easily persuade myself that I had an official claim on him, but I loathed going to him, as I would to the GPU. I thought I had the courage and skill to treat most human problems as personal ones, but the moment I appealed to authority to help me out I was like a man on a tightrope who thinks of falling. Could I convince myself that the consul was a friend as well as an official? I hesitated and all at once the light went out in the consulate. My mind was made up.

I rang the bell on the first landing, but there was no answer. I rang again and knocked. After half an hour of waiting I came down into the street. I walked on towards the Admiralty and sweeping aside by St Isaac's I tried the Astoria and finally ended up on the Neva. It was no good. When I got back to the Kazan Cathedral I was shivering with cold and the workmen round the brazier whom I intended to ask for a night's lodgings had gone. I walked back to the consulate and banged at all the doors in the building. Bullard emerged from one of them. 'You were knocking at the offices, which closed at four,' he explained. 'The private part of the house is on this side.'

I had no self-reproaches as I got into bed, for I was persuaded that I was going to be desperately ill.

The next morning I woke up feeling remarkably well. I had an English breakfast with eggs and bacon, marmalade and toast and coffee. Afterwards I went out and bought the commissar's coat with the short sleeves. The sun was shining. The palaces on the canals, freshly colour-washed in buff or pink, were framed in snow and draped with broad red banners. I felt wonderfully detached from it all. The palaces wore their banners with the patient suffering look of domestic pets wearing bows for a birthday party. About everything there was an impromptu, impermanent and almost innocent look.

It was with a feeling of insolent well-being that I returned to Chernishev Pereulok. After I had rung the bell I felt ashamed of my new coat and folded it into a bundle. Kolya was in bed. We were polite and constrained. He handed me a postcard from Vaishlé, the Pole. 'Gubert Georgievitch. Congratulations on the Fifteenth Anniversary of Socialist Construction and the termination of the fourth year of the five-year plan! I also invite you to my house for the latter half of tomorrow, the first day of the holidays.'

The kitchen was full of smoke, for everybody in the flat was having a bath for the Anniversary. No one trusted the cleanliness of the bath itself but put a stool inside and balanced a basin of hot water on the stool. Darya Andreyvna even placed in it a trough for her feet. I used to prefer to wash in the communal baths, where there was constant hot water and elderly people lashed themselves with birch twigs.

Darya Andreyvna was going to lead the procession for the theatre. Kolya was marching for the Oriental Institute. The Director of Techmass had rung up to find if I would march with them, but I had been out and did not know where to meet them. Kolya, instead of being flippant as he usually was about processions, was important and treated me as if I was Lane-Tuckey. I would never be forgiven that night at the consulate. As we went out he made a stately, unfriendly apology. He had been in a Manichean mood, he said. He insisted that I should come back that night. I agreed I would and said that I would see that his wife Connie in Eastbourne would get the same rent that he had to pay when he worked for the Soviet Embassy and lived in Torrington Square, but I said I must have the phortochka shut. We discussed the matter in a business-like way, as if Chernishev Pereulok was in fact a Bloomsbury lodging-house.

As we were going down the stairs we met the Pole coming up. He had a big peony in his buttonhole with slogans stamped in gold on each petal. 'I came to see if you had got my invitation', he said. 'Yes, and I'm coming.' 'Good! And I brought you this.'

It was another letter. Handing it to me, he bolted down the stairs and disappeared. When I unstuck it, a packet of roubles tumbled out with a note: 'Lent for an indefinite period, in case you are short for the celebration of the Fifteenth Anniversary of Socialist Construction.' I went to Torgsin and bought some bottles of wine to take to the party.

It was difficult pressing my way through the crowds in the Nevsky and, at the corner of the Sadovya, I was brought to a halt by a fresh tributary coming in from the Neva docks and the English Quay. I had to wait there wedged against a parapet for several hours. I was told that a million men and women passed along the Nevsky that day. In each group of this endless pro cession two men on either flank held up a flapping red streamer with a slogan on it, or grotesque figures of European statesmen. It was fully an hour before the students' and teachers' procession passed. I wanted to see if there was anyone I knew, and how they were affected by this performance. Organized in processions, those whom we have known as complex individuals shed colour and character. Also there is some unconscious tabu that we violate every time we look at our friends in their public moments, which are often the moments of deepest privacy. The violation may be easy and pleasant, but it delays us for that split second between perceiving and observing. Kolya passed close by but not till he had gone did I realize that I had seen him. A column of sailors went by and I looked in vain for Lihachev. A little later I noticed a dislocation in the procession, people moderating their step behind and on either side of the baroness. She walked slowly enough for me to watch her. Her companions on either side, keeping step, held a pole from which a banner was stretched: WE ARE MARCHING TOWARDS THE CONQUEST OF TECHNICAL EFFICIENCY IN A SOCIALIST WORLD. She did not look either ironical or embarrassed. It was as if she was half asleep but sufficiently awake to enjoy her dream. She did not seem conscious of her lameness, imposing her pace with confidence on those around her.

I have thought that just as half our physical lives passes in sleep, it is perhaps intended that our mental life should be equally distributed between the assertion of our uniqueness and its renunciation. If that trance-like state of submersion in a public or collective mood bears an analogy to sleep, it would reflect our individual and self-centred lives by very simple images and phrases in dream-like sequences. In such a way, the caricatures and slogans that floated above them would complement, like dreams, the intricate, logical natures of Kolya and the baroness. The slogans were the shadows of human thinking in which their thoughts merged restfully, just as their footsteps concurred in the broad beaten track upon the snow, and we do not expect faithfulness in tone or form or colour from shadows.

All I remember of the Pole's party is the food and a tall thin guest with a bald head, a geologist like Vaishlé. As he shook hands, he said, 'I am bald and thin because I think very much; my Polish friend is round and jolly because he never thinks. I have been prospecting in Turkestan and I will show you some photographs. Later still I will recite you some poems of the French poet, Béranger.' All happened as he predicted. As for the food, there were golubtsi (mince and rice wrapped in cabbage leaves and fried), hard cakes covered with stewed apple, soft cakes covered with poppy seeds, glasses of vodka mixed with lemonade and chilis. I saw the aunt and her bed, but I had decided to leave Russia and the desperate significance they would have had for me a week before was no longer there.

The last few weeks before the schools closed I spent at Chernishev Pereulok. Kolya submerged himself in his translation of Lenin and began to take his Communism and his professional functions much more seriously. I was a foreign critic now not a friend and he would step coldly from argument to argument, like rungs on a ladder. His English obsession only flared up now and again, as when every Saturday he laid a neat bill on my bed for me to forward to my wife. Several times we made up parties to Sestroretsk or Pavlovsk or Gatchina. He was never unfriendly but he had become a different person, conscientious, informative and rather dull. He provoked in me all the qualities I had detested in the Lane-Tuckeys.

I took many solitary walks under the lovely alleys of lime and maple round Leningrad. Lihachev was away but sometimes Yegunov came with me. He had a big dog which was in the stud book and therefore had a ration book of its own, and despite the rigours of the Five-Year Plan ate more than its master. We usually exercised it in the Kamenny Ostrov, the island in the Neva, where the wealthy merchant families, whose houses are now rest-homes and hospitals, once lived. It was criss-crossed by little birch-lined canals and bridges. Sometimes I went with one or two of my pupils to the Yussupov Palace, to which as a teacher I had access. It was a Students' Recreation Centre, with rooms for chess and cards and billiards. It had also a small theatre. Down in the basement in the winter of 1916 Rasputin, who was hard to kill, was beaten to death by Prince Yussupov and his companions. The vast china chandelier in the hall surely dated from those days. There were robins and canaries perched on its branches, which dripped with blue convolvulus.

For my last evening Kolya decided to have a party and, setting enough money aside for my droshki to the station, I gave him the remainder of my roubles. I was pleased when he said, 'I will arrange it all,' and then spent more than half on smoked fish, a favourite delicacy of his. It was like a return to ordinary humanity. Lihachev was back home again and when our guests had gone in the early morning, he and Yegunov spread their shubas on the floor and slept on them. My train left very early, so I did not bother to sleep. Kolya and I left without rousing the others.

At the station, the Pole and Guzelimian and Tihomirov and two of my pupils were waiting. The Pole gave me a box of liqueur chocolates, Guzelimian asked me to remember his fishing-rod. Then there suddenly flashed into my mind, 'My blue carriage rug!' I exclaimed aloud, and promptly Kolya said, 'I'll fetch it!' and darted away. I shouted after him, 'For God's sake keep it!' but I paused for one greedy moment before I said this and I was too late. The blue rug, which I had brought from Ireland, had stood between me and pneumonia; now it meant nothing to me, but it could have meant a great deal to the Archangelskys. They got it in the end, but how ungraciously.

I kept looking at the station entrance while the others were talking, because I was wondering how I could keep in touch with my Russian friends. Would it be safe to write letters to each other? Could we send newspapers? I had left all this to the last moment, for I intended to ask Kolya and hear him say, 'I will arrange.' But the train went out. Alexander Ivanitch and the Pole looked at the wheels, which meant, I had been told, that they wanted me to come back.

The train went through lonely swamp, thinly wooded with birch and alder. Here and there a solitary Soviet soldier guarded the line until, as we appraached the frontier, the main roads slowly became cart tracks and petered out into grass and barbed-wire entanglements.

* * *

In the autumn of 1956 I went with seven other Irishmen on a 'cultural delegation' to China. On the way back I parted from the others in Moscow because I wished to go to Leningrad to see if any of my old friends were alive. As the translator of Leonov's *The Thief,* I had good contacts with the Union of Writers and, when I told them my reasons for wishing to go to Leningrad, I met with understanding. They said they would look out for a guide to take me on the night train the following day. But would I in the meantime give them a talk on Irish Writing? I went back to the Hotel National and spent the day in my room writing and was ready for my appointment with them in the afternoon. There were about a dozen people there, mostly teachers and translators. They asked me searching and intelligent questions. One of them was translating O'Casey's autobiographical series and he asked me to interpret a passage in O'Casey's idiosyncratic idiom, which always seemed to me to obscure what was otherwise lucid. I did badly but recovered a little of my credit when I said that in *Sunset and Evening Star* O'Casey had written a couple of friendly pages about me and the 'Insult' to the Papal Nuncio.

As I left them I was told that my guide, Anna Shelestova, would meet me at the National late that evening and take me on the night train to Leningrad. On the train I reflected on my chances of finding any of my friends alive. There was only a thin hope. What I had heard as rumour at home had been confirmed in Moscow. In 1934, three years after I had left, Kirov, the Leningrad Party Boss, whom many thought would be Stalin's successor, had been murdered. Foreign influence was suspected and many thousands of arrests were made on the flimsiest of evidence. I heard how the elderly vet who treated the German consul's dog, and the woman who sold eggs to the Polish consul, had been hauled off to prison. It was obvious that all foreign-language teachers would be under suspicion. Five years later the war had broken out, and after that came the invasion of Russia and the terrible siege of Leningrad. It was a forlorn hope.

Almost all my friends in Leningrad had had telephones, so the first thing we did when we arrived was to look up their names in the telephone book. Only one familiar name was there, the one I most wanted to see, Nikolai Mihalitch Archangelsky. He was not in Chernishev Pereulok but in the southern suburb of Narva. When Anna telephoned, a female voice said that he was out but would be back at two.

We leapt into a cab and, as Anna was a native of Leningrad, we quickly found the Archangelsky's flat. It was in a large new tenement block and No. 32 was on the third storey. When the door was opened by a big blowsy woman, there was a babel of children's voices and kitchen smells. She did not ask us in but said that if we cared to wait, Nikolai Mihalitch would be along in twenty minutes. 'Does he still work at the Oriental Institute?' I asked. 'No, he works at the Kirov Factory.' 'That was the Putilov in your time,' interjected Anna. 'Does he write at all now?' I asked. The woman looked puzzled. 'He's an engineer,' she said. It took me a moment to grasp that there were two Nikolai Mihalitch Archangelskys, and that this was the wrong one. I could not stay there a second longer. 'Let's at least try Chernishev Pereulok,' I said to Anna. My disappointment had turned into relief, for the Nikolai Mihalitch I knew would have been miserable in such surroundings.

I was no help to Anna in finding our way to Chernishev Pereulok. All the familiar landmarks had gone, and when we arrived and stopped at No. 59 I got out in perplexity. Even in the hallway it was different. The lift was working. Could these be the stairs that I had run down with Nina Gavrilovna shouting after me that night I had spent at the consul's? It was not possible. We went up in the lift all the same and stopped on the fifth floor.

Darya Andreyevna's mirror had gone and so had the mat. A stranger came to the door when I rang the bell. No, he had never heard of anyone called Nikolai Mihalitch Archangelsky, but there was a very old lady in the flat still who had been there since before the war. She might know. 'Is it Darya Andreyevna?' I asked. 'Yes, that's her name.' I described myself and he said he would find out if she would see me. He came back and said the old lady remembered me – an Englishman – but she was bed-ridden and did not want to see a strange man; she'd see the woman who came with me. So Anna went alone. I waited for a long time on the landing till Anna came out. She said Darya Andreyevna remembered the Archangelskys well. The mother had died and sometime in the mid-thirties Nikolai Mihalitch had been taken away to Gorohovaia Prison for quite a short period. He had come back and after three weeks had died in the flat.

I could not leave it like that. It seemed to me that Tihomirov, as a Red Army man, was the one who was likely to have survived the purge that followed Kirov's murder. By a strange chance I had in my notebook the number of the two old women with whom he lodged, and in a moment I was talking to the one who had survived. Yes, she remembered Alexander Ivanitch talking about me, the Englishman. 'Poor Alexander Ivanitch! He died you know three years ago. I always told him he drank too much coffee.' This seemed a very old-ladyish diagnosis, but I asked her did she remember Lihachev and Yegunov and Kolya. Indeed she did, but Alexander Ivanitch had not been seeing anything of them for a very long time before he died. 'How long?' 'Oh, maybe fifteen or twenty years ago. I think something may have happened to them.' She was not going to tell me more and maybe she did not know. When anyone went to prison in those days, their relations used to bring them parcels, until one day they were told no more parcels were necessary. You were not informed whether they had died or been moved to another prison.

I had learnt very much what I had expected to learn, which was nothing. I was sad not only for my friends but for anyone who leaves the world anonymously, surrounded by hostile or uncaring people.

Anna had done her best for me. There was still half a day. What would I like to see? I did not want to go sight-seeing, and in any case most of the Intourist sights had been destroyed by the Germans. The imperial palaces in the southern environs of the city, Peterhov, Gatchina, Pavlovsk, Tsarskoye Selo, had all lain in the path of the German advance and had been looted and burned. All the trees in their parks had been cut down. 'But we're restoring them,' said Anna, loyal to Intourism, 'and we're getting all the pictures and sculptures back again, or their equivalents. And we've replanted the trees.'

In the end she took me to a hill overlooking the city and the Gulf of Finland. There was a slot-machine telescope there and with a running commentary from Anna I turned it round. To the west I saw the island of Kronstadt and the wooded coast of Finland, and Anna told me how, backed by the Finns, the Germans had flung forty-five divisions against the city. After the victory at Kingisepp, in which her brother had died, they forced their way across the Estonian frontier, confident that the city would fall to them in a couple of days, but the siege had lasted twenty-nine months and had ended in a Russian victory. Moving the telescope towards the city, I saw the Nevsky Prospekt thrusting eastwards to the Champs de Mars. The biggest fire from the incendiary bombs, Anna said, had been in the Gostiny Dvor. That was the shopping-centre in the Nevsky where I had eaten pirozhkies the night I slept at the consulate. She told me about the famine and how her brother's family had eaten carpenter's glue and yeast with hot water, till the fierce winter of 1941-42 when they had made a road across the ice on Lake Ladoga and transported food across from the east. I traced the Neva till it veered southwards by the Finland Station and the Summer Palace. To the north I saw the islands where I had walked with Yegunov and his dog. They were now called the Kirov Islands, Anna told me, and the great highway that led to them was called Kirov Avenue. Thousands of honest men and women died because of Kirov, but their names are nowhere recorded.

I have forgotten much of what Anna told me but I am more inclined to apologize for writing about great events, which touched me not at all, than for tracing again the tiny snail track which I made myself.

Is it not obvious that when through the modern media far things are brought near, the near things must be pushed far to make room for them.? Imperceptibly, we become Lilliputians wandering in a Brobdignag of our own contrivances and persuading ourselves that through contact with greatness we ourselves become greater. Then something happens to jerk us back to thoughts and people of our own size and significance. Most of the time when I was looking through that telescope, I was thinking not of the tremendous disasters that had befallen Leningrad and all Russia, but of the small stupidities, the acts of laziness or greed I had committed myself. Why had I not given the blue rug to Kolya's mother instead of leaving it behind by mistake? Why hadn't I sent Guzelimian his fishing-rod?

[1984]

APPENDIX

A STATEMENT TO THE COMMITTEE AND MEMBERS OF THE KILKENNY ARCHAEOLOGICAL SOCIETY BY THE HONORARY SECRETARY, HUBERT BUTLER

November 10th, 1952

A Committee Meeting is being summoned on Wednesday next, at 8.30 p.m., in the Technical Schools, Kilkenny, to discuss the effects upon the Society of the incident at the International Affairs Association. I think it would leave you freer to discuss the matter if I did not come to the meeting myself but sent to each of you a statement which you could study before you reached the meeting.

I expect that some of you will think I ought to resign without more ado and others, who bear me no ill will and realize that I spoke without any intention to give pain to anyone, will think I ought to give up the secretaryship in order to tide things over and prevent the Society from dissolving.

I need not emphasize how desperately sorry I would be if the Society did break up along sectarian or other lines, and how ready I shall be to co-operate in any effort to keep it going. We are, I think, unique in having survived so long without a trace of bitterness or dissension. So I have to think hard what is the right thing to do.

In the first place, I do not believe that my resignation now would save the Society as an interdenominational one to which people of every shade of opinion could belong. Secondly, pressure has been exercised to make me resign. That makes resignation impossible for me for it would imply that I admitted that what I did or said was wrong, and that I cannot admit.

As I have been secretary for seven years, of which the recent year, in which we organized the exhibition in the Tholsel and the visit of the Belfast Field Club, has been the most successful,

I should have to consider the request to resign as a mark of disapproval. I could not take it in any other way.

Before you make a decision I would like you to look back over the many pleasant summer afternoons we have spent together in the past seven years, and how often we might have split upon just such issues as this and yet we survied. Do you remember, for instance, the outing to Carrickshock, when Father Clohosey spoke to us on the Tithe War at the memorial to the three men who had been killed in an attack on the tithe collector, Edmund Butler, who, with twelve policemen, lost his life? Most of the Protestants went home from the bottom of the hill, but I went to the top, because I knew that Father Clohosey could be relied on to give an impartial account of this bitter controversial event. And that is just what he did do. And, if you remember, it was I who offered him the thanks of the Society when the evening ended at Ballybodan. Yet that was an issue which, had I been a bigotted person, might have affected me strongly. My great grandfather, Richard Butler, the Rector of Burnchurch, near Bennettsbridge, had been mobbed and molested so frequently by the agitators that in the end he had to leave his home for several years. Yet in fact, he thought, as I think, that the tithe agitators had right on their side. He did not, and no more could I, make a sectarian issue of it.

I mention myself because I have been attacked, but each one of us has acted in the same way. Our little Society, under our chairman, John O'Leary, has been doing Christian work healing the sores of history and reconciling conflicting opinions. I am quite certain that His Excellency, the Nuncio, could not possibly wish it to come to grief.

It would not have been surprising if we had split on some local issue of Kilkenny history, the Confederation, Cromwell, the Penal Laws, but it is to me almost unbelievable that we should be in danger of disintegrating because of two different interpretations of tragedies that happened eleven years ago in the plains of Slavonia and the wild hills of Bosnia and Herzegovina.

As I would like you to understand something of the issues at stake, I will quote you the letter I wrote to the Nuncio, but I gather at present he does not want it to appear in the press.

Maidenhall,
Bennettsbridge,
Co. Kilkenny.

Nov. 2, 1952.

Your Excellency,

I would like to express my regret at any embarrassment or pain I may have caused you by my remarks after Mr O'Curry's talk. I felt, as I have felt for six years, that vital facts were being suppressed and that, though their discussion might at first be very bitter, worse would follow if they were ignored.

I think the enclosed letter from Mgr Stepinac, which I translated and published Dec. 29, 1950 in *The Church of Ireland Gazette,* discloses a complex situation in Yugoslavia, which could not possibly be ignored in any discussion on 'Yugoslavia, the Pattern of Persecution'. You are not, I think, likely to have seen this letter, because it was never published in Yugoslavia or mentioned at the Archbishop's trial by his accusers. The Communists were at that time holding him responsible for the barbarities of the conversion campaign and this letter shows too clearly that he was not responsible for them.

Nonetheless, it also shows (the quotation from Mgr Mishitch in particular) that force was being used to affect opinion, or, to put it differently, the violence of the times was being exploited for the purpose of proselytism. Since these were the methods used then and later by the Communists for their proselytism too, an unfair and unbalanced view of persecution in Yugoslavia would have been obtained if Mr O'Curry's paper had not been discussed in the light of these facts.

The International Affairs Association with its membership drawn from all creeds seemed the only forum in which these delicate issues could be soberly discussed. I went as the guest of a foundation member, who assured me that unfettered discussion had always been the order of the day.

I had gone, I admit, with the intention of disputing Mr O'Curry's interpretations, which I already knew, but, believe me, the last thing I wished to do was to insult you, your Church or Mr O'Curry.

My family is Irish, I was born here and have lived here most of my life. My experience and the experience of most Irish Protestants is that the kindliness, toleration and good will of Irish Catholics towards their Protestant fellow countrymen is such that is is hard for us even to conceive what bitterness and violence can exist in other lands.

In conclusion I would like to assure your Excellency of my sincere esteem and good will.

Yours sincerely,
HUBERT BUTLER.

As for the charge that I spoke uncharitably of Mgr Stepinac, I hope that one of the Kilkenny papers will print the account which I published over a year ago in *The Church of Ireland Gazette,* 20 April 1951, of a visit I paid to Mgr Stepinac with four Quakers. It will show that I never thought him 'a dupe' (a misreporting) and that my feelings towards him have always been respectful.

I will here quote one extract: 'Mgr Stepinac in prison is a figure, who commands respect. What he did, he did in the belief that it was right. Christians, who think otherwise – and there are millions of them – would mostly agree that while he remains in prison, the focus of violent emotions, there is little hope of a dispassionate enquiry into the tragic story of 1941.'

I attach also a translation of the letter from Mgr Stepinac to Pavelitch, which I have sent to the Nuncio. It is long and difficult, but I took great pains to translate it accurately from the Serbo-Croatian, and I am rather surprised that here, where Mgr Stepinac is so greatly venerated, it excited so little interest on publication nearly two years ago. No Irish paper asked permission to republish it, yet I believe it is the most important letter the Archbishop ever wrote. The facts to which he refers are all corroborated in the publications of the Serbian Orthodox Church.

Those who read the letter will admire Mgr Stepinac for his courage and humanity, though some may share the views of the Serbian Orthodox Church, expressed very strongly in their wartime publications, that he could have helped them best by witholding his recognition from the Government which decreed their compulsory conversion. But I do not think we are likely to divide on this point along the obvous lines. It is a question upon which each person will have his own individual opinion.

The Archbishop's letter will show that Count O'Brien, who is quoted against me in the Dublin and Kilkenny papers, is a wholly unreliable historian. Of the gigantic compulsory conversion campaign he writes on page 16 of his book on Mgr Stepinac, published by *The Standard*, 'It was through Mgr Stepinac's firm stand that Pavelitch's endeavours to impose the Catholic faith by force ended in complete failure.' Mgr Stepinac, who is modest as well as brave, shows in the attached letter how wildly untrue this statement is. The compulsory conversion campaign in Croatia, 1941, was one of the most terrible in the history of Europe.

I am glad to say that these problems do not touch us here, where for several generations we have shown tolerance and not tried to force our faith upon each other. Yet, at the meeting in Dublin, having expert knowledge relating to a subject which was being very seriously investigated, I felt it my duty to speak as I did. I could not have done otherwise.

HUBERT BUTLER